Shipping and Ports in the Twenty-first Century

Shipping and port systems are vital to societies and lifestyles around the world. In the late twentieth century, however, assumptions concerning the robustness of these systems were severely shaken by economic shocks largely triggered by oil crises.

This volume explores the resolution of many of the consequent uncertainties, and how adapted systems have been shaped to meet the challenges of the new millennium, focusing particularly on three closely interrelated themes: globalisation, technological change and the environment. Contributors examine subjects as diverse as:

- economic integration of emerging economies – in particular China
- the cruise tourism phenomenon and global integration
- new conceptual perspectives on port and shipping development
- technological drivers in the high-speed ferry and offshore oil industries
- pollution management challenges for shipping and ports.

Contributors' investigations make for a rewarding book of value to academics working in many fields including transport studies, marine and coastal studies, business, economics and economic geography. Organisations, practitioners and policy-makers in public- and private-sector professions ranging from coastal and port management to environmental regulation will also appreciate the volume.

David Pinder is Emeritus Professor of Geography, University of Plymouth, UK. He is also a Foreign Member of the Royal Netherlands Academy of Arts and Sciences. **Brian Slack** is Professor of Geography, Concordia University, Montreal, Canada.

Ocean management and policy series
Edited by H.D. Smith

Shipping and Ports in the Twenty-first Century

Globalisation, technological change and the environment

Edited by David Pinder and Brian Slack

For the International Geographical Union's Commission on Marine Geography

Routledge
Taylor & Francis Group

LONDON AND NEW YORK

First published 2004
by Routledge
11 New Fetter Lane, London EC4P 4EE

Simultaneously published in the USA and Canada
by Routledge
29 West 35th Street, New York, NY 10001

Routledge is an imprint of the Taylor & Francis Group

Typeset in Galliard by Wearset Ltd, Boldon, Tyne and Wear
Printed and bound in Great Britain by MPG Books Ltd, Bodmin

British Library Cataloguing in Publication Data
A catalogue record for this book is available from the British Library

Library of Congress Cataloging in Publication Data
A catalog record for this book has been requested

ISBN 0-415-28344-2

To our wives, Pam and Mabel

Contents

Figures

Tables

Contributors

Mark Cleary is Professor of Human Geography and Dean of Social Science and Business at the University of Plymouth, UK. He has research interests in South-East Asia, with a particular interest in the relationships between development and environmental management, and has published widely on the region. Recent publications include *Borneo: Change and Development* (Oxford University Press, 1995) and *Environment and Development in the Straits of Malacca* (Routledge, 2000) co-authored with Goh Kim Chuan. Address for correspondence: Faculty of Social Sciences and Business, University of Plymouth, Plymouth PL4 8AA, UK. Email: mcleary @plymouth.ac.uk

Claude Comtois is Professor of Geography at the Université de Montréal, Canada. He has held Visiting Professorships in France, China and Australia. His most important work addresses issues of maritime and intermodal transport, mostly in East Asia. Consultant to municipal and provincial agencies, he has also served as project director for the Canadian International Development Agency. He is the author of over 100 scientific publications in French, English, German and Chinese. His latest publications focus on the strategies of the international corporate transport sector. He currently supervises a government project on sustainable port and water transport systems. Address for correspondence: Centre d'Études de l'Asie de l'Est, Centre Research sur les Transports, Université de Montréal, Montréal, QC, Canada H3C 3J7. Email: claude.comtois@umontreal.ca

Peter de Langen has worked for over six years as a transport, port and regional economist at Erasmus University Rotterdam. He is active in teaching, contract and academic research. He specialises in port economics and has studied various aspects of ports, including trade forecasting, entrepreneurship and innovation, labour relations, long-range planning, economic clustering, and port competition. He has participated in a number of contract research studies as both a researcher and a project manager. His PhD thesis deals with the performance of seaport clusters, a topic about which he has published in journals such as *Maritime Policy and Management* and the *Journal of Maritime Economics*. Address for correspondence: Faculty of Economics,

Erasmus Universiteit Rotterdam, Burg, Oudlaan 50, 3062 PA Rotterdam, The Netherlands. Email: delangen@few.eur.nl

Goh Kim Chuan is Professor of Physical Geography at Nanyang Technological University, Singapore. He has research interests in the fields of hydrology, environmental management and pollution, and has carried out a range of research and consultancy activities in Singapore and Malaysia in this field. Along with his research on land degradation, agricultural change and water management, he was co-author of *Environment and Development in the Straits of Malacca* (Routledge, 2000). Address for correspondence: National Institute of Education, Nanyang Technological University, 1, Nanyang Walk, Singapore 637616. Email: gohkc@nie.edu.sg

Derek Hall is Professor of Regional Development at the Scottish Agricultural College, Ayr Campus, UK. He has published on conceptual approaches to tourism transport, transport policy, transport and development in Central and Eastern Europe, and EU enlargement. His work also includes gendered approaches to tourism and travel. He is a former Chair of the Royal Geographical Society/Institute of British Geographers Transport Research Group. Address for correspondence: Management Division, SAC, Auchincruive, Ayr KA6 5HW, UK. Email: D.Hall@au.sac.ac.uk

Robert McCalla is Professor of Geography at Saint Mary's University in Halifax, Canada. His research and teaching interests are in maritime transportation. He has published in journals such as the *Journal of Transport Geography*, the *Canadian Geographer*, *Maritime Policy and Management*, *Geoforum* and *Tijdschrift voor Economische en Sociale Geografie*. He is the author of *Water Transportation in Canada* (Formac, 1994). Currently, he is an external examiner of the World Maritime University in Malmö, Sweden, and also Chair of his department. Address for correspondence: Department of Geography, St Mary's University, Halifax, Canada B3H 3C3. Email: robert.mccalla@stmarys.ca

David Pinder is Emeritus Professor of Economic Geography at the University of Plymouth, where until recently he was Head of the School of Geography. His research centres on the closely related themes of ports, shipping and energy. In 2003 he was elected to foreign membership of the Royal Netherlands Academy of Arts and Sciences in recognition of his work in these contexts. In addition to numerous papers, his edited books include *Cityport Industrialization and Regional Development* (1981, with B.S. Hoyle); *Revitalising the Waterfront* (1988, with B.S. Hoyle and M.S. Husain; and *European Port Cities in Transition* (1992, with B.S. Hoyle). He has also guest-edited several journal special issues with a marine focus: *Geostrategy, Naval Power and Naval Port Systems* (1997, with H.D. Smith, *Marine Policy*); *Heritage Resources and Naval Port Regeneration* (1999, with H.D. Smith, *Ocean and Coastal Management*); and *Coastal Cultural Heritage and Sustainable Development* (2003, with A. Vallega, *Journal of Cultural*

Heritage). He is currently Chair of the International Geographical Union's Commission on Marine Geography. Address for correspondence: School of Geography, University of Plymouth, Plymouth PL4 8AA, UK. Email: david_pinder@ramolhaus.freeserve.co.uk

Gillian Reynolds is Principal Environmental Specialist at Lloyd's Register in London. She has a degree in biochemistry, an MSc in oceanography and a PhD awarded for research in the field of freshwater ecology. She spent the early part of her career at Imperial College, London, where she was responsible for a variety of research projects on air quality and water treatment. In 1990 she joined Lloyd's Register to develop its environmental activities in the marine field. Her work has included research into most of the topical areas of interest regarding the impact of shipping on the environment, including the development of the first classification society rules for environmental protection in the shipping industry. In 1999 she was awarded the Duke of Edinburgh Marine Environment Protection Award for her work in this field. Address for correspondence: Lloyd's Register of Shipping, 71 Fenchurch Street, London EC3M 4BS, UK. Email: gill.reynolds@lr.org

Giovanni Ridolfi is Professor of Geography at the University of Parma, Italy. A transport geographer, his fields of interest also include marine geography, with special reference to coastal management and regional issues. His primary area of research is the Mediterranean Sea, about which he has undertaken studies of usage change including cruising, new container routes and transshipment hubs, maritime jurisdiction, and military and geostrategic issues. He has published in journals such as *Ocean and Coastal Management*, *Tijdschrift voor Economische en Sociale Geographie*, *Maritime Policy* and *GeoJournal*. He is a Corresponding Member of the IGU Commission on Marine Geography. Address for correspondence: Faculty of Letters and Philosophy, University of Parma, 43100 Parma, Italy. Email: giovanni.ridolfi@unipr.it

Peter J. Rimmer is Emeritus Professor and Visiting Fellow in the Division of Pacific and Asian History, Research School of Pacific and Asian Studies, The Australian National University, Canberra. His main academic interests are centred on examining the economic integration of the Asia-Pacific region through an analysis of the region's air, shipping and telecommunications networks within a global context (with particular attention to the urban nodes). He has over 260 publications. His latest, with Professor Howard Dick, is entitled *Cities, Transport and Communications: The Integration of Southeast Asia since 1850* (Palgrave Macmillan, 2003). Also in preparation with Professor Dick is a second book: 'Rethinking the Southeast Asian City: Patterns, Processes and Policy'. Address for correspondence: Division of Pacific and Asian History, Research School of Pacific and Asian Studies, Australian National University, Canberra ACT 0200, Australia. Email: Peter.Rimmer@coombs.anu.edu.au

Jean-Paul Rodrigue is Assistant Professor of Geography in the Department of Economics and Geography at Hofstra University, Hempstead, New York. Specific topics investigated by Dr Rodrigue cover global change, urban regions, economic integration, international trade, regional development, transport systems and logistics. He serves on the editorial board of the *Journal of Transport Geography*. His recent book about the global economic space (*L'Espace économique mondial*) received the 2001 Pricewaterhouse Coopers award for the best French business-related book published in North America. Address for correspondence: Department of Economics and Geography, Hofstra University, Hempstead, New York 11549, USA. Email: Jean-Paul.Rodrigue@hofstra.edu

Brian Slack is Professor of Geography at Concordia University, Montreal, Canada. He has had a long-standing interest in intermodal transport, with an emphasis on ports and shipping. His recent research has focused on how globalisation is reshaping containerisation and on the regional differences that are evident. He has published extensively in journals such as *Maritime Policy and Management* and *GeoJournal,* and has contributed to edited books such as *Modern Transport Geography* (Wiley, 1998) and *Handbook of Logistics and Supply Chain Management* (Pergamon, 2001). He is the Honorary Secretary of the IGU's Commission on Marine Geography. In 2002 he received the Edward Ullman Award from the American Association of Geographers for outstanding contributions to transportation geography. Address for correspondence: Department of Geography, Concordia University, 1455 Boulevard Maisonneuve W, Montréal H3C 1M8, Canada. Email: slack@vax2.concordia.ca

Stefano Soriani is Associate Professor in Economic and Political Geography at the Department of Environmental Sciences (Università Ca' Foscari, Venice) and a member of the Steering Committee of AGEI (the Association of Italian Geographers). He currently teaches economic geography, coastal systems and conflicts for the use of natural resources, cost–benefit analysis and economic valuation of the environment. His main fields of research include port development and transportation, urban waterfront redevelopment, and integrated coastal zone management. Address for correspondence: Dipartimento di Scienze ambientali, Università Ca' Foscari, Calle Larga Santa Maria, 2137, 30123 Venezia, Italy. Email: soriani@unive.it

Tim Stojanovic is a Research Associate of the Department of Earth, Ocean and Planetary Sciences, Cardiff University. He gained his PhD from Cardiff Business School with a study of integrated coastal management in England and Wales. His research interests include environmental management and information science and the coastal environment, and he has conducted research projects with maritime partners in these fields as a member of Cardiff's Marine and Coastal Environment Research Group (MACE). He is presently working within the EcoPorts consortium, a European research programme sponsored by the European Union Directorate of Transport and Energy. With a team of scientists and practitioners, he is responsible for the development of port-specific auditing and environmental management tools. Address for correspondence: School of Earth, Ocean and Planetary Science, Main Building, Park Place, Cardiff University, Cardiff CF10 3YP, UK. Email: stojanovic@cardiff.ac.uk

Chris Wooldridge is a Senior Lecturer in the School of Earth, Ocean and Planetary Science at Cardiff University, where he is Director of Studies for the BSc degree scheme in Marine Geography. He is Science Coordinator for the EC *EcoPorts* Project (a ports sector-inspired initiative aimed at environmental protection and sustainable development), and his research activities and publications are focused on the environmental management of port and shipping operations. He has contributed to the design and implementation of the new standard for the Port Environment Review System (PERS) administered by the EcoPorts Foundation. Address for correspondence: School of Earth, Ocean and Planetary Science, Main Building, Park Place, Cardiff University, Cardiff CF10 3YP, UK. Email: wooldridge@cardiff.ac.uk

Preface and acknowledgements

This book originated in two meetings – *Oceans at the Millennium* (2000) and *Oceans of Change* (2002) – both held at the National Maritime Museum, Greenwich, UK, and organised jointly by the Museum and the International Geographical Union's Commission on Marine Geography. The object of both meetings was to create forums for discussion of the problems associated with the use and protection of the world's seas and oceans, and the implications of these problems for future economic and conservation strategies. Shipping and ports are major forces in this arena, and the shipping and port literature already contains numerous case studies. The meetings at the National Maritime Museum were designed to move towards a more integrated systematic approach through the juxtaposition of ideas, analysis and results. Papers were presented on contextual and methodological issues, on recent and current research, on policies and on planning experiences. Both events brought together a wide range of participants from international organisations, government agencies, the shipping and port industries, environmental groups, and academia.

While the chapters in this volume are mainly based on selected papers from these meetings, all have been extensively revised and edited. Rather than produce a general overview, the policy of the editors has been to be selective and work closely with the contributors to produce a book structured around three key, and closely interrelated, themes currently of great importance in relation to shipping and ports: globalisation, technological change and the environment. We should like to record our gratitude to the contributors for their collaboration, and also to the many organisations around the world whose cooperation was essential for much of the research presented here.

Individual authors whose work has been supported by grants acknowledge this in their chapters. Acknowledgement or permission to reproduce illustrative material, particularly photographs, is similarly given at appropriate points in the text. In addition, we wish to recognise the generous financial sponsorship provided by the following organisations: the Crown Estate, Associated British Ports and the Institute of Marine Engineering, Science and Technology. Without this support, the conferences that have led to this book might not have taken place, and would certainly have been on a much reduced scale. Here it is also appropriate to thank Dr Jonathon Potts of the National Maritime Museum for his excellent work in raising sponsorship and proposing speakers.

Some contributors have supplied their own illustrative material, but most has either been adapted, or produced completely, by members of the Cartographic Unit in the School of Geography at the University of Plymouth. The advice, skills and effort invested so willingly by Tim Absalom, Brian Rogers, Gareth Johnson and – most recently – Jamie Quinn have been crucial to the quality of the volume's presentation. Thanks are also due to Andy Elmes, the School's Technical Manager, for his support and assistance in coordinating the final steps in the production of the manuscript. We also record our admiration for the School's secretarial staff – chiefly Kate Hopewell, but also Naomi Swales and Linda Ware – who coped so calmly and uncomplainingly as chapters swirled in and out by email, and yet more revisions were proposed.

David Pinder
School of Geography
University of Plymouth
October 2003

Brian Slack
Department of Geography
Concordia University
October 2003

Abbreviations

ASEAN	Association of South East Asian Nations
BOD	biological oxygen demand
btoe	billion tonnes of oil equivalent
CEO	chief executive officer
CFC	chlorofluorocarbon
CIS	Commonwealth of Independent States
CLIA	Cruise Lines International Association
COSCO	China Ocean Shipping (Group) Company
COSCON	COSCO Container Lines Company Ltd
CRISP	Centre for Remote Imaging, Sensing and Processing
DGPS	differential global positioning system
DPS	dynamic positioning system
DWR	deepwater route
dwt	deadweight tonnes
ECEPA	Environmental Challenges for European Port Authorities
ECNA	east coast of North America
EIS	environmental information systems
EMAS	Eco-Management and Audit Scheme
EMIS	environmental management information systems
EMS	environmental management systems
ESPO	European Sea Ports Organisation
EU	European Union
FDPSO	floating drilling, production, storage and offloading system
FLNG	floating liquefied natural gas system
FOC	flag of convenience
FONG	floating oil and natural gas system
FPSO	floating production, storage and offloading system
GPS	global positioning system
GRT	gross registered tonnage
GWP	greenhouse warming potential
HCFC	hydrochlorofluorocarbon
HFC	hydrofluorocarbon
HPH	Hutchison Port Holdings

ICT	information and communications technology
IMO	International Maritime Organization
ISO	International Organization for Standardization
IT	information technology
KCRC	Kowloon–Canton Railway Corporation
lo/lo	lift on/lift off
MEAP	Marine Emergency Action Procedures
MIDA	Maritime Industrial Development Area
MPA	Maritime and Port Authority (of Singapore)
mtoe	million tonnes of oil equivalent
NAFTA	North American Free Trade Agreement
NGO	non-governmental organisation
NPV	net present value
ODP	ozone depletion potential
OOCL	Orient Overseas Container Line
PAH	polyaromatic hydrocarbon
PANYNJ	Port Authority of New York and New Jersey
PATH	Port Authority Trans-Hudson railway
PCB	polychlorinated biphenyl
PCDD	polychlorinated dibenzodioxin
PCDF	polychlorinated dibenzofuran
PERS	Port Environmental Review System
ppm	parts per million
PPSA	Prevention of Pollution of the Sea Act (Singapore)
ro-ro	roll-on/roll-off
SCR	selective catalytic reduction
SCSPA	South Carolina State Port Authority
SDM	Self-Diagnosis Methodology
TBT	tributyl tin
TEU	twenty-foot equivalent unit
TRESHIPS	Technologies for Reduced Environmental Impact from Ships
TSS	Traffic Separation Scheme
TTEG	Tripartite Technical Expert Group
ULCC	ultra-large crude carrier
UNCLOS	United Nations Convention on the Law of the Sea
VECS	vapour emission control system
VLCC	very large crude carrier
VOC	volatile organic compound
VTIS	Vessel Traffic Information System
WCNA	west coast North America
WTO	World Trade Organisation

1 Contemporary contexts for shipping and ports

David Pinder and Brian Slack

Introduction

The twentieth century was a period of transformation for ports and shipping. At the dawn of the last century, coal-fired ships were the norm; tramp steamers scoured the world for business; European-registered vessels dominated seaborne commerce; ships of all kinds spent much time in port; ports themselves were labour-intensive; complex and extensive port communities were consequently distinctive elements of urban docklands; and concerns over the environmental impacts of ports and shipping were virtually non-existent. As the century progressed, each of these features changed, some steadily, others rapidly. Writing in 1981, the editors of *Cityport Industrialisation* reviewed this dynamism through the work of a wide range of shipping and port specialists, and speculated on the issues likely to be encountered towards the end of the century (Pinder and Hoyle 1981). More than two decades later, in the early years of the twenty-first century, this present volume provides an opportunity to build on that analysis. In doing so, attention is focused on three recurrent, interrelated and key contexts highlighted by the 1981 review: globalisation, technological change and the environment.

As we demonstrate, in the early 1980s the reciprocity between these contexts and the shipping and port systems was already evident. Globalisation, technology and the environment were impacting in many fundamental ways on maritime industries, and were in turn being shaped by feedback channels from the industries themselves (Figure 1.1). Yet while this was clear, the early 1980s was also a time of great uncertainty. Long-established assumptions had been shaken by economic crisis, to the extent that likely future interaction between the shipping and port systems, on the one hand, and globalisation, technology and the environment on the other, was now highly debatable. Against this background, important issues to be considered today are the questions of how this uncertainty was resolved, and how the outcomes contributed to radical developments that are currently reshaping the maritime and port industries of the new millennium.

To explore these questions, the contributions to this volume have been structured into three sections, each concerned primarily with one of the main

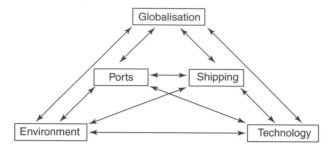

Figure 1.1 Globalisation, technology and the environment: interlinkages with ship-
       ping and ports.

contexts. But while globalisation, technological change and the environment
make useful part titles, it is important to stress that – because of the themes'
inherent interrelationships – most chapters touch on more than one theme and
would, indeed, be incomplete unless they did so. Within each chapter the
authors have naturally adopted individual approaches, so that the reader is confronted with issues as diverse as corporate strategy, port governance, performance evaluation, cultural change, technological adoption and adaptation, citizen
participation, and strategic response to the environmental movement. This
diversity adds greatly to the relevance, interest and value of this book; without it
there would in many instances be the danger of misleading oversimplification.
Yet diversity also makes the case for an overarching view of the volume, a task
we aim to undertake in this chapter. In doing so, we set the various contributions in a broader perspective, starting with the contextualisation of globalisation, technological change and the environment in the climate of uncertainty
that was so pervasive less than a quarter of a century ago.

Shipping, ports and late-twentieth-century uncertainty

Globalisation today is a very broad concept – many would say vague. A recent
book provided 35 different definitions (Streeton 2001). In the economics and
business literature it is recognised as promoting the financial and commercial
expansion of a world economy that has become increasingly integrated (Dicken
2003). In politics, global issues are seen to shape the relationships between
states (Dunn 1995). As regards the environment, many forces of change
operate at the planetary scale. In culture, the influence of television, cinema and
the Internet are diffused across the globe (Friedman 1995; Scott 1997). Even
terrorism has gone global, thanks to al-Qaida!

In the early 1980s, however, well before the term 'globalisation' gained popularity with politicians and the public, its focus was clearly on global economic
restructuring. Within this context, shipping and port developments were key
enablers of the globalisation process. The emergence of oil supertankers had

facilitated the unprecedented growth and modernisation of advanced economies from Western Europe to Japan (van den Bremen 1981; Molle and Wever 1984a, b; Odell 1986; Pinder 1992). Adaptation of supertanker principles had created dry-bulk carriers, greatly enhancing global trade in commodities such as coal, iron ore and bauxite (Takel 1981). To meet the demands of these trends, major ports had invested heavily in Maritime Industrial Development Areas (MIDAs). And ports were also investing extensively in the relatively new concept of containerisation, creating and equipping the terminals for the new generations of container ships that were already globalising trade in manufactured goods and components through dramatic efficiency gains and transport cost reductions.

Yet while the past interaction of shipping, ports and globalisation was clear, in 1981 the future seemed highly uncertain. The post-1945 growth era, remarkable for both its length and its strength, had been ended by the oil crises of 1973–4 and 1978–9 (Odell 1986). It was by no means evident that energy consumption in the advanced economies would rebound from the post-crisis slump. Large-scale investment in heavy industries had been scaled down rapidly, as plans were abandoned and many major corporations contemplated plant closures to rationalise their production systems. In these post-Fordist circumstances, what did the future hold for ports whose recent development had been dominated by the growth culture? Was it even safe to assume that the most spectacular recent advance – containerisation's emergence and rapid take-off – would not succumb to a worldwide slump in trade caused by the economic shocks of the 1970s?

Technological change, meanwhile, lay at the heart of almost everything that had driven the unprecedented advance of shipping and port systems between the 1950s and the 1980s. Bulk carriers for oil and dry commodities would have been imposssible without major new insights into loads, stresses and their management through progress with ship design and construction techniques (Figure 1.2). They would also have been pointless without technological advances in handling that enabled bulk commodities to be loaded, unloaded, organised and stored in port areas on a much greater scale, and with far greater efficiency, than had previously been possible. Containerisation echoed and reinforced all this: new types of ship based on radically different design concepts; a revolution in the nature and capacity of the quayside crane; and equally impressive advances in other handling equipment to improve the speed, rationality – and therefore the cost – of quayside storage. But how, and on what fronts, would technological change proceed in the new and highly uncertain post-1970s investment climate? On the one hand, weak economic conditions seemed highly likely to be coupled with the rapid advance of information technologies (IT) to achieve greater levels of computerised automation and, consequently, cost economies. This could be envisaged with respect to both the manning of ships and port-based cargo handling and industrialisation. In other respects, on the other hand, it was far from evident how the driving force of technological change would, or could, evolve. Had not the imperative for further advance of

Figure 1.2 The bulk coal carrier *El Carribe C* discharging in Le Havre. (Courtesy of the Port Autonome du Havre.)

the bulk commodity trades been undermined by the economic crisis? And if recession was to be a feature of the post-Fordist era, could the economic climate sustain the continued acceleration of containerisation technologies?

So far as the environmental costs of shipping and port system development are concerned, it cannot be argued that in 1981 their scale and significance were fully understood. Science was far less advanced than today. Public understanding of the environmental issues was commensurately lower. The Fordist ethos, prioritising economic growth, still tended to dominate debate. Yet despite these handicaps, appreciation of the environmental costs of trade expansion, industrialisation and port growth was taking root. In particular, Fordist growth had impacted on cityport populations through negative externalities such as air pollution (Figure 1.3) and traffic congestion, while the seemingly remorseless creation of new port areas had eroded ecologically rich estuarine and coastal wetlands on an unprecedented scale (Pinder and Witherick 1990). On these foundations, movements had begun which posed the first serious challenges to the postwar ambitions of port authorities and their shipping industry clients. But, once again, these movements were surrounded by uncertainty in the early 1980s. Would they wither away as economic crisis swung the pendulum firmly in favour of economic development rather than environmental pro-

Figure 1.3 Emissions to air from a Rotterdam refinery, 1978. (Photo David Pinder.)

tection? Might they simply become redundant as ports, industries and the new breed of container shipping companies backed away from serious investment plans whose economic rationale had now become questionable?

The twenty-first century: global and local in the maritime sector

Experience over the past two decades points clearly to the conclusion that uncertainty surrounding port industrialisation and containerisation has been resolved in dramatically different ways. Although there are naturally exceptions, in general the impetus for heavy port industrialisation has never re-emerged in the post-Fordist era. On the contrary, MIDAs have slipped from the research agenda, and partial port de-industrialisation – to which we return in relation to

Figure 1.4 Two generations of container crane: Rotterdam (1978) and Oakland (1996).
     (Photos David Pinder.)

ports and the environment – has not been unusual (Harcombe and Pinder 1996). Consequently, the imperative for change in shipping systems and ship technologies in order to facilitate the heavy industrial globalisation process has also failed to recover. Containerisation, however, contrasts sharply with this experience. Fears that recession might halt the advance of this sector proved entirely ill-founded as the global marketplace continued to develop rapidly, with the result that, as Slack details in Chapter 2, container shipping has been transformed (Figure 1.4).

Slack demonstrates how the need to serve the global marketplace has exerted enormous pressures on the shipping lines to extend their services and increase capacity. For most lines the costs of meeting these challenges have been considerable, and have dictated reorganisation of the industry. Concentration, achieved through mergers and the formation of strategic alliances, has been necessary to gain significant advances with service networks, ports of call and vessel size. These are changes with far-reaching spatial consequences, including new configurations of shipping services, the emergence of hub-and-spoke networks and, through the port selection process, resultant impacts on the growth prospects of ports. Here we see both an extension of the spatial scale of linkages and a deepening of the intensity of services, classic responses to the demands of globalisation as highlighted by Beresford[1] (1997) and Giddens[2] (1990). Beyond this, however, the influence of globalisation in the restructuring of container shipping should not be allowed to obscure the fact that containerisation itself is helping to shape globalisation. The multi-ocean networks of alliances that now exist, and the integration of lesser markets into mainline services, are powerful forces contributing to the expansion of the global economy. The new patterns identified by Slack form an evolving architecture helping to define the actual spatial character of contemporary globalisation.

What we also see emerging from these restructuring processes is the issue of conformity or homogenisation. As indicated earlier, the globalisation concept is now very broad, as evidenced by cultural studies in which the homogenising impact of global media, commerce and their values on human activity and experience – from food to cinema and television – is seen as a significant threat. In the maritime context the emergence of global carriers and the formation of strategic alliances is interpreted by Slack as a signal that diversity in container shipping is being lost as a result of competitive pressure. His analysis is that container shipping companies have become more uniform as they have striven to serve the global marketplace, calling at the same hub ports, with vessels of the same type and offering similar service frequencies.

Further evidence of the extent of this homogenisation trend emerges strongly from research by Comtois and Rimmer into container shipping developments in China, the most dynamic market in the world (Chapter 3). Over the past ten years, China has become the centre of very considerable growth in container traffic, and has been drawn increasingly into the global economic system. What is notable about these shifts is not only the scale of integration into the global economy, but also how this is being played out in an economic system that is transforming itself from a command economy to one that is becoming increasingly open. Comtois and Rimmer reveal the strategies employed by the major Chinese shipping group COSCO in order to adjust to the competitive pressures of globalisation and the internal political changes in China. As a company that was originally a state-owned enterprise, COSCO has implemented a programme of modernisation that has transformed the organisation into a corporation that is commercially based and characterised by an impressive new range of horizontal and vertical linkages. The outcome is that it has become one of the major container carriers in the world, and an actor in other fields ranging from container leasing to joint ventures for container terminal development. While achieving this, COSCO has stayed apart from the main global alliances and network structures, but at the same time has relied heavily on lessons learned from their growth experiences. Consequently, the company's development strategies have to a great extent been modelled closely on those pursued by western container corporations, with the result that the 'new' COSCO could increasingly be mistaken for a clone of its homogenised western counterparts.

While globalisation has frequently led to such convergence at the global scale, a great deal of social science research has concluded that global processes impact differentially at the local or regional levels. Cultural distinctiveness shapes issues or processes as varied as advertising (Hannerz 1996) and production technologies (Gertler 1997). In the environmental field we are urged to 'act locally', even if we 'think globally'. Global political and economic processes have been shown to play out differently in different states and regions.

The importance of region and locality cannot be over-estimated in shipping because, as much as markets may be globally linked, each retains a great deal of uniqueness and specialisation. Ports, too, possess distinctive features of site and market accessibility. Partly for these reasons, the globalisation part of the book includes contributions concerned with locality issues. Thus, in Chapter 4, Rodrigue, in a study of the Port of New York and New Jersey, reveals some of the challenges that globalisation is imposing at the local scale. Channel dredging has become a very critical issue in many ports around the world, and New York is no exception. If it is to expand its role as a hub, the port must be able to accommodate the largest container ships. At the same time, it must also serve the broad marketplace of the north-eastern United States, because the port is a vital link between global production systems and this dynamic focus of regional demand. Fulfilling this role is, however, increasingly challenging because of local failure: poor connectivity between the US rail system and port facilities embedded deep in the conurbation.

Beyond this, Rodrigue also spotlights a quite different locality issue often associated with globalisation: port governance. The rise of globalisation has run parallel to the liberalisation movement, which has in turn stressed the superiority of privatisation over public sector ownership and management. Following this thesis, the Port Authority of New York and New Jersey (PANYNJ) should arguably perform poorly in meeting the needs of the port because, reflecting its status as a public institution *par excellence*, the authority has numerous other responsibilities that at best are only indirectly connected with port activity. These range from bridges and tunnels, through aspects of public transport, to power generation and waste disposal. The result is that port activity is responsible for a only small part of the authority's asset portfolio and income. This vast jurisdiction, plus the fact that the port is but one element in the total mandate, could be used as 'evidence' that the PANYNJ is no longer appropriate to serve the port's interests as it strives to meet the demands of globalisation and thus overcome severe competition from other east-coast ports. Rodrigue's analysis, however, demonstrates that such an assumption would be entirely groundless. Slow growth in the past can be attributed to structural shifts in the local economy, rather than port authority failure. Infrastructural needs such as terminal expansion and channel dredging have been identified and met despite the Authority's disparate responsibilities, clearly calling into question the natural superiority of privatised management. Indeed, one of the advantages of this form of governance may be to ensure access to the very large sums required to invest in new projects.

De Langen (Chapter 5) approaches locality issues from a quite different, and primarily methodological, perspective. Many studies focus on understanding processes of change, creating a gap relating to the evaluation of success (or failure) at the locality level. De Langen's argument that there should be a more overt focus on performance evaluation draws upon a growing body of literature in economics that seeks to understand how competition is spatially constructed. Following Krugman's (1991) 'new economic geography' and Porter's (1990) diamond model of competition, de Langen provides an evaluative framework based on cluster analysis. In some respects this is a development of linkage studies of the type that once sought to quantify the complexity and scale of the networks of commercial and industrial activity generated by port activity (Witherick 1981). This ancestry can be observed in de Langen's application of the cluster concept to Rotterdam, whereby statistical data are employed to rank the agglomeration tendencies of an extensive range of port-related activities.

However, the main contribution of de Langen's form of cluster analysis lies in the emphasis placed on qualitative research. In the process of cluster definition, substantial weight is given to the views of key actors in port-related activities. Evaluation of cluster performance entails recognition of the qualitative distinction between cluster structure and cluster governance. In the exploration of both these concepts, qualitative questions are to the fore. Structure is related, for example, to agglomeration effects, the degree of internal competition, perceived barriers to entry and exit, and the degree of heterogeneity. Governance issues, meanwhile, centre on factors such as levels of trust between cluster members, the presence of industry leaders, and the ability to find collective solutions. An important extension of this approach is that conclusions on cluster strengths and weaknesses are not drawn from statistical analysis of data sets of the type that proliferate in association with ports, but are instead based on the insights of substantial samples of key actors within the cluster, insights naturally derived from qualitative investigations. This emphasis on insights and perceptions is intimately connected with de Langen's search for understanding and explanation rather than description, and the results produced again cause us to recognise that locations and local conditions still count, even in such global industries as container shipping.

Containerisation – the chief concern of early chapters at either the global or the local scales – is by no means the only facet of the shipping industry that is intertwined with globalisation. The opening part of the book concludes, therefore, with a contribution aiming to demonstrate the necessity of adopting wider perspectives. Here the focus is a newly emerged major maritime industry: cruise shipping. As might be anticipated, Hall's analysis in Chapter 6 draws out the cruise industry's distinctiveness. While the thrust of container shipping is towards homogeneity, cruise shipping is characterised by a post-Fordist search for product differentiation as companies offer different kinds of cruise services to different clientele. One important current trend is to grow by moving away from exclusivity, a hangover from the 1920s when cruising was a very specialised sector catering to the affluent. In the process, the experience of cruising has itself become a marketing device, in which fantasy and escapism are components. Some new cruise ships are designed to provide the complete vacation experience, largely obviating the need to venture into the real world. Others call at company-owned islands where idealised environments are populated by fake (company-employed) residents. This is globalisation at its most extreme, deeply enmeshed with postmodernism.

Despite this distinctiveness, Hall's analysis also highlights striking parallels with containerisation in the globalisation era. Driven by the affluence of western lifestyles, both have experienced rapid recent growth. Having achieved an annual average growth rate of more than 8 per cent over the past 20 years, cruising now handles more than 10 million passengers a year and generates revenues of US$14 billion. By 2010, passenger numbers are predicted to reach 22 million. Like container ships, cruise liners have increased dramatically in size. Hall reports that more than 50 new ships are on order, many of them over 100,000 dwt. A further similarity lies in the outcome of industry restructuring: the emergence of containerisation's extensive vertical and horizontal integration is echoed strikingly in the cruise industry. Beyond this, the experiences offered by cruise packages are becoming increasingly global – not least through widespread adoption of the fly-and-cruise concept, which enables many cruise ships to maximise returns in major regional markets such as the Caribbean, Alaska and the Mediterranean. And, also to maximise returns, companies routinely redeploy vessels from one global region to another in response to seasonal market conditions. Most controversially, the global cruise industry raises major locality issues relating partly to the environment – especially the disturbance caused by cruise ships in remote, ecologically rich regions – but also to the equity of the balance between social impact and economic benefit among local communities subject to continual influx.

Technology the enabler

In *Global Shift*, Dicken (2003: 85) refers to technology as 'the great growling engine of change'. It is now evident that this engine has operated in various ways to resolve the uncertainty that surrounded shipping and port technologies in the early 1980s. While some formerly dominant forces have never recovered from economic crisis, new forms of technological advance have not been slow to emerge. In the oil industry, for example, emphasis on the upscaling of supertankers has evaporated completely, to be replaced by progress with double hull construction and other design advances – reflecting environmental regulation – and significant improvements in small-scale products tankers to bolster the efficient distribution of oil derivatives by sea (Hysing and Torset 1994). While one theme has been shifts in technological emphasis, however, another has been consistency: technology continues to underlie a great deal of globalisation. Most obviously, as demonstrated in the chapters by Slack and Hall, it is advances in naval architecture, shipbuilding engineering and construction materials that have made possible the economies of scale achieved by, for example, post-Panamax container ships (see pp. 31–32) and modern cruise liners. Indeed, at the start of the twenty-first century such technological advances sometimes seem to be running ahead of economics, with shipping lines hesitant (at present) to order the ever-larger ships appearing on the designers' drawing boards.

Although this consistency promotes general recognition of the importance of technological change, on two counts there is a case for more searching analyses. The first is a common tendency to treat technological change as a 'black box', the contents of which need only be appreciated in general terms. Here the problem is a widespread failure to understand not simply the technologies themselves but, more importantly, the processes through which they promote economic and social change. Second, technological advance goes far beyond the relatively well-known progress with containerisation and the cruise industry noted above. This demands broader perspectives than are often adopted. For example, container shipping requires significant applications of information technology to plan and manage the global distribution of boxes. Similarly, at the local scale, many ports are now crucially dependent on information technologies for traffic management and safety. The importance of these largely invisible technologies was graphically demonstrated when problems with the Port of Houston's computer denied pilots, and others responsible for ship safety, access to crucial navigational information (Allison 2003a, b)[3].

All three technologically oriented chapters in Part II demonstrate the gains to be made by broader perspectives and closer examination of the contents of the 'black box'. McCalla's thesis in Chapter 7 is that decades of study of technological advances associated with containerisation have focused on the trees rather than the wood, creating a major conceptual gap with respect to our understanding of the interrelationships between technologies and port systems. Bird's *Anyport* model of 1963 was well suited to the pre-containerisation world, but should be complemented by a new model encompassing the quite different forces, and outcomes in port development, that have subsequently prevailed. Like Bird, McCalla proposes an evolutionary model based on stages: the development of initial container terminals; their subsequent expansion; further growth achieved by investment in additional terminals; terminal consolidation aimed at efficiency improvements; and, finally, the development of 'superterminals' to overcome the limitations of earlier investments and cope with the gigantism of the latest generation of container ships.

McCalla tests his *Superterminal* model by drawing on empirical evidence at two spatial scales: regionally via the east-coast ports of North America, and locally through the single port of Charleston, South Carolina. Detailed analyses of infra-structural investments in various technologies throughout the east coast demon-strate a variety of experiences, yet none the less highlight the general validity of the model's first four stages. In contrast, the final stage – progression to *Superterminal* investment – is revealed to be predictive. Although the economic case and the potential benefits are recognised, as yet no east-coast port has risen to the chal-lenge of this stage. Indeed, Charleston's efforts to do so suggest that the transition to *Superterminal* may be substantially more difficult than is the case with earlier developmental stages. Viewed as a whole, McCalla's contribution does much to bring the detailed and complex history of containerisation into sharper focus through ideas that clearly warrant further testing elsewhere in the global system.

While McCalla's perspective is port oriented, the following two chapters explore the dynamics of technological change in the shipping sector, but well beyond the familiar territory of containerisation. In Chapter 8, Ridolfi focuses on the impressive advances that have transformed the high-speed ferry from a concept to a widely applied transport medium. Around the world there are now some 1,500 of these fast ferries in service, many with cruising speeds of 40 to 50 knots (about 70–90 kph). A main thrust of Ridolfi's work is that progress has not come about simply through stepwise improvement of a single innovation. Instead, the goal of achieving high speed at sea has generated a series of altern-ative solutions – hydrofoils, hovercraft, catamarans and monohulls – to over-come the limitations of other innovations, and thus deal with challenging operational conditions as effectively as possible. An important outcome has been the emergence of a competitive environment between the various forms of fast ferry. Not all the solutions have thrived in these circumstances – mainstream hovercraft, in particular, have not proved popular. But one form of hovercraft, the sidewall variety, survived early unpopularity and difficulties to be developed into the catamaran, and the rivalry between catamarans and hydrofoils has been highly productive in forcing progress with both speed and carrying capacity.

Two further features of Ridolfi's contribution should be highlighted. First, he reveals clearly the manner in which technological change can be harnessed to target a broader market than originally identified, in the process increasing significantly the potential earnings on investment. Thus, from an early narrow focus on high-speed passenger travel, the sector has moved on via, first, the development of car carrying capacity and, more recently, progression to freight carriage. Monohulls (Figure 1.5) are currently particularly important in this latter context, and Ridolfi envisages significant further development in this respect. Most immediately, there is a role for fast ferries to complement advances in containerisation by providing rapid distributor services from major hub ports. In the longer term, however, there is the potential for further technological progress to bring direct long-distance competition between fast ships and 'traditional' container traffic. As Ridolfi notes, transatlantic fast con-tainer vessels and services are already being proposed.

Figure 1.5 The high-speed monohull *Aquastrada TMV 114*. (Courtesy of Rodriquez
Cantieri.) With an overall length of 113.4 metres, and powered by three
waterjets, the *TMV 114* can carry 928 passengers and 200 cars at 50 knots.
Pitching and vertical motion are kept within ISO standards in waves of up to
5-6 metres by its Seaworthiness Management System. Hull construction is of
high-tensile steel, with a superstructure of aluminium alloys, carbon fibre and
titanium.

Second, this long-term evolution has implications for the relationships
between fast ferries and globalisation. Although, as Ridolfi demonstrates, fast
ferries have spread widely around the world, so far their limited range, plus
restrictions imposed by sea conditions, have meant that they have not contributed directly to globalisation processes. In the main, their impacts – chiefly
accelerated economic and social integration – have been at either the regional
scale, typified by operations in Mediterranean and South-East Asian waters, or
locally in densely populated areas such as the Bay of Naples. If these ferries
evolve as Ridolfi anticipates, however, they will clearly become a significant
additional globalisation force, especially with respect to the future of containerisation.

Pinder (Chapter 9) examines a very different segment of the shipping industry that is crucially dependent on technological advance. Crude oil and gas production are shifting increasingly to offshore sites, which currently account for at
least a third of the oil and a quarter of the gas 'lifted' globally. The search for
new reservoirs is being focused in ever-deeper offshore waters, with depths of
3,000 m (10,000 feet) now being widely adopted as the target. Operations in

such depths are at present primarily concerned with the search for oil and are heavily dependent on a range of technologically sophisticated vessels, as Pinder demonstrates through studies of drillships and Floating Production, Storage and Offloading systems (FPSOs). Drillships have been made possible by a host of technological breakthroughs, including dynamic positioning systems and drilling methods capable of working in ocean depths of up to 2,500 m. They can also be repositioned rapidly and are easily moved from one site to another. These features produce significant advantages over fixed drilling platforms, even if these were technically feasible in extreme depths. FPSOs are similarly ever more sophisticated devices that not only permit production and storage operations in deep water without the need for extremely challenging pipeline or platform construction, but also undertake the extensive processing *in situ* that a normal platform would provide.

While the focus of Pinder's chapter is the technological breakthroughs that are pushing the frontiers of oil exploration and production steadily further into the ocean realm, it also provides another reminder of the character and influence of globalisation. Because of its scale and scope, oil production has become a global phenomenon in which more and more of the ocean bed is seen to offer potential exploration opportunities. As in the container and cruise shipping industries, new types of vessel – highly specialised, laden with advanced technologies, and often larger and more efficient than their predecessors – are being brought into service to exploit the potential. This trend, however, is by no means issue-free. For example, Pinder demonstrates that the link with globalisation is not simply through the increasingly global efforts to find and exploit deep-sea oilfields; also of central importance is the complex global pattern of shipbuilding and fitting out. In this context, major questions arise in relation to who gains and loses in the globalisation process. In value terms, virtually no construction work goes directly to developing countries in whose waters the industry is working, such as those on the currently very active West African frontier. Although hull construction is typically contracted to newly industrialised countries such as South Korea, most of the work is straightforward and is neither high value nor technologically challenging. Conversely, the provision of technologically sophisticated systems, and their installation at the fitting out stage, are high-value activities dominantly performed in the West.

Ports, shipping and the environment: towards a new harmony?

A striking feature of the post-crisis period has been the absence of frequent confrontations between expansionist ports and environmental groups, the focus of so much earlier friction. In many developing areas this might be attributed to the 'priority gap': continuation of the long-recognised low priority attached to environmental issues compared with western economies. In the latter, however, quite different forces are arguably responsible. As noted earlier, economic crisis blocked the impetus for large-scale industrial investment that had previously

Figure 1.6 The post-crisis land bank: Rotterdam's Maasvlakte port extension in the early 1980s. (Photo David Pinder.) Covering 2,000 ha and reclaimed in the late 1960s, it attracted only an oil storage tank farm (far distance) and a gas-fired power station before economic crisis halted industrial investment and consequently consigned the expensively reclaimed Maasvlakte to the port's land bank.

underpinned the development of so many environmentally damaging MIDAs. Because ports had expected the demand for MIDAs to continue, many were constructing new expansion areas when the crisis struck. Because these areas were never colonised by the industries for which they were intended, 'land banks' were created that could be drawn upon when additional space for new port activity was eventually needed (Figure 1.6). In many ports the scale of these land banks was substantially increased by industrial disinvestment following the economic crisis. In Europe, for example, 25 coastal refineries – nearly a fifth of the total – were closed between the late 1970s and the mid-1980s (Harcombe and Pinder 1996). These refineries naturally varied in size, but it was not unusual for 2, 3 or 4 km² of land to become redundant (Figure 1.7). As economic growth resumed in the post-crisis period, therefore, it was frequently possible for many ports to add new facilities – particularly container terminals – without returning to the earlier strategy of encroachment on the undeveloped coastal zone. Indeed, as McCalla's analysis of events in Charleston in Chapter 7 reveals, any port proposing greenfield development could easily face great public pressure to opt instead for a brownfield site from the land bank.[4]

McCalla's study is a clear indication that, despite the period of quiescence in

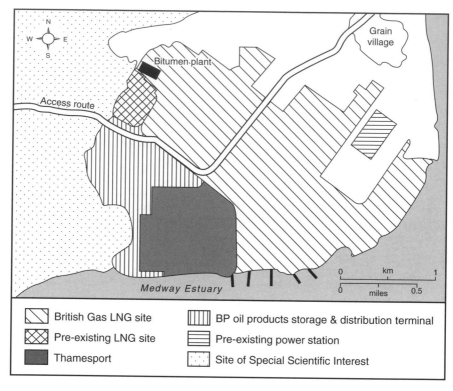

Figure 1.7 The former BP Isle of Grain oil refinery site in the early 1990s. Most of the 600-ha site remained derelict, British Gas having failed to pursue its proposed expansion of LNG facilities.

the 1980s and 1990s, the potential for confrontation between port expansion and environmental protection remains real.[5] While this is undoubtedly the case, however, the contributors to Part III are primarily concerned to highlight the argument that the interface between ports, shipping and the environment should be explored on a much broader front and from alternative perspectives. To present this case, their studies have been paired: for both ports and shipping, one investigation provides a wide-ranging overview, complemented by a second with a locality or regional focus. Linking all four chapters (Chapters 10–13) is a background question: to what extent can we claim to be progressing towards a more harmonious relationships between ports, shipping and the environment?

Wooldridge and Stojanovic (Chapter 10) question the stereotypical view that ports are extremely reluctant guardians of the environment. Using evidence drawn widely from Western Europe, they argue that, at the very least, pioneering ports have shown considerable, and mounting, concern for environmental management. Moreover, as the level of this concern has grown, there has been a significant improvement in the number of ports adopting a positive stance on environmental protection. Thus, whereas in the 1970s concern was generally limited to the requirements of health and safety legislation, the 1980s witnessed a growing interest in waste management and environmental impact assessment. Environmental auditing and participation in coastal zone management rose to the fore in the 1990s, while current concern prioritises integrated port environmental management supported by the development of IT-based environmental management systems. A particularly important shift identified is the growing belief among ports that the environment should be a pre-competitive issue. Agreement and collaboration should establish the environmental standards to be met, ensuring that low standards in some quarters do not result in unfair competition that is damaging to the economic prospects of ports that are environmentally more rigorous.

Although Wooldridge and Stojanovic make the case for a revised interpretation of European seaports' attitudes to the environment, they also highlight the fact that progress has been far from problem-free. Nor has it been achieved solely through the activities of well-motivated ports. To a degree, the obstacles have been – and still are – technical. For example, individual ports have generally developed their own environmental management structures, creating major difficulties for the pooling of information via linked IT systems. Beyond this, behavioural issues are commonly encountered: existing port employees frequently lack both IT expertise and scientific education relevant to environmental monitoring and protection. In general, therefore, a clear need for capacity building exists. Meanwhile, there is little doubt that progress has been dependent on institutional initiatives as well as the catalytic effect of pioneering ports. To a degree, this institutional influence has come from within the ports industry, particularly via the European Sea Ports Organisation (ESPO). But external influences, exerted chiefly by the European Commission, have also been extremely important. While this institution has naturally stimulated change via its regulatory function, in addition it has promoted progress through substantial investment in research projects and initiatives designed to alleviate ports' environmental impacts. One of the major messages to emerge from Wooldridge and Stojanovic's work, therefore, is that any attempt to transfer western European achievements to other world regions cannot rely simply on the leadership of progressive ports. Major obstacles will be encountered, and their solution will depend, to a considerable extent, on the creation of an appropriate institutional context.

In Chapter 11 Soriani continues the theme of ports' improving environmental performance, focusing especially on a perception problem: the difficulty of achieving external recognition of improvement and, in consequence, greater weight in key planning debates. Taking Venice as his case study, Soriani demonstrates first the port's poor past record of environmental degradation. Expansion schemes – not all of which were ultimately needed – consumed extensive wetlands on the margins of the lagoon. Channel deepening and regularisation impacted further on the aquatic environment. And, through groundwater abstraction, industries in the new port areas made a major contribution to accelerated subsidence of the lagoon floor. This not only eroded the wetlands still further, but also exacerbated flooding problems in the culturally unique historic city of Venice.

Soriani's second thrust is to assemble the evidence that this poor record has, to a great extent, been overcome. Thanks to industrial closures forced by economic restructuring, water abstraction has been sharply curtailed, slowing lagoon subsidence. Former industrial sites are being recycled for new port uses. Programmes have been launched to recreate wetlands. Yet although these trends are all highly positive from the viewpoint of local environmental protection, they have largely failed to register with either the public or major institutions with which the port must interact. What prevails is the old image and, as a result, the port must still argue from a position of weakness in key negotiations such as those surrounding the proposed periodic closure of the lagoon for flood protection purposes. From a strategic viewpoint, therefore, it is evident that objective improvements in a port's environmental performance may be insufficient for its goals to be met in full. The challenge can also be subjective: control must be gained over what may be growing divergence between image and reality.

Like Wooldridge and Stojanovic, Reynolds (Chapter 12) challenges widely held assumptions, in this case the belief that the dominant environmental threat from shipping is the danger of catastrophic accidents, particularly involving crude oil. Her argument is that all stages of a ship's life cycle, from construction to scrapping, impact on the environment, with day-to-day operations having the greatest significance in terms of emissions and discharges. Concentrating on these relatively neglected everyday impacts, Reynolds demonstrates the breadth of the problems, countermeasures undertaken and the extent of the difficulties to be overcome. Systematic analysis reveals a wide range of significant emissions to air, discharges to water and waste streams, many of which have yet to be effectively controlled by regulation. Thematically, the argument reveals strong links with globalisation, suggesting the power of economic forces operating at the world scale to induce other forms of globalisation in the environmental arena. For example, pollution, and the risk of ecological damage, can be globalised through factors such as the concentration of shipping in the world's major shipping lanes, or the capacity of inappropriately discharged ballast water to introduce non-native or pathogenic organisms into vulnerable local ecosystems. Equally evident are the relationships with technological change, primarily because in many instances regulation can be made effective only through technological advances controlling, for example, exhaust emission content, cargo vapour emissions or the marine ecological impact of antifouling paints. Although Reynolds's review establishes that progress is being made on many fronts, it is equally evident that a great deal remains to be done if reality is to be brought into line with the common perception that – while there may be intermittent severe accidents – the shipping sector is fundamentally environmentally benign.

Cleary and Goh close the environmental part of the book with a regional study – centred on the Straits of Malacca – of marine pollution control in the developing world. Here the theme of global and local re-emerges, since navigation pressures in the congested Straits are to a great extent generated by globalisation-related demand arising elsewhere, but have major local implications in the event of, for example, a supertanker disaster. What also re-emerges is the need to question received wisdom concerning the environmental 'priority gap' – in part, at least. Even though the regional emphasis is on economic development, the environment is on the agenda: pollution dangers not only have been recognised but also have prompted a range of control initiatives. These depend partly on regulatory penalties, but also on management measures such as traffic separation schemes and investment in the tracking and information technologies to implement them. A further positive sign is the degree of international cooperation between Singapore, Malaysia and Indonesia that this progress has required. But there are also indications that conversion to the goal of environmental protection is still far from complete. Measures taken to combat pollution relate dominantly to the threat of tanker collisions and oil spillages. Recognition of wider threats appears limited. Although there is international cooperation, it is evident from Cleary and Goh's analysis that the pace is set by Singapore – the region's most advanced economy – with Malaysia and Indonesia trailing in their neighbour's wake. And while Singapore performs this leadership role on the one hand, on the other it continues to pursue – largely unopposed – wetland reclamation projects for port development that would provoke a storm of protest in the West.

Conclusion: towards an evolving research agenda

How may we summarise the collective research arguments advanced by the contributors? One common theme to emerge is the scale and pace of change that characterised the closing decades of the twentieth century. The reordering of priorities has been extensive and has resolved many of the uncertainties that originally prevailed. Economic challenges associated with industry and the global movement of raw materials have largely slipped from the agenda, giving way to new dominant centres of interest overwhelmingly concerned with service provision. Outstanding among these is the containerisation phenomenon, with its imperative for rapid, low-cost movement of goods. But as the exploration of the cruise industry demonstrates, this service-oriented momentum has also developed on a significantly broader front. As this has happened, both shipping and ports have become ever more entwined with globalisation – both as facilitators of globalisation processes and as economic entities that must constantly strive to succeed in an increasingly competitive globalised economic environment.

This shift is in turn a signpost towards a second major theme to emerge from the analyses: the research opportunities that exist on an increasingly broad front. While these opportunities relate in part to shipping systems and port operations narrowly defined, they go well beyond this in the contexts of technological change and the environment. Environmental factors are playing an increasingly important role in shaping port and shipping operations, and these maritime activities are themselves sources of multi-faceted environmental problems. These relationships open a very broad range of research possibilities. Similarly, it is evident that new technologies are an enabling force in many branches of the shipping sector, quite apart from the crucial technological advances associated with containerisation. Moreover, the examples explored in this volume – high-speed ferries and the offshore oil industry – amply illustrate their relevance to the day-to-day lifestyles, and indeed life chances, of very large populations. Even so, they are seriously under-researched.

Complementing this emphasis on the potential breadth of the research front is an equivalent appreciation of the importance of progress towards new con-ceptual and methodological bases. McCalla's *Superterminal* model, Slack's identification of homogenisation as a questionable force in the container indus-try, de Langen's concern for both the cluster concept and qualitative research, and Pinder's use of database methodologies to conceptualise 'model' offshore vessels can all be seen as steps in that direction. Conceptualisation is essential in a subject area such as this, because both shipping and ports have the capacity to generate great complexity through case studies exploring numerous, yet usually unrelated, channels. While some progress has been made, however, what is pro-vided here is indicative rather than exhaustive. All three of our overarching themes – globalisation, technological change and the environment – continue to offer major opportunities in this arena.

Finally, much of our contributors' work highlights the importance of continuing to question received wisdom. This is implicit in the general argu-ment for diversification of the research agenda, but also explicit in various other respects. Examples include questioning of the increasingly firmly rooted assumption that privatisation will deliver more efficient ports than 'outmoded' public ownership; the argument that excessive concern for containerisation risks the neglect of equally significant technological advances elsewhere in the ship-ping and port sectors; rejection of the idea that the chief environmental threat posed by shipping is the danger of catastrophic oil pollution; and championing of the view that port authorities are increasingly establishing a record as guardians, rather than enemies, of the environment. Such healthy attitudes are, of course, essential for progress. In noting them, however, we are acutely aware that what is offered here is – like the *Cityport Industrialization* review in 1981 – only a limited snapshot taken at a particular point in time. Change is continu-ous, and we look forward to the alternative perspectives that other generations of shipping and port geographers will undoubtedly offer in the future.

Notes

1 One main dimension of globalisation is the issue of scope, whereby relationships of all kinds, from trade to refugee flows, have become extended. These extended relation-ships are seen to produce a state of affairs in which the roles and importance of locali-ties and even nation-states are reduced. Beresford (1997) captures this by arguing that the concept 'reflects a more comprehensive interaction than has occurred in the past,

suggesting something different from the word "international". It implies a diminishing importance of national boundaries and the strengthening of identities that stretch beyond those rooted in a particular region or country'.

2 Globalisation's second dimension is the intensification of relations, whereby disparate elements are drawn ever more closely together. This is captured in Giddens's (1990) definition of globalisation: 'an intensification of world-wide social relations which link distant localities in such a way that local happenings are shaped by events occurring many miles away, and vice-versa'. This intensification of relations is not restricted to social linkages, but also includes economic, cultural and political associations.

3 The affected information systems were described as a 'a critical part of the country's infrastructure' (Allison 2003a). It was alleged that the incident occurred because a computer hacker in the United Kingdom, whose target was a private individual in the United States, needed to go through intermediary computers to build strength. One of these computers happened to be the Port of Houston's system. When the case came to court, however, the accused was found not guilty.

4 In this case the brownfield site in question was created not by industrial decline, but by restructuring of the US Navy. Naval reorganisation has been responsible for making large tracts of land redundant, particularly – but not exclusively – in the United States. For examinations of this topic, see the papers in two journal theme issues: Smith and Pinder (1997) and Pinder and Smith (1999).

5 The potential for confrontation will obviously increase as land banks are exhausted. Moreover, evidence is emerging that conservationists and the public are starting to regard areas remaining in the bank as ecologically valuable. On the United Kingdom's Southampton Water, for example, a substantial wetland zone in Dibden Bay was completely destroyed in the 1950s to create a dumping ground for dredged material, ground intended to be available in the long run for port expansion (Pinder and Witherick 1990). Having stood idle for several decades, the in-filled bay is now the subject of a public inquiry provoked by vociferous opposition, much of it environmental, to a proposed new container terminal (Planning Inspectorate 2003). Similarly, on the Seine estuary a major environmental confrontation has arisen because of Le Havre's plans for containerisation on land reclaimed for a failed MIDA project (Port Technology International 2002).

References

Allison, R. (2003a) 'Hacker attack left port in chaos', *Guardian*, 7 October, p. 7.

—— (2003b) 'Youth cleared of crashing American port's computer', *Guardian*, 18 October, p. 7.

Beresford, S.V. (1997) *President's Message*, New York: Ford Foundation.

Dicken, P. (2003) *Global Shift*, London: Guilford.

Dunn, J. (ed.) (1995) *Contemporary Crisis and the Nation State*, Oxford: Blackwell.

Friedman, T.L. (1995) *Cultural Identity and Global Process*, London: Sage.

Gertler, M. (1997) 'Between the global and the local: the spatial limits to productive capital', in K. Cox (ed.) *Spaces of Globalization*, New York: Guilford.

Giddens, A. (1990) *The Consequences of Modernity*, Stanford, CA: Stanford University Press.

Hannertz, U. (1996) *Transnational Connections: Culture, People, Places*, London: Routledge.

Harcombe, S. and Pinder, D.A. (1996) 'Oil industry restructuring and its environmental consequences in the coastal zone', in B.S. Hoyle (ed.) *Cityports, Coastal Zones and Regional Change*, Chichester, UK: Wiley.

Hysing, T. and Torset, O.P. (1994) 'Reduction of oil outflows at collisions and ground-ings through improved vessel design arrangement', *Marine Pollution Bulletin*, 29: 368–374.

Krugman, P. (1991) *Geography and Trade*, Leuven: Leuven University Press.

Molle, W. and Wever, E. (1984a) *Oil Refineries and Petrochemical Industries in Western Europe: Buoyant Past, Uncertain Future*, Aldershot, UK: Gower.

—— (1984b) 'Oil refineries and petrochemical industries in Europe', *GeoJournal*, 9: 421–430.

Odell, P.R. (1986) *Oil and World Power*, Harmondsworth, UK: Penguin.

Pinder, D.A. (1992) 'Seaports and the European energy system', in B.S. Hoyle and D.A. Pinder (eds) *European Port Cities in Transition*, London: Belhaven, pp. 20–39.

Pinder, D.A. and Hoyle, B.S. (1981) 'Cityports, technologies and development strat-egies', in B.S. Hoyle and D.A. Pinder (eds) *Cityport Industrialization and Regional Development: Spatial Analysis and Planning Strategies*, Oxford: Pergamon, pp. 323–338.

Pinder, D.A. and Smith, H.D. (eds) (1999) *Heritage Resources and Naval Port Regener-ation*, theme issue of *Ocean and Coastal Management*, 42(10–11).

Pinder, D.A. and Witherick, M.E. (1990) 'Port industrialization, urbanization and wetland loss', in M. Williams (ed.) *Wetlands: A Threatened Landscape*, Oxford: Black-well, pp. 234–266.

Planning Inspectorate (2003) *Dibden Bay Inquiry*, available at www.planning_inspectorate.gov.uk/dibden/ (accessed 21 February 2003).

Porter, M.E. (1990) *The Competitive Advantage of Nations*, London: Macmillan.

Port Technology International (2002) 'Port of Le Havre sets sights on 3 million Teus at "Port 2000"', online, available at http://www.porttechnology.org/industry.news/2002/mainnews/07.05.01.shtml (accessed 18 December 2002).

Scott, A. (ed.) (1997) *The Limits of Globalisation*, London: Routledge.

Smith, H.D. and Pinder, D.A. (eds) (1997) *Geostrategy, Naval Power and Naval Port Systems*, theme issue of *Marine Policy*, 21(4).

Streeton, P. (2001) *Globalization: Threat or Opportunity?* Copenhagen: Copenhagen Business School.

Takel, R.E. (1981) 'The spatial demands of ports and related industry and their relation-ships with the community', in B.S. Hoyle and D.A. Pinder (eds) *Cityport Industrial-ization and Regional Development: Spatial Analysis and Planning Strategies*, Oxford: Pergamon, pp. 47–68.

van den Bremen, W.J. (1981) 'Aspects of maritime transport and port development under the influence of changes in the energy supply in the next decades: Western Europe as a case study', in C. Muscara, M. Soricillo and A. Vallega (eds) *Changing Maritime Transport*, vol. 1, Naples: Istituto Universitario Navale and Istituto di Geografia Economica for the International Geographical Union, pp. 40–73.

Witherick, M.E. (1981) 'Port developments, port-city linkages and prospects for mar-itime industry: a case study of Southampton', in B.S. Hoyle and D.A. Pinder (eds) *Cityport Industrialization and Regional Development: Spatial Analysis and Planning Strategies*, Oxford: Pergamon, pp. 113–132.

Part I
Global and local in the maritime sector

2 Corporate realignment and the global imperatives of container shipping

Brian Slack

Introduction

Globalisation and container shipping enjoy a reciprocal relationship. There is little doubt that the expansion of international commerce and the establishment of global manufacturing systems would have been impossible without the efficiencies and economies that containerisation has brought. Container shipping is a facilitator of globalisation. It provides the means to connect markets and customers with a safe, reliable and cost-effective transportation system. At the same time, global forces have impacted on the shipping industry itself. Shipping lines have been forced to provide more services to more markets with larger ships than ever, and this has placed very considerable financial pressures on lines. Customers demand a global service, but in order to satisfy this imperative, the carriers have had to enter new markets and add extra capacity in an environment of heightened competition. This has resulted in an unprecedented consolidation of many of the carriers. While a degree of cooperation between carriers in the container shipping industry has always existed, in the latter part of the 1990s there occurred a significant *rapprochement* of most of the major actors. Two types of groupings are evident. First, there are multinational mergers involving complete financial integration, such as between the British-based P&O and the Dutch line Nedlloyd, and the acquisition of the US line APL by NOL of Singapore. Here, the merged companies operate under a single management structure. Second, strategic alliances have been formed, whereby firms pool resources (vessels) and operate joint services, while retaining their independence. An example of a recent alliance in container shipping is the Grand Alliance, made up of the German Hapag-Lloyd, the Anglo-Dutch P&O Nedlloyd, the Malaysian MISC, the Japanese NYK and the Hong Kong OOCL.

This chapter examines how globalisation is shaping the container shipping industry. It begins by describing the new organisational structures that have emerged as a result of global pressures. The fundamental reorganisation of the industry has significant spatial consequences. The main part of the chapter analyses how shipping services, port selection and vessel deployments have been restructured. In coming together in strategic alliances or through mergers, companies have been forced to make adaptations. At no time in the history of containerisation has the geography of shipping services changed so much. The chapter concludes by considering the future implications of a restructured container shipping industry.

Restructuring of container shipping

The explosion of international trade that occurred during the last decade of the twentieth century, a growth that is generally explained by globalisation (Dicken 1998; Dunning 1997), presented significant opportunities for container shipping. As a transport service that provides the means to carry large quantities of goods with security at a low cost, container shipping was uniquely positioned to take advantage of the new commercial opportunities. The intensification of trade between North America, Europe and East Asia, and the opening up of new markets in South Asia and Latin America, resulted in a growth of container traffic worldwide from 61 million TEU (twenty -foot equivalent units) in 1986 to 225 million TEU in 2000 (*Containerisation International Yearbooks*).

Inevitably, this growth created significant challenges for container shipping. The companies had to add capacity in a relatively short period of time. The world fleet of container ships grew from 1.4 million TEU in 1986 to 5.3 million TEU in 2000 (*Containerisation International Yearbooks*). Ever-larger ships provided most of this new capacity and, despite the operational scale economies, were more costly to purchase. At the same time that companies were facing significant financial pressures to acquire new vessels and establish new services in more markets, they also were confronted by increased competition. During the latter part of the last century, many new carriers appeared on the world scene, many of them from Asia, seeking to exploit the enormous trade opportunities made possible by regional manufacturing growth. In this way, the Korean Hanjin, the Chinese COSCO and the Malaysian MISC emerged as competitors to the established lines. Despite the growth in international maritime trade, therefore, shipping lines faced unprecedented financial demands and enhanced competitive pressures.

It was these competitive pressures arising out of globalisation that forced most of the leading shipping lines to seek some form of cooperation with erstwhile competitors. Companies that found themselves weakened by competition, or unable to afford needed investments, became targets for takeover, while others sought to expand into new markets by acquiring firms already present there. There emerged during the 1990s, therefore, a series of mergers and acquisitions that has served to transform the industry (Table 2.1). Examples of mergers include that of P&O and Nedlloyd in 1996 and that between SeaLand and Maersk in 1999. The former comprised two long-established European firms that had been experiencing financial difficulties (Brooks 2000). The latter involved two of the most important container shipping lines, which had come together in 1991 in the first strategic alliance in the industry, an alliance that exploited the different market strengths of the two carriers. The merger came about because the parent company of SeaLand, CSX, sought to focus on its

Table 2.1 Alliances and mergers in the ocean container industry, 1990–2000

Alliances	Mergers
Grand Alliance Hapag-Lloyd – MISC – NYK – OOCL – P&O Nedlloyd	Maersk-SeaLand
New World Alliance APL/NOL – HMM – MOL	NOL – APL
United Alliance CY – DSR/Senator – Hanjin – UASC	CP Ships – CAST – TMM – Lykes – Contship – ANZDL – Italia
Cosco – K-Line – Yangming	P&O Nedlloyd
Maersk-SeaLand	CMA-CGM

Source: *Containerisation International Yearbook*, 2002.

core business – railroads – and hive off its shipping assets, enabling them to be purchased by Maersk (Brooks 2000).

Examples of acquisitions include that of NOL's purchase of APL. APL was a major US shipping line that focused only on the transpacific trade route. It had been experiencing financial difficulties in the 1990s and became a takeover target. In fact, it was acquired by the smaller, though more globally exposed, national shipping company of Singapore in 1997 (Brooks 2000). The new company now operates under the name of APL. The most dramatic example of acquisition is that of CP Ships, which, starting in 1995, has purchased six shipping lines – CAST, Lykes, ANZDL, Contship, TMM and Italia – and has become one of the top 10 container carriers in the world (Alix *et al.* 1999).

Strategic alliances represent looser forms of association whereby independent companies come together and share resources to operate jointly in some markets, while continuing to compete separately in others (Goold and Campbell 1998). As mentioned earlier, the first such alliance in container shipping was between SeaLand and Maersk in 1991. In 1995, however, the Global Alliance between APL, OOCL, MOL and Nedlloyd was formed. It was quickly matched by the Grand Alliance between NYK, P&O, Hapag Lloyd and NOL, and by a grouping between Hanjin, DSR-Senator and Cho Yang. Subsequent mergers (already discussed) forced a realignment of alliance membership, as newly merged companies found themselves in different alliances. In 1997, therefore, the present groupings were established (Table 2.1).

Organisational restructuring has involved most of the major shipping lines in the world. Only Evergreen, MSC and Zim among the 20 carriers have not been involved in some form of consolidation, and even these are party to looser forms of association such as slot charters. Whether the restructuring has taken the form of a merger or a partnership in an alliance (or both), it has resulted in a spatial transformation of the industry over a very short period of time. Services have been extended and reconfigured, vessels redeployed, and the ports of call adjusted, changes that ultimately affect every facet of the maritime industry. Against this background, the way services, ships and ports have been impacted is now explored in detail.

The new service networks

In operational terms both alliances and mergers have produced a transformation of service networks. Indeed, the opportunities of rationalising vessel deployments are one of the advantages claimed for sharing or merging fleets that are increasingly expensive to operate in a global environment. The intensity and frequency of container shipping services have changed as a direct result of the consolidation. Slack *et al.* (2002) report that the number of shipping services mounted by alliance members increased by a third in ten years, from 422 services in 1989 to 545 in 1999. The proliferation of services has given rise to an inevitable spatial adjustment in the configuration of shipping networks. Prior to the formation of the alliances, container shipping networks exhibited three broad characteristics. Foremost was the differential concentration of services and capacities of the carriers. Except for NYK and Nedlloyd, all the companies that were to join an alliance provided services that were regionalised and, with the exception of Maersk, were based largely on nationality. The Asian carriers maintained services that were oriented to North and East Asia, while the European carriers, with the exception of Maersk, had an emphasis on services focused on North-West Europe. Similarly, the US carriers were weighted towards east- and/or west-coast markets (Figure 2.1).

A second feature of the pre-alliance service structure was the general simplicity of the services. Most were range-to-range; that is to say, they linked two continental facades. This is particularly evident if North, East and South-East Asia are combined and treated as one range. The number of services that extended beyond two maritime ranges was very small (Figure 2.2). The third feature of the earlier services was the heavy allocation of capacity to the main markets of North-West Europe, North America and North and East Asia. The

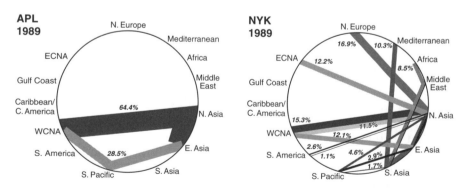

Figure 2.1 Regional/national concentrations of container shipping services, 1989.

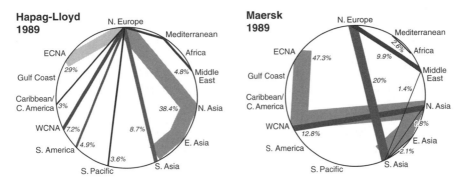

Figure 2.2 Range-to-range services and the dominance of east–west trade routes.

pre-eminence of the east–west trades was evident. Lesser markets had few services and the slot capacity allocation was markedly inferior.

When the geographical spread of the pre-alliance services is examined, significant differences between companies are evident. Table 2.2 tallies the number of services for each line in 13 major market areas (ranges). From a low

Table 2.2 Number of maritime ranges served by alliances and alliance members, 1989–99

Company	1989	1999
Grand Alliance		10
MISC	5	6
NYK	11	13
Hapag-Lloyd	12	12
P&O	10	13
Nedlloyd	13	13
OOCL	9	11
New World Alliance		8
HMM	6	8
APL	4	12
NOL	9	
MOL	10	13
United Alliance		11
Hanjin	4	11
Cho Yang	6	11
DSR	6	11
Senator	7	
Maersk	10	13
SeaLand	7	
K-Line	10	9
Yangming	9	10
COSCO	11	11

Source: Slack *et al.* (2002) (data drawn from *Containerisation International Yearbooks*).

of 4 ranges served in the case of Hanjin and APL, to a full complement of 13 ranges for Nedlloyd, there was a wide variation, but with an average of 7.3 regions served. These results confirm that most container shipping services prior to the alliances were regionally concentrated.

By 1999, after the mergers and alliances had taken place, a growing conformity of shipping services had become evident. This is reflected in the ranges served (Table 2.2). The mean number of ranges served per company rose from 7.3 in 1989 to 10.3 in 1999. Services became more extensive. Companies that had a wide market coverage in 1989 – such as P&O, MOL and Maersk – became global operators, and others that were more regionally based in 1989 – such as APL, Hanjin and HMM – also emerged as world players (Figure 2.3).

Alliance membership has in every case but one (MISC) facilitated the expansion of services. The alliance sailings permitted many carriers to enter markets that they could not serve independently. Thus, HMM gained access to the east coast of North America (ECNA) and the Caribbean as a result of its membership in the New World Alliance. Through its acquisition by NOL and its membership in the New World Alliance, APL now provides service to Europe. In a similar fashion, P&O, through its merger with Nedlloyd and membership in the Grand Alliance, is involved in services to the west coast of North America (WCNA) for the first time (Figure 2.4).

It should be noticed that the alliance services form an integral, though by no means complete, part of the services of member carriers. These alliance services tend to be between the major trading blocks (Table 2.2) and, because of the pooling of resources, they deploy the largest ships. This has permitted the individual members to mount separate or joint services into lesser markets such as Central and South America, thereby enhancing further the global character of container shipping. In addition, the industry is developing new feeder services, especially in Asia and the Mediterranean, where a new hub structure has been established, based on new pivot ports in the southern basin (Zophil and Prijon 1999). While the industry is still dominated by the east–west trades, a more north–south alignment is becoming evident.

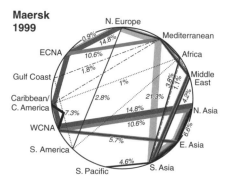

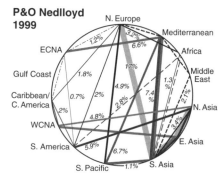

Figure 2.3 Global multi-range networks.

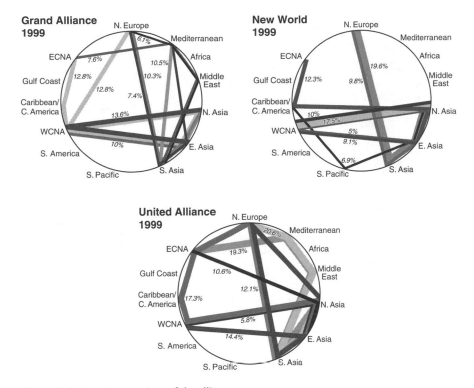

Figure 2.4 Container services of the alliances.

Vessel size and numbers

One of the most remarkable developments in container shipping over the past ten years has been the explosion of vessel capacity. This is reflected in the actual number of ships comprising the fleets of the companies that formed alliances in the late 1990s. In 1989 the total number of vessels they deployed was 728. Ten years later, the fleet had grown to 1,100 (Slack *et al.* 2002). This growth in vessel numbers is explained by the expansion of services described earlier in the chapter. However, it provides only a partial picture of the growth in capacity, since it is the increase of vessel size that has been one of the most remarkable features of the past ten years. For the first 30 years of containerisation there was a modest growth in vessel size, from the first- and second-generation ships of 2,000 TEU capacity, to the fourth generation vessels of the late 1980s, whose capacity reached 4,000 TEU. Because there was an operational limit to the size of the ships, due to the dimensional constraints of the locks of the Panama Canal, the largest vessels at this time were referred to as Panamax. In 1989 the first post-Panamax vessel entered service. It was slow to be accepted, but the economies of scale of large ships have proved subsequently to be very attractive, and since 1995 there has been a very significant growth in post-Panamax vessel

Figure 2.5 The *Hamburg Express.* (Courtesy of Hapag-Lloyd). With a capacity of 7,500 TEU, this is one of the world's largest container ships.

numbers and capacity (Figure 2.5). By 2000 the majority of ships on order were of post-Panamax dimensions, and the debate in shipping circles has been about what the limits might be. By 2002, vessels of 8,000 TEU capacity were in service, and vessels in excess of 15,000 TEU are considered by some experts to be feasible (Cullinane and Khanna 2000), though not by others (Gilman 1999).

The role of the alliances in shaping the progression of vessel size is debatable. The debut of the post-Panamax ships pre-dates the alliances. But it is note-worthy that the alliance services employ ships that are larger than the average for the fleets of individual carriers. Members have contributed their largest vessels to alliance services, a pooling of assets that ensures a service capacity that few would be able to justify as separate operators. The alliances and mergers have clearly given the impetus to the progression of vessel capacity in the con-tainer shipping industry.

Changing patterns of port selection

The choice of ports of call is directly related to how the carriers seek to exploit markets. The changes made to container shipping networks over the last decade of the twentieth century impact on port selection. Expansion into new markets brings with it the inevitable addition of new ports but, even on ranges where service is being maintained, new joint services have the potential to bring about a rationalisation of port selection. The different companies in an alliance might have formerly called at different ports, but the new joint services will necessitate realignment.

The late 1990s was a period of significant change and adjustment for the carriers' services. Table 2.3 summarises the changes for a sample of carriers. The most impressive feature is the scale and magnitude of the shifts in ports of call that took place in a very short time. All companies experienced a large adjustment in port services coinciding with the establishment of the alliances. However, the character of the changes differed between the carriers. Some companies, such as APL and MISC, greatly enlarged their port networks, while others, such as MOL and Hapag-Lloyd, experienced some retrenchment. There is no consistency within alliance structures, with some members expanding the number of ports of call, and others reducing service.

Some of the changes are very striking. In a five-year period, HMM added 43 new ports to its schedule, while maintaining service to 24 and dropping only 10. A similar pattern is found for OOCL. Conversely, alliance co-member MOL ceased service to 57 ports, while adding only 47. Companies that underwent equity mergers during the period, as well as alliance membership, experienced some of the largest adjustments. P&O added 106 ports to its network and APL 71, both increases being greater than the number of ports retained between 1994 and 1999. On a smaller scale, DSR added 29 ports. This leads to the question of whether the mergers led to the increases. In the case of P&O it appears that the merger with Nedlloyd was an important factor in the addition of ports, because Nedlloyd had served 60 of the 106 new additions previously. On the other hand, for APL only 8 of its new ports had been served previously by NOL, and in the case of DSR, none of the new additions was previously served by Senator. This suggests that the mergers themselves did not always bring about change.

There appear to be two elements regarding the effects of the alliances on

Table 2.3 Turnover of ports in three alliance networks, 1994–9

Carrier	Port dropped	Port continued	of which are alliance ports	Port added	of which are alliance ports	of which are from merged partner
HMM	10	24	21	43	16	n.a.
APL	6	35	19	71	18	8
MOL	57	92	29	47	8	n.a.
P&O	14	89	29	106	14	60
NYK	41	112	34	30	9	n.a.
Hapag	31	67	30	20	13	n.a.
MISC	6	42	21	29	14	n.a.
OOCL	11	39	26	49	17	
DSR	25	58	27	29	11	0
Hanjin	2	25	21	35	16	n.a.
Cho Yang	8	33	27	32	10	n.a.

Source: *Containerisation International Yearbooks.*

port selection. First, in every case the majority of the ports included in alliance networks were previously called at by its members individually. For the Japanese carriers, which were already offering services to a wide spectrum of ranges, the alliance ports were overwhelmingly part of their existing networks. For HMM, APL, MISC, DSR, Cho Yang, OOCL and Hanjin, the alliance ports represented at least half the ports for which service was maintained between 1994 and 1999, and in the case of Hanjin and HMM, nearly all the retained ports were those that were part of alliance services.

The second aspect of the alliances is that they helped open up new markets and ports. They provided every member with additional market coverage, and all the carriers added ports of call that were components of alliance networks. Examples are numerous, including MISC accessing the east coast of North America, DSR the west coast, P&O the Pacific North-West, APL Europe and Hapag Lloyd the Far East. Of particular interest is the way the alliance services enabled carriers to tap directly into the Chinese market, replacing earlier networks based entirely on transshipments via Hong Kong (Wang and Slack 2000). A further way the alliances helped members open up new markets arose from the fact that the joint services linked the major markets, which enabled freed capacity to be allocated to establish individual services in other ranges. Thus, during the latter half of the 1990s MOL restructured its services in Japan, and MISC extended new services to lesser markets such as Australia.

If the actual ports served by alliance services are examined, two features stand out (Table 2.4). As is implied above, the alliance services are concentrated on the main market ranges. It is also evident that the alliances have sought to provide services to each range by selecting the largest ports. Multi-port services are thus the feature of alliance operations on each range.

Globalisation, consolidation and container shipping

The features of the container shipping industry described in this chapter provide some indication of the effects of alliances on shipping services. Of basic significance is the diversity of the firms that have come together in various forms during the review period. Differentiated by nationality, capitalisation and capacity, the container shipping companies that operated independently prior to the consolidations of the mid-1990s served different markets in different ways. Most were regionally concentrated, operating range-to-range services between ports on the east–west trades. As they have come together through mergers and/or membership in strategic alliances, there has been a marked tendency for the services to become more similar. The former regional market differences have diminished, as all the companies are now serving most market areas in the world. There are still some differences in the relative capacity allocations to the different markets, but there is far greater conformity of market coverage today than in the early 1990s.

Conformity is an expected outcome of globalisation. Companies serving global markets adopt standardised operational and marketing procedures that

Table 2.4 Ports served by the major alliances, 2001

New World Alliance	Grand Alliance	United Alliance
Northern Europe		
Bremerhaven, Felixstowe, Hamburg, Le Havre, Rotterdam, Southampton	Antwerp, Bremerhaven, Hamburg, Le Havre, Rotterdam, Southampton, Thamesport	Antwerp, Felixstowe, Hamburg, Le Havre, Rotterdam, Thamesport
Mediterranean		
Genoa, Marseilles, Barcelona	Barcelona, Damietta, La Spezia, Marsaxlokk, Marseilles	Giaio Tauro, La Spezia, Marseilles, Valencia
Middle East		
Aden, Jeddah, P. Said	Jeddah, Dubai	Jeddah, Khor Fakkan
South Asia		
Colombo, Laem Chabang, Port Kelang, Singapore	Tanjung Priok, Colombo, Laem Chabang, Port Kelang, Singapore	Colombo, Port Kelang, Singapore
East Asia		
Chiwan, Hong Kong, Kaohsiung, Keelung, Kwangyang, Ningbo, Quingdao, Shanghai, Yantian	Hong Kong, Kaohsiung, Ningbo, Quingdao, Shanghai, Shekou, Xiamen, Yantian	Chiwan, Hong Kong, Kaohsiung, Kwangyang, Quingdao, Shanghai, Xingang, Yantian
North Asia		
Busan, Hakata, Kobe, Nagoya, Shimzu, Tokyo, Yokohama	Busan, Hakata, Kobe, Nagoya, Sendai, Shimzu, Tokyo	Busan, Hakata, Osaka, Tokyo
West Coast N. Am		
Dutch Harbor, Los Angeles, Oakland, Portland, Tacoma, Seattle, Vancouver	Long Beach, Los Angeles, Oakland, Seattle, Vancouver	Long Beach, Oakland, Portland, Seattle, Vancouver
East Coast N. Am		
Charleston, New York, Miami, Norfolk, Savannah	Charleston, Halifax, Miami, New York, Norfolk, Savannah	Norfolk, New York, Savannah
Central America		
Balboa, Puerto Manzanillo	Balboa, Cristóbal, Puerto Manzanillo	Balboa, Cristóbal, Manzanillo, Puerto Manzanillo

Source: *Containerisation International Yearbook*, 2002.

allow them to carry on business in disparate regions (Dicken 1998). Providing transportation services across the world's oceans has necessitated constructing networks that are interlinked, using comparable vessels in similar marketplaces, employing common handling operations, and applying standardised information and documentation processing systems. In turn, these developments in the container shipping industry help shape globalisation itself. The strategies of intensifying services between the main markets, and extending container services into smaller markets that used to be outside main intermodal networks, have greatly enhanced the international trade and investment that are essential features of globalisation.

While container shipping services were becoming more similar, there occurred a massive change in the selection of ports of call. All the companies that joined alliances have undergone a very large turnover in port service calls since the mid-1990s. All have shed ports from their networks, while at the same time adding many new calls. This has produced a radically different set of ports of call in each carrier's services. These changes can be ascribed directly to the alliances. The groupings forced the companies to rationalise and integrate services, and thus required a greater coordination of port selection for the mainline alliance services. At the same time, the cooperation freed resources that provided opportunities to enter new markets outside the alliance structure or serve existing markets in different ways.

The radical changes in the ports of call paradoxically contributed to the growing similarity between the separate companies. Because the core services of the different alliances use many of the same ports, the differences in the ports of call of the alliances listed in Table 2.4 are surprisingly few. Not only are the alliance carriers serving the same ranges, but they are also calling at the same set of ports on each range. Differences occur in the non-alliance services and in the feeder networks, but even here port selection is quite uniform. The explanation is that, while globalisation forces the companies to have a presence in every major world market, within many of these markets the availability of ports with adequate facilities, suitable water depths and acceptable operational conditions is limited. The global carriers thus end up serving the same ports.

Container shipping futures

Making predictions about the future of container shipping is hazardous. The industry has evolved very rapidly over the past decade, and it would be foolish to believe that further unforeseen changes are unlikely. There are certain developments, however, that are likely to come about, while others are more debatable.

A central question is the durability of the alliances. Some economists see alliances as fundamentally unstable (Midoro and Pitto 2000), and in other industries alliances have been shown to exhibit very limited success (Bleeke and Ernst 1995). Supporters of mergers claim that alliances are too loose to generate the savings and growth potential that only equity mergers or acquisitions can provide (Brooks 2000). However, in spite of a significant turnover in membership during the first years of the earliest shipping alliances, they have proved to be extremely stable. Members have gained advantages by pooling resources, and there appears to be some satisfaction with the results (Ryoo and Thanopoulou 1999). Even though there have certainly been difficulties in working together because of the different corporate cultures that are thrown together in the alliances, for the most part these complications have been managed.

There is a growing concentration of ownership and capacity in container shipping. By 2001 the top 20 container lines accounted for 83 per cent of vessel capacity. Alliances and mergers are an important part of the trend, but it is being reinforced by the dynamic internal growth of some lines. Maersk has become the industry leader through its merger with SeaLand, but the parent firm, the privately owned A.P. Moller of Denmark, has been very aggressive in expanding services and capacity. COSCO, the Chinese carrier, has similarly embarked on a growth strategy, explored by Comtois and Rimmer in Chapter 3. At present it appears that this concentration is likely to continue as a result of over-capacity and market uncertainty. The impact of the concentration of capacity on competition will become a very important question in the future.

The growth in the size of container ships seems set to continue, despite over-capacity concerns. The larger vessels are cheaper to operate and, because of downturns in the shipbuilding industry, their capital costs are actually falling. Companies have been quick to take advantage of these conditions and order more ships. Moreover, despite the views of some sceptics, the growth in the size of ships seems to have no limit. It is rumoured that Maersk is presently building a ship with a capacity of 12,000 TEU, and Delft University has designed one of 18,000 TEU. The growth in vessel size has enormous implications for ports that have to establish facilities that can accommodate these ships, especially in terms of the provision of equipment that can work the ships, terminal sites that are large enough and channels that are deep enough. This issue is explored further by Rodrigue in Chapter 4 and McCalla in Chapter 7.

Ports have already had to adjust to unprecedented changes in the configurations of shipping services. Whereas in the past they could have expected several calls by different lines, they now face fewer visits (albeit with larger vessels) because of the combined services of the alliances. As mentioned above, the costs they face in adjusting to increasing vessel size represent an unwelcome burden at a time when there is growing uncertainty as to whether the carriers will continue to maintain their service or switch to another port. This uncertainty has meant that port competition is likely to be enhanced, and the ability of ports to meet the financial and environmental costs imposed by the forces of globalisation will become issues of great public concern.

If these developments are likely to take place as a result of the factors discussed in this chapter, there are bigger changes on the horizon that are shaped by other considerations. The effects of 11 September are likely to play a critical role in shaping container shipping in the near future. The events of that day have already accentuated a slowdown in the world economy. The shipping industry had added capacity in anticipation of pre-2001 rates of growth being maintained. There is presently serious over-capacity on most trade routes, and the forecast is for the situation to deteriorate as new ships on order enter service. By 2004 an additional 1.5 million TEU of capacity will be added to the world container fleet, with over 60 per cent accounted for by post-Panamax ships (*Containerisation International Yearbook*, 2002). It will be interesting to see how well members of alliances manage to cope, or whether – as is suspected – some firms may collapse and either fail completely or be acquired by others. Whatever the outcome, the trend towards concentration of ownership in container shipping is likely to accelerate further.

The events of 11 September are likely to have other, less obvious impacts. As a result of the threat of terrorist attacks, the United States has become aware of the vulnerability of its ports. Containers are seen as especially at risk, since so few are inspected upon entry. The United States now places its security and customs inspectors in major overseas ports to pre-clear containers before they are shipped to the United States. Agreements have now been made with many local port authorities, and several that were initially reluctant to allow US personnel to operate in their terminals – such as Hong Kong – have been forced to accede. To have remained outside the system would have been a severe competitive disadvantage to their shippers. One implication of this is that because ports without local screening may find their containers held up for security clearance, traffic may avoid them, thus accentuating the already marked pattern of concentration of container flows through a small number of hub ports.

Conclusion

Globalisation has contributed to the remaking of container shipping networks of many of the largest carriers. The imperative of serving markets in all parts of the world has forced the carriers to extend and reconfigure their services. Yet doing so has meant that the differences between the lines have diminished, and globalisation appears to be imprinting a great deal of conformity on the industry. This conformity is being accentuated by the creation of alliances, because of the common alliance services, and because the alliances themselves are serving the same market regions.

The scale and scope of changes in port selection by alliance members represent one of the most remarkable developments in container shipping since the mid-1990s. As services have been restructured, the changes have been amplified at the level of the individual ports. All the carriers have used alliance membership as a means of coordinating services, many of which have involved new ports of call. At the same time, companies have been afforded opportunities to expand services outside the alliance structure.

If change has been the overriding feature of container shipping over the past decade, in the immediate future it is likely that the trend will be maintained.

Conformity, concentration and competition are likely to be the three 'C' watchwords of the present decade. As much as the changes imply significant structural and organisational causes and effects, many of the most important changes will have spatial dimensions. The geography of container shipping appears set to continue as a vital element in shaping world trade and economic development.

Acknowledgements

I wish to thank the Social Science and Humanities Research Council of Canada for its financial support of my research. I am indebted to my colleagues Claude Comtois and Robert McCalla and my students Emmanuel Guy and D'Arcy Ryan for their intellectual support and enthusiasm.

References

Alix, Y., Slack, B. and Comtois, C. (1999) 'Alliance or acquisition? Strategies for growth in the container shipping industry, the case of CP Ships', *Journal of Transport Geography*, 7: 203–208.
Bleeke, J. and Ernst, D. (1995) 'Is your strategic alliance really a sale?', *Harvard Business Review*, 73: 97–105.
Brooks, M.R. (2000) *Sea Change in Liner Shipping*, Oxford: Pergamon.
Containerisation International Yearbook, various years, London: Informa Group.
Cullinane, K.P.B. and Khanna, M. (2000) 'Economies of scale in container shipping: optimal size and geographical implications', *Journal of Transport Geography*, 8: 181–196.
Dicken, P. (1998) *Global Shift*, London: Guilford.
Dunning, J. (1997) *Alliance Capitalism and Global Business*, New York: Routledge.
Gilman, S. (1999) 'The size economies and network efficiency of large containerships', *International Journal of Maritime Economics*, 1: 39–59.
Goold, M. and Campbell, A. (1998) 'Desperately seeking synergies', *Harvard Business Review*, 76: 130–143.
Midoro, R. and Pitto, A. (2000) 'A critical evaluation of strategic alliances in liner shipping', *Maritime Policy and Management*, 27: 31–40.
Ryoo, D.K. and Thanopoulou, H.A. (1999) 'Liner alliances in the globalisation era: a strategic tool for Asian container carriers', *Maritime Policy and Management*, 26: 349.
Slack, B., McCalla, R.J. and Comtois, C. (2002) 'Strategic alliances in container shipping: a global perspective', *Maritime Policy and Management*, 29: 65–79.
Wang, J. and Slack, B. (2000) 'The evolution of a regional container port system: the Pearl River delta', *Journal of Transport Geography*, 8: 263–276.
Zophil, J. and Prijon, M. (1999) 'The MED rule: the interdependence of container throughput and transhipment volumes in Mediterranean ports', *Maritime Policy and Management*, 26: 175–193.

3 China's competitive push for global trade

Port system development and the role of COSCO

Claude Comtois and Peter J. Rimmer

Several chapters in this volume – particularly those by McCalla, Rodrigue and Slack (Chapters 7, 4 and 2) – explore current containerisation issues and trends largely in the context of western economic development. In the late twentieth century, however, political shifts thrust other types of economy into the global trade system that is so dependent on containerisation as a transport mode. In part this reflected the collapse of socialism, especially in the Central and East European contexts. But it was also a consequence of decisions within the surviving communist world. Given this trend, an over-narrow focus on western trade systems carries with it the danger of neglecting these important developments elsewhere in the global economy. This chapter, therefore, aims to counteract that neglect.

To do so, its attention is centred on China, the country expected to become the prime focus of world maritime activity during the first decade of the twenty-first century. Since 1978 China has undergone massive restructuring. Its open door policy has led to explosive economic growth, while the introduction of market reforms has created new production and trade linkages between expanding urban centres. Much of this new economic activity has been underpinned by the extension of China's sea–land connections. Ernst Frankel (1998) has provided a broad overview of this development. However, there is now a pressing need to go beyond this conspectus and examine the domestic *and* international aspects of sea–land development in more detail. We contribute to this objective primarily by studying changes in the structure, networks and activities of the state-owned China Ocean Shipping (Group) Company (COSCO). The choice of this group is appropriate partly because it includes China's leading container carrier, but also because its strategic adjustments closely mirror shifts in the country's economic geography and in the world at large.

Analysis focuses on the group's two main entities, COSCO Container Lines Company Ltd (COSCON) and COSCO Pacific, the arm of the business now dominantly engaged in container leasing and container terminal operations. The main time-frame is the period since 1990, a seminal period marked by further market reforms in China and the country's increased participation in the world economy. Evidence is drawn primarily from detailed fieldwork, with supporting information from trade journals, port consultants' reports and international development agencies. Attention centres on the challenges created by the early development strategy of China's original state-owned carrier, COSCO; on the post-1990 emergence of COSCON and COSCO Pacific in response to these challenges and the increasingly competitive global economic environment; and on the strategies pursued by these companies to secure success in this increasingly harsh environment. The main thrust is to judge the extent to which – in an ever more privatised world – state-owned companies may still engage effectively with the market to the substantial benefit of the national economy. Before concentrating on this issue, however, the chapter provides essential background by reviewing the national context which both influences, and is influenced by, COSCON and COSCO Pacific. This is achieved through analyses of, first, China's container port system and its constituent port ranges and, second, intermodality structures and connectivity with the hinterland.

The system: port ranges, the hinterland and intermodal split

Table 3.1 shows that the top ten container ports in China handle over 98 per cent of the country's entire container throughput. The dynamism of the system is demonstrated by the fact that total container traffic increased from 6.4 million TEU in 1990 to over 35 million TEU in 2000 (CIY 2002). Dynamism is also highlighted by the significant number of changes in port rankings in this period, as well as by a lessening of Hong Kong's domination. Geographically, the

Table 3.1 Top ten container ports of China, 1990 and 2000

1990			2000		
Port	Traffic (1,000 TEU)	Percentage in port system	Port	Traffic (1,000 TEU)	Percentage in port system
Hong Kong	5,100.6	79.6	Hong Kong	18,100.0	51.0
Shanghai	456.1	7.1	Shanghai	5,613.0	15.8
Tianjin	286.0	4.5	Yantian	2,148.0	6.1
Qingdao	135.4	2.1	Qingdao	2,120.0	6.0
Dalian	131.3	2.1	Tianjin	1,708.4	4.8
Jiuzhou	85.2	1.3	Guangzhou	1,429.9	4.0
Guangzhou	80.7	1.3	Xiamen	1,084.7	3.1
Nanjing	41.8	0.7	Dalian	1,011.0	2.8
Chiwan	40.0	0.6	Ningbo	902.0	2.5
Xiamen	30.0	0.5	Shekou	720.3	2.0
Top 10	6,387.1	99.6	Top 10	34,837.3	98.2
China total container port system	6,411.6	100.0	China total container port system	35,483.0	100.0

Source: *Containerisation International Yearbook*, 1990–2002.

container port system is composed of three port ranges: the northern range around the Bohai Rim, the central range centred on the Yangzi River delta, and the southern range comprising a cluster of ports in the Pearl River delta (Figure 3.1).

The northern range, or Bohai Rim, has three major container ports: Qingdao, Tianjin and Dalian. Their relative proximity has led to the concentration of traffic on them and, therefore, to a negligible role for small or medium-sized container ports. Gini coefficient analysis (Table 3.2) reveals that container flows in the Rim are relatively evenly distributed between these three ports. Even so, in absolute terms Qingdao and Tianjin (ranked fourth and fifth in the Chinese container port hierarchy) each have roughly twice the container throughput of Dalian (Table 3.1). The ports' twin traditional roles as major industrial centres and gateways for China's northeastern foreign trade are reviving through increasing exchanges eastwards across the Yellow Sea with South Korea and Japan. Also influential is the proximity of Beijing, within 200 km of Tianjin. Given these circumstances, Bohai Rim ports have been highly successful in becoming commercially attractive to foreign investors. For example, Sea-Land Orient (Tianjin) Terminals, a joint venture between CSX World Terminals and Pacific Ports, operates four container berths in Tianjin. International and domestic container terminal operations in Dalian are managed by a subsidiary of the Maritime and Port Authority of Singapore (PSA) (Cass 2001), and in 2000 Qingdao signed an agreement with P&O Ports to form a joint venture company to develop and operate a new container terminal on a 30-year concession. Analysis of changes such as these suggests that the region is ripe to become a testbed for further deregulation and separation of the regulatory and commercial functions of ports.

The central port range is currently dominated by Shanghai, but with Ningbo – approximately 200 km to the south – emerging as a new load centre in Hangzhou Bay. Because of Ningbo's growth, the range's Gini coefficient shows moderate deconcentration (Table 3.2). As a city, Shanghai is progressively redefining its production functions. The trend is to relocate the production of components to neighbouring provinces with lower space rental costs and other conditions of comparative advantage. This modifies, but does not reduce, the structure of exchanges and their demands on the port system (Comtois 1993). Local authorities are substituting industrial transformation functions by trade- and service-related functions, giving a strong impetus towards increasing container traffic and strengthening Shanghai as a hub port. Because depth problems are now limiting hub development here,[1] the central government has approved the construction of a new deepwater port on the Yangshan Islands in Hangzhou Bay (Wang 2001). This project, scheduled to take 20 years to complete at an estimated cost of US$12 billion, includes a 52-berth container terminal and the construction of a 32-km bridge to connect the new port with the planned town of Luchaogang on the mainland. Ningbo, meanwhile, has experienced an annual average rate of growth of over 40 per cent since 1990. The increasing demand for container traffic has already led the port authority, in a joint venture with Hong Kong-based Hutchison Port Holdings (HPH), to

Figure 3.1 Selected container ports along China's maritime ranges, 2003.

Table 3.2 Gini coefficient for the container port ranges of China, 1990 and 2000

Range	Gini coefficient, 1990	Gini coefficient, 2000
Top ten container ports	0.6956	0.4807
Northern range	0.1842	0.1244
Central range	0.4160	0.3616
Southern range	0.7557	0.5708

Source: *Containerisation International Yearbook*, 1990–2002.

begin construction of new container terminals.[2] The expansion of facilities at both Ningbo and Shanghai is a signal of the magnitude of the expected traffic growth in the Yangzi River delta. To deal with this it may be necessary to consider the creation of a system-wide solution in which multi-site shipping centres will permit each port to exploit a particular niche function.

The southern range still displays the highest concentration level of all China's port ranges (Table 3.2). This reflects the continuing pre-eminence of Hong Kong. With its strategic location in the south, Hong Kong secures a large volume of transshipment traffic, and has also prospered because of its burgeoning industrial sector supported by massive export-oriented foreign investments (Rimmer 1992). With this foundation, its position as the world's leading container port and China's main transshipment hub has been maintained following the former colony's reversion to the People's Republic of China in 1997. While Hong Kong remains dominant, however, the decline in the southern range's Gini coefficient from 0.76 to 0.57 in only ten years is an indicator that new ports in the Pearl River delta have sharply increased their container market share.[3] These ports have built their success on two factors: the efficiency and liberalisation of commercial exchanges with Hong Kong, and the trade performance of Guangdong Province. Their development appears to challenge the role of Hong Kong, and this is partly the case. They include the deepwater ports of Chiwan, Shekou and Yantian in the eastern delta, all of which compete directly with Hong Kong by offering international calls. But ports in the western delta are complementary because they are feeder ports and not accessible to large container ships (Wang and Slack 2000). Organisational linkage between these ports and Hong Kong is also a consequence of the actions of Hong Kong terminal operators who have hived off container operations to alternative locations in the Pearl River delta (Comtois and Slack 2000). This diversion of cargo from Hong Kong to other ports in the southern range naturally introduces the question – highly relevant to all three port ranges – of the consolidation and development of hinterland connections through logistics.

Hinterland relations and intermodality

Key features of the evolution of hinterland connections based on intermodality are provided in Table 3.3 in the form of modal split data for water transport and road haulage for the three lead ports of Qingdao, Shanghai and Hong Kong. The table's most striking feature is the increasing use of water transport (i.e. sea–inland navigation and sea–sea feeder activity). By 2000 this accounted for almost half the movements to and from the three ports, compared with only 11 per cent in 1990.[4] Most of this growth focused on Shanghai and Hong Kong in the central and southern ranges. In Shanghai it was so marked that water transport now easily exceeds that by road. Shanghai's strong showing in river-based container transport is related to investments in berthing facilities along the Yangzi for container loading and unloading. These facilities support an increasing amount of containerised cargo shipped to Shanghai, on a multiporting basis, from Chongqing and downstream locations. In Hong Kong, meanwhile, the increase in river-borne traffic stems from the significant changes in the geographical distribution of container shipping in the Pearl River delta noted earlier. In particular, it reflects the use of ports in the western delta as feeder ports complementary to Hong Kong (Wang and Slack 2000). Organisationally, the modal split of container movements in the region is increasingly controlled by HPH, which has deliberately tailored the distribution system to the needs of its regional network (Rimmer and Comtois 1996).

Shanghai and Hong Kong hold key positions as the main conduits for riverine cargo vessels linking China's hinterland with its external markets. However, this model of intermodality based on high-density inland navigation cannot become a China-wide alternative to road haulage. This is partly because none of the container terminals on the Yangzi and in the Pearl River delta serves as an inland hub for other river ports. There is no river-linked hub-and-spoke formation. But what is also crucial is that many distant hinterland locations are in landlocked regions that have no, or limited, inland waterway facilities. This is exemplified by Qingdao's hinterland, where 87 per cent of container movements are carried by road. Moreover, with China's entry into the World Trade Organisation (WTO), business opportunities will arise in small and medium-sized cities inland, not in the most important coastal cities already dominated by international players. As investments focus on inland regions, the need for

Table 3.3 Container traffic by waterway and highway to and from China hub ports, 1990 and 2000

	1990			2000		
	Total TEU	Waterway TEU	Highway TEU	Total TEU	Waterway TEU	Highway TEU
Qingdao[a]	50,800	28,800	22,000	2,072,700	275,900	1,796,800
Shanghai	102,800	17,500	85,300	9,326,300	5,602,600	3,723,700
Hong Kong	905,631	70,941	834,690	8,105,002	3,462,000	4,643,002

Source: Zhongguo Jiaotong Nianjian (1990–2001); Hong Kong Marine Department (1997–2001).

Note
a Estimated.

increasing logistics and distribution requirements will lead to the emergence of inland hubs in the road business.

Given the scale of the Chinese hinterland, it is perhaps surprising that rail transport has not figured in the intermodality analysis. Rail's role is certainly on the increase. Before 1990 rail movement of containers was essentially confined to non-ISO boxes restricted to the domestic market. Subsequently the need for fully fledged intermodal operations has been recognised and encouraged by the Ministry of Railways, the World Bank, COSCO and other shippers (Wu and Nash 2000). Intermodal rail depots have been developed close to the main container ports and in inland provinces (Loo and Hook 2001). COSCON has established a range of weekly shuttles within China, based on Qingdao. Similarly, the first intermodal trains connecting China's deep hinterland with Hong Kong started service in 1995. By 2000, the Kowloon-Canton Railway Corporation (KCRC) had established services between Hong Kong and 23 locations in China. On the international scale, in conjunction with the Ministry of Railways, KCRC is offering a new service to Russia and the Commonwealth of Independent States (CIS).[5] COSCON's equivalent to this is a container rail service with the Russian hinterland through Dalian.

These indicators suggest that increasing competition will emerge between rail and other modes, particularly road transport, in the economic hinterland. As yet, however, this competition is essentially potential. Currently, container movement by rail ranks behind fuel, agricultural goods, military supplies and commuter traffic. By 2000, the number of containers transported by rail was only 87,468 (Zhongguo Jiaotong Nianjian 2001: 583).[6] Factors responsible for this are both national and local. Nationally, the issue is largely one of transport pricing policy: rail's share of container traffic is limited by the high transport charges imposed by the Ministry of Railways. Local obstacles include infrastructural lags. For example, in Hong Kong a key problem in shifting the modal balance is the absence of a rail line to the Hong Kong Kwai Chung container terminals (Woodbridge 2001). Although plans are in hand to eliminate this gap, containers currently have to be barged or road-hauled to and from KCRC's rail freight yard in Kowloon – a slow and expensive business.[7]

From COSCO to COSCON and global player status in container shipping

The Chinese government established COSCO in 1961. At that time the company's organisation was based on domestic ports from Dalian to Guangzhou, with an ocean-going merchant fleet comprising only 20 ships aggregating 196,300 dwt and calling at only 13 foreign ports (Leung 1981). Pursuing the central planning paradigm, for almost 30 years China's shipping planners worked consistently to establish COSCO as a maritime corporation with virtual ministry status (Heine 1989). In this phase the carrier established a self-owned and diversified container fleet. Ocean-going vessels were purchased progressively from abroad, and also at home as local shipbuilding capabilities increased (Song 1990; Flynn 1999; Lu and Tang 2000). Extensive strategic use was made of Hong Kong to earn much-needed foreign currency and to base the container fleet. Apart from the currency advantages, this enabled the company to circumvent restrictions on Chinese vessels entering hostile overseas ports. In addition, a related strategic thrust was diversification through subsidiaries: off-shore companies acquired included the charterers Ocean Tramping and Yick Fung, as well as Ming Wah, the shipping arm of China Merchants' Holdings. The latter company invested in port development, insurance and shipping under China's Ministry of Communications (Rimmer and Comtois 2002).

By 1990, COSCO was experiencing steady growth and had become a diverse conglomerate involved in shipping, port and terminal management, inland haulage and storage, shipbuilding and repair, freight forwarding, financial services and real estate. It occupied seventh place among the world's container line operators. It provided 1,220 sailings on 41 routes, called at 58 ports and deployed 146 vessels aggregating 108,772 TEU (CIY 1990). Despite the apparent success, however, its pattern of shipping services indicated that its monolithic organisational structure within a planned economy was ill-suited to the imperative of enabling the company to compete effectively with the dominant firms in the global container trade. Here the most diagnostic feature was the marked imbalance between intra-Asian and extra-Asian shipping services.

An emphasis on intra-Asian shipping services highlighted the importance of proximity in company activity (Figure 3.2). Six routes operated between North-East and South-East Asia, including a weekly service between Bangkok and Singapore. Marked ties between China and Japan were revealed by more than 37 monthly services, the Kobe–Yokohama–Hong Kong triangle being pivotal to the network. Inland, the domestic links were limited, and the network's threshold did not extend beyond China's coastal area. Only three inland water-borne connections existed and all radiated from Hong Kong. These linked the hub port with Zhangjiagang and Wuhan in the Yangzi River delta, and Huangpu in the Pearl River delta.

In sharp contrast, a striking feature of the pattern of extra-Asian services was relative simplicity (Figure 3.3). Only three ports – Xingang, Shanghai and Hong Kong – were dominant as the national hubs. Very few services extended beyond two port ranges (i.e. Europe and west-coast North America). While the company transited the Panama and Suez canals, it did not serve the transatlantic route and had no round-the-world services. Even though these east–west trades were limited, however, in terms of capacity and services the carrier's investment was distinctly biased towards them. Approximately 68 per cent of its shipboard capacity was allocated to the three transpacific and three trans-Suez routes. The slot capacity of the North–South trade was markedly inferior, even though six routes served the Middle East and smaller markets in the South Pacific, Africa and South America.

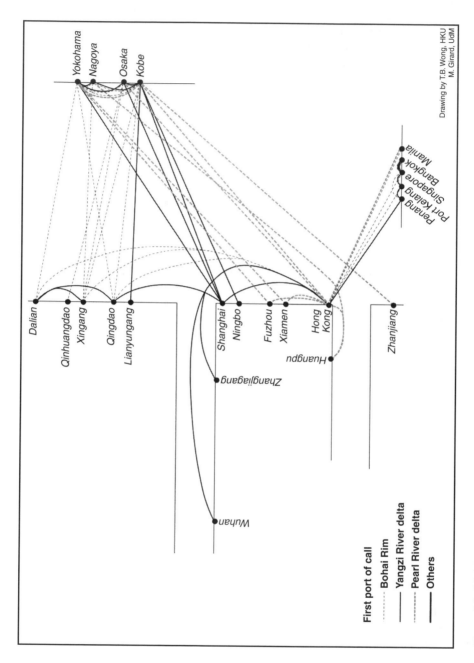

First port of call
········· Bohai Rim
———— Yangzi River delta
········· Pearl River delta
———— Others

Drawing by T.B. Wong, HKU
M. Girard, UdM

Figure 3.2 COSCO intra-regional traffic and ports of call, 1990.

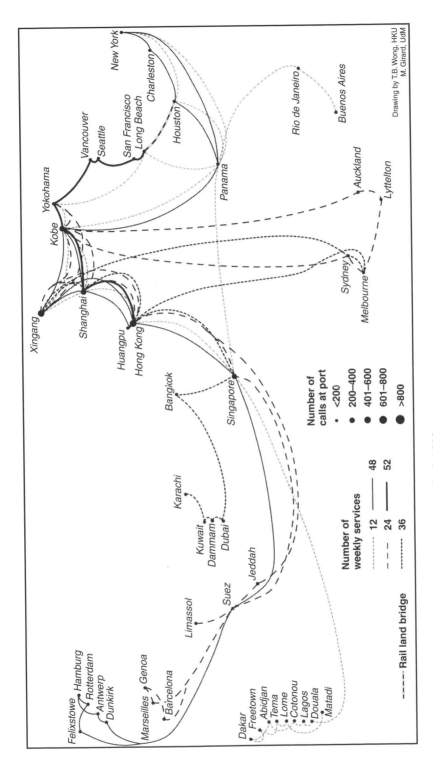

Figure 3.3 COSCO extra-regional traffic and ports of call, 1990.

Drawing by T.B. Wong, HKU
M. Girard, UdM

Number of
calls at port
· <200
● 200–400
● 401–600
● 601–800
● >800

Number of
weekly services
········· 12
– – – 24
········· 36
——— 48
——— 52

– – – Rail land bridge

Corporate restructuring

In response to this challenge of an ill-developed global network, and in line with a new government policy of separating state-owned enterprises from the ministries to increase their effectiveness in the marketplace, the COSCO Group was subjected to corporate restructuring. Operations were streamlined, and responsibilities for the various core businesses were assigned to specialised entities. Currently, the new shipping group has 80 companies under its umbrella, plus links with more than 300 other companies involved in all aspects of shipping. In this restructured framework, the key shipping element is COSCON. In pursuing the goal of growth in an environment of intense competition and consolidation, this core company has adopted an offensive development strategy mirroring those of the world's most important maritime carriers. This aggressive emulation strategy has had four dimensions.

The first relates closely to corporate approach and image. COSCON has transformed itself from a wholesaler of port-to-port services into a retailer of door-to-door services by building a network comprising four regional centres – Beijing, New York, Hamburg and Shanghai – and over 300 branch offices in coastal cities and inland transportation hinges. The unfavourable image of a state-controlled organisation securing market share through price cutting has been shrugged off and replaced by one based on service quality. Now COSCON participates in trade lane discussions and shipowners' associations to offer transpacific, trans-Suez and transatlantic services (CIY 2002). There have also been clear echoes of the consolidation movement so prevalent among western container carriers: in 1998 the company reinforced its position through a merger with the Shanghai Ocean Shipping Company.

The second thrust has been large-scale fleet modernisation. Between 1990 and 2000, COSCON reduced its fleet to 118 vessels – a 19 per cent cutback. Many small cellular vessels of less than 1,000 TEU were phased out, while 21 container ships with capacities exceeding 3,000 TEU joined the fleet and six post-Panamax vessels with capacities of 5,200 TEU were ordered (Table 3.4).

Table 3.4 COSCON's fleet development, 1990–2000

Vessel size (TEU)	1990		2000		On order	
	Capacity (TEU)	Number	Capacity (TEU)	Number	Capacity	Number
Under 1,000	35,786	108	35,769	69		
1,000–1,999	46,659	34	68,049	47		
2,000–2,999	16,412	6	31,313	13		
3,000–3,999	0	0	54,097	15		
Over 4,000	0	0	31,200	6	31,200	6
Total	98,857	148	220,428	150	31,200	6

Source: *Containerisation International Yearbook*, 1990–2002.

On balance, this combined disinvestment and investment strategy more than doubled capacity and maintained the company's position as the world's seventh-largest carrier (CIY 2000).

Third, the new corporate outlook and modernised fleet were combined to change dramatically the geography of the company's international shipping service and thus gain benefit from the increase in world trade with Asian markets, the new growth centres in the global economy (Comtois 1999). Consequently, compared with the limited network in 1990, the company's global operations in 2000 revealed a weekly service network structure, with pendulum services between three or more ranges (Figure 3.4). Outside Asia the carrier added 23 new ports to its schedules, while maintaining services to 24 and dropping only 11 (Table 3.5).

The trunk east–west trades have undergone an ambitious expansion programme. The new pattern is marked by an intensification of activities across the Pacific through seven weekly services. A rail land bridge from North American west-coast ports reduces global transit time (Slack 2001). There are greatly strengthened links between Hong Kong, Singapore and Europe, with Suez established as a pivot port. Based on Suez, there are four weekly services through the canal towards the Mediterranean and North European ports, including one weekly service that extends to the east-coast ports of North America. Operations have also expanded into new markets, with two weekly services originating and terminating in the Atlantic. In effect, a 'Main Street' has emerged between the hub ports of Rotterdam, Antwerp, Felixstowe, Suez, Singapore, Hong Kong, Shanghai, Busan, Kobe and Long Beach.

Fourth, the feeder North–South network pattern in Africa and South America has similarly been restructured and augmented. Thus, a weekly service from Hong Kong to South America, with important stopovers in Durban and Cape Town, is complemented by another weekly service between Durban and other African ports. Other features are the persistent links between China and Australia and New Zealand, together with weekly services between ports in Japan, South Korea and Australasia. Although most of COSCON's slot capacity is committed to the east–west routes, the new alignment of the north–south trades clearly highlights the carrier's interplay between global and regional traffic patterns. For example, in addition to its global function, the rail land bridge to Houston permits Asian freight to and from the Gulf Coast region of North America to be handled by west-coast ports (Slack 2001). More generally, container flows at the hub ports on the 'Main Street' have been reorganised, allowing ships travelling between Europe, Asia and North America to be loaded with north–south traffic.

While much restructuring has been at the world scale, a quite different dimension of COSCON's strategic response to globalisation pressures has been defensive rather than offensive: the consolidation of its previously extensive intra-Asian trades (Figure 3.5). Faced with sharply intensifying competition as weekly intra-Asian services increased from 29 to 42 between 1990 and 2000, the company established partnership arrangements to pool resources with a cluster of

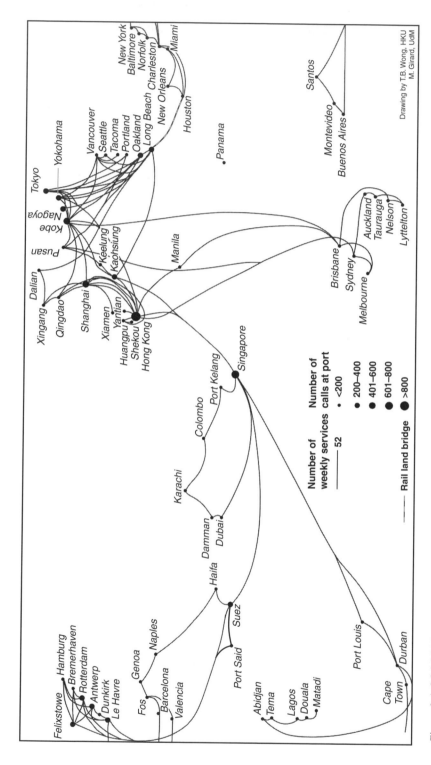

Figure 3.4 COSCON extra-regional traffic and ports of call, 2000.

Table 3.5 Turnover of ports in COSCON maritime ranges, 1990–2000

Range	Ports in 1990	Ports dropped	Ports added	Ports in 2000	COSCON ports in global alliance services	COSCON ports services by global terminal operators
ECNA	2	0	3	5	3	1
Gulf	1	0	1	2	0	0
Caribbean	0	0	0	0	0	0
WCNA	4	1	3	6	5	6
S. America	2	1	2	3	0	1
S. Pacific	4	0	3	7	0	3
S. Asia	6	1	1	6	3	4
China	13	2	29	40	7	9
N. Asia	4	0	6	10	6	0
Middle East	4	2	3	5	1	1
Africa	9	4	3	8	0	0
Mediterranean	4	2	2	4	2	2
N. Europe	5	1	3	7	5	4
Total	58	14	59	103	32	31

Source: *Containerisation International Yearbook*, 1990–2002.

market-economy carriers: Japan's 'K' line; the Taiwan-based Yangming Line and Evergreen Group; the Hong Kong-based Orient Overseas Container Line (OOCL); and the Korean-based Hanjin Shipping. As with other strategic alliances, this association has led to some service gains, particularly nine weekly sailings to Korea and the extension of COSCON's services to Taiwan within a conference agreement with OOCL.[8] But a more striking feature of change has been retrenchment. For example, in sharp contrast to COSCO's network pattern of the previous decade, COSCON has ceased operations on five routes in South-East Asia, only maintaining a weekly service between Bangkok, Huangpu, Hong Kong and Shekou. Similarly, the company has cancelled seven itineraries with Japan, consolidating this traffic on to the new Korea services.

As COSCON addressed its network weaknesses through this mixture of offensive and defensive strategies, it did so in a highly dynamic environment which quickly posed new challenges. Central to these was the new state policy allowing other maritime carriers to compete with COSCON by operating within the booming China hinterland and have access to the country's maritime gateways. Foreign companies have acquired the right to engage in a wide range of transport activities. Major liners on the east–west routes make direct calls at China's main ports. State forwarders and foreign groups compete for the business of moving containers through the Chinese hinterland (Drewry 1996). Moreover, intensified competition within the domestic port system has not been confined to the state-facilitated entry of foreign companies. COSCON's success has even led the Ministry of Communications to seek a second Chinese

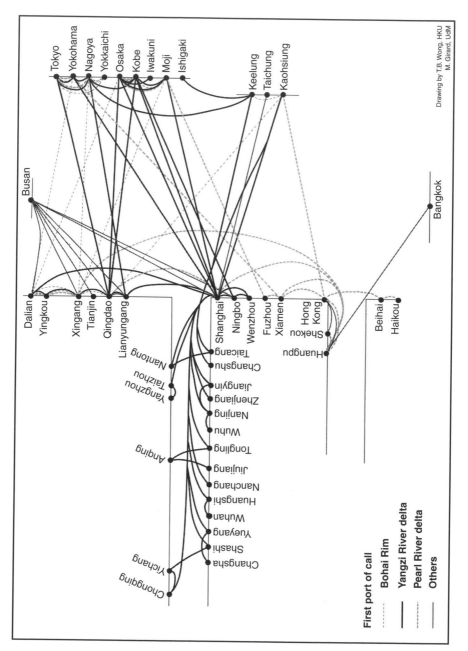

Figure 3.5 COSCON intra-regional traffic and ports of call, 2000.

Drawing by T.B. Wong, HKU
M. Girard, UdM

First port of call

- Bohai Rim
- Yangzi River delta
- Pearl River delta
- Others

player: in 1999 the Shanghai-based China Shipping Container Lines was established to compete with the company by offering mirror-image schedules and cheaper prices. Thus, COSCON's monopoly over China's main container ports has been broken by both foreign and domestic competition.

As with the company's aggressive investment in a new fleet, its strategic response to these challenges has been primarily offensive. Above all, feeder services have been mounted within China to ports as yet ignored by foreign carriers. No fewer than 29 additional Chinese ports were brought into the network between 1990 and 2000 (Table 3.5). In this way, within a fully fledged domestic cabotage maritime circuit COSCON has intensified traffic between the three port ranges of the Bohai Rim, the Yangzi River delta and the Pearl River delta. This process has confirmed Qingdao, Shanghai and Hong Kong as national hubs, the indisputable foci within these ranges for a large number of domestic links, and also the bases for tangential services to secondary ports. Moreover, reinforcing this trend, the company has increasingly integrated its new Chinese ports into its schedules as direct ports of call on the trunk transpacific and trans-Suez routes.

COSCO Pacific, growth and the diversification of core business

COSCO Pacific is the descendant of the Florens Group, purchased by COSCO in order to secure a container supplier. Subsequent transformation of the company reflects, to a degree, the strategic development of this role. By 1990 the fact that it was not operating in the free market had allowed a situation to emerge in which containers were being leased to COSCON at higher than market rates. As a first step towards the market economy, from 1991 the company gradually reduced its rental rates to bring them more into line with competitors'. Then, capitalising on China's rapid trade growth and increasing demand from COSCON, COSCO Pacific was listed on the Hong Kong Stock Exchange in December 1994. Widening of the customer base was the linked strategic step, with company expansion driven by more customers leasing more containers. Between 1995 and 2000 the number of containers owned by COSCO Pacific grew by 81 per cent, while the number of customers rose from 20 to 155 (Table 3.6). Fostering this, by 1997 a network of five overseas sales offices had been established, in Tokyo, San Francisco, New York, London and Genoa. Similar support growth has taken the number of container depots to 200 in 153 locations around the globe. The result has been that COSCO Pacific has become the world's sixth-largest container leasing company. Although COSCON continues to be the largest customer (a role likely to be consolidated by COSCON's introduction of post-Panamax container vessels, noted earlier), the diversification benefits for COSCO Pacific are none the less clear. The wider customer base reduced dependence on leasing income from COSCON from 92 per cent in 1995 to 68 per cent in 2000 (Table 3.6), significantly increasing income in the process.

Table 3.6 COSCO Pacific container leasing operations, 1995–2000

Year	Containers owned and operated (TEUs)	Number of customers	Leasing income from COSCON (%)	Leasing income from first five lessees (%)	Container purchase attributable to COSCON (%)	Container purchase attributable to first five lessees (%)
1995	291,083	20	92.2	97.1	14.5	60.9
1996	343,245	38	92.3	97.7	27.9	86.6
1997	469,951	86	84.7	92.0	21.6	58.8
1998	505,954	150	75.3	83.2	55.4	92.0
1999	500,899	175	70.7	79.1	22.7	61.0
2000	527,982	155	67.7	75.8	11.7	48.4

Source: COSCO Pacific (1995–2000).

A quite different but, in profit terms, similarly significant strategic thrust has been the pursuit of a vertical integration policy. Aspects of this have been investment in container and container-paint manufacturing operations in Shanghai and Tianjin, plus the acquisition of Plangreat Ltd – a container services group that provides handling, stevedoring, storage and repair, as well as trailer transport. These steps, however, have been modest compared with COSCO Pacific's core excursion into vertical integration: direct investment in port terminal operations. Stakes have been established in a geographically balanced portfolio of port terminals that enjoy unique competitive advantages due to their favourable geographical locations, enhanced infrastructures, advanced management services and plentiful sources of cargo. The result has been that whereas terminal operations accounted for only 4 per cent of operating profits in 1995, by 2000 the proportion exceeded one-third (Table 3.7). Moreover, as the China trade continues to grow, the company is in an unrivalled position to benefit through its terminals from the increasing demand generated by COSCON and other maritime carriers in the country's northern, central and southern ranges (Table 3.8).

How has this been achieved? Much of COSCO Pacific's shift into terminal operations has involved acquisitions. In part, these have been made through asset reorganisation within the COSCO Group. In 1995 the company acquired the entire equity interest in Frosti International from the group holding company. With this takeover came a 50 per cent equity holding in COSCO-HIT Terminals (Hong Kong) – a company engaged in the provision of container terminal operations, management and development at Terminal 8 (East) in Kwai Chung, Hong Kong. Similarly, in 1997 terminal handling capacity on the Yangzi River was boosted through the acquisition of the group's shareholdings in Zhangjiagang and Shanghai. Logically, this asset reorganisation has

Table 3.7 COSCO Pacific operating profits by principal activity, 1995–2000 (US$ '000)

Activity	1995	1996	1997	1998	1999	2000
Container leasing	44,505	44,663	80,237	86,961	84,891	75,549
	96%	59%	65%	67%	63%	53%
Terminal operations	1,855	31,038	38,267	38,938	41,772	49,891
	4%	41%	31%	30%	31%	35%
Container handling and	–	–	2,468	2,596	2,695	2,851
storage	–	–	2%	2%	2%	2%
Industrial	–	–	1,235.5	2,596	2,695	2,851
	–	–	1%	2%	2%	2%
Financial services	–	–	1,235.5	9,086	9,433	12,829
	–	–	1%	7%	7%	9%
Corporate expenses	–	–	–	(10,383)	(6,737)	(1,425)
	–	–	–	(8%)	(5%)	(1%)
Total	46,360	75,701	123,443	129,794	134,749	142,546
	100%	100%	100%	100%	100%	100%

Source: COSCO Pacific (1995–2000).

Table 3.8 COSCO Pacific container terminal throughput in China, 1995–2000 (TEU)

Terminal	Pearl River delta			Yangzi River delta		Bohai Rim	
	COSCO-HIT Terminals (Hong Kong) Ltd	Yantian International Container Terminals	River Trade Terminal Holdings Ltd	Shanghai Container Terminal	Shanghai Waigaoqiao Terminal	Zhangjiagang Win Hanverky Container Terminals	Qingdao Cosport International Container Terminals
Equity interest	50%	5%	10%	10%	20%	51%	50%
1995	1,190,000	n.a.	0	n.a.	0	n.a.	n.a.
1996	1,154,021	353,509	0	1,438,322	0	116,780	274,562
1997	1,302,409	638,396	0	1,766,590	0	119,384	300,332
1998	1,206,572	1,038,074	0	2,027,188	0	105,051	350,126
1999	1,220,002	1,588,089	357,941	2,593,995	925,000	113,114	401,029
2000	1,412,854	2,147,476	980,759	2,950,500	1,200,000	136,778	502,119

Source: COSCO Pacific (1995–2000).

also involved profit transfer within the group, raising COSCO Pacific's profits but not necessarily those of the group as a whole. Other acquisitions, however, have taken the company outside the group and increased earning capacity. In 1997 a 5 per cent share in Yantian, one of four deepwater ports planned by the Chinese government, was purchased. Further inroads in developing a domestic network of container terminals also came in 1997 through the purchase of shareholdings in Qingdao in the Bohai Rim.

A second route into vertical integration, one that is physically influencing port system development, has been participation in joint ventures to invest in new facilities and operate existing terminals. So far as new facilities are concerned, this process began – and to date has advanced furthest – in Hong Kong. In 1996, COSCO Pacific joined Sun Hung Kai Properties, Hutchison International Port Holdings and Jardine, Matheson & Co. to form a consortium to build and operate the River Trade terminal at Tuen Mun Area 38, Hong Kong. The integrated 60-berth terminal facilities at Tuen Mun commenced operations in 1999 to service 100 river-borne vessels. This large-scale expansion in river traffic, central to the southern range's modal split between movement by road and water noted earlier, has been made possible by the extensive and innovative use of mid-stream operations to supplement the land-based terminals. These operations have much lower costs and charges than land-based terminals, and hence they increase Hong Kong's competitiveness *vis-à-vis* the southern China deepsea ports. In 2000 COSCO Pacific's joint venture strategy was extended to Shanghai in the central port range. Control of container port facilities here was secured by signing an agreement, involving a 20 per cent stake, to operate the Shanghai Pudong International Container Terminal as a joint venture. This terminal has three berths with 900 m of quay and a total storage area of 500,000 m². Additionally, the company has strengthened its position in the northern range by signing letters of intent with the ports of Qinhuangdao, Qingdao and Dalian to operate other joint-venture terminal operations.[9]

While its joint-venture activity is as yet clearly biased towards Hong Kong, therefore, the strategy has secured footholds in all three port ranges, with all that that implies in terms of benefits to be gained from the widespread rapid upswing in container traffic. Moreover, to maximise these opportunities the company has formed alliances with major manufacturing distribution enterprises in China and overseas. In China this is in anticipation of a rise in the flow of goods between eastern and western parts of the country, stemming from government efforts to boost economic activities in the latter region. As the Chinese government formulates concomitant plans for improving transport infrastructures to meet the rising demand for cargo distribution, this will bring increased container business to coastal ports, which will in turn benefit COSCO Pacific's container terminals.[10]

One final feature of COSCO Pacific's development strategy must be noted. The analysis of the company's entry into terminal operations has emphasised capacity acquisition and consequently has focused on quantitative change. However, there has also been a clear quality dimension to the corporate strategy. Anticipating trade growth from China's entry into the WTO, and arguing that information technology causes structural changes to trade systems by creating additional demand for intermodality, the company has expanded investments in hub ports with the aim of developing a comprehensive container-related logistics business. Thus, for example, its logistical services now incorporate tracking software, enhancing its ability to meet customers' requirements for online container leasing. This system simultaneously strengthens the global network of sales offices and depots, and provides a platform for further development of e-commerce to maximise benefits from operating an integrated chain of services.

Conclusion

This study of China's leading shipping company has demonstrated that state ownership does not lead necessarily to decision-making processes that are radically different from those of the private sector. After 1990, the original company, COSCO, restructured its corporate activities in such a way that the group now participates in global alliances and trade lane associations on an equal footing with private shipping companies. This successful restructuring is reflected both in COSCON's international and domestic shipping patterns, and in COSCO Pacific's container port operations.

The analysis of shipping patterns reveals that international shipping companies now share an increasing proportion of China's foreign shipping business. Yet COSCON still holds a dominant position in the domestic market and matches its rivals through its increasing dependence on the ports of Hong Kong, Shanghai, Singapore, Kobe, Suez and Kaohsiung. COSCO's strategy of spinning off core assets in container shipping and terminal operations has permitted the resultant COSCON and COSCO Pacific to operate as sharply focused business entities free of many of the trappings of state control. Moreover, their interlocking partnership has allowed COSCON to emerge as a global supplier of container services.

Residual elements of the group's state-owned roots persist, but these remaining differences between the group and its privately owned and operated competitors are likely to evaporate. Currently, 1,500 domestic freight forwarders (including 450 Sino-foreign joint ventures) monopolise China's inland transport movements to and from seaports. With China's accession to the WTO, however, foreign freight forwarders will be allowed to conduct domestic business in China, covering distribution, wholesaling, retailing, after-sales service, repair, maintenance and transport. As their China operations will be integrated into their global intermodal network – combining container movements by ship, plane, truck, water or train – the development of supply-chain management will become the main driver of traffic growth. Both COSCON and COSCO Pacific will have to respond to, and converge on, these changes. This will require, for example, further development of their hub ports of Hong Kong, Shanghai and Qingdao, as well as revamping of their logistics systems. In the process, their operations will become indistinguishable from the activities of privately owned foreign competitors. The increased growth in container shipping, concentration in selected hubs, and a multiplication of freight distribution centres by state-owned and privately owned shipping companies will be integral to the reordering of China's spatial economy in the third millennium.

Notes

1 These limitations are, of course, significant for COSCON as well as other shippers.
2 Although the subject is beyond the scope of this chapter, new terminals in Shanghai and Ningbo – and, indeed, elsewhere in China – raise important issues related to environmental impact, including the loss of wetland ecosystems.
3 It is also an indicator that, despite the impressive absolute growth in Hong Kong's container traffic, its market share in the total Chinese container port system dropped from 79 per cent in 1990 to 51 per cent in 2000.
4 This trend has an important environmental dimension. Water transport has not reduced the volume of more environmentally damaging road transport, but it has ameliorated its rate of growth.
5 These services provide transit times between south China and Ulan Bator of 15 days, Almaty in 20 days, Moscow in 28 days and Kiev in 30 days.
6 Environmental issues are again important in this context, since low rail usage is counterbalanced by substantially higher road haulage.
7 This problem is strikingly similar to the deficiencies in cross-harbour rail links between New Jersey and New York, highlighted by Rodrigue in Chapter 4.
8 The introduction of a direct trade agreement between China and Taiwan has considerably strengthened the growth of unitised traffic. The decision to extend services to Taiwan has long-term implications for the use of Chinese coastal hubs and maritime regions (Rimmer 1997, 1998; Robinson 1998). It has also prompted speculation about a merger of Chinese shipping lines.
9 The fact that COSCON has been calling at these ports gives COSCO Pacific a competitive advantage in each of these locations.
10 COSCO Pacific is also establishing strategic partnerships with international logistics operators that will facilitate entry into this new business arena focused on the Hong Kong multimodal gateway.

References

Cass, S. (2001) 'The Chinese dragon roars on', *Cargo Systems Supplement*, 9–60.

CIY (1990–2002) *Containerisation International Yearbook*, London: Informa Group.

Comtois, C. (1993) *The Restructuration of Transportation in China: The Emergence of a New Transactional Environment*, Centre de Recherche sur les Transports, publication no. 946, Montreal: Université de Montréal.

—— (1999) 'The integration of China's port system into global container shipping', *GeoJournal*, 48: 35–42.

Comtois, C. and Slack, B. (2000) 'Terminaux de transport et grande région urbaine: l'intégration de Hong Kong dans les performances de la Chine', *Perspectives Chinoises*, 58: 12–20.

COSCO Pacific (1995–2000) *Annual Report*, Hong Kong: COSCO Pacific Limited.

Drewry Shipping Consultants (1996) *Global Container Markets: Prospects and Profitability in a High Growth Era*, London: Drewry.

Flynn, M. (1999) 'PRC maritime and the Asian financial crisis', *Maritime Policy and Management*, 26: 337–347.

Frankel, E.G. (1998) 'China's maritime developments', *Maritime Policy and Management*, 25: 235–249.

Heine, I.M. (1989) *China's Rise to Commercial Maritime Power*, New York: Greenwood Press.

Hong Kong Marine Department (1997–2001) *Summary of Hong Kong Port Statistics*, Hong Kong: Hong Kong Marine Department.

Leung, C.K. (1981) 'Shipping and port development for modernisation', in E.K.Y. Chen and S.S.K. Chin (eds) *Development and Change in China*, Hong Kong: Centre of Asian Studies, University of Hong Kong, pp. 127–143.

Loo, B.P.Y. and Hook, B. (2001) 'Interplay of international, national and local factors in shaping container port development: a case study of Hong Kong', *Transport Reviews*, 22: 219–245.

Lu, B.Z. and Tang, A.S. (2000) 'China shipbuilding management challenges in the 1980s', *Maritime Policy and Management*, 27: 71–78.

Rimmer, P.J. (1992) *Hong Kong's Future as a Regional Transport Hub*, Canberra Papers on Strategy and Defence no. 87, Canberra: Australian National University.

—— (1997) 'TransPacific oceanic economy revisited', *Tijdschrift voor Economische en Sociale Geografie*, 88: 439–456.

—— (1998) 'Impact of global shipping alliances on Pacific Rim seaports', *Maritime Studies*, 98: 1–30.

Rimmer, P.J. and Comtois, C. (1996) 'Refocusing on China: the case of Hong Kong's Hutchison Whampoa', *Pacific Viewpoint*, 37: 89–102.

—— (2002) 'China's transport and communication firms: transforming national champions into global players', *Pacific Viewpoint*, 43: 93–114.

Robinson, R. (1998) 'Asian hub feeder nets: the dynamics of restructuring', *Maritime Policy and Management*, 25: 21–40.

Slack, B. (2001) 'Intermodal transportation', in A.M. Brewer, K.J. Button and D.A. Hensher (eds) *Handbook of Logistics and Supply-Chain Management*, Oxford: Elsevier Science, pp. 141–154.

Song, Y.H. (1990) 'Shipping and shipbuilding policies in PR China', *Marine Policy*, 1: 53–70.

Wang, J.J.X. (2001) 'Regional governance of port development in China: a case study of Shanghai International Shipping Center', paper presented at the conference Logistics Hubs and Outsourcing Centres: The New Functions of Asian Port Cities, Hong Kong, 24 November 2001.

Wang, J.J.X. and Slack, B. (2000) 'The evolution of a regional port system: the Pearl River Delta', *Journal of Transport Geography*, 8: 263–275.

Woodbridge, C. (2001) 'Planning a modal shift', *Containerisation International Regional Review: Hong Kong and Southern China*, pp. 12–13.

Wu, J.H. and Nash, C. (2000) 'Railway reform in China', *Transport Reviews*, 20: 25–48.

Zhongguo Jiaotong Nianjian (1990–2001) *Yearbook of China Transportation and Communications*, Beijing: Yearbook House of China Transportation and Communications.

4 Appropriate models of port governance

Lessons from the Port Authority of New York and New Jersey

Jean-Paul Rodrigue

Globalization has been one of the dominant paradigms of maritime shipping and port terminal development since the mid-twentieth century. The emergence of a global economy has focused on three poles – North America, Western Europe and Japan – where most of the commercial, financial and distribution functions take place. Substantial changes have concomitantly occurred in the manufacturing sector, with production capabilities spread over vast territories (Rodrigue 2000), resulting in extensive shifts in the geography of freight distribution. Ports, from gateways to feeders, have been influenced by increased competitive pressures, by their integration with inland freight distribution systems, and by technical and technological changes in maritime and land transportation alike (Rodrigue *et al.* 1997). Global change has frequently inflicted severe local pains (McCalla 1999).

All this is now well known. But how ports should respond and adjust to these externally driven changes is much less well understood. Later in this volume (Chapter 7), McCalla aims to compensate for this gap through a theoretical approach to container port development, based on detailed analysis of the defensive and offensive strategies pursued by ports and shippers on the North American eastern seaboard. In the present chapter a complementary analysis is offered, focusing on a related issue. The globalization of trade has been closely linked with the rise of neo-liberal thinking and associated post-Fordist policies. In places this has been a driving force for port privatization, and more widely for managements to focus on ports' essential core business. But what has not been tested as this trend has emerged is the growing implication that publicly owned ports, not subject to the full rigour of the market, are unable to respond effectively to the new competitive pressures of globalization. Exploring this issue is the main aim of this chapter.

The port of New York serves as an excellent testbed to examine the thesis that in a neoliberal, privatized world, adherence to public agency port governance is outmoded and disadvantageous. The Port Authority of New York and New Jersey (PANYNJ) not only remains firmly in public control, but also has a remit extending well beyond a governance model focused narrowly on the management of port land use, support for terminal operators, and traffic regulation activities such as safety. In fact, the PANYNJ is responsible for a wide array of infrastructure ranging from office space[1] to bridges and tunnels, industrial development zones, waterfront developments, four airports and one heliport, transit systems and port terminals (Doig 2001).

No other port authority in the world manages such a diversified portfolio of activities, infrastructure and terminals within a coterminous geographical and administrative entity.[2] As a result, it is one of the largest public agencies in the United States, one which serves a region of more than 20 million persons and 600,000 businesses, representing one of the most extensive accumulations of economic activity in the world. To present it as the ultimate in the survival of Fordist governance, or a state within a state, seems little exaggeration. Consequently, the success with which this complex and diffuse organisation has coped with the port's development needs can be seen as a key question relevant to port systems around the world. How strong is the evidence that continued public ownership, and the demands of an extremely diverse portfolio of interests, have dissipated the PANYNJ's attention and consequently worked to the detriment of what should be its core business, the port?

To explore this question, the chapter begins by placing the port of New York in the wider contexts of change in the global trading environment and associated pressures on the US port system. Attention then turns to the long-term development of the PANYNJ and, in particular, the impressive diversification of its activities into non-port investments. Finally, with the breadth of diversification established, the spotlight turns to the needs of the port *per se*, and the degree to which these have been prioritized and met by the Authority.

The global and US contexts

As one of the poles of the global economy, the United States has been significantly affected by restructuring of its international trade in terms of its nature, volume and direction. While accounting for 22 per cent of global GDP, the national market is substantial, but international trade is taking a growing part of the economy, a trend particularly underlined by trade agreements such as the North American Free Trade Agreement (NAFTA) and the explosion of transpacific trade. Since the mid-1970s the US economy has systematically produced a negative goods trade balance, which reached a record $484.5 billion in 2002 (US Department of Commerce 2003). This is jointly the result of a growth of national consumption; an appreciation of the value of the US dollar, making foreign products cheaper; and a shift of labour-intensive manufacturing activities outside the United States. While exports of goods have consistently grown to reach $682.3 billion in 2002, this growth has been outpaced by imports, which totalled $1,166.9 billion the same year.

Such a negative balance is reflected in port operations, which have seen a sizeable growth in traffic, but a shift in its direction. About 44 per cent of the world's merchant fleet calls at a US port each year. However, the maritime façades of the United States, having different functions and market areas, are each being affected in a different manner as the changing trade structure that is

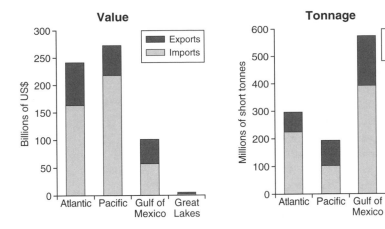

Figure 4.1 Value and tonnage of foreign cargo handled by maritime façade, United States, 1999. (Source: US Corps of Engineers, Navigation Data Center.)

tied to globalization generates varied regional adjustments. Ports on the Pacific coast handle the highest value of foreign cargo, while the Gulf of Mexico takes the most tonnage, mainly oil and agricultural products (Figure 4.1). The highest imbalance in cargo value is along the Pacific façade. This is an indication of value added inbound cargo from Pacific Asia coupled with a significant inland distribution function, notably through a rail land bridge using double stacking. The highest tonnage imbalance is along the Atlantic façade, where all the petroleum, most of the raw materials and significant shares of the manufactured goods are imported for regional consumption (US Department of Transportation 2001). At a local scale this imbalance is also reflected in every major port, where imports dominate significantly (Figure 4.2). In New York's case, 75 per cent of the value and 90 per cent of the tonnage are import/inbound related. This includes 11 per cent of all ocean-borne general cargo imported into the United States and 40 per cent of the Midwest-bound cargo transshipped through North Atlantic ports (PANYNJ 2001).

New York and its Port Authority

New York's role as one of the world's true global cities and the main gateway of the eastern seaboard of North America is widely acknowledged (Abu-Lughod 1999; Sassen 1991). This role emerged at the beginning of the nineteenth century, was mainly the consequence of the advantages of its port location, and initially was associated with nothing unusual with respect to port governance.

The port's hinterland initially developed to include the resource-rich regions of the US heartland through the Erie Canal, which opened between 1821 and 1825. The canal linked New York to Albany and Buffalo and initiated a new era of growth for inland freight transportation. At that time, New York was only

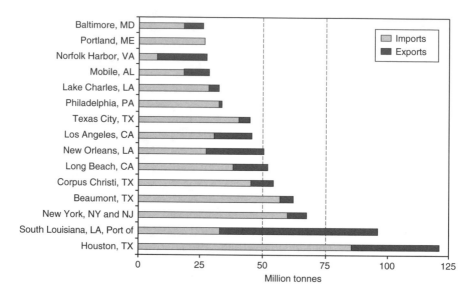

Figure 4.2 Cargo handled by the top 15 American ports, 2001 (tons). (Source: US Corps of Engineers, Navigation Data Center.)

the fifth-largest US seaport, behind Boston, Baltimore, Philadelphia and New Orleans. But by 1850 New York had evolved to become the most active port in the United States, as well as its prime city handling maritime traffic. By this time, its throughput exceeded the amount handled by Boston, Baltimore and New Orleans combined (New York State Canal Corporation 2001). The latter part of the nineteenth century focused on rail infrastructure developments, undermining the importance of the canal system but confirming the function of New York as the hub of the national transport system. This growth of port activities was on a par with the consolidation of foreign trade, wholesaling, and financial, shipbuilding and industrial activities. At this time, too, New York became the immigration gateway of North America.[3]

Since the New York harbour and the lower Hudson River are the boundary between the states of New York and New Jersey, port development occurred on both sides but under different jurisdictions. This process led to conflicts between the two states concerning the usage and jurisdiction of harbour facilities on the Hudson River, and by the early twentieth century these were becoming increasingly difficult to manage. In 1917, as the United States entered the First World War, an interstate conflict arose over the issue of rail freight rates. Most of the rail lines coming from the west ended on the New Jersey side of the harbour, while most ocean shipping was calling at Manhattan and Brooklyn. Freight had to be transferred on barges across the Hudson, exacerbating delays and congestion in the harbour. New Jersey petitioned the Interstate Commerce Commission to lower freight rates on its side of the Hudson in order to attract more port calls, but was overruled on the ground that the whole region was one functioning harbour. This was the stepping stone that led to the creation of the Port Authority, modelled initially on that already established in London.

The institutional setting

Founded in 1921, the PANYNJ became responsible for a region of 1,500 square miles (3,880 km²), overlapping two powerful states and centred around New York harbour (Figure 4.3). From the outset, a key feature was that it received a very broad governance mandate enabling it to undertake any project concerning any transport mode as long as it would promote commerce, trade and public good. To finance its activities the PANYNJ can issue bonds, charge user fees and collect rent. These arrangements have combined to ensure that it now has vested interests in a wide array of infrastructure developments, only some of which are port facilities. The emergence of this diversity is charted in the following section through a review of non-port infrastructure projects undertaken by the authority through the 80 years of its existence.

The most noteworthy achievements of the PANYNJ in its early years (the 1920s and 1930s) were not the development of port terminals, but the construction or the takeover of a succession of bridges and tunnels linking the two states, an urgent need on which both sides of the Hudson agreed. The issue of connectivity between New York and New Jersey was thus addressed, by road if not by rail.[4] Goethals Bridge and Outerbridge Crossing were the first to be constructed (1928), followed by the George Washington and Bayonne bridges (1931). These projects were completed ahead of schedule and below estimated costs, which boosted the reputation of the PANYNJ as an efficient legal and administrative body. The authority also opened the Lincoln Tunnel in 1937, having taken over in 1930 the jurisdiction of the Holland Tunnel (completed in 1927) (PANYNJ 2001).

The post-Second World War era marked tremendous technological and spatial changes for transport activities in New York. The most overt changes concerned the development of air transport terminals: by 1948 the PANYNJ was responsible for New York's three major airports, Newark, La Guardia and John F. Kennedy.[5] These it began to transform into world-class terminals. But the 1950s and 1960s also saw a commitment to public transit. As New York, like all American cities, was suburbanizing, a growing demand for passenger movements between both sides of the Hudson was being felt, and the PANYNJ believed it had the responsibility to help accommodate this increase in interstate interactions. This led to the opening of the Port Authority Bus Terminal (1950), the Port Authority Trans-Hudson railway (PATH) (1962) and the George Washington Bridge Bus Terminal (1963).

In the 1970s and 1980s, New York's economy was compromised by de-industrialization and the flight of head offices of major corporations. Now the PANYNJ became more specifically involved in regional economic development

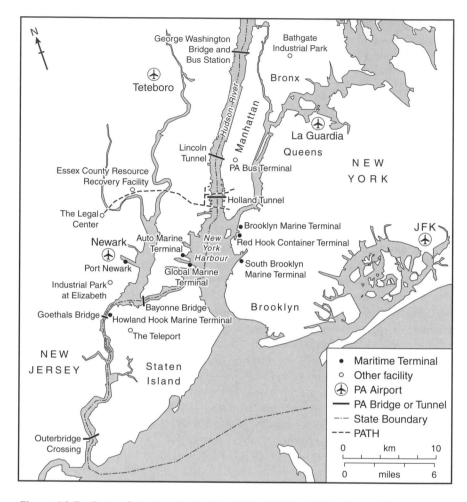

Figure 4.3 Facilities of the Port Authority of New York and New Jersey, 2003. (Source: PANYNJ, 2001; Bureau of Transportation Statistics (2003).)

with the construction of the World Trade Center (1970), plus the creation of industrial and telecommunications parks and a power plant (1990). But more efficient and sustainable land transit has also been a major theme, particularly with respect to the notorious problem of connectivity between its two main airports and Manhattan, which until recently could be reached only by road. Air-Train services connecting the Newark airport with regional rail transit opened in late 2001, and another service linking JFK with rail lines into Manhattan commenced operation in 2003.

Figure 4.3 provides an overview of the facilities under the jurisdiction of the Port Authority in 2003. Beyond this, the extent, diversity and importance of long-term investment in non-port activity are readily highlighted:

- *Bridges and tunnels.* Every river crossing between the city of New York and the state of New Jersey is operated by the PANYNJ. Together they carry more than 250 million vehicular crossings each year, and the George Washington Bridge is the most heavily used in the world, with about 300,000 crossings a day.[6] To improve the efficiency of regional vehicle circulation, the PANYNJ has implemented since 1997, in collaboration with several state and transportation authorities, an electronic toll system[7].

- *Airports.* The three major airports – Newark, John F. Kennedy and La Guardia – handled 34.2, 32.8 and 25.5 million passengers respectively in 2000, making New York a global air transport hub ranking alongside London and Tokyo. The combined air passenger traffic of all four airports[8] was 92.4 million, making the authority the largest direct overseer of air traffic in the world. In addition, air cargo amounted to 2.8 million tons.

- *Public transit.* The PATH heavy rail line, linking New Jersey with downtown Manhattan, carried 73.4 million passengers in 2000. The same year, the Port Authority Bus Terminal handled over 2.3 million bus movements and 58 million passengers. On a typical weekday, approximately 7,200 buses and 200,000 people use the bus terminal. Because the George Washington Bridge Bus Station is more oriented to longer-distance commuting, its figures are lower. Even so, it handled 5.7 million passengers in 2000.

- *Regional development initiatives* include both the industrial parks (Bathgate in the Bronx and Elizabeth, New Jersey[9]) and commercial developments offering office space (the Staten Island Teleport and the Legal Center, New Jersey). The PANYNJ is also involved in two waterfront development projects contributing to the reduction of inner-urban problems by converting centrally located maritime terminals to mixed urban land use. The power plant's contribution to regional development is via sustainability: on average, 2,500 tons of refuse is converted into electricity every day.

The PANYNJ's diversification is, therefore, impressive. Moreover, its extent is underlined by the Port Authority's financial profile. Operating revenues in 2002 were about $2.7 billion, of which 57 per cent was derived from air terminal operations and 30 per cent from interstate transportation in the form of bridge tolls and transit fares. In sharp contrast, port activities accounted for only 5 per cent of revenue income (Figure 4.4). The asset picture differs in detail, but port infrastructures now account for only 11 per cent of the PANYNJ's total assets. This remarkable situation strongly underlines the importance of the central issue this chapter seeks to explore. Is there evidence that the massive and diversified involvements of the Port Authority have worked to the detriment of the port function, for example by drawing away funding from the core business of port development? Does it appear likely that the authority will respond adequately to current trends that seem set to make improved regional freight distribution a priority in the next phase of development in the early twenty-first century?

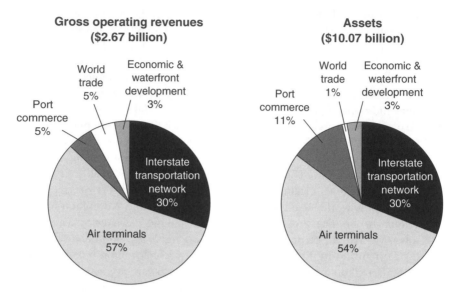

Figure 4.4 Financial profile of the Port Authority of New York and New Jersey, 2002. (Source: Port Authority of New York and New Jersey, Annual Financial Report (2002).)

The PANYNJ: meeting the port's key needs?

At first sight, there are signs of Port Authority failure. By the 1970s, New York was the largest container port in the world, handling just under 1 million TEU in 1975, 1.9 million in 1980 and 2.3 million in 1985. From this peak, however, a period of stagnation and relative decline endured, with the result that in the early 1990s the port was handling roughly the same amount of containerized traffic as it had in the early 1980s (1.8 million TEU). During this period, Asian container ports such as Hong Kong, Singapore, Kaohsiung and Pusan surpassed New York, while on the Pacific coast Los Angeles and Long Beach also boomed and topped it.[10] Similarly, the hubbing role of New York on the Atlantic coast was challenged by traditional rivals such as Baltimore, Philadelphia and Montreal.

Warf and Kleyn (1989) have argued that local factors, particularly inadequate intermodal rail access and high labour costs, played a significant part in this relative decline. Yet the period in question was also the time when the local economy was subject to sharp international trade changes that were beyond local control. De-industrialization began in the 1950s but was still a major force at this time, culminating in a devastating recession in 1989–92 and impacting sharply on the port's export function. Meanwhile, although a new regional economy was developing new directions of trade, at first these could not fully compensate for lost exports. As the 1990s progressed, however, regional economic adjustment gathered pace, fed through to the port, and demonstrated that it was not the port itself that had checked throughput growth. Instead, port dynamism had become increasingly dependent on the demands of the regional economy, which were in turn spurred by the globally linked functions of New York.

Port traffic reorientation and recovery arose in part from New York's new wave of development, which relied increasingly on activities global in scale, including finance and banking, international investment, information technologies, and marketing and media services (Lakshmanan and Chatterjee 2000; Warf and Cox 1989). But recovery was also a consequence of expanding regional consumption: while the New York metropolitan area houses 20 million people, an extra 80 million can be reached within 24 hours. This makes the direct market area of the port of New York one of the largest in North America and one of the most extensive in the world. Against this background, the key trade figures are that while cargo exports increased by 38 per cent in tonnage in the period 1991–2002, cargo imports – overwhelmingly containerized – boomed by 70 per cent. Its national share has also improved in the past five years, as the Port of New York/New Jersey accounted for 13.5 per cent of all containers handled by American ports in 2002 and 59.6 per cent of all containers handled by North Atlantic ports (PANYNJ 2003). This was the result of rapidly accelerating regional freight demand (Figure 4.5). Similarly, New York's Auto Marine Terminal handled 588,000 vehicles in 2002, 94 per cent of which were inbound. Thus, freight transportation and distribution in the eastern seaboard became increasingly consumption related, as opposed to the traditional production-related role, and the resumption of port growth hinged on the successful structural shift New York's hinterland, which globalization *regionalized*.

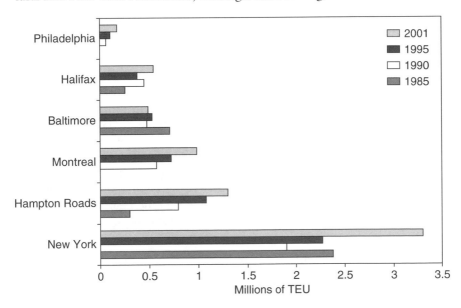

Figure 4.5 Main container ports of the North Atlantic façade, 1985-2001 (millions of TEU). (Source: American Association of Port Authorities (2002).)

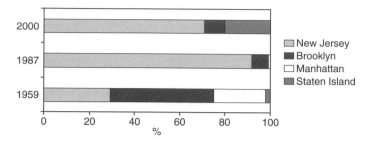

Figure 4.6 Distribution of general cargo operations, Port of New York, 1959, 1987 and 2000. (Sources: for years 1959 and 1987 Moss (1988); for 2000, and PANYNJ (2001–3).)

The conclusion that port growth was not strangled by inadequate facilities is also borne out by a review of infrastructural investments. Over a lengthy period, most port terminals were relocated from the general cargo wharves of Manhattan, Brooklyn, Hoboken and Jersey City to specialized and more spacious locations. By the early 1980s almost all maritime cargo transshipment in Manhattan had ceased, and traffic was dominantly handled in New Jersey and Staten Island, a complete reversal in the port's geography of freight (Figure 4.6). There are now seven public terminals that are managed by the PANYNJ in these new sites. While the South Brooklyn Marine Terminal is a warehousing facility, and the Auto Marine Terminal is exclusively for vehicles, the remaining five are dedicated container facilities (the Port Elizabeth, Port Newark, Howland Hook, Red Hook and Global Marine terminals). Moreover, as McCalla demonstrates in Chapter 7, since these container terminals were established it has been standard practice to increase their capacity in various ways – especially by extending the stacking area, by adding additional berths and by investing in more cranes.

The consequence of this long-term programme of relocation and investment has been to ensure that the supply of handling facilities has kept ahead of demand. In 2000, for example, New York's potential container throughput (approximately 4 million TEU) was used to 75 per cent of capacity. This was the case even though the growth of containerized traffic between 1995 and 2000 exceeded the combined growth of all competing ports of the North Atlantic. Handling facilities were not restricted, despite the fact that New York received the largest number of container ship calls in the United States and had consolidated its position as the country's third-largest container port.

The PANYNJ, the port and the future

Evidence of the PANYNJ's continuing commitment to the port, despite its other varied interests, comes also from future plans. In the port system generally, the global and regional forces dictating change will continue to impact at the local level (Slack 1994; McCalla 1999). Given this reality, the PANYNJ recognizes that the major challenge is to continue to upgrade facilities to meet the needs of port operations in the early twenty-first century. Above all, the goal is to enable container traffic to realize its potential and double to 6 million TEU by 2015. Consequently, in 2000 the PANYNJ committed $1.8 billion for port redevelopment under a five-year plan, encouraging local marine operators to commit another $500 million in marine terminal investments. Targets of this new investment are mainly added terminal capacity, dredging and improved access to inland transportation (O'Neill and Moss 1998).

Capacity expansion is proceeding on two main fronts:[11]

- *Howland Hook*. This terminal closed in the late 1980s when its user, the container shipping line United States Lines, went bankrupt. In 1996 it was reopened, extending the operational capacity of the Port of New York by about 500,000 TEU per year. Already the terminal handles about 20 per cent of the port's total cargo, and is being expanded by the addition of a 124-acre (50-ha) site to increase freight-handling and warehouse space.[12] By 2006, Howland Hook's capacity will have been doubled to 1 million TEU per year, or about 25 per cent of all container traffic. Because this added transshipment traffic would clog the already highly congested highway system of Staten Island, the upgrading of rail connections and on-dock rail services is under way to mitigate this problem. Eventually, however, growing pressure could force the construction of a new crossing to New Jersey, next to the Goethals Bridge. While the main purpose of developing Howland Hook is to ensure port – and thus regional – growth, its position in the State of New York also makes it a political 'equaliser' in the distribution of port activities in the metropolitan area (Figure 4.4).
- *Port Elizabeth*. Port Elizabeth, which handles about 60 per cent of containerized traffic, will be extended into a new 350-acre (142-ha) terminal with 6,000 ft (1,800 m) of berthing linked to a 70-acre (28-ha) on-dock express rail facility. This should be ready in 2004. This terminal offers the only double-stack rail link within the PANYNJ, and is thus a high-priority investment. Once completed, the rail-to-ship capacity should be able to transship about 1 million containers per year. Maersk-SeaLand, the world's largest container shipper, is mainly based at Port Elizabeth. Although this company's decision in 1999 to maintain New York as its east coast hub partly reflected the perception that the port is now cost-competitive with other Atlantic ports, it also acknowledged Port Elizabeth's continuing growth potential.

Planned channel deepening reflects the worldwide driver that, as the global container fleet is upgraded with larger ships, major ports face the challenge of accommodating deeper vessel draughts (Slack 1994). While a typical Panamax container ship could be accommodated by a 35-foot (10 m) channel, the new generation of post-Panamax vessels – carrying between 4,000 and 5,000 TEU – requires a channel depth between 42 and 52 ft (13–16 m).[13] New York's

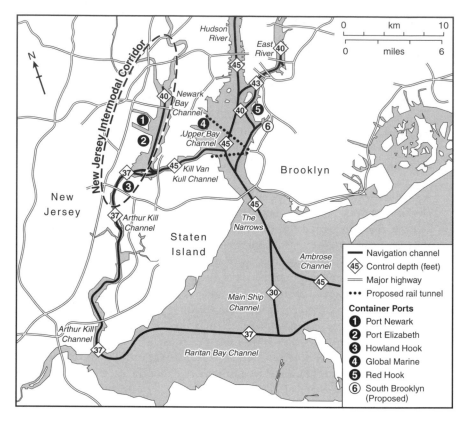

Figure 4.7 Intermodal facilities and navigation channels of the Port of New York, 2003.
(Source: Bureau of Transportation Statistics (2003).)

late-1990s clearance of 40 ft (12 m) for its container terminals was consequently a threat, especially as several North American ports already had better access (Figures 4.7 and 4.8). Channel deepening has thus become an important issue relating to the port's ability to keep and enhance its containerized traffic. This was emphasized in July 1998, when the newly merged Maersk-SeaLand company was negotiating with the Port Authority over its choice of New York as its east coast container hub, and brought pressure to bear by arranging for the post-Panamax container ship *Regina Maersk* to call at Port Elizabeth half-empty. Fully loaded it could not have navigated the Kill van Kull channel linking Port Elizabeth with New York harbour.

From this chapter's perspective, the PANYNJ's most significant response to the *Regina Maersk* episode was to include in its agreement with Maersk-SeaLand a clause undertaking to deepen the Kill van Kull to accommodate the shipping line's new fleet of post-Panamax container ships. As early as 1999 the Army Corps of Engineers[14] started dredging work on a 45 ft Kill van Kull

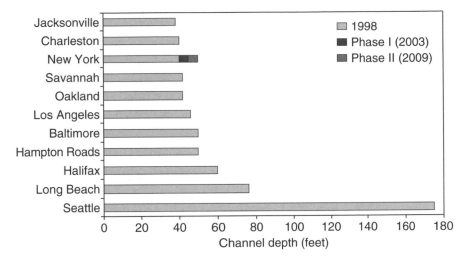

Figure 4.8 Channel depth at selected North American ports, 1998. (Source: adapted from O'Neil and Moss (1998).)

channel costing $700 million and completed in 2003. But in 2001 the PANYNJ went well beyond this by accelerating and expanding the dredging project. Plans now envisage a depth of 50 ft (15 m) for the whole harbour access channel,[15] and an improved depth of 41–45 ft (12.4–13.6 m) in the approach to the Howland Hook terminal (compared with the current 37 ft (11.2 m). This work is expected to be completed by 2009, with dredging costs of around $1.8 billion, of which about 50 per cent is to be provided by the Port Authority.

In addition to terminal development and sea access improvements, the PANYNJ's continuing commitment to the port may be tested by its land transport proposals. Here the essential background is the problem of intra-urban movement by road and rail. Since 85 per cent of containers bound for the port are carried by 15,000 truck movements each day,[16] local accessibility to marine terminals is a fundamental issue. The problem is further exacerbated by congestion and very high local transportation costs, which are on average 30 per cent higher than in other US metropolises. Freight movements across the harbour are limited by two bridges, George Washington and Verrazano, handling crossings of more than 30,000 trucks per day. One survey found that it costs roughly the same to move a container by truck from Port Elizabeth to Manhattan (straight distance 1.5 miles (2.5 km), although the truck must go via the George Washington Bridge) as it does to go from Connecticut to Ohio (a distance of 500 miles (800 km) (Holguin-Veras and Paaswell 2000). Moreover, road congestion is expected to increase by 50 per cent by 2020 (NYCEDC 2000).

The conclusions to be drawn from the Port Authority's response are admittedly mixed, even though it has widespread jurisdiction over key road and rail infrastructures. Recognising the road congestion drawback in inland accessibility, the PANYNJ has for some time been attempting to promote better intermodal rail connectivity. Not all these efforts have yet borne fruit, particularly in relation to the major problem of cross-harbour rail accessibility between Brooklyn, where rail access is primordial, and New Jersey. On this route, traffic must either take a 140-mile (225 km) detour north through Albany or be floated by rail barges. The preferred solution is a cross-harbour rail tunnel, either from Greenville Yard in New Jersey or from Staten Island[17] Figure 4.7; NYCEDC 2000). Additional attractions of this solution are that it would increase port capacity by supporting the construction of a major container terminal in south Brooklyn and – through modal diversion – would alleviate road freight movements between New Jersey and Long Island[18]. But this project is controversial because of very high construction costs (ranging anywhere between $1.3 billion and $2.4 billion) and poor terminal accessibility in Brooklyn. Consequently, as an alternative, further expansions of rail float barge services have been initiated (NYMTC 2001).

Elsewhere, however, progress in the promotion of local rail transport has been more concrete, especially at Port Elizabeth. In 1991 a 35-acre (14 ha) ExpressRail terminal, built by the intermodal freight operator Maher Terminals, opened. This offers direct doublestacking ship-to-rail and rail-to-ship transshipment capabilities, functions which grew at a phenomenal rate from 43,000 containers handled in 1992 to 228,000 in 2002. Although this facility is reaching the limits of capacity, a new terminal with improved truck and rail access opened in 2003 (PANYNJ 2001). It is now expected that rail's share of intermodal movements will climb to 25–30 per cent of transhipped containers by 2010, resulting in clear economic and environmental benefits for the locality (NYMTC 2001).

One final important initiative, launched by the Port Authority in 2002, must be noted: the creation of a Port Inland Distribution Network (Figure 4.9). This aims to relieve regional road congestion in the metropolitan area, expand port throughput, increase the efficiency of freight distribution, and favour inland development by using a set of inland rail and port terminals to handle containers (PANYNJ 2003). A wider market area should emerge, with about 82 per cent of the regional container market located within 50 miles (80 km) of the proposed terminals. The strategy is that at least some of the ocean-going container ships arriving in New York could be unloaded directly on to barges that would then be shipped to regional barge ports, such as Albany, Davisville, Bridgeport, New Haven, Camden, Salem and Wilmington. In addition, because the channel depth on the Hudson between New York and Albany is at least 32 feet (10 m) and available all year, a high-capacity lo/lo (lift on/lift off) container barge system could increase the port's market area in south-eastern Canada, particularly in Ontario and Quebec. Apart from the economic benefits, the modal shift achieved by diverting freight from road to water would bring environmental gains not only in the metropolitan area, but also in the wider region. Although the initiative is recent, an agreement to use the Port of Albany as the first regional freight distribution centre has already been signed.

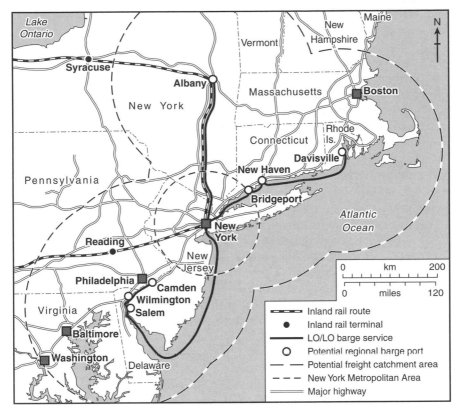

Figure 4.9 Port inland distribution network and regional 'sub-harborization' of container terminals by the Port of New York, 2003. (Source: PANYNJ (2003) and US DOT-FHWA Office of Freight Management (2003).)

Conclusion

The Port Authority of New York and New Jersey represents a unique example of port governance with vested interests in a wide range of activities ranging from real estate to road transportation and transport terminals (road, air and port). Because of its mandate, it has greater room for manoeuvre than most port authorities in the allocation of its development priorities.

The investigation has demonstrated that in spite of a diversified portfolio of activities dominated by air and road transportation, the PANYNJ has an enduring commitment to port development. Recent development projects underline this long-term commitment, as they mainly aim at improving the efficiency of regional freight distribution with added terminal capacity, channel deepening and improved access to inland transportation. The evidence gathered points clearly to the conclusion that the PANYNJ can be labelled an efficient example of public port authority governance, despite the widespread neo-liberal view that effectiveness is best achieved through privatization. The following major factors behind the efficiency of the port's governance can be identified:

- *A regional focus.* The PANYNJ has been strongly embedded in the regional economy for over 80 years. There is consequently great coherence in coordinating regional development policies, as it is well placed to anticipate future transportation needs and provide a coordinated response. Although bi-state governance may trigger 'turf wars' in the geographical allocation of funding, the size of the PANYNJ's jurisdiction and the scope of its mandate enable it to mitigate these conflicts effectively. Comparatively, a private port authority tends to have a focus that is either too narrow or global.
- *A broad mandate.* A public authority such as the PANYNJ has the objective of promoting 'public good', which can be multi-dimensional (social and economic) in its interpretation. By its mandate, it is able to focus on a variety of projects, not necessarily port operations, which can serve regional development and provide additional revenue generation. Bridge tolls, for instance, ensure a very stable revenue stream that can be allocated to support development priorities. PANYNJ's vast assets support the financing of ambitious projects with limited, if any, federal or state government involvement. The PANYNJ is able to capture revenue opportunities unavailable to other port authorities under a different governance regime.

It is acknowledged that the PANYNJ is an outcome of local political geography, which resulted in the creation of an entity that would otherwise have been unlikely to have existed. In this sense, its governance model has limited applicability to other port authorities. However, its success at continuously re-inventing itself and – most importantly – deploying its diversified mandate to serve the needs of the port, suggests that public-sector control continues to merit consideration as the reform of port authority governance is debated in the twenty-first century.

Acknowledgements

The author would like to thank David Pinder, Jose Holguin-Veras and Barney Warf for their useful comments on earlier drafts of this chapter.

Notes

1 New York's premier financial centre, the World Trade Center, belonged to the PANYNJ and was destroyed on 11 September 2001 by a terrorist attack. Although the final impact of this event on the Authority is as yet unclear, it is evident that it will be far-reaching. In addition to the loss of annual operating revenues of $342 million and real estate valued at $1.04 billion (2001 figures), the PANYNJ lost 74 employees, its head offices, the PATH rail station under the complex (ridership

65,000 people a day) and a power substation. Meanwhile, the airports and the port were closed for one week and PATH ridership was reduced on undamaged parts of the system. Overall, it was estimated that the authority's losses from the terrorist attack amounted to $2.4 billion (Smothers 2001). It must be anticipated that these huge losses will have an impact on future port projects. However, the attack itself does not invalidate the basic aim of the chapter: to assess past performance and strategic intentions in order to determine the ability of a diverse publicly owned authority to prioritize the needs of the port.

2 While the PANYNJ is a vertically integrated port authority, the Marine and Port Authority of Singapore (MPA), probably the world's second-largest port authority, is integrating horizontally by building and contracting the management of container terminals around the world with a focus on China, the Middle East and Western Europe. In 2000 the MPA handled about 25 per cent of the world's container transshipment throughput.

3 The port still has this role, but changing migration patterns have made California and Texas prime gateways.

4 The problem of rail connectivity was to emerge much later, in the 1990s. The initial focus on road reflected a shift in priority in US land transportation development with the funding of regional and national (Interstate) highway systems. This shift accelerated in the 1950s.

5 Known at that time as New York International.

6 Congestion on these crossings is now a major issue because of the intensity of use.

7 Known as E-Zpass, these electronic tags are valid for all major tolls in the states of New York, New Jersey, Pennsylvania, Delaware, Massachusetts and Maryland.

8 The fourth airport, Teteboro, handled fewer than 200,000 passengers a year.

9 The Elizabeth industrial park, adjacent to the container terminal, is not a pure industrial development and was completed in 1997 with the addition of a giant IKEA store.

10 Hong Kong and Kaohsiung surpassed New York in 1986, Singapore in 1987, Pusan and Los Angeles in 1989 and Long Beach in 1993.

11 The PANYNJ is considering a third initiative: reactivating the South Brooklyn Marine Terminal. Currently used for storage and to handle some bulk cargo, the site could provide additional container capacity. However, it is seriously impeded by lack of space and accessibility to the highly congested local road network. Moreover, rail access to New Jersey is currently provided indirectly via a float barge system.

12 The land was purchased from Procter and Gamble.

13 Larger container ships are on the drawing board, including a 'Malacca-max' concept that could carry between 16,000 and 18,000 TEU. This would require a draft of about 69 feet (21 metres), and currently no port on the eastern seaboard could accommodate such a ship.

14 The Army Corps of Engineers is the sole agency authorized to undertake dredging projects in the United States.

15 Various environmental and technical problems arise from this project as a 50 ft (15 m) channel involves cutting into the bedrock at several points.

16 The national average for truck carriage is 44 per cent.

17 Proposals of this type are of long standing: construction of a rail tunnel has been under consideration by the PANYNJ and other agencies since 1936.

18 The prediction is that trucking trips would be reduced by 6 per cent.

References

Abu-Lughod, J. (1999) *New York, Chicago, Los Angeles: America's Global Cities*, Minneapolis: University of Minnesota Press.

American Association of Port Authorities (2002) [untitled], available at http://www.apa-ports.org/ (accessed 20 February 2002).

Bureau of Transportation Statistics (2003) *Transportation Atlas of the United States*, available at http://www.bts.gov (accessed 3 April 2003).

Doig, J.W. (2001) *Empire on the Hudson: Entrepreneurial Vision and Political Power at the Port of New York Authority*, New York: Columbia University Press.

Holguin-Veras, J. and Paaswell, R.E. (2000) 'New York regional intermodal freight transportation planning: institutional challenges', *Transportation Law Journal*, 27: 453–473.

Lakshmanan, T.R. and Chatterjee, L. (2000) *New York: Gateway City to the Global Economy*, online, available at http://www.bu.edu/transportation/NY.pdf (accessed 12 April 2003).

McCalla, R. (1999) 'Global change, local pain: intermodal seaport terminals and their service areas', *Journal of Transport Geography*, 7: 247–254.

Moss, M.L. (1988) 'New York vs. New Jersey: a new perspective', *Portfolio*, Summer.

New York City Economic Development Corporation (NYCEDC) (2000) *Cross Harbor Freight Movement Major Investment Study*, online, available at http://www.newyork biz.com/Library/Studies/CrossHarbor.html (accessed 15 February 2002).

NYMTC (2001) *NYMTC Regional Freight Plan: Task 2 – Description of Freight Transportation System in the Region*, prepared by Cambridge Systematics, Inc., online, available at http://webservices.camsys.com/nymtcfreight/documents/nymtc_task2_complete.pdf (accessed 18 January 2002).

New York State Canal Corporation (2001) *The Erie Canal: A Brief History*, online, available at http://www.canals.state.ny.us/history/index.html (accessed 6 December 2001).

O'Neill, H. and Moss, M.L. (1998) *Tunnel Vision: An Analysis of the Proposed Tunnel and Deepwater Port in Brooklyn*, New York University, Taub Urban Research Center, online, available at http://urban.nyu.edu/archives/tunnel-vision/tunnel-vision.pdf (accessed 9 August 2003).

Port Authority of New York and New Jersey (PANYNJ) (2001–3), various press releases, online, available http://www.panynj.gov.

—— (2003) *PortViews*, 2 (1).

Rodrigue, J.-P. (2000) *L'espace économique mondial: les économies avancées et la mondialisation*, Quebec: Presses de l'Université du Québec.

Rodrigue, J.-P., Slack, B. and Comtois, C. (1997) 'Transportation and spatial cycles: evidence from maritime systems', *Journal of Transport Geography*, 5: 87–98.

Sassen, S. (1991) *The Global City: New York, London, Tokyo*, Princeton, N.J: Princeton University Press.

Slack, B. (1994) 'Pawns in the game: ports in a global transport system', *Growth and Change*, 24: pp. 597–598.

—— (1998) 'Intermodal transportation', in B. Hoyle and R. Knowles (eds) *Modern Transport Geography*, New York: Wiley, pp. 263–289.

Smothers, R. (2001) '$2.4 billion in losses are detailed in report', *New York Times*, 21 September.

US Corps of Engineers, Navigation Data Center. [no date, untitled], available at http://www.iwr.usace.army.mil/ndc/wcsc.htm (accessed 9 August 2003).

US Department of Commerce (2003) *U.S. Foreign Trade Highlights*, online, available at http://www.ita.doc.gov/td/industry/otea/usfth/ (accessed 8 September 2003).

US Department of Transportation, Federal Highway Administration, Office of Freight

Management (2003) [untitled], available at http://www.marad.dot.gov/ (accessed 4 September 2003).

Warf, B. and Cox, J. (1989) 'The changing economic impacts of the Port of New York', *Maritime Policy and Management*, 16: 3–11.

Warf, B. and Kleyn, L. (1989) 'Competitive status of US ports in the mid-1980s', *Maritime Policy and Management*, 16: 157–172.

5 Analysing the performance of seaport clusters

P. W. de Langen

Defining clusters

The contention underpinning this chapter is that, while the pressures of globalisation naturally encourage research into the reaction of entire port systems, this should not be at the expense of investigations at the locality level. Moreover, these investigations should go beyond the consideration of the development of individual ports, narrowly defined. There is instead a need to inject more assessment into port studies and to apply this assessment-based approach to the whole agglomeration of activities generated by the port. How are they performing in the changed economic environment created by continuing globalisation? Achieving this goal, it is argued, can be achieved by introducing the cluster concept to port studies.

The concept of clustering has become central for analysing the competitiveness of nations (Porter 1990), industries (Panniccia 1999) and firms (McEvily and Zaheer 1999). Here, clusters are defined as a population of geographically concentrated and mutually related business units, associations and public (or private) organisations centred around a distinctive economic specialisation. Clusters have four main characteristics:

1   A cluster is a population of interdependent organisations. These organisations – predominantly firms – operate in the same value chain and have to some extent a shared competitive position. For that reason, they are interdependent: when one firm attracts business, other firms benefit, and when a firm goes bankrupt, other firms lose a customer or supplier. Apart from economic relations (transactions between firms in the cluster), firms are also 'socially related', for instance through meetings between CEOs in business clubs and networks (Mistri 1999).

2   Clusters are geographically concentrated. Different clusters have different relevant cluster regions and can occur at a variety of scales: local, regional or interregional. The issue of the geographical delimitation of the region is not addressed in this chapter (for a discussion see de Langen 2001), but the geographical concentration of clusters sets them apart from networks. Networks can be international, clusters are spatially concentrated networks.

3   The cluster population consists of four kinds of organisations: business units, associations, public–private organisations and public organisations. Business units may be organisational units of firms as a whole. For instance, business units of banks or insurance firms dealing with ships are included in a maritime cluster, not the bank or insurance firm as a whole. Furthermore, 'parent firms' outside the cluster can own business units.

4   The cluster population is linked by a core specialisation. This notion is implicit in most studies on clustering and is necessary since the 'chain' of input–output relations is in principle endless. For instance, high-tech research centres are part of a 'technology cluster', but restaurants in the vicinity of these research centres are not, because they are not related to the core specialisation.

Thus, the seaport cluster population consists of business units, associations and public and/or private organisations that are relatively strongly interrelated, are functionally linked to the core specialisation of the cluster, and are located in the proximity of the seaport. Indicators of the strength of linkages include:

*   Use of common cluster resources, such as labour. Clusters have in general a joint labour pool. The usage of these resources indicates that firms are related to the cluster.
*   Membership of cluster associations. Regional cluster associations arise in many clusters, and membership of such associations shows that firms are included in the cluster networks.
*   Inclusion in 'regional learning systems' (Cooke 1998). Clusters are characterised by relatively extensive flows of knowledge and information. The inclusion in such learning networks also demonstrates the existence of strong linkages.

Ports as clusters

The geographical concentration of similar and complementary economic activities is a widespread phenomenon (Krugman 1991). Firms in various industries cluster together in specific regions. Yet even though the role of ports as drivers of agglomeration is widely acknowledged (Krugman 1991; Fujita and Mori 1996), the cluster concept has not been used to analyse seaport clusters in particular.

The cluster concept is, therefore, a new theoretical perspective for analysing seaports. Seaports are not just nodes in a transport chain, which is the focus of studies of intermodal transport, but may be seen as regional clusters of economic activities. Central in the cluster perspective is the recognition that the development of individual firms in a cluster depends crucially on the development of the cluster as a whole. Employing a cluster perspective allows new research questions to be addressed, such as what factors drive the development of seaport clusters? What is the nature of inter-firm relations in seaports? And under what conditions, and to what extent, do firms in clusters cooperate?

Even though the term 'cluster' may not have been used, and the literature on clusters not considered, there have been some studies that have addressed issues that are centre stage in a cluster perspective, such as the 'port community' (Martin and Thomas 2001) and the port service industry (Slack 1988, 1989). The port regarded as a cluster is of practical interest for actors in the port industry, and of theoretical interest for regional economists, because ports have always been clusters of economic activity. The arrival of cargo and ships in ports has always attracted related economic activities. Furthermore, port activities themselves are highly concentrated in a limited number of locations. Eighty-three per cent of the total thoughput in the current 15 European Union countries[1] is concentrated in the 75 largest ports. The 10 largest ports handle 40 per cent of all cargo (RMPM 2002).

Economic activities included in a port cluster

Cargo handling – including all activities such as pilotage and stevedoring which together facilitate the loading and unloading of cargo – is the core specialisation of seaport clusters (Teurelincx 2000). All economic activities related to the arrival of goods and ships are included in the port cluster. Cargo handling functions are intrinsically linked to transport activities, such as shipping and forwarding. These activities locate in seaports precisely because seaports are transport nodes. Thus, transport firms are included in the port cluster population. As centres of goods handling and storage, and because of the abundant presence of transport services, seaports are attractive locations for logistics activities. These logistics services, such as storage, assembling, repacking and consolidating, are strongly related to transport and cargo handling activities. Many firms offer cargo handling, transport and logistics services in one integrated 'package'. This shows the strength of the linkages between these activities. Figure 5.1 illustrates the relations between cargo handling, transport and logistics activities.

Ports are also industrial zones. Because of their ability to handle and store bulky industrial raw materials such as oil, coal and iron ore, seaports are frequently centres of manufacturing production activities, such as chemicals and steel. A seaport location greatly reduces cargo-handling and transport costs. When cost minimisation is crucial for competitive production, industrial activities locate in seaports, and production activities are closely integrated with logistics and transport. In addition, ports are centres of trade. For some commodities, such as agricultural products, steel and oil, trading takes place in the same place as storage, either because buyers and sellers want to see the product, or because information on shipping prices is elementary for trading companies. When trade and storage are related, trade activities are included in a port cluster.

Thus, cargo handling, transport, logistics, specific production functions and certain trading activities are strongly interrelated and comprise the 'port cluster'. Table 5.1 shows the strength of relations between these five activities, according to a group of 43 industry experts in Rotterdam. It is evident that in this case the

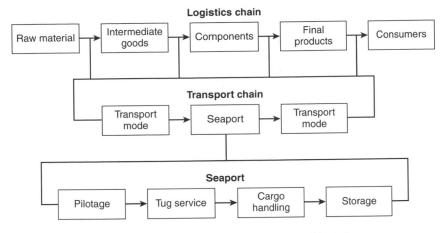

Figure 5.1 The linkages between cargo handling, transport and logistics.

five activities are relatively strongly interrelated. Although trade is consistently the least linked part of the cluster, cargo handling, transport and logistics are all centrally related to the other cluster activities. Further detail on all these activities, indicating the types of firm they comprise, is provided by Table 5.2.

A framework for analysing the performance of clusters

In this section a framework for analysing the performance of clusters is presented. The performance of a cluster can be measured by the value added that is generated in the cluster. This measure is similar to established measures of regional or national economic growth. For an explanation in more detail, see de Langen (2004). A review of the economic literature related directly or indirectly to clusters suggests that cluster studies can be classified into one of four schools

Table 5.1 Average strength of relationships between firms engaging in different activities

	Cargo handling firms	Transport firms	Logistics firms	Manu-facturing firms	Trading firms
Cargo handling firms	4.2	4.0	3.5	2.9	2.5
Transport firms	4.2	4.2	3.5	2.8	2.3
Logistics firms	4.0	4.0	3.6	2.8	2.6
Manufacturing firms	4.3	4.0	4.0	4.0	2.7
Trading firms	3.4	3.8	3.6	3.4	3.0

Source: Interviews.

Note
Scale: 1 = very weak; 5 = very strong. Number of respondents = 43.

Table 5.2 The principal activities comprising a port cluster

Cargo handling system	Transport system	Logistics system	Production system	Trade system
Stevedoring Stevedoring suppliers Rail terminals Towage and pilotage Storage of goods Port engineering	Shipping companies Transport companies Ship suppliers Ship agents Forwarding agents Maritime services Transport services Ship repair	Logistics service providers Warehouse facilities Logistics consultancy and ICT services Value added services	Production activities related to commodities Supplier services for production	Trading companies for commodities Trade centres Commodity auctions

(Table 5.3). These schools yield complementary insights for understanding the performance of clusters.

Population economics, because it is predominantly used to analyse populations of firms in the same industry, does not consider clusters themselves. However, it provides several insights that can be applied to clusters. Population economics recognises that the behaviour of firms in a population is strongly interdependent, that populations of firms evolve over time, and that changes in a population of firms are strongly influenced by entry and exits (Staber 1998). Furthermore, a population perspective indicates that diversity in a population can add to the performance of that population.

Table 5.3 Different schools: their focus and leading authors

School	Leading author(s)	Focus of school
'Diamond school'	Porter (1990)	A holistic approach to understanding the competitiveness of national industries
New economic geography	Krugman (1991); Fujita, Krugman and Venables (1999)	Spatial equilibria of forces leading to, and opposing, spatial concentration
Population economics	Metcalfe (1998); Hannan and Freeman (1977)	The dynamics of a population
Industrial district school	Piore and Sabel (1984); Staber (1998); Harrison (1992)	Explaining the characteristics of industrial districts and the relative success of this organisational mode

The 'new economic geography' approach explains agglomeration in all kinds of industries as the result of two opposing forces: agglomeration economies and disagglomeration economies. There are three agglomeration forces: the presence of customers and suppliers, a qualified labour force and 'knowledge spillovers'. The two main diseconomies are congestion and land scarcity. This approach is useful for analysing whether geographic clustering is likely to increase or decrease.

The 'industrial district' school focuses on the behaviour of firms in clusters and the embeddedness of firms in regional environments. This school deals with issues such as innovation regimes in clusters, the balance between cooperation and competition, and the role of 'leader firms'. Consequently, it provides a basis for analysing the governance of clusters.

Finally, Porter's 'diamond school' presents a holistic approach to analysing cluster performance. Porter's framework has been criticised by some scholars for being vague and theoretically unsound (Krugman 1991), but it is widely used in practice by policy makers. It considers a large number of 'variables' that influence performance, and these are grouped into four central factors: internal competition, a demanding home market, the presence of customers and suppliers, and beneficiary factor conditions.

From these four approaches a framework for analysing the performance of clusters can be developed. Central to this framework is a distinction between cluster governance and cluster structure. *Cluster governance* is a broad term. It includes all the actors (public and private) that are involved in projects to improve the competitive position of the cluster. Cluster governance may be defined as the mix of, and relations between, various mechanisms of coordination used in a cluster, and it is different in each cluster. For example, in some clusters strong linkages between firms and research centres have been created, while in others they have not. Such differences influence the development of a cluster. *Cluster structure* is defined as the composition and economic characteristics of the cluster population. The four schools provide several useful insights into the character of both cluster governance and cluster structure (Table 5.4).

A proposed framework for analysing the performance of clusters, based upon the insights derived from the four schools, is presented in Figure 5.2. The framework suggests that the structure and the governance of a cluster are interrelated. For instance, the number and role of associations in a cluster (governance) are likely to be different in a heterogeneous cluster than in a homogeneous one (structure). Regarding the structure of a cluster, the model identifies four variables that influence performance: the strength of agglomeration economies, the presence of entry and exit barriers, the degree of heterogeneity, and the level of internal competition. All four variables are derived from the schools discussed above. Similarly, the four governance variables influencing cluster performance are factors drawn from the literature. The presence of intermediaries, embedded leader firms, levels of trust, and solutions to problems of collective action are all important factors in cluster governance. It must be

Table 5.4 Cluster insights from the schools incorporated in the theoretical framework

School	Insights with regard to cluster structure	Insights relevant to cluster governance
'Diamond school'	Internal competition enhances cluster performance Presence of critical customers increases the cluster performance	Clusters can be characterised by 'vibrant environments', with fierce internal competition
New economic geography	Presence of agglomeration economies enhances cluster performance Presence of agglomeration diseconomies hampers cluster performance	Knowledge spillovers are an important advantage of clusters. Such knowledge spillovers depend on cluster governance.
Population economics	Heterogeneity of cluster population enhances performance Spatial exit and entry barriers influence cluster performance	
Industrial district school	Heterogeneity of the cluster population enhances performance[a]	Quality of governance regimes enhances performance

Note
a The kinds of firms that are beneficial for a cluster are discussed in most studies by the industrial district school.

recognised, however, that these four variables do not capture the whole complexity of cluster governance. The performance, the structure and the governance of a cluster may be affected by external factors, such as national and international policies and the development of the region as a whole. These factors are not incorporated in this model since the framework focuses on the internal characteristics of clusters themselves.

Performance of seaport clusters: an empirical application

The theoretical framework proposed above opens up a large field for empirical application to seaports. This section focuses on two key elements – agglomeration economies and internal competition in seaport clusters – and explores them in relation to the port of Rotterdam.

The data presented here were gathered by interviewing 'port experts' in Rotterdam. An initial list of 30 experts comprised the chairpersons of four important associations in Rotterdam, senior managers of the largest firms in the port, and others suggested by Professor Welters, a professor of port economics and former director of the employers' association. This initial list was subsequently expanded by including others who were suggested by at least two of the initial

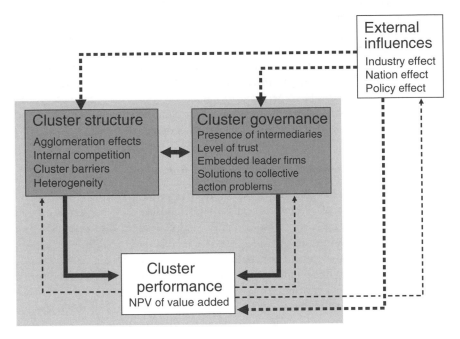

Figure 5.2 A framework for analysing clusters.

experts. In total, 49 experts were asked to participate. Forty-three agreed, representing a response rate of almost 90 per cent. Individual interviews were held with these senior business executives between autumn 2001 and spring 2002.

The port cluster in Rotterdam

Rotterdam is the largest port in the world, with a throughput of roughly 320 million tonnes (RMPM 2002). The port cluster population consists of some 2,000 firms generating about 61,000 jobs. The cluster population is identified on the basis of the following sources:

1   The membership of a port cluster association (Deltalinqs). This organisation has about 1,600 'members', active in cargo handling, transport, logistics, production and trade.
2   The leaseholders of land in the port. These firms are active in cargo handling, transport, logistics, production and trade.
3   Data from the 'economic census' of the Netherlands, providing details on the location of firms, the number of firms and firm size in different industries.
4   The opinions of the port experts on which economic activities belong to the cluster and which do not.

Leading firms in the port of Rotterdam cluster include chemical production firms. Some 90 chemical firms generate about 15,000 jobs. Transport firms are another important part of the cluster. There are some 1,600 firms in this sector, including transport intermediaries, shipping lines, container repair firms, inland shipping and road freight transport firms. These firms are predominantly small or medium sized, generating in total about 23,000 jobs (RMPM 2002). Other important groups include some 50 cargo handling firms that generate about 7,000 jobs, approximately 200 logistics firms employing about 15,000 and some 30 trading firms that employ about 2,000 people.

Agglomeration economies and diseconomies in Rotterdam

The literature indicates that the concentration (clustering) of economic activities is the outcome of the interaction of two opposing forces: agglomeration economies that foster concentration, and agglomeration diseconomies that encourage deconcentration. An analysis of the relative strength of the two forces allows us to understand the spatial dynamics of activities in port clusters. It is evident that the importance of the two forces varies for different economic activities and changes over time.

Table 5.5 shows the opinion of the port experts with regard to the relevance of agglomeration economies and agglomeration diseconomies for Rotterdam's port cluster. Respondents agree strongly that the presence of a labour pool, customers and suppliers, and knowledge and information attract firms to the cluster. They are divided over whether wage pressures are a decentralising force, but disagree with the proposition that congestion induces firms to leave. Overall, these results suggest that agglomeration economies prevail over diseconomies in Rotterdam.

These findings are, of course, for the cluster as a whole, and we may ask whether they are equally valid for individual sectors within it. Although the expert interviews did not involve this level of detail, this question can be approached through the use of data for firm populations. Rotterdam accounts for 7 per cent of firms in the Netherlands, and this may be used as a yardstick with which to measure degrees of clustering (Table 5.6). It is immediately evident that there is a great deal of intersectoral variation in clustering tendencies. Maritime services, inland shipping and port services – with between 45 per cent and 49 per cent of their firms concentrated in the region – are all strongly concentrated. This can be verified from other data sources, such as employment statistics. For maritime services, for example, 1,600 of the 2,000 jobs in the Netherlands as a whole are located in Rotterdam (RMPM 1994). Shipbuilding and shipping display only slightly lower degrees of clustering, with 35 per cent and 29 per cent, respectively, of Dutch firms located in the conurbation.

The lesser degree of concentration of logistics and chemicals is somewhat surprising. Logistics is given a high profile in port publicity because of three logistics parks in the vicinity of the port, and the presence of Asian and US firms that have selected Rotterdam as their base (NDL 2001). However, van Klink

Table 5.5 Expert opinion with regard to six propositions on agglomeration

Proposition	Agree	Disagree	No opinion
The presence of a cluster specific labour force in Rotterdam is a reason for firms to locate in Rotterdam's port cluster.	29[a]	11	3
The presence of cluster related customers and suppliers in Rotterdam is a reason for firms to locate in Rotterdam's port cluster.	42[a]	1	0
The presence of cluster related knowledge and information in Rotterdam is a reason for firms to locate in Rotterdam's port cluster	35[a]	7	1
Relatively high land prices and scarcity of land in Rotterdam's port cluster induce firms to leave the cluster.	24	14	5
A relatively high level of congestion in Rotterdam induces firms to leave the cluster.	9	32[a]	2
The high wage level and power of labour organisations in Rotterdam's port cluster induce firms to leave the cluster.	21	20	2

Source: Interviews.

Note
a Significant majority.

(1995) has already demonstrated that logistics activities in Rotterdam are lagging behind the development of these activities elsewhere because of the growing importance of disagglomeration forces. Land prices and congestion in the port area are inducing firms to decentralise logistics, and this possibly explains the more moderate degree of concentration of the sector in Rotterdam.

Table 5.6 Concentration of port cluster activities in Rotterdam

Activity	Proportion of firms located in Greater Rotterdam
Share of Greater Rotterdam in the national economy	6–7%
Maritime services	49%
Port services	48%
Inland shipping	45%
Shipbuilding	35%
Shipping	29%
Logistics activities	20%
Chemical production	15%
Transport activities	5%

Source: Bureau van Dijk (2001).

Chemical industries are closely associated with Rotterdam, occupying over 2,400 ha or about 60 per cent of the port area. Even though most chemical activities were developed in the 1950s and 1960s, and are therefore 'mature', investments are still substantial, and there is the objective of attracting more 'downstream' functions, such as the manufacture of plastics, plastics products and medicines. Yet despite this image, the degree of clustering is less than for other cluster sectors because it competes for investment with other major chemical clusters, partly within the Netherlands but also at the international scale. Antwerp, for example, is a particularly strong, and geographically close, competitor. Similarly, transport firms are relatively footloose, include many modes, and have widespread markets. Thus, they are not attracted to seaports by agglomeration forces, and consequently have a proportionately low degree of concentration in Rotterdam.[2]

These findings clearly suggest that future studies of port clusters should not simply focus on the cluster as a whole; they should also adopt a more detailed analytical approach to explore intersectoral contrasts in cluster attractiveness and performance.

Internal competition in Rotterdam's port cluster

In this subsection the positive effects of internal competition in the seaport cluster performance are examined. Three assumptions from the literature are tested. First, economic rents exist if external competition is imperfect (Goss 1998). Thus, internal competition adds to the performance of a seaport because it prevents monopoly pricing. Second, internal competition fosters specialisation. In general, internal competition is competition on a 'perfect' level playing field, because the competitive environment is virtually the same for everyone: competitors have the same hinterland access, the same regulations and the same labour market. Because all these conditions are identical, firms with internal competitors have incentives to differentiate, in order to reduce competitive pressure. Such differentiation adds to the competitiveness of clusters, because it increases their 'product diversity'. The third argument for the positive effect of internal competition on the performance of a port cluster is the 'vibrant environment' argument (Porter 1990). The essence of this is that internal competition leads to a fertile environment for innovation.

Experts participating in the study were asked to assess four propositions relating to these theoretical assumptions. In all cases, significant majorities agreed that internal competition has positive impacts. More than two-thirds believed internal competition to be a more powerful force than external competition in encouraging specialisation. And there was a near-unanimous view that it lowers switching costs, promotes a dynamic environment conducive to innovation, and generally enhances port cluster performance (Table 5.7).

Here it must be noted that while most firms in seaport clusters face relatively strong internal competition, there are exceptions. These include cargo handling firms and maritime service providers (tugboat firms and pilotage, lashing and

Table 5.7 Expert opinion with regard to four propositions on internal competition

Proposition	Agree	Disagree	No opinion
Since the competitive environment is practically the same for competitors in the same port cluster, internal competition is a stronger force inducing firms to specialise than external competition.	32[a]	10	1
Internal competition leads to low 'switching costs' for port users; switching costs are higher when port services only face external competition.	36[a]	4	3
Internal competition leads to dynamism and a 'vibrant competitive environment'. Such an environment is conducive for innovation.	40[a]	3	0
The presence of internal competition adds to the performance of the port cluster.	41[a]	1	1

Source: Interviews.

Note
a Significant majority.

mooring services). These are unlikely to face strong internal competition because the large minimum size needed for viability ensures that the number of competitors is limited (Table 5.8).

Table 5.8 shows that in most cargo handling segments in Rotterdam, internal competition is indeed restricted. However, because of special conditions applying to various commodity types, this is not necessarily disadvantageous for cluster performance. For example, in the markets for dry bulk handling and oil, shippers jointly own the terminals. This joint ownership structure counters the threat that operators will charge high prices and 'appropriate the economic rent'.

Table 5.8 Expert evaluation of the strength of internal competition in the most important cargo handling markets

Market segment	No internal competition	Limited internal competition	Strong internal competition
Container handling	3	33[a]	4
Dry bulk handling	1	37[a]	2
Liquid bulk handling	5	32[a]	2
Breakbulk handling	1	28[a]	11
Pilotage	38[a]	4	0
Tug services	2	28[a]	11
Mooring services	30[a]	12	0

Source: Interviews.

Note
a Significant majority.

The sector where a lack of internal competition is potentially the most detrimental to the performance of the port cluster is the container businesss. Container handling is one of the most dynamic sectors of port activity and contributes significantly to the local economy. Here, too, however, it is arguable that the danger is more apparent than real. In the container handling market, monopoly pricing is likely to occur not simply when internal competition is absent, but when three additional conditions are also met:

1   The market should be non-contestable (entry barriers prevent firms entering the market). In container handling, entry barriers are substantial: specific (non-recoverable) investments are required, customers have long-term contracts, and immediate entry is impossible since terminals have to be constructed and cranes ordered. Furthermore, in many ports legal barriers to entry exist as well, and suitable sites are unavailable.
2   Switching costs for shippers should be substantial. External competition is perfect when shippers can switch their cargo to a different port without (or with very minor) costs. Switching costs for cargo originating from, or destined for, a contestable hinterland are low. In a captive hinterland switching costs are substantial. Thus, the threat of operators raising prices (for captive cargo) exists.
3   The 'price effect' – for example, the increase of revenue from price increases – should be larger than the 'substitution effect' (the reduction of revenue because shippers switch to different ports). If this is the case, revenues increase when prices increase. When the captive hinterland is relatively large, or when operators can use price discrimination to charge high prices for captive cargo and offer competitive prices for contestable cargo, raising prices above the prices of competitors leads to increasing revenues.

Given the fact that shipping lines pay terminal operators a flat fee per container, and can shift cargo easily between ports, a system of price discrimination is inconceivable. Thus, in container shipping external competition is perfect except where the captive hinterland is substantial. In Rotterdam, just as in the other ports in the Hamburg–Le Havre range, this is not the case. There is considerable inter-port competition. As a consequence, from a monopoly point of view, internal competition in Rotterdam's container handling market is unnecessary.

This does not imply that container firms discount the significance of internal competition. Table 5.9 is derived from a survey of the four managing directors of the container operators in Rotterdam, a survey focusing on the effects of internal competition on specialisation. The responses demonstrate that there are strongly felt pressures from within the cluster to respond effectively with respect to factors such as pricing, reliability, speed and flexibility. But external competition generally provoked still higher scores from respondents, and raised additional factors towards the top of the list. Three of the four most important competitive factors (hinterland connections, geographical location and political

Table 5.9 Factors of competition for internal and external competition

Internal competition	Score	External competition	Score
Price of services	4.8	Hinterland connections	5
Reliability	4	Price	4.8
Speed of handling	4	Geographical location	4
Flexibility	3.8	Political factors	4
Image of company	3.3	Reliability	3.8
		Speed of handling	3.5
		Flexibility	3.5

Source: Interviews.

Note
Scale: 1 = not important; 5 = very important. Number of interviewees = 4.

factors) are uneven between ports: their geographical locations and hinterland connections differ and, especially in North-West Europe, government policies differ also, both between countries and between regions. Thus, the playing field for external competition is considered to be more uneven than for internal competition. These results suggest that the competitiveness of operators *vis-à-vis* external competitors is uneven and, as a consequence, does not automatically trigger firms to specialise in order to establish, maintain or improve competitive advantage.

Against this background, Table 5.10 sheds further light on what actually motivates the container companies with respect to specialisation within the cluster. The four container operators in Rotterdam have developed mutually distinctive strategic specialties of one form or another. For ECT it is reliability and high throughput; for RST the short sea market; for Hanno flexibility; and for Uniport cost competitiveness. What emerges clearly from the table is that there is a strong relationship between the firms' market share and the importance of internal competition as a motivator. At the extremes, external competition is dominant for the largest operator (ECT), but internal competition is

Table 5.10 Size and competitive focus of container terminal operators in Rotterdam

Operator	Market share	Importance of external v. internal competition on a scale from 1 (internal) to 5 (external)	Specialisation
ECT	71%	External (5)	Reliability, large volumes
RST	14%	Mixed (3)	Short sea market
Hanno	9.5%	Mixed (3)	Focus on flexibility
Uniport	5.5%	Internal (1)	Cost fighter

Source: Interviews.

overriding for the smallest one (Uniport). Between these extremes, RST and Hanno claim to respond to pressures from both directions, but certainly view internal competition as significant. On the basis of these results it may be concluded that internal competition does foster specialisation among terminal operators. For this reason, internal competition contributes to the competitiveness of the port as a whole, even when external competition prevents monopoly pricing.

Conclusion

This chapter has presented a conceptual framework for the analysis of clustering in seaports, emphasising the value of recognising the difference between cluster governance and cluster structure. In a practical application the population of the substantial Rotterdam port cluster – comprising cargo handling, transport, logistics, production and trade – was identified. Expert opinion was shown to believe that cluster membership is advantageous in a variety of ways, with most forces continuing to encourage agglomeration. Additional analysis, however, revealed strikingly contrasted concentration levels on the part of different activities, suggesting that a more refined interpretation of cluster strengths and weaknesses could be achieved through investigations at the sectoral level within the cluster.

Expert opinion was also shown to believe that the promotion of internal competition can be a significant factor driving improvements in the performance of a cluster. Even when the 'monopoly argument' is an apparent danger, as with containerisation in Rotterdam's case, fierce external competition can be sufficient to prevent companies from charging monopoly prices. Most significantly of all, it can also be sufficient to encourage container handling firms to specialise in specific market segments in order to reduce the fierce internal competition.

It is suggested that this approach to the analysis of clustering provides a 'new' perspective for assessing seaport performance. This perspective allows a wide number of relevant issues to be addressed, including:

- What centripetal and centrifugal forces are relevant for seaports and what processes of (de)concentration result from these forces?
- How can the competitiveness of seaport clusters, both *vis-à-vis* other seaports and *vis-à-vis* other locations, be analysed and compared?
- What is the nature of linkages of different activities clustered in seaports and how do such linkages develop over time?
- How do governance structures for clusters develop and how do these structures affect the competitiveness of seaport clusters?
- How does internationalisation of the port industry affect the importance of local linkages and the nature of cluster governance?

These questions form an important research agenda for port economics, an agenda that in most instances could be fruitfully addressed using an international comparative approach.

Notes

1 Austria, Belgium, Denmark, Finland, France, Germany, Greece, Ireland, Italy, Luxembourg, the Netherlands, Portugal, Spain, Sweden and the United Kingdom.
2 It could be added that trading activities do not cluster together in Rotterdam, either. Only 6 per cent of all Dutch trading activities are located there. The figures are slightly higher for firms trading in chemical products (about 8 per cent) and those trading in coffee, tea, etc. (about 9 per cent). But even these are lower than those for seven of the eight categories listed in Table 5.6.

References

Bureau van Dijk (2001) *Reach database*, The Hague: Government of the Netherlands (review and analysis of companies in the Netherlands; for more information, see http://www.bvdep.com/).

Cooke, P. (1998) 'Regional systems of innovation: an evolutionary perspective', *Environment and Planning A*, 30: 1563–1584.

Fujita, M. and Mori, T. (1996) 'The role of ports in the making of major cities: self-agglomeration and hub-effect', *Journal of Development Economics*, 49, 93–120.

Fujita, M., Krugman, P. and Venables, A.J. (1999) *The Spatial Economy: Cities, Regions, and International Trade*, Cambridge, MA: MIT Press.

Goss, R. (1998) 'British ports policies since 1945', *Journal of Transport Economics and Policy*, 32: 51–71.

Hannan, M. and Freeman, J. (1977) 'The population ecology of organisations', *American Journal of Sociology*, 82: 929–964.

Harrison, B. (1992) 'Industrial districts: old wine in new bottles?', *Regional Studies*, 26: 469–483.

Krugman, P. (1991) *Geography and Trade*, Leuven: Leuven University Press.

Langen, P.W. de (2004) *The Performance of Port Clusters: A framework to analyze cluster performance and an application to seaport clusters in Durban, Rotterdam and the lower Mississippi*, ERIM PhD Series no. 34, Rotterdam: ERIM.

McEvily, B. and Zaheer, A. (1999) 'Bridging ties: a source of firm heterogeneity in competitive capabilities', *Strategic Management Journal*, 20: 1133–1156.

Martin, J. and Thomas, B.J. (2001) 'The container port community', *Maritime Policy and Management*, 28: 279–292.

Metcalfe, S. (1998) *Evolutionary Economics and Creative Destruction*, London: Routledge.

Mistri, M. (1999) 'Industrial districts and local governance in the Italian experience', *Human Systems Management*, 18: 131–139.

NDL (2001) *Van EDC naar ELC*, The Hague: NDL.

Panniccia, I. (1999) 'The performance of industrial districts: some insights from the Italian case', *Human Systems Management*, 18: 141–159.

Piore, M. and Sabel, C. (1984) *The Second Industrial Divide*, New York: Basic Books.

Porter, M.E. (1990) *The Competitive Advantage of Nations*, London: Macmillan.

RMPM (1994) *Scheepvaartgebonden Maritieme Dienstverlening in Rotterdam*, Rotterdam: Rotterdam Municipal Port Management.

—— (2002) Homepage statistics, available at http://www.port.rotterdam.nl/.

Slack, B. (1988) 'The evolution of a port service industry complex', *Canadian Geographer*, 32: 124–132.

—— (1989) 'Port services, ports, and the urban hierarchy', *Tijdschrift voor Economische en Sociale Geographie*, 80: 236–243.

Staber U. (1998) 'Interfirm cooperation and competition in industrial districts', *Organization Studies*, 19: 701–24.

Teurelincx, D. (2000) 'Functional analysis of port performance as a strategic tool for strengthening a port's competitive and economic potential', *International Journal of Maritime Economics*, 2: 119–140.

van Klink, H.A. (1995) *Towards the Borderless Mainport Rotterdam: An Analysis of Functional, Spatial and Administrative Dynamics in Port Systems*, Amsterdam: Thesis Publishers.

6 Ocean cruising

Market dynamics, product responses and onshore impacts

Derek Hall

Introduction

Cruising has become an important part of the global tourist industry. As a specialised sub-market, it possesses very distinctive characteristics with specific geographical dimensions (Table 6.1). This chapter appraises the nature, development and impacts of ocean cruising, essentially the last two categories of the typology. It begins by outlining the industry's growth as a global tourism phenomenon. The chequered history of ocean cruising is described, culminating in its recent regeneration and spectacular growth. The chapter goes on to examine the products and markets that are behind this regeneration. The structure of the ocean cruise industry is examined in detail, and the industry as a whole is situated in the wider process of globalisation. While it is an ocean-based phenomenon, ocean cruise tourism has significant onshore impacts. The nature and scope of these impacts are presented and assessed. The chapter concludes by

Table 6.1 Simple typology of cruises

Location/type	Products/markets
River, canal and lake cruises	Small, shallow-draught vessels, often domestic markets, cabotage-limited
Special interest (such as sail, education or exploration)	Often purpose-built vessels, specialist crews, a degree of monopoly through differentiation. Worldwide markets, highly differentiated
Extended ferry 'mini-cruises'	Joint product with car ferry services. Often between country pairs, taking advantage of 'duty free' availability
Short ocean cruises	Mostly large vessels, usually purpose-built for mass-market cruising. World market, but thus far heavily dominated by US demand. Differentiated by location, dominated by the Caribbean
Long-distance ocean cruises	Large vessels, often relying on 'tradition' and luxury, resources acquired internationally. Single world market

Source: After Bull (1996: 29).

evaluating the prospects for ocean cruising in the early years of the twenty-first century.

Nearly two decades ago, Foster (1986) commented on the lack of attention paid in the academic literature to ocean cruising, despite the substantial expansion of the industry and its growing importance. Wood (2000) made the same observation more recently. Exceptions include a handful of maritime geographers who have recognised the distinctive nature of cruising, which involves specialised ships (Charlier 1997a, 2000b) with particular routing patterns (Charlier 1997b, 1999), and distinctive port selection characteristics in specific market areas (Charlier 1996a, b; Marti 1990, 1991; Marti and Cartaya 1996; McCalla 1998).

The academic tourism literature has been even more reticent in addressing ocean cruising as a rapidly growing element of the global tourism phenomenon. Geographically oriented tourism texts have either ignored it (Pearce 1989; Hall and Page 1999) or alluded to it only peripherally (e.g. Ioannides and Debbage 1998b). Even a number of forward-projecting global tourism texts have failed to acknowledge its significance (e.g. Theobald 1994; Faulkner *et al.* 2000).

On the other hand, economic evaluations of the ocean cruise industry have gradually increased in number and scope (e.g. Mescon and Vosikis 1985; Hall and Braithwaite 1990; Dwyer and Forsyth 1996, 1998; Wild and Dearing 2000), while more general papers on industry structure and evolution have been produced for some time (e.g. Beth *et al.* 1984; Lawton and Butler 1987; CLIA 1992; Hobson 1993). Issues relevant to the ocean cruise industry addressed in the wider maritime literature include safety (e.g. Li and Wonham 2001; Alderton and Winchester 2002), crew structure and supply (e.g. Li and Wonham 1999; Lin *et al.* 2001), ship technology (e.g. Wang and McOwan 2000), port competition (e.g. Fleming and Baird 1999; Helling and Poister 2000), and globalisation and the influences of global political change (e.g. Thanopoulou *et al.* 1999; Wrona and Roe 2002).

The growth and regeneration of ocean cruising

The ocean cruise industry came into being as a distinct industry in the 1920s. It developed as a result of two main factors:

- The search for new ways to commit conspicuous consumption to leisure activity.
- The post-First World War restrictions imposed by the US government on the flow of immigrants. Ships that had been used for migrant transport now had to find alternative roles, and many were refitted as cruise liners (Lundberg and Lundberg 1993).

Ocean cruising arguably began in 1922 when the Cunard ship *Laconia* made her first circumnavigation of the world. This set a trend for the rest of the decade, whereby cruises became the preferred mode of travel for the world's social elite. This trend was, however, inhibited by the economic depression of the 1930s, and then curtailed by the onset of the Second World War. Ocean cruising resumed in the 1950s, notably in the Caribbean, largely sustained by the wealthy elderly, who had the time, inclination and disposable income to take advantage of the particular attractions of cruising.

While the specific market circumstances of river cruises and 'duty-free' short cruises such as those in the Baltic Sea experienced an increase in importance, it was not until the early 1980s that ocean cruising witnessed a significant resurgence. This regeneration was encouraged by a combination of factors:

- aggressive marketing campaigns and popular media images, including the television series *The Love Boat* (United States) and *Traumschiff* (Germany) (Ward 1992: 61);
- increasing disposable wealth (Dwyer and Forsyth 1998);
- changing demographic profiles in the world's leading economies; and
- nostalgia for a slower pace of leisure travel.

While rising levels of wealth and an ageing population structure in developed economies appear to confirm the image of the typical cruise passenger as being old and wealthy, in fact cruise lines have sought to expand the market and their range of products by targeting middle-income, middle-aged groups. This was achieved by offering shorter cruises, introducing fly-cruise options, and increasing ship capacities. As a result, the profile of cruise passengers has seen average income and age diminishing, while world demand grew from 1.5 million passengers in 1980 to over 10 million in 2000, rendering ocean cruising one of the world's leading tourism sectors. With an 8 per cent annual growth rate since 1980, participation in ocean cruising has increased at almost twice the rate of tourism overall, and is predicted to double to 22 million passengers by 2010 (Cruise Information Service 2001). It is estimated that 150,000 people are now employed in the sector, compared to just 15,000 in 1976 (Mather 2002). North America accounts for 80 per cent of the world cruising market, much of which has focused on the Caribbean (Morrison *et al.* 1996; Dickinson and Vladimir 1997).

Ocean cruising trends took on a new scale in the 1990s. By the middle of the decade, US$9 billion was being invested in new cruise ships (Peisley 1995), including the largest passenger ships in history. This has continued into the new millennium, with more than fifty new ships, worth US$40 billion, being constructed, which will expand global capacity by 55 per cent by 2006 (Cruise Information Service 2001). While this growth in fleet capacity is seen as largely demand led, it has been stimulated also by state subsidies provided to shipbuilding industries in France, Finland, Italy and a number of Asian countries. These subsidies represent up to 30 per cent of construction costs, rendering cruise ships a competitive capital purchase (Bull 1996).

A downturn in bookings and prices, reflecting a slowdown in the US economy, was already being experienced in the cruise and airline sectors before the events of 11 September 2001 (Douglas 2001), but the terrorist attacks exacerbated and provided cover for a pre-existing trend. In apparent response to public perceptions, several companies cancelled sailings in Europe and the Middle East and repositioned their vessels to 'safe' North American and Caribbean waters to encourage Americans to travel again, with embarkation from the nearest ports for passengers, thereby reducing the need for flight connections (Salles 2002).

By early 2002 there were signs of recovery, with most companies cutting prices in an effort to retain their markets. For example, Orient Lines was offering up to 30 per cent discounts on early bookings for its revised 2002 Mediterranean programme for individual passengers, alongside various discounts and upgrades for group passengers (Orient Lines 2002). Within a year of '9/11', several of the lines that had altered their European itineraries were reinstating programmes in Europe, particularly the Mediterranean, for 2003, largely in response to consumers' requests. Others that had shifted their focus to itineraries departing from North American ports were expanding those programmes as well.

Despite short-term instability events forcing disruption on the ocean cruising industry – others have included piracy on the *Achille Lauro* (1985), the Gulf War (1991) and the Kosovo conflict (1999) – the advantages of ocean cruising compared to alternative holiday modes are seen to include:

- ease of planning, with convenience of booking enhanced through rapidly increasing electronic availability (e.g. Travelocity.com 2001);
- virtually totally inclusive package prices;
- self-contained ships, with high-quality food and high levels of staffing to ensure that passengers have positive experiences, including maximum relaxation;
- programmes for children;
- opportunities to visit a variety of places in a short period of time with minimum inconvenience (Morrison *et al.* 1996).

Ocean cruise markets

The ocean cruise market was worth US$14.4 billion in 2000 (Cruise Information Service 2001). Geographically, it is still dominated by North Americans, who made up 75 per cent – 7.5 of 10 million – of the global market in 2001, compared to a less than 20 per cent share for Europeans and just over 5 per cent for the rest of the world (Salles 2002). Indeed, although a majority of cruise vessels fly non-US flags, an evaluation of the total economic impact of the cruise lines, their passengers and their US suppliers suggested that in 1999 it was worth $15.5 billion to the US economy. In addition, the cruise industry was responsible for generating 214,901 full-time jobs for US citizens (ICCL 2000).

As noted earlier, in recent years the industry has been targeting younger potential customers with more modest incomes, such that by the early 1990s it was found that:

- a quarter of all passengers were under 40 years of age, with just a third over 60 years of age;
- only a third of clients had incomes above US$60,000 per annum;
- a quarter of passengers still had children at home (Santo 1994).

The fastest-growing passenger segment is now the 25–39 age group (Morrison *et al.* 1996). The US Cruise Lines International Association (CLIA) has identified the 'hot prospect' market segments of 20- to 39-year-olds, US$20,000–40,000 income groups and families with children as groups most likely to seek, or at least respond to, shorter and cheaper products. A younger and lower-income clientele with more family commitments is now the target of the middle-market cruise lines. They have developed specific products tailored to such markets, notably mega-ships that embrace a wide range of entertainment facilities which, because of economies of scale, keep costs down (Peisley 1995). There is now a growing vertical differentiation in the industry, ranging from the less-expensive 'fun' cruises of Carnival Cruise Lines to the prestigious, sophisticated, premium-priced Cunard product.

Although US seniors represent a $200 billion leisure travel market, and it is projected that by 2030 there will be about 65 million older adults in the United States – two and a half times the number in 1980 (van Harssel 1994) – the average age of cruise passengers during the 1990s fell further to 44. Perceptions of cruising as a retirement activity have shifted towards viewing cruising as a choice for honeymooners, families and other young adults. Mutually reinforcing this trend, a number of companies have developed products with strong niche roles. For example, Miami-based The Wedding Experience is a company that specialises in arranging and performing cruise-ship wedding ceremonies. Looking to expand the market, the company's services have diversified into bar mitzvahs, vow renewals, anniversary celebrations and party planning (The Wedding Experience 2001).

Ocean cruising products

The search to broaden the market base of ocean cruising has given rise to an industry that is increasingly segmented. The CLIA, a marketing and promotional trade organisation formed in 1975 (McIntosh *et al.* 1995: 112), divides the ocean cruise market into seven segments: budget, contemporary, premium, luxury cruise, luxury sailing, exploration/soft adventure and niche. The mass-market contemporary and budget categories account for 53 per cent of passenger capacity, and the premium category for 36 per cent. It should be noted, however, that this segmentation has been largely confined to the North American market until very recently. In Europe, for example, although steady growth has taken place, the market in the later 1990s could still be characterised as elderly, elitist and expensive. One US cruise executive claimed it to be 20 years behind North America, with a lack of capacity to achieve critical mass, although it was on the threshold of change (Verchere 1997).

Despite the recent growth of the industry overall, only 12 per cent of Americans and less than 2 per cent of Europeans have been on a cruise, although surveys suggest that more than half would like to go on one (Connon 2002). Regional initiatives have been developed in Far East Asia and Oceania to further develop cruise passenger markets.

New market products are being developed. The 1980s and 1990s saw growth in speciality markets such as adventure travellers, sports enthusiasts and those seeking an educational experience (Hobson 1993; CLIA 1997). Silversea Cruises has partnered National Geographic Traveller to provide cruises offering wider opportunities to learn about destinations visited. Norwegian Cruise Line has operated 'sports afloat' theme cruises featuring football, hockey and other activities (Ioannides and Debbage 1998a: 114). More recently, cruise lines have been entering the market for motivational conferences and incentives for top business as a means of expanding the upper echelon of the cruise industry (Buchanan 2001, 2002). A number of new vessels have been fitted out to meet the requirements of this sector, with the provision of single-seat dining, large theatre-style auditoriums and technically advanced production facilities, including video teleconferencing facilities and multiple laptop stations. The potential of this sector is reflected in the production of dedicated corporate cruising brochures by several cruise companies.

In the past two decades, new product development to broaden cruise appeal has included:

- development of creative and diverse itineraries that encompass a variety of ports and anchorages;
- packaging flight, cruise and land options;
- development of quality shore attractions and add-on tours (Dwyer and Forsyth 1996: 41).

The most popular cruise destination region in the world is the Caribbean. This popularity can be attributed to an ideal cruising environment – the region's varied geographical, cultural and physical characteristics (Lawton and Butler 1987: 333) – and close proximity to the world's largest cruise market, the United States. The Caribbean is the destination for half of all North American cruise activities. The port of Miami serves as the major gateway to the Caribbean and is the largest cruise port in the world (Charlier 1989; Marti 1990, 1991; Marti and Cartaya 1996). Annually, some 70 cruise ships from 24 lines operate in the Caribbean, such that for some time a number of islands have received substantially more cruise visitors than stopover tourists (Hodder 1993). The region is likely to maintain its dominance as a cruise destination for the foreseeable future. It is predicted for the Caribbean that by 2006 there will be more passenger ship berths than hotel rooms, and that cruise arrivals will outnumber stopover arrivals (Wood 2000).

Other significant cruising areas include the Mediterranean, the Pacific, Alaska, North Africa and the South China Sea, although the aftermath of the events of '9/11' in the United States has led to a medium-term review of some destination areas. Competition between cruise lines to add exotic ports of call has been intense (Wood 2000). For example, Cunard added 55 and Crystal Cruise Lines 24 in 1998, and in that year 130 cruise ships called at over 1,800 ports (Godsman 1999).

Cruise lines often deploy their vessels in different regions according to the season, ensuring all-year deployment of substantial pieces of capital investment. For example, for its 2002 programme, Crystal Cruises was offering a series of 15- and 16-day themed East Asian cruises between mid-April and early June. Orient Lines offer 24- to 40-day voyages 'designed for baby boomers and active seniors...who seek enriching, educational and soft adventure cruise-tour experiences' (Orient Lines 2001) to Africa, Asia, South America and the South Pacific between October and April. US companies such as Celebrity Cruises usually cruise the Caribbean during the northern hemisphere winter, Europe in the summer, and increasingly Asia and the Pacific during the shoulder periods.

The overall regional distribution of cruise liner activity and interseasonal movements is revealed in Table 6.2. Noteworthy is the dramatic difference in the northern hemisphere's summer and winter deployments. Alaska, Bermuda and the North Atlantic have no cruise activity in winter, and Europe has very little. This contrasts with summer market peaks of 17 per cent of global share

Table 6.2 Cruise liner overall and seasonal capacity by regional deployment, 1999

	Total bed-days ('000s)	Total share (%)	First quarter (%)	Second quarter (%)	Third quarter (%)	Fourth quarter (%)
North America	**36,067**	**54.8**	**62.8**	**52.1**	**49.2**	**57.3**
Caribbean & Bahamas	25,111	38.1	52.8	30.7	23.3	47.5
Mexican Riviera & Panama	4,333	6.6	10.0	6.7	2.9	7.7
Alaska	4,702	7.2	—	11.2	17.1	—
Bermuda & N.E. Atlantic	1,921	2.9	—	3.5	5.9	2.1
Europe	**15,913**	**24.2**	**4.2**	**32.2**	**38.8**	**18.1**
Mediterranean	11,303	17.2	3.2	23.6	24.9	16.8
N.W. Europe & transatlantic	4,610	7.0	1.0	8.6	13.9	1.3
Rest of the world	**13,857**	**21.0**	**33.0**	**15.7**	**12.0**	**24.6**
Far East & S.E. Asia	5,228	7.9	5.0	7.5	7.7	8.8
Hawaii & S. Pacific	3,418	5.2	6.0	4.1	3.8	7.1
S. America & Antarctica	1,678	2.5	6.4	0.3	0.2	3.6
Africa & Indian Ocean	2,031	3.1	5.5	2.2	0.2	4.5
Round the world	1,502	2.3	7.1	1.6	0.1	0.6
Total	**65,837**	**100.0**	**100.0**	**100.0**	**100.0**	**100.0**

Sources: after Charlier (2000a: 17, 18).

for Alaska and 39 per cent for Europe. The latter represents a share higher than that of the Caribbean at that time of year. Most vessels cruising in Europe between April and October are repositioned from a wide range of global locations. By December, the Caribbean has a dominant 58 per cent share of the world market. Of course, these figures will have been modified by the events of 11 September 2001, with Americans substituting cruises within the Americas for those in European waters.

Rapid increases in passenger capacity have been made possible by the increasing scale of new vessels brought into use. In turn, their economies of scale, coupled with the market expansion, have helped to raise profit levels for the largest cruise lines. In November 1999, Royal Caribbean's *Voyager of the Seas* became the largest ever cruise liner at 130,000 tonnes, accommodating 3,840 passengers and with a crew of 1,181. Such huge vessels are categorised as 'post- (or over) Panamax' ships since they are too large to pass through the Panama Canal (Charlier 1997a, 2000b). The new ships, with their vast atriums and inward-looking architecture, are essentially floating resorts, with onboard leisure facilities ranging from casinos and shopping malls to golf courses, climbing walls and ice-skating rinks (Figure 6.1).

One benefit of the new tonnage is increased speed and therefore ability to

Figure 6.1 The Royal Caribbean Radiance-class cruise liner *Brilliance of the Seas*. Seen here in Venice, the *Brilliance of the Seas* entered service in July 2002. With an overall length of 290 m and 13 decks, her passenger capacity is 2,501. Particular design features are glass elevators facing the sea, and a nine-storey glass-enclosed 'centrum'. The vessel's cruising speed is 25 knots (46 kph) and the liner alternates seasonally between the Caribbean/Panama Canal region and Europe. (Photo courtesey of David Pinder.)

cover greater distances between ports of call. However, for the volume market there is an increasing problem of ever-larger vessels being unable to enter the smaller ports of an ever-expanding menu of destinations. This paradox raises significant logistical questions, since cruise lines do not like using tenders, and it is important for the port to convince an operator that its offshore moorings are secure. Further, such arrangements are vulnerable to disruption due to weather. For example, in July 1999 the *Queen Elizabeth II* could not land passengers at Peterhead in north-east Scotland (Fraser 1997) because of high winds. The ship's captain refused to give permission for anyone to leave or enter the liner (although one man had to be airlifted off with suspected appendicitis). As a consequence, 700 passengers had to cancel organised coach tours to local attractions, resulting in a clear loss of income for local economies. However, in this particular instance an estimated 30,000 people visited Peterhead to view the liner and to take part in carnival events organised in conjunction with its visit (Anon. 1999a).

Structure of the ocean cruise industry

Cruise lines are relatively footloose businesses which source inputs from a range of countries, and this has been an advantage to countries that otherwise would earn little from tourism (Bull 1995). For example, CTC Lines, now Ukrainian owned, was developed by the former Soviet Union to earn foreign exchange by operating cruise ships in a number of regions and supplying services to passengers from the major markets (Peisley 1995).

In terms of operating economies:

- Capital costs are high: cruise ships are much more expensive capital items than are cargo ships of a comparable size.
- Fixed running costs are also high: the staffing factor can be 20 to even 100 times higher than for a cargo ship of comparable size (Bull 1996: 31).

Although at the turn of the century, the 'Big Three' cruise lines – Carnival, Royal Caribbean International and P&O/Princess – collectively controlled over two-thirds of the North American market and approaching half of global capacity (Table 6.3), the most rapidly growing line was Star Cruises, a Malaysian-based company catering primarily to Asian tourists. Its goal is to become the world's fourth-largest cruise company. Even during the Asian financial crisis, Star Cruises ordered two further 85,000 tonne ships in 1998 to add to the seven in its fleet and three others already on order. Asia has huge potential as a cruise destination region, and this has been recognised for some time (PATA 1995; Heung 1997). For example, the 1993 Singapore Tourist Promotion Board strategic plan for growth identified the cruise market as a growth niche (STPB 1993; Low and Heng 1997). Significant growth is also taking place in the Australasian market (e.g. Hall and Kearsley 2001: 33).

Table 6.3 Cruise lines' market share, 2000

Major cruise lines	Global market share (%)
Carnival	18.3
Royal Caribbean	15.1
P&O/Princess	10.1
Holland America	8.9
Norwegian Cruise	8.1
Celebrity Cruise	6.2
Costa Cruises	5.6
Premiere Cruise	3.9

Source: US Business Reporter (2002).

Vertical integration

As cruise lines have emulated theming from the entertainment and hotel sectors, so hotel and entertainment conglomerates have been increasing their presence in the cruise industry. Needing to maintain market share following competitive pressures on its resorts, Club Med entered the cruise sector in the early 1990s with the construction of luxury sailing boats. Hyatt Hotels took a half-stake in Royal Caribbean in 1988. Radisson Hotels International owns Radisson Seven Seas Cruises. Ramada Hotels has leased Premier's ships for short cruises from the Ramada Plaza resort near Orlando, Florida. The Disney Corporation entered the cruise business in 1998 after a long-previewed publicity campaign promoting cruising as a complementary product to theme park visits in Florida (Zbar 1995).

As traditionally staid cruise tourism has become more like non-cruise mass tourism, its distinctive characteristic of sea-based mobility has enabled it to exhibit major characteristics associated with processes of globalisation (Wood 2000). A cruise liner's size – taking advantage of internal economies of scale and sourcing on-board products globally – represents a very visible concentration of multinational capital. Its physical mobility gives it the capability to be 'repositioned' anywhere in the world at any time, and cruise liners spend much of their time in non-territorial waters, only briefly 'touching down' in their ports of call. Indeed, cost savings can be made by sailing slowly, and thus saving fuel, and by including ports of call which have cheap or low-tax fuel bunkering (Bull 1996).

Ship crews represent a compact yet highly diverse labour force (originating from up to 50 countries on a single ship). Such globally recruited labour is rigidly stratified into three groups: officers, staff and crew. These groups have separate living areas, segregated dining areas, different levels of restrictions about interacting with passengers, and vastly different pay levels, with usually a clear ethnic cast to this hierarchy (Mather 2002; Wazir and Mathiason 2002). Recruitment policies, while acknowledging tourist images and expectations, are critically influenced by industry interests of employment control, cost minimisation and public relations. Most shipboard employees work seven days a week for six months at a time.

Avoidance of national or international regulations is a major characteristic of cruise lines (Wood 2000: 352–353, 365). The use of flags of convenience (FOCs) circumvents home-country employment laws, taxes and maritime regulations (Mentzer 1989). Over half the tonnage of leading maritime nations flies FOCs. For cruise ships this is even more pronounced. Indeed, cruise development has been assisted by the climate of deregulation and the pool of migrant labour on which the industry increasingly relies. Not a single cruise ship plying the Caribbean flies the US flag. Although both are based in Florida, Carnival Cruise Lines is registered as a Panamanian corporation and Royal Caribbean flies the Liberian flag. In the latter case the company is estimated to save around US$30 million annually in US taxes by registering its ships under FOCs (Frantz 1999). FOC ship crews are subject to the employment laws neither of their countries of origin nor to those of the country of their employer, but they are subject to the laws of the country in which the ship is flagged, most commonly Panama, Liberia or the Bahamas. Employment laws protecting the rights of workers are virtually non-existent in FOC countries (Alderton and Winchester 2002).

Horizontal integration

Globalisation of the cruise sector has also led to increased internationalisation of ownership and further concentration, with a massive shake-out steadily reducing the number of industry participants.

Norwegian Capricorn Line joint venture company aimed at the Australian market by establishing Norwegian Cruise Lines, which acquired Orient Lines two months later (1998). Carnival purchased Europe's largest cruise line, Costa Cruises, in June 1997 as part of the company's effort to develop a global position. These trends represent an accentuation of long-standing processes (Wood 2000: 350).

Cunard was acquired by Trafalgar House, a British multinational conglomerate, in 1971. In the 1980s and early 1990s Cunard purchased several Norwegian ships and the Royal Viking name, but in 1996 Trafalgar House was taken over by the Norwegian company Kvaerner ASA. Two years later, Kvaerner sold Cunard to the US-based Carnival Corporation, which promptly merged it with its luxury-end Seabourn Cruise Line (Wood 2000: 350).

As a result of a rapid pace of mergers, acquisitions and bankruptcies in the sector over the past two decades, Carnival Corporation – which in 1980 owned just three ships with fewer than 4,000 berths – was able to acquire Holland America, Seabourn, Costa, Windstar and Cunard Lines, comprising a fleet of 43 ships with a capacity of over 50,000 passengers; it also has a part-interest in Airtours' Sun Cruises.

Industry agglomeration has been particularly marked since the second half of the 1990s (Table 6.4). In most cases, separate brands have been maintained to

Table 6.4 Agglomeration during the late 1990s and early 2000s

Company	Took over
Royal Caribbean	Celebrity Cruises
Cruise Holdings	Dolphin Cruise Line (merged with its Premier brand)
Norwegian Cruise Line	Majesty Cruise Line; Orient Lines
Carnival	Costa Cruise Lines; Cunard
P&O Princess	Seeking merger with Royal Caribbean[a]

Note
a At the time of writing, this agreed merger was being compromised by a hostile bid for P&O Princess from Carnival.

compete in different cruise market segments, although at least a dozen cruise brands have disappeared during this period.

Destination promotion and the commodification of cruising

Many ports and regions have departments or sections of their tourist boards or economic promotion agencies whose function is to promote their area as a potential cruise line destination. For example, the Cruise Scotland marketing consortium was set up in 1998 to promote Scotland as a cruising destination to the worldwide market by encouraging more companies to include it in their itineraries. It comprises 16 port authorities together with the Scottish tourist board (VisitScotland), 14 area tourist boards, the National Trust for Scotland, Historic Scotland (responsible for 300 historic properties spanning five thousand years) and Simply the Best (a retailing group). The cruise industry contributes an estimated £10 million (US$12.5 million) annually to Scotland's tourism revenue, and this partnership approach, coupled to coordinated onshore support, is thus seeking to maximise shore expenditure by passengers and crew. Further, local tourist boards and ground handlers constantly review shore excursions, particularly for repeat passengers, and look to niche markets such as German passengers who express environmental awareness and are keen on walking (Figure 6.2).

However, as with any form of tourism, a number of factors may deflect tourists (and deter cruise lines) from using certain destinations on either a temporary or a permanent basis. These include:

- crime: well-publicised murders of tourists in the Miami area led to a decline in international tourist arrivals in south Florida in the early 1990s (Schiebler *et al.* 1996);
- political instability: the 1987 military coup in Fiji resulted in a sharp decline in tourist arrivals (Miller and Auyong 1991);
- natural disasters: Hurricane Hugo hit many Caribbean islands in 1989, causing an immediate decline in tourism (Orams 1999: 40).

Figure 6.2 The cruise liner *Berlin* off Portree, Isle of Skye, Scotland. (Photo courtesy of D.H. Hall.)

An important part of the strategy of the mass-market cruise companies has been to define land-based resorts such as Orlando and Las Vegas as their real competition and to market their ships as superior, crime-free and safe resort destinations. In this way, the ship is sold as the primary destination, rather than the ports it docks at. Indeed, 'destination cruising' – where the ports of call are central to consumer choice and experience – is now considered by some to be a niche market rather than the end objective.

Indeed, if the experience economy (Pine and Gilmore 1998) is an explicit characteristic of post-industrial society, then the way in which the cruise liner has been transformed – from tourism transport providing a means to an end, to a self-contained eclectic experience set in an internal landscape of fantasy providing an end in itself – represents one of the most potent, spatially mobile and globalised symbols of post-industrialism.

Fantasy has been the core of the internal environment of cruising for a long time. Carnival's 'fun-ship' marketing, aimed squarely at the middle-class mass market, helped to turn the company into a dominant force in the industry. While US-based cruising grew at an average rate of 8.4 per cent in the two decades to 2001, Carnival increased its number of berths by 11 per cent per annum over the past decade and its earnings growth by 15 per cent per year. The introduction of the company's first specially constructed vessel in 1985, *The Holiday*, was branded as 'Disney World for adults' (Showker and Sehlinger 1998). In the case of Caribbean cruises, however, Wood (2000) argues that the ultimate in 'fantasyscapes' is not the ship itself, but the 'fantasy islands' privately owned by the cruise companies, which perpetuate myth and the sense of 'else-whereness' by manipulating the external environment. These islands are off-limits to all but passengers and employees, and are marketed as 'the true Caribbean experience – only better'. Six cruise lines now own private islands in the Caribbean which they include in their itineraries.

In this fantasy world, an island with no Caribbean people living on it can be marketed as 'the best of the Caribbean', claiming to offer, not a little paradoxi-cally, 'the total experience that can be found in the West Indies'. This social – commercial – reconstruction of reality as an exclusive, almost hermetically sealed vision of paradise provides some interesting parallels with the self-imagery and 'front-stage' fantasy construction surrounding foreign tourism development generated under autarkic communism in such countries as North Korea and Albania (Hall 1984, 1990). Contact with local people is viewed as being dis-turbing to passengers (Orenstein 1997), so this is minimised or excluded. Thus, for example, the 'safe', carefully selected 'islanders' at Disney's Castaway Cay are hired through casting agencies, and may come from as far away as Australia (Sloan 1998). Complementing reconstruction, sanitisation and control of the cruise passengers' Caribbean social and cultural environment, cruise lines further their deific, totalitarian role by 'enhancing' – re-engineering – the Caribbean's natural environment in order to fulfil fantasy images. Thus, at Cast-away Cay Disney dredged sand from the bay and then ground it up further to make the island's beaches conform to (the company's perception of) the hedon-istic tourist image and desire to consume a physical construction of 'paradise' (Antoni 1999). Arguably, such contestable commodification cannot be sustain-able. It represents not so much MacCannell's (1976: 91–107) notion of 'staged authenticity' as an ideologically inspired holistic reinvention of place, harnessing and focusing the totalitarian potential of corporate capital (see also, for example, MacCannell 1992; Lash and Urry 1994; Rojek 1995; Rojek and Urry 1997; Urry 1990, 1992a, b, 1995).

The development of private island destinations has an explicit twofold negat-ive impact on Caribbean countries' cruise-derived income, as:

- in practice a local destination port is being removed from the cruise itiner-ary process.
- the cruise company monopolises the economic rewards of renting to its passengers a comprehensive range of supplementary requirements such as snorkelling equipment, cabanas and small boats, and selling them drinks and souvenirs at company-owned shops and markets.

The already limited contribution of cruise passengers to local Caribbean economies is thereby further eroded. For example, the proportion of North American tourists in the Caribbean spending at least one night on land declined from 61.8 per cent in 1987 to 48.6 per cent in 1998 (McDowell 1999). In response, some ports have attempted to re-image themselves to become an extension of the fantasy environment of the ship, reproducing a new form of mass tourism enclave development, albeit not as hermetically self-contained or corporately dominated as the likes of Castaway Cay.

Cruise residence – the ultimate product development?

Over the past decade, world cruises lasting three or four months have become increasingly popular. One of the consequences of this has been a tendency for passengers to treat their cabins as their own property, hanging paintings on the walls and filling them with bric-a-brac purchased at different ports of call. Some even leave their possessions to be stored on the ship ready for their next trip, to return to their cabins exactly as they left them. A logical extension of this trend is the provision of cruise apartments, permitting the actual ownership of a cruise liner cabin for permanent use. Thus in March 2002 the US$262 million 40,000 tonne *The World* set out on its maiden voyage with 110 luxury furnished apartments costing upwards of US$2 million each (Dinnigan 1999; Wilson 2002). The ship aims to sail almost continuously around the world; its first two years' itinerary included the South Seas, Alaska, the Falklands, China, the Cannes Film Festival, Carnival in Rio and the Monaco Grand Prix (The World of ResidenSea 2002).

The target buyer of an apartment on this liner is a successful businessman aged around 50 who already has several homes around the world. A residents' committee, together with the ship's captain, has authority to sell property and remove undesirables. Forty per cent of early sales were in the United States with the majority of the remainder in Britain and Scandinavia. The high level of security, and the scale of the vessel, are intended to deter piracy or potential terrorism. The company plans to build two further vessels (Hulse 1999), while a French shipbuilding company (Chantiers de l'Atlantique, part of the Alsthom group) has published plans to construct a self-propelled 'leisure island' capable of accommodating 10,000 residents (Lichfield 2002).

Major onshore impacts

The onshore impacts of ocean cruise tourism are particularly acute. In contrast to other forms of mass tourism, onshore visits tend to be for relatively short periods of time – typically morning to early evening – and produce a unique set of impacts, including:

- short-term pressure on retailing and other services;
- congestion in port-related and passenger-activity areas, requiring significant impact management strategies (for example, Kirkwall in the Scottish Orkney Islands banned cars from the town centre and set up a park-and-ride bus service when the *QE2* visited, to cope not just with the cruise passengers landing but also with landward visitors arriving to view the liner);

- loss of economic benefit from visitors not staying in local onshore accommodation; and
- wider economic leakages resulting from the organisation of onshore visits by the cruise company or its agents, and from the fact that such excursions may take visitors some distance away from the point of disembarkation.

Adverse 'seasonality' effects can thus result from concentrated periods of diurnal visitor activity, as well as from the periodicity and annual seasonal changes in patterns of cruise liner arrivals.

Second, there is the potential for local inflation and functional change in the provision of services to result from relatively high-income visitors demanding certain types of goods which may gradually usurp the role of traditional retailing needed by local people. This can clearly impose economic hardship on host communities, particularly those that do not enjoy enhanced income as a result of tourism (Young 1973; Mathieson and Wall 1982).

Third, possible demonstration effects can arise, particularly for younger local people, including:

- attempted tourist lifestyle emulation;
- rebellion against traditional beliefs and norms; and
- opportunities for crime, not least against tourists themselves.

Economic 'leakage' is common in marine tourism situations, because visitors often arrive in vessels that have been provisioned with supplies elsewhere. In many coastal and island areas, marine tourism operators may not be local but will be seasonal businesses that have their base elsewhere. Consequently, much of the income generated by the business does not stay within the host community.

Exemplifying a number of these impacts is the case of Juneau, capital of Alaska. With a population of 30,000, this city sees as many as 600,000 cruise visitors during the short summer months, a figure which has risen from 250,000 since 1990. Cruise tourists crowd the city's streets and generate a feeding frenzy among local businesses. Even more annoying to many locals are the fleets of helicopters passing overhead ferrying visitors to the mile-thick Juneau Icefield north of the town. As a consequence, in October 1999 the population voted for a US$5 per head tax on cruise passengers to help defray the expense to the local community of handling such crowds (Anon. 1999b).

Bermuda presents a different model of attempts to reduce impact problems. Prior to 1984, up to seven cruise ships a week were docking here. Several adverse impacts, including traffic congestion, led to the introduction of limitations on cruise ship passengers by restricting the number of ships in port at any one time, and preventing weekend cruise ships from docking. The number of ships is limited to five of four–star ranking or higher, with the aims of not only controlling visitor numbers but also preserving the island's up-market image, and thereby ensuring a relatively high onshore visitor expenditure (Teye 1992; Peisley 1996).

The onshore impacts of marine pollution resulting from cruise liner activity may be significant. For example, in 1999 Royal Caribbean Cruise Lines and Carnival Corporation's Holland America Line were fined several million US dollars for dumping untreated bilge water, oil and other waste into Alaskan waters. Royal Caribbean, which is based in Miami, was fined US$6.5 million by a federal court for offences committed in 1995 and 1996, including the dumping of dry-cleaning chemicals, the rigging up of special pipes that by-passed on-board pollution-control equipment, and the falsification of records. The company has also been fined for dumping waste near ports of call in other parts of the world. It has been quoted subsequently as promising to establish a better environmental culture, emphasising that new ships have on-board water-cleaning systems that far surpass (US) government standards and turbine engines that generate less smoke (Anon. 1999b).

Ocean cruising futures

The prospects for ocean cruising in the early years of the twenty-first century suggest that the limits of vessel size may have been reached, with the present vessels on order reaching maximum scale economies (crucial for pricing policy), while beginning to face operational limits in terms of port choice and customer service. Second, greater market penetration in Europe (notably in the United Kingdom, Germany and Spain) and other developing markets can be expected as company expansion and consolidation looks beyond North America for mass market development. Nonetheless, particularly following the events of 11 September 2001, considerations of security, alongside those of access, level of interest, and climate, will impose constraints on the pursuit of new destinations.

The ocean cruise industry is likely to remain a dynamic oligopoly with high global concentration among a handful of mass market operators of large ships complemented by a relatively large number of smaller specialist operators. The latter will continue to differentiate their products and market to dynamic niche segments based upon such considerations as family life cycle stage, income and geographical location.

Despite an underlying global economic downturn (Douglas 2001), cruising for business and as incentive tourism is likely to develop further (Peisley 2001; Buchanan 2001), reflecting trends within the wider tourism industry and business environment. As a new direction in the mutual relationship between cruising and global influences, the tapping of a potentially inexhaustible source of cheap labour from China could drive ship wages down further. Overseas ship employment is seen as a way of raising maritime skills to international standards in China, and by comparison with, for example, the Philippines, China's programme is more integrated into its national development policy (Fong 1997).

As one of the most innovative maritime sectors, and one of the most dynamic elements of global tourism development, ocean cruising presents a range of substantial yet dynamic issues and characteristics which deserve closer attention from both researchers and policy makers.

References

Alderton, T. and Winchester, N. (2002) 'Flag states and safety: 1997–1999', *Maritime Policy and Management*, 29(2): 151–162.

Anon. (1999a) 'QE2 all at sea during Peterhead carnival', *Press and Journal* (Aberdeen), 23 July.

—— (1999b) 'Trash overboard: pollution in Alaska'. *The Economist*, 18 September, p. 73.

Antoni, R. (1999) 'Blackbeard doesn't come here anymore', *Outside*, 24(1): 62–69.

Beth, H.L., Hader, A.H. and Kappel, R. (1984) *25 years of World Shipping*, London: Fairplay.

Buchanan, G. (2001) 'Business on board', *Conference and Incentive Travel*, July/August, pp. 65–69.

—— (2002) 'The perfect package', *Conference and Incentive Travel*, March, Supplement, p. 7.

Bull, A.O. (1995) *The Economics of Travel and Tourism*, 2nd edn, Melbourne: Longman.

—— (1996) 'The economics of cruising: an application to the short ocean cruise market', *Journal of Tourism Studies*, 7(2): 28–35.

Charlier, J. (1989) 'Miami, capitale mondiale des croisières', *Transports*, 337: 286–292.

—— (1996a) 'Cruise shipping in the eco-tourism era', in W. Roehl (ed.) *Second Environment for Tourism Conference*, Las Vegas: University of Nevada Department of Tourism, pp. 45–50.

—— (1996b) 'Current cruise activity in the Mediterranean: a geographical overview', *Seatrade Mediterranean Ferry and Cruise Convention*, Genoa, 17–20 September, pp. 18–20.

—— (1997a) 'La Croisière à l'heure overpanamax', *Journal de la Marine Marchande*, 4038: 1047–1052.

—— (1997b) 'Seasonal repositioning strategies: current and future trends for the main cruise markets', in *Cruise + Ferry 97*, Vol. 1, Rickmansworth, UK. Business Meeting Ltd, pp. 24–32.

—— (1999) 'The seasonal factor in the geography of cruise shipping', *The Dock and Harbour Authority*, 79: 214–219.

—— (2000a) 'An introduction to the geography of cruise shipping, main cruise areas and regional seasonal migrations', in R. Castejón and J. Charlier (eds) *El renacer de los cruceros: la mundialización de los negocios turísticos y marítimos*, Madrid: Fundación Portuaria/Universidad Internacional Menéndez Pelayo, pp. 15–28.

—— (2000b) 'De la norme panamax à l'essor des overpanamax', *Acta Geographica*, 121(1): 102–111.

Connon, H. (2002) 'High noon looms in battle for the high seas', *Observer*, 13 January.

Cruise Information Service, 2001, *Annual Cruise Review 2000*, available at http://www.cruiseinformationservice.co.uk/html/press/five/index.htm (accessed 5 July 2002).

Cruise Line Industry Association (CLIA) (1992), *The Cruise Line Industry: An Overview*, New York: CLIA.

—— (1997) 'Cruise news. Surprise! You – yes, you – might be in the market for a cruise', New York: CLIA, available at http://www.ten-io.com/clia/news/ (accessed November 9 1999).

—— (2002) 'Cruise industry rebounding at record pace in 2002', New York: CLIA, available at http://www.cruisecritic.com/newsletter/newspopup.cfm (accessed 30 September 2002).

Dickinson, B. and Vladimir, A. (1997) *Selling the Sea: An Inside Look at the Cruise Industry*, Chichester, UK: John Wiley.

Dinnigan, L. (1999) 'Consider the notion of life on the ocean', *Travel Agent*, 6 December, http://www.findarticles.com/cf0/m0VOU/10297/58381986/print.jhtml (accessed 18 February 2002).

Douglas, H. (2001) 'Profits dip as cruisers sail close to the wind', *Scotland on Sunday*, 29 July.

Dwyer, L. and Forsyth, P. (1996) 'Economic impacts of cruise tourism in Australia', *Journal of Tourism Studies*, 7(2): 36–45.

—— (1998) 'Economic significance of cruise tourism', *Annals of Tourism Research*, 25: 393–415.

Faulkner, B., Moscardo, G. and Laws, E. (eds) (2000) *Tourism in the 21st Century: Lessons from Experience*, London: Continuum.

Fleming, D.K. and Baird, A.J. (1999) 'Some reflections on port competition in the United States and western Europe', *Maritime Policy and Management*, 26(4): 383–394.

Fong, Y.M. (1997) 'China wants Singapore to hire more of its seafarers', *InforMare*, available at http://www.informare.it/news/review/1997/st0009.htm (accessed 10 April 1998).

Foster, G.M. (1986) 'South Seas cruise: a case study of a short-lived society', *Annals of Tourism Research*, 13: 215–238.

Frantz, D. (1999) 'Gaps in sea laws shield pollution by cruise lines', *New York Times*, 3 January.

Fraser, S. (1997) 'Luxury liners land rich catch at fishing capital', *Scotland on Sunday*, 4 May.

Godsman, J.G. (1999) 'President's message', Cruise Lines International Association, available at http://www.cruising.org/clia/pres.html (accessed 9 November 1999).

Hall, A.J. and Braithwaite, R. (1990) 'Caribbean cruise tourism: a business of transnational partnerships', *Tourism Management*, 11: 339–347.

Hall, C.M. and Kearsley, G. (2001) *Tourism in New Zealand: An Introduction*, Melbourne: Oxford University Press.

Hall, C.M. and Page, S.J. (1999) *The Geography of Tourism and Recreation*, London: Routledge.

Hall, D.R. (1984) 'Foreign tourism under socialism: the Albanian "Stalinist" model', *Annals of Tourism Research*, 11(4): 539–555.

—— (1990) 'Stalinism and tourism: a study of Albania and North Korea', *Annals of Tourism Research*, 17(1): 36–54.

Helling, A. and Poister, T.H. (2000) 'US maritime ports: trends, policy implications, and research needs', *Economic Development Quarterly*, 14(3): 298–315.

Heung, V.C.S. (1997) 'Hong Kong: political impact on tourism', in F.M. Go and C.L. Jenkins (eds) *Tourism and Economic Development in Asia and Australasia*, London: Cassell, pp. 123–137.

Hobson, J.S.P. (1993) 'Analysis of the US cruise line industry', *Tourism Management*, 14(6): 453–462.

Hodder, J.S. (1993) 'The Caribbean Tourism Organization in historical perspective', in D. Gayle and J. Goodrich (eds) *Tourism Marketing and Management in the Caribbean*, London: Routledge, pp. 20–27.

Hulse, T. (1999) 'Is it a ship? Is it a floating country? Or just the jet set's favourite tax dodge?', *The Independent*, 24 November.

International Council of Cruise Lines (ICCL) (2000) 'Cruise industry economic impact tops $15 billion in U.S. in 1999', Arlington, VA: ICCL, available at http://www.iccl.org/pressroom/press39.htm (accessed 11 May 2001).

Ioannides, D. and Debbage, K.G. (1998a) 'Neo-Fordism and flexible specialization in the travel industry: dissecting the polyglot', in D. Ioannides and K.G. Debbage (eds) *The Economic Geography of the Tourist Industry*, London: Routledge, pp. 99–122.

—— (eds) (1998b) *The Economic Geography of the Tourist Industry*, London: Routledge.

Lash, S. and Urry, J. (1994) *Economies of Signs and Space*, London: Sage.

Lawton, L.J. and Butler, R.W. (1987) 'Cruise ship industry: patterns in the Caribbean 1880–1986', *Tourism Management*, 8(4): 329–343.

Li, K.X. and Wonham, J. (1999) 'Who mans the world fleet? A follow-up to the BIMCO/ISF manpower survey', *Maritime Policy and Management*, 26(3): 295–303.

—— (2001) 'Maritime legislation: new areas for safety of life at sea', *Maritime Policy and Management*, 28(3): 225–234.

Lichfield, J. (2002) 'French shipbuilder plans to build Jules Verne's "dream isle"', *The Independent*, 28 September, p. 17.

Lin, C-T, Wang, S-M. and Chiang, C.-T. (2001) 'Manpower supply and demand of ocean deck officers in Taiwan', *Maritime Policy and Management*, 28(1), 91–102.

Low, L. and Heng, T.M. (1997) 'Singapore: development of gateway tourism', in F.M. Go and C.L. Jenkins (eds) *Tourism and Economic Development in Asia and Australasia*, London: Cassell, pp. 235–254.

Lundberg, D.E. and Lundberg, C.E. (1993) *International Travel and Tourism*, Chichester, UK: John Wiley.

McCalla, R.J. (1998) 'An investigation into site and situation: cruise ship ports', *Tijdschrift voor Economische en Sociale Geografie*, 89(1): 44–55.

MacCannell, D. (1976) *The Tourist: A New Theory of the Leisure Class*, London: Macmillan.

—— (1992) *Empty Meeting Grounds: The Tourist Papers*, London: Routledge.

McDowell, E. (1999) 'Fewer jet flights in Caribbean skies', *New York Times*, 10 January.

McIntosh, R.W., Goeldner, C.R. and Ritchie, J.R.B. (1995) *Tourism Principles, Practices, Philosophies*, 7th edn, Chichester, UK: John Wiley.

Marti, B. (1990) 'Geography and the cruise ship port selection process', *Maritime Policy and Management*, 17: 157–164.

—— (1991) 'Cruise ship market segmentation: a "non-traditional" port case study', *Maritime Policy and Management*, 18: 93–103.

Marti, B. and Cartaya, S.A. (1996) 'Caribbean cruising: an analysis of competition among U.S. homeports', *Maritime Policy and Management*, 23: 15–25.

Mather, C. (2002) *What It's Really Like to Work on Board Cruise Ships*, London: War on Want/International Transport Workers' Federation.

Mathieson, A. and Wall, G. (1982) *Tourism: Economic, Physical and Social Impacts*, Harlow, UK: Longman.

Mentzer, M. (1989) 'Factors affecting cruise ship fares', *Transportation Journal*, 29(1): 38–43.

Mescon, T. and Vosikis, G. (1985) 'The economic impact of tourism at the port of Miami', *Annals of Tourism Research*, 12: 515–528.

Miller, M.L. and Auyong, J. (eds) (1991) *Proceedings of the 1990 Congress on Coastal and Marine Tourism*, Corvallis, OR: National Coastal Resources Research Institute.

Morrison, A., Yang, C., O'Leary, J. and Nadkarni, N. (1996) 'Comparative profiles of travellers on cruises and land-based resort vacations', *Journal of Tourism Studies*, 7(2): 15–27.

Orams, M. (1999) *Marine Tourism: Development, Impacts and Management*, London: Routledge.

Orenstein, C. (1997) 'Fantasy island: Royal Caribbean parcels off a piece of Haiti', *The Progressive*, 61(8): 28–31.

Orient Lines (2001) 'Orient Lines introduces "Grand Voyages" itineraries', *Tutto Crociere*, available at http://www.cybercruises.com/oringrvoitjul01.htm (accessed 23 July 2001).

—— (2002) 'Introducing new Mediterranean brochure for 2002', Orient Lines, available at http://www.orientlines.com/news/prdetail.lassö?id=34455 (accessed 18 February 2002).

Pacific Asia Travel Association (PATA) (1995) 'Hong Kong', *Pacific Asia Travel News*, March/April, pp. 14–16.

Pearce, D. (1989) *Tourist Development*, 2nd edn, Harlow, UK: Longman.

Peisley, T. (1995) 'Transport: the cruise ship industry to the 21st century', *EIU Travel and Tourism Analyst*, 2: 4–25.

—— (1996) *The World Cruise Ship Industry to 2000*, London: Travel and Tourism Intelligence.

—— (2001) 'Shipping forecast: new ships ahead', *Conference and Incentive Travel*, Supplement, May, pp. 2–3.

Pine, B.J. and Gilmore, J.H. (1998) 'Welcome to the experience economy', *Harvard Business Review*, July–August, pp. 97–105.

Rojek, C. (1995) *Decentring Leisure: Rethinking Leisure Theory*, London: Sage.

Rojek, C. and Urry, J. (1997) *Touring Cultures: Transformations of Travel and Theory*, London: Routledge.

Salles, B.R. (2002) 'The cruise market in 2001', *InforMare*, available at http://www.informare.it/news/forum/2002/brs/cruise-auk.asp (accessed 30 September 2002).

Santo, J. (1994) 'The cruise market', *The Travel Counselor*, 8: 70–78.

Schiebler, S.A., Crofts, J.C. and Hollinger, R.C. (1996) 'Florida tourists' vulnerability to crime', in A. Pizam and Y. Mansfeld (eds) *Tourism, Crime and International Security Issues*, Chichester, UK: John Wiley, pp. 37–50.

Showker, K. and Sehlinger, B. (eds) (1998) *The Unofficial Guide to Cruises*, New York: Macmillan.

Singapore Tourism Promotion Board (STPB) (1993) *Strategic Plan for Growth 1993–1995*. Singapore: STPB.

Sloan, G. (1998) 'When you're young at heart: Disney makes big magic on the high seas', *USA Today*, 31 July.

Teye, W.B. (1992) 'Land transportation and tourism in Bermuda', *Tourism Management*, 13(4): 395–405.

Thanopoulou, H.A., Ryoo, D.-K. and Lee, T.-W. (1999) 'Korean liner shipping in the era of global alliances', *Maritime Policy and Management*, 26(3): 209–229.

Theobald, W. (ed.) (1994) *Global Tourism: The Next Decade*, Oxford: Butterworth-Heinemann.

Travelocity.com (2001) 'Travelocity.com booking boatloads of cruises: Web site sees more than 300% increase in cruise bookings', *Tutto Crociere*, available at http://www.cybercruises.com/trbobocrwejul01.htm (accessed 23 July 2001).

Urry, J. (1990) *The Tourist Gaze*, London: Sage.

—— (1992a) 'The tourist gaze and the environment', *Theory, Culture and Society*, 9: 1–26.

—— (1992b) 'The tourist gaze "revisited"', *American Behavioral Scientist*, 36: 172–186.

—— (1995) *Consuming Places*, London: Routledge.

US Business Reporter (2002) *Cruise Line Market – Yr 2000*, available at http://www.activemedia-guide.com/mrk44112.htm (accessed 18 February 2002).

van Harssel, J. (1994) 'The senior travel market: distinct, diverse, demanding' in Theobald, W. (ed.) *Global Tourism: The Next Decade*, Oxford: Butterworth-Heinemann.

Verchere, I. (1997) 'Not just for geriatrics', *The European*, 31 July.

Wang, J. and McOwan, S. (2000) 'Fast passenger ferries and their future', *Maritime Policy and Management*, 27(3): 231–251.

Ward, D. (1992) *Cruising and Cruise Ships*, New York and Oxford: Berlitz.

Wazir, B. and Mathiason, N. (2002) 'Cruise liner crews slave below decks', *Observer*, 8 September, p. 14.

Wedding Experience, The (2001) 'The Wedding Experience offers cruise ship weddings, vow renewals and anniversary programs around the world', *Tutto Crociere*, available at http://www.cybercruises.com/weexofcrshjul01.htm (accessed 23 July 2001).

Wild, P. and Dearing, J. (2000) 'Development of and prospects for cruising in Europe', *Maritime Policy and Management*, 27(4): 315–333.

Wilson, J. (2002) 'Mobile home "floating town" docks in London', *Guardian*, 8 April.

Wood, R.E. (2000) 'Caribbean cruise tourism: globalization at sea', *Annals of Tourism Research*, 27(2): 345–370.

World of ResidenSea, The (2002) 'Residensea announces christening and itinerary updates for the world, February 13, 2002', Freeport: ResidenSea Ltd, available at http://forum.residensea.com/forms/press_releases.html?id=28 (accessed 18 February 2002).

Wrona, A. and Roe, M. (2002) 'The Polish maritime sector under transition', *Maritime Policy and Management*, 29(1): 17–43.

Young, G. (1973) *Tourism: Blessing or Blight?*, Harmondsworth, UK: Penguin.

Zbar, D. (1995) 'Disney glides into cruises', *Advertising Age*, 66(19): 38.

Part II
Technology the enabler

7   From 'Anyport' to 'Superterminal'

Conceptual perspectives on containerization and port infrastructures

Robert J. McCalla

Introduction

In the past, geographers have developed various 'stages of growth' models to analyse port development processes. Three of the most widely applied are those relating to waterfront revitalization, the evolution of internal port infrastructure and the development of complete port systems. These models share common ground in that the idea of change over time and space lies at their heart, but all three adopt quite different perspectives of scale and content. At the micro scale – that is, within the port and generally in historic docklands – waterfront redevelopment models seek to understand responses to the separation of port and other urban functions at the water–land interface, the separation that has become so common over time (Hoyle *et al.* 1988; Hayuth 1989). They explore the city's rediscovery of its waterfront as old port facilities were abandoned and new cargo handling areas were built on greenfield sites, usually towards the open ocean and especially on deeper water. At the city scale, meanwhile, the classic interpretation of internal port infrastructure development is Bird's (1963) *Anyport* model. This postulates five stages of port development and migration, driven by the impact of growing cargo throughput and improved land transportation – especially railroads – on the demand for port facilities in the form of more and larger docks and greater storage space. And at the scale of the coastal region, various models have focused on port system development, particularly in terms of interport competition and hinterland evolution (Taaffe *et al.* 1963; Rimmer 1967; Hayuth 1981).

Despite their popularity, all three perspectives on port development are now dated to some degree, especially the *Anyport* model. Moreover, the fact that change is central to their approaches implies a need for continued appraisal to reflect the influence of today's highly dynamic world. Consequently, this chapter aims to add to the analytical armoury by proposing an additional model relating specifically to container port development. The most obvious need for this focus is that *Anyport* pre-dates the current containerization era, and consequently cannot deal with the dramatic effects of containerization technologies on the assessment of existing port infrastructures. Nor can it encompass the impacts of decisions relating to the scale and location of new investments in these technologies and their associated infrastructures. Less obviously, yet still importantly, the container age is now so advanced that it is no longer appropriate to assume the homogeneity of container terminals, as is done so frequently. If we are to understand processes of change in general cargo ports today and in coming decades, a conceptual perspective on this dimension of technological advance is essential to give greater depth to our understanding of terminal evolution and the external imperatives that drive it.

The chapter postulates that, just as there have been milestones in waterfront redevelopment, internal port development and port systems development, there have been significant stages of container port development into 'Superterminal'. Five stages are proposed: start-up, expansion, addition, consolidation and redevelopment. Each one of these stages can be thought of as a process that the port passes through in order to exploit technological change by providing and upgrading its container facilities. To assess the applicability of the model, it is applied at two scales: first, at the macro scale, to ports on the North American eastern seaboard and then, at the micro scale, to the port of Charleston. Charleston provides a highly appropriate case study because its embrace of containerization has raised it to the position of second-largest container handling port on the east coast behind New York, with aspirations to take on dominant load centre status on the eastern seaboard, especially in the southern range.

The model

The model is set out here in purely conceptual terms, accompanied by only essential illustration of the reality on the ground, and with most exemplification incorporated in subsequent sections. A schematic representation linking space with process is shown in Figure 7.1. Stage 1 is the construction of the first purpose-built container terminals (T_1). Since the concept of containerization was new in both theory and practice when this occurred in the 1960s, and since the shipping industry by its very nature is conservative, Stage 1 terminals were small. Most comprised one or two cranes, with limited back-up land, and had restricted access to inland areas by existing land networks, rather than by specially built road and rail lines. No one foresaw the great demands that would be put on the inland transport system as containerization became the norm for general cargo transport internationally. In contrast, there was usually good sea access to Stage 1 terminals since containerization was designed with sea transport in mind. Their locations were, in fact, dictated by connections to the sea, not the land.

Stage 2 envisages three options for the future of the initial terminal: closure, no change or expansion. Although it will be demonstrated later that *closure* has been rare, theoretically it has been possible in the event of a terminal being found to be deficient for some reason. Perhaps the site was poor: congestion became a problem and there was no room for expansion. Perhaps the situation was wrong: other competing ports were better located to serve the overseas

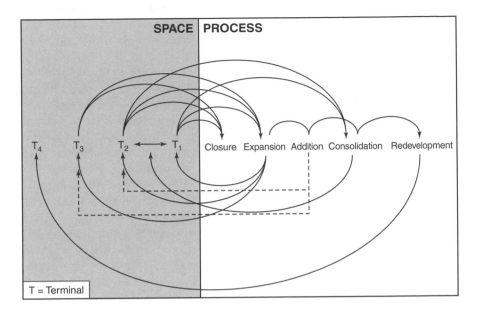

Figure 7.1 Container terminal development model.

forelands and inland hinterlands. Perhaps trade routes changed and the port, with its trial terminal, found itself outside the shipping lanes. But regardless of the specific driving force, terminal closure would signal either the end of containerization at the port in question, or a marked delay in its reintroduction and permanent adoption.

The *no change* option represents continuance of the terminal with no increased investment in facilities. In this scenario the initial decision to establish the facility was justified, but there was no need to expand it yet. Once again, however, the conceptual need to incorporate this option in the model should not be seen as an indication that it was a common outcome. In fact, it was unlikely that the status quo could remain for long, as larger ships and expanding trade became the norm. If expansion did not occur, then the terminal, and the port, would be left behind. For this reason the model proposes *expansion* as the usual practice in Stage 2. Typically, expansion will have been required to deal with technological developments in ships (larger, faster); to deal with changes in land-based transportation systems (unit container trains and inland marshalling yards); and, generally, to handle the increases in container trade which came about with the universal adoption of the concept. In investment terms, expansion can be conceptualized as additional cranes, larger storage areas, more berths and better land access. Spatially it usually meant either the removal of adjacent existing port infrastructure (typically, storage sheds and warehouses that were no longer required because the container served as its own storage unit) or encroachment on to reclaimed land. Such land was often built up with dredged material from the harbour as the port deepened its channels to cater to the larger ships. This process commonly had major environmental implications, a point to which we return later. At this stage, however, these impacts normally went unrecognized (Pinder, 1981; Pinder and Witherick, 1990).

Most ports were limited with respect to how much expansion the early terminals could accommodate. Decisions to construct them were made in the infancy of containerization. As already indicated, the consequence was that often they were not in the 'best' places in the port, and so they suffered restricted back-up areas, limited room for expansion and poor land access. Moreover, although satisfactory at first, water depth in the access channels or at the terminals themselves often became an issue as container ships evolved. To encompass these deficiencies, Stage 3 allows for *additional* terminals to be provided for ports to remain competitive in the expanding container world. The new terminals (T_2, T_3 in Figure 7.1) were larger in size than the original. They were often designed with expansion in mind. They could be adjacent to the original terminal, but more often than not were in a new area of the port where the water was deeper and land access, by road and rail, could be constructed. Moreover, while the early terminals were established with sea access in mind, the planners of subsequent terminals were more aware of the need for large open areas to take full advantage of the technologies and ensure fast and efficient transfer to land-based transportation systems. The advent of intermodality (Hayuth, 1987; Slack, 1998), in which the port was but one player in the seamless transfer of goods from inland locations on one continent to inland destinations on another, meant that container terminals were as much about land as about water transportation. In fact, in this stage container terminals came to be called intermodal terminals to reflect the transfer function they facilitated between modes.

The process of intermodal container terminal development took place continually at the port. One can envisage Stage 3 as a constant process of facility reappraisal and development, deciding policy on closures (rare), retention of the status quo and expansion in relation to existing terminals; and, depending on how those terminals performed, also deciding on additional terminals to serve expanding trade. Eventually, though, the fourth stage of the model would be reached as some type of *consolidation* of facilities became needed. This consolidation could be geographical – that is, the combination of adjacent terminals to create a larger facility with greater economies of scale; or it could be corporate, as one terminal operator came to dominate terminal operations in the port.

These four options of terminal development – closure, expansion, addition and consolidation – resulted in multi-terminal port landscapes, which grew over time in a rather piecemeal and almost uncoordinated fashion. Terminals were expanded where they could be; new terminals were built when they had to be to cater for changing circumstances. But a review of many ports today would demonstrate that this rather *ad hoc* terminal development has now been replaced by integrated port planning which takes into account the circumstances of the port, inland transportation companies and shipping lines; incorporates forecasts of trade development; and also acknowledges the new environmental reality – that port facilities must be sited so as to minimize negative environmental externalities. As a result, a fifth process of terminal development, *redevelopment*, is suggested in the model. This is the stage many ports are at now.

Redevelopment is a coordinated effort of expansion, addition and consolidation. It is more than just adding to existing facilities, or upgrading those facilities with technologically more advanced equipment. It is more than just building another terminal, or of consolidating what is in the port presently. Redevelopment creates a new geography of container facilities in the locality, a refocusing of where container activity is to take place. It represents a concentration of container handling at a *Superterminal*. This redevelopment is generated by events external to the port – detailed by Slack in Chapter 2 – and is both reactionary and anticipatory. Particularly, redevelopment is being brought about by the trend towards container cargo consolidation in hub ports. This consolidation is occurring because shipping alliances are reducing the number of port calls they make along a coastal range. Larger ships, of 6,000 TEU capacity and more, mean that only certain ports will be able to serve as hub ports. If the redevelopment of container facilities does not occur in these ports, it is likely that they will lose status relative to competitors, and a decline in shipping activity will occur.

Redevelopment may represent a radical approach to port investment and administration. No longer are old practices acceptable; a new approach must be tried to make the port competitive and expand its container throughput. However, this process proceeds in an environmentally aware society, very different from that encountered in the early stages. Not everyone may share the port's enthusiasm for increasing its scale of operations. Consequently, in the attempt to refocus container handling operations in the port, opportunity is given to environmentalists and local residents to challenge the redevelopment. Thus, the development–environment interface can become a key issue obstructing the model's progression.

Theory into practice on the US eastern seaboard

The applicability of the model is illustrated by analysing container terminal developments along the North American eastern seaboard (Figure 7.2). After an overview of the seaboard developments in the context of the model, Charleston is used as an example to show how a single port fits the model. As would be expected, there is a complex history of terminal openings, expansions and additions in the eastern seaboard ports over the years since container technologies were introduced at New York in 1956. Tables 7.1–7.7 detail this history. A close examination of each of the tables gives an appreciation of what happened in each of the ports. In addition, each table offers insights into the collective development of containerization on the eastern seaboard.

Table 7.1 highlights the post-*Anyport* development of containerization, with the majority of ports building their initial terminals in the 1960s. Terminals

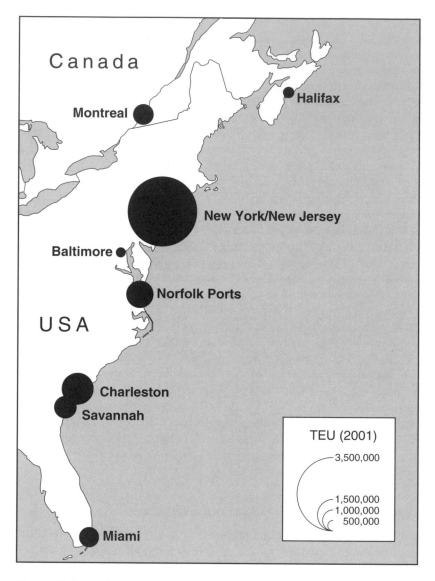

Figure 7.2 Selected container ports on the North Atlantic eastern seaboard.

were predominantly single berth and small (average less than 10 ha). The typical
initial terminal had one berth and at most two cranes. All the evidence points to
a very guarded and conservative introduction of container technologies in
eastern seaboard ports.

Expansion of the initial terminals is shown to be typical (Table 7.2). Only
one (Baltimore's SeaLand terminal) was not expanded. Only the Quebec termi-

Table 7.1 Initial container terminal developments at selected eastern seaboard ports

Port	Terminal	Year	Description
Halifax	Halterm	1970	2 berths, 2 cranes, 22.7 ha
Quebec	CP Ships	1969	2 berths, 2 cranes, 7.28 ha
Montreal	Manchester	1968	1 berth, 2 cranes, 5.8 ha
New York	Port Newark/Elizabeth	1959	2 berths, no dockside cranes, 7 ha
Baltimore	SeaLand	Mid-1960s	1 berth, 1 crane, 11.1 ha
Norfolk	Norfolk International	Mid-1960s	1 berth, 2 cranes
Charleston	Columbus Street	1966	1 berth, 1 crane, 6 ha
Savannah	Garden City	1969	1 berth, 1 crane, 6.5 ha

Source: Personal communication with the ports.

nal closed (Table 7.5), when CP Ships moved its operations upriver to Montreal. Expansions were of three types of investment: in additional berths, cranes and space. All three did not necessarily occur simultaneously; often it would be a new berth or new crane, or sometimes additional space, separately. Altogether there were over 100 separate investments in cranes, berths or additional terminal areas. From small and timid beginnings came large and bold investments resulting in substantial areal increases in a series of phased expansions. Particularly of note are the areal increases at Port Elizabeth (to more than 300 ha), Norfolk (210 ha) and Savannah (138 ha). It would seem that the initial small terminals were small not because of limited space, but because investors were unsure about containerization's future and they were, in effect, 'testing the waters'.

As Table 7.3 shows, all except one port (Savannah) received investments in additional terminals. Altogether, 18 additional terminals were opened in six ports. Typically these new terminals were opened within four to six years after the initial terminal, certainly within 10 years. The evidence suggests both boldness and caution on the part of investors. Boldness can be seen in the number of cranes installed in the new terminals (2–3 versus 1–2 in the initial terminals), as well as in the average number of berths (2–3 versus 1–2). Also, between five and six times as much land was devoted to the additional terminals as in the initial developments (over 330 ha compared with less than 60 ha). Caution, though, can also be seen. Although the average size of the additional terminals was quite high (22 ha), this disguised contrasts. A few were very large (e.g. Howland Hook, Wando Welch and Seagirt), but the majority were not much larger than the initial terminals. Moreover, the total area added by the additional terminals was actually quite small compared with the expansions to the initial terminals which were ongoing at the same time.

Expansion of the additional terminals took the same form as expansion of the initial terminals: in additional berths, cranes and space (Table 7.4). Again, closure of terminals was not common (Table 7.5). No fewer than 37 expansion phases can be identified at the selected ports. Often, additional investment came

Table 7.2 Expansion of initial container terminals

Port	Terminal	Year	Description
Halifax	Halterm	1987	3rd crane
		1988	Additional berth
		1991	4th crane
Montreal	Manchester	1970	2nd berth, expansion to 7.8 ha
		1987	Combined with Cadillac Terminal to create Maisonneuve Terminal with 5 cranes, 17.2 ha
New York	Port Newark/ Elizabeth	1961	Port Elizabeth opened with 5 berths, 18.6 ha
		By 1977	Port Newark/Elizabeth consisted of 26 berths, 22 cranes and 307 ha. Individual terminal operators were: ACL, International Terminal, Maersk, Maher, Navieras de Puerto Rico, Pittson, SeaLand and Universal.
		1983	Maersk expanded to 22 ha Universal expanded to 44.5 ha
		1985	Maersk 2nd crane
		1986	ACL expanded to 41.4 ha, 3rd berth, 3rd crane SeaLand expanded to 91 ha
		1990	Mahar Fleet Street expanded to 81 ha
		1991	Maersk 3rd crane SeaLand 7th crane
		1993	Maersk expanded to 6.4 ha
		1994	Maersk 4th crane
Norfolk	Norfolk International	1973	Expanded to 81 ha, 2nd berth, 3rd and 4th cranes
		1981	3rd berth
		1988	Expanded to 194 ha, 4th berth, 5th–7th cranes
		2000	Expanded to 210 ha, 8-10th crane
Charleston	Columbus Street	1973	2nd berth
		1974	2nd crane, expanded to 27.3 ha
		1986	Expanded to 49.8 ha
		1989	3rd crane
Savannah	Garden City	1974	Expanded to 19.4 ha, 2nd berth, 2nd crane
		1978	Expanded to 40.5 ha, 3rd berth, 3rd and 4th cranes
		1983	Expanded to 49 ha, 4th berth, 5th and 6th cranes
		1986	Expanded to 97 ha, 5th berth, 7th–9th cranes
		1992	Expanded to 109 ha, 6th berth
		1996	10th and 11th cranes
		1999	Expanded to 138 ha, 7th berth, 12th and 13th cranes

Source: *Containerisation International Yearbooks* and personal communication with the ports.

Table 7.3 Additional container terminal construction after initial terminal

Port	Terminal	Year	Description
Halifax	Fairview Cove	1982	1 berth, 2 cranes, 21 ha
Montreal	Cast	1972	2 cranes, 5 ha
	Boucherville	1972	1 crane, 5 ha
	Racine	1978	3 cranes, 7.3 ha
	Cadillac	1979	1 crane, 4.1 ha
	Bickerdike	1980	1 crane, 5.3 ha
New York	Northeast Marine (South Brooklyn)	196?	2 berths, 2 cranes, 26.5 ha
	Global Marine	1970	2 berths, 3 cranes, 34 ha
	Howland Hook	1972	3 berths, 4 cranes, 75.7 ha
	Red Hook	1981	2 berths, 2 cranes, 16.4 ha
Baltimore	Dundalk	1971	1 berth, 2 cranes
	South Locust Point	1979	3 berths, 2 cranes, 9.3 ha
	Seagirt	1991	3 berths, 7 cranes, 46 ha
Norfolk	Newport News	1972	1 berth, 1 crane
	SeaLand	1975	1 berth, 1 crane
	Portsmouth	1970s	2 berths, 20.2 ha
Charleston	North Charleston	1970	1 berth, 1 crane, 5.3 ha
	Wando Welch	1982	3 berths, 4 cranes, 50.5 ha

Source: *Containerisation International Yearbooks* and personal communication with the ports.

quickly. It is true there were some long time lags between initial investment and the first expansion (e.g. Howland Hook – 14 years, Newport News – 16 years) but in 9 of the 15 additional terminals for which we have information, the first expansion came within five years. Although expansions in the additional and initial terminals took similar forms, there were differences (Table 7.6). Expansions to additional terminals placed less emphasis on berths and more on terminal size. As ships have increased in size and capacity, it has not been the number of berths that has been important, but the size of the terminal to handle the increased volumes. The expansions to the new terminals have been geared to this reality. This fact has important consequences for the model. It points out the importance and differences between expansions to initial terminals and expansions to additional terminals. They are distinct stages in the model's development.

Consolidation of terminals has not occurred at all the eastern seaboard ports, but it is an established process at over half the ports studied (Table 7.7). As suggested in the model description, the consolidation has taken the form of spatial joining (at Montreal, New York and Baltimore) or corporate linkage (at Norfolk). In temporal terms, the evidence seems to be that consolidation has replaced the process of expansion to additional terminals, but detailed examination of Tables 7.7 and 7.4 shows that there is considerable temporal overlap between the two. Consolidation runs in parallel with expansion.

Table 7.4 Expansions to additional container terminals

Port	Terminal	Year	Description
Halifax	Fairview Cove	1986	2nd berth
	Fairview Cove	1990	3rd crane
Montreal	Cast	1976	Expanded to 9.5 ha
	Racine	1981	Expanded to 11.2 ha
		1983	Expanded to 16.8 ha, 3rd crane
	Cadillac	1984	Expanded to 4.7 ha
	Bickerdike	1988	Expanded to 9.6 ha, 2nd crane
	Cast	1989	Expanded to 15.5 ha
	Racine	1992	Expanded to 21 ha, 4th crane
New York	Global Marine	1981	Expanded to 38 ha
	Port Seatrain	1981	Expanded to 35.2 ha
	Global Marine	1983	Expanded to 40 ha
	South Brooklyn	1983	Expanded to 44.5 ha
		1985	3rd crane
	Howland Hook	1986	Expanded to 75.7 ha, 6th and 7th cranes
	Red Hook	1986	Expanded to 32 ha, 3rd crane
	Global Marine	1987	4th crane
	Red Hook	1990	4th crane
Baltimore	Dundalk	1973	3rd crane
		1977	4th and 5th cranes
		1983	6th–9th cranes
	South Locust	1987	Expanded to 14.9 ha
		1988	Expanded to 35 ha, 3rd crane
	Dundalk	1988	10th crane (one crane was moved to North Locust Terminal in 1990, leaving 9 cranes)
	Seagirt	1993	Expanded to 55 ha
	Dundalk	1996	10th crane, now 230 ha
	Seagirt	2000	4th berth
Norfolk	Portsmouth	1981	Expanded to 22.4 ha, 3rd berth
		1984	3rd and 4th cranes
	Newport News	1988	Expanded to 20 ha, 2nd berth, 2nd-4th cranes
	Portsmouth	1992	5th crane
Charleston	North Charleston	1972	2nd crane
		1979	Expanded to 38 ha, 3rd crane
		1986	Expanded to 77.5 ha, 4th crane
	Wando Welch	1986	Expanded to 60.5 ha
	North Charleston	1990	5th and 6th cranes
	Wando Welch	1996	Expanded to 90 ha, 5 berths, 9 cranes

Source: *Containerisation International Yearbooks* and personal communication with the ports.

Table 7.5 Closures of container terminals at selected eastern seaboard ports

Port	Terminal	Year	Comments
Quebec City	CP Ship	1975	Terminal operations moved to Montreal
New York	Port Seatrain	1982	
	South Brooklyn	1986	Terminal closed while the Port Authority looked for a new operator. Operating again in 1990.

Source: *Containerisation International Yearbooks.*

Table 7.6 Expansion characteristics at initial terminals compared to additional terminals

	Cranes	Berths	Additional areas
Expansion of initial terminals	+39	+25	+15
Expansion of additional terminals	+37	+11	+22

Source: Derived from Tables 7.2 and 7.4.

The evidence from the eastern seaboard does not yet demonstrate a clear move to *Superterminal* development, termed redevelopment in the model. Although very large intermodal terminals serving the major shipping lines of the world have emerged, for example at Baltimore (Dundalk, 230 ha), Savannah (Garden City, 138 ha) and Port Elizabeth (over 300 ha), no one terminal has recently been constructed which demonstrates the qualities of the redevelopment postulated in the model. Here the model is predictive, rather than interpretative of the past. Looking ahead, as the following section suggests, it is likely that current terminal developments at Charleston will be the first illustration of the redevelopment phase of the model on the eastern seaboard.

The Charleston experience

The first containers were handled at Charleston's initial Columbus Street Terminal (Figure 7.3 and Table 7.8) on 12 March 1966, when the SeaLand vessel *Gateway City* loaded 35 boxes bound for Puerto Rico (Moise 1991: 151). Demonstrating how rudimentary the Stage 1 terminal could be, this was a break-bulk general cargo facility dating back to the nineteenth century. Only 6 ha was allocated for container handling, and the one berth earmarked for containers was equipped with a general-purpose crane rather than one built specifically for container handling. Within two years, however, SeaLand was using Columbus Street to serve European and South-East Asian trade as well as that with Puerto Rico. This growth led to the transition into Stage 2 expansion. The

Table 7.7 Consolidations of container terminals at selected eastern seaboard ports

Port	Terminal	Year	Comments
Montreal	Manchester and Cadillac	1987	Combined to form Maisonneuve Terminal with 5 cranes and 17.2 ha
New York	SeaLand and Pittson Stevedoring	1986	Pittson Terminal taken over by SeaLand to create a larger SeaLand Terminal
	Mahar and International Operators	1986	International Terminal taken over by Mahar to create the Mahar Fleet Street Terminal with 4 cranes and 38 ha
	Mahar and Navieras de Puerto Rico Terminal	1988	Navieras de Puerto Rico Terminal taken over by Mahar to create a larger Mahar Fleet Street Terminal
	ACL Terminal	1994	Combined with Mahar Fleet Street Terminal
Baltimore	Seagirt and SeaLand	1991	Sea-Land Terminal incorporated into newly opened Seagirt terminal
Norfolk	Newport News and Norfolk International	1982	Virginia International Terminals took over the operation of both terminals
	Portsmouth	1983	Joined Newport News and Norfolk International Terminal under the Virginia International Terminals umbrella

Source: *Containerisation International Yearbooks* and personal communication with the ports.

year 1973 saw the addition of a second, common-user, container berth, followed in 1974 by the installation of a container crane and extension of the terminal to 27.3 ha. Moreover, Stage 2 lasted into the 1980s as throughput growth continued with the success of lines such as Maersk. The mid-1980s witnessed a virtual doubling of the terminal's area, to 49.8 ha, and 1989 the commissioning of an additional container crane (Table 7.2). In 1999, 1.9 million tonnes of containerized cargo passed through Columbus Street (Port of Charleston 2000).

At the same time as SeaLand was beginning to use this initial terminal, other container lines – notably Seatrain – were calling at the port. This encouraged the South Carolina State Port Authority (SCSPA) to propose two additional (i.e. Stage 3) terminals, even while Stage 2 expansion at Columbus Street was still being planned.

The first lay on the Cooper River and was on a site that had originally been

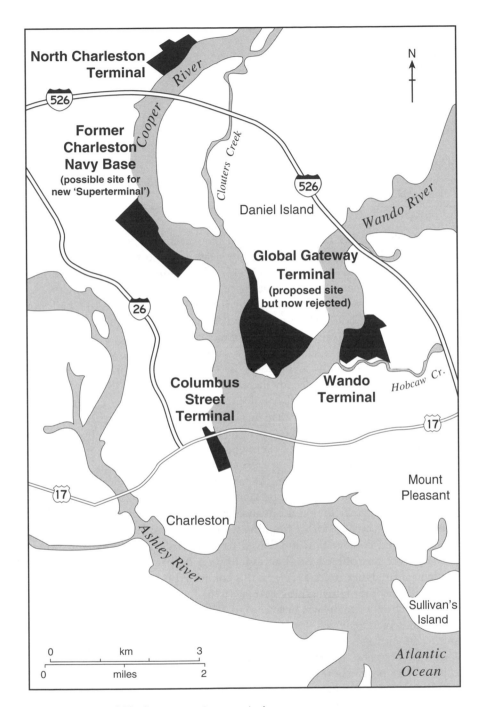

Figure 7.3 Port of Charleston container terminals.

Table 7.8 Port of Charleston, SC, container terminal development

---

Initial terminal (T₁)
Columbus Street – 1966
   Expansion: 1973, 1974, 1986, 1989

Additional terminals (T₂ –T₃)
North Charleston – 1970
   Expansion: 1972, 1979, 1986, 1989

Wando Welch – 1982
   Expansion: 1986, 1996

Redevelopment (T₄)
   Global Gateway Terminal – proposed 1999, abandoned 2003
   Former Navy base – proposed 2003

---

developed by the US Army in 1918, had then been totally rebuilt during the Second World War to become a major army east-coast port of embarkation, and had finally passed to the SCSPA in 1945. This ex-military port site provided convenient and cheap development space, albeit 14 km further from the sea than Columbus Street, and consequently it now became the North Charleston Terminal (Moise 1991: 46). Opened in 1970 with one berth, one container crane and only 5.3 ha of container storage land, this Stage 3 development quickly followed the model by moving into the expansion phase. A second crane was installed as early as 1972, followed by two others in 1979 and 1986, when the terminal was also vastly increased in size – first to 38 ha and then to 77.5 ha. By 1999 the terminal handled 2.59 million tonnes of containerized cargo, nearly 40 per cent more than its Columbus Street counterpart.

The second Stage 3 terminal was in many ways a response to both the site limitations at Columbus Street – hemmed in by other port users – and North Charleston's unfortunate situation 25 km from the sea buoy up the long, twisting and silt-laden Cooper River. At first, the SCSPA considered developing facilities east of Coulters Creek on Daniel Island, but in 1972 it came to settle on another greenfield site on the Wando River at Hobcaw Creek (Figure 7.3). While this was actually further from the sea than Columbus Street, and, surprisingly, required containers to be drayed to a railhead 15 km away, the Wando site none the less offered good accessibility on deep water, which limited the amount of dredging needed. It was also connected directly, via its own access road, with the interstate highway system (I526).

Although its opening was delayed until 1982, for reasons to which we shall return, the Wando Welch Terminal was at the outset equipped more impressively than either its Columbus Street or North Charleston counterparts – with 3 berths, 4 cranes and 50.5 ha. But despite this large early capacity, it soon echoed their progression into expansion mode. Within four years the area was increased by 20 per cent, followed by a further 50 per cent increase in 1996. By then it was one of the eastern seaboard's best-equipped container terminals, with 5 berths and 9 cranes. The traffic attracted reflects this clearly: total throughput in 1999 (6.27 million tonnes of cargo) easily exceeded the combined figure for the Columbus Street and North Charleston terminals.

From this analysis it is evident that Charleston exemplifies extremely well three dimensions of the model: start-up, expansion and addition. But it is also clear that it does not demonstrate the processes of terminal closure, stagnation or consolidation. These departures from the model are readily explained. The absence of closure or stagnation at any of the terminals reflects the great success Charleston has had as a container port (Figure 7.4). Between 1978 and 2000 there were only three years – 1981, 1990 and 1993 – when the port did not experience an increase in container throughput. Over that period the average *annual* growth in TEU was 21.2 per cent. Moreover, although the recent annual growth rate has been lower (7.1 per cent over the 1990s), this does not imply that the port is moving steadily towards a no-growth situation. In the financial year 2000, for example, the port experienced a 16 per cent increase in container handling.

The lack of consolidation, meanwhile, points to the conclusion that Stage 4 of the model is not inevitable; it may be sidelined if local conditions so dictate. Geographical consolidation has not occurred, partly because the existing terminals are spread widely around the city, with no contiguity between them that could be exploited (Figure 7.3). It also reflects the fact that even the large-scale Wando Welch Terminal has insufficient capacity to divert significant traffic from other terminals and still have a realistic margin left for future growth. And ownership consolidation is not possible in Charleston because all terminals already belong to the SCSPA. Beyond this, however, the Charleston case also demonstrates that failure to consolidate does not preclude a port from embarking on the final redevelopment stage. On the contrary, Charleston illustrates

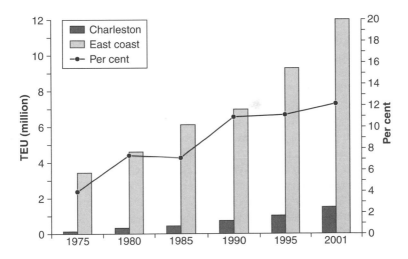

Figure 7.4 Container handling in the port of Charleston compared to east-coast ports generally.

very effectively the emergence of Stage 5 *Superterminal* ambitions – and their consequences.

Charleston has turned to the *Superterminal* strategy for three main reasons. First, its existing terminals are nearing capacity. Second, future traffic projections envisage a 5.8 per cent annual increase in container throughput by existing shipping lines using the port (Port of Charleston 2002a). Third, the port aims to add to this growth by becoming a major hub centre for eastern seaboard containers. Most of the largest container lines in the world serve Charleston, and if the port wishes to keep these lines and take on an even greater eastern seaboard role, then it must make a steep change to its facilities.

Charleston's *Superterminal* project, the Global Gateway Terminal, was originally destined for Daniel Island (Figure 7.3), where the SCSPA acquired land during the 1990s. Early in that decade, 323 ha was purchased on the Cooper River side of the island. Then, in 1997, the island's remaining 202 ha was bought in secret (Bartelme 2002). The plans for Global Gateway were published in 1999. The new terminal was to be connected to the interstate highway system by a 3-km access road. A 13-km railroad spur was to be built to link the terminal to existing rail lines. Dredging would take Charleston's entrance channel down to 14.3 m (47 ft), and the approach to Daniel Island down to 13.5 m (45 ft). On land, although the first phase was to be quite modest – no more than two berths with 40 ha of storage by 2006 – subsequent phases would have involved all the island's 525 ha.

Current plans, however, are very different. Indeed, the port abandoned the Daniel Island proposal in the summer of 2002, replacing it with an alternative *Superterminal* proposed to be built on newly acquired land on the west side of the Cooper River opposite Daniel Island (Port of Charleston 2003). Community opposition to the Daniel Island proposal forced the port to rethink the development of its new terminal, but not before it attempted to appease local concerns. The first concession was to propose a drastic reduction in the Global Gateway project by limiting it to the Cooper River side of Daniel Island only. Dock construction on the Wando River side would not take place, and port development there would be permanently restricted. Much of the east side of the island would continue to serve as a dredge material disposal area, and 22 ha at the northern end of the site was to be transferred to the city for public use on completion of Phase 1. In addition, there was to be a new emphasis on maintaining the viability of the three existing terminals well into the future, primarily through the channel-deepening programme from which they, too, would benefit. Deeper channels to the Wando Welch and Columbus Street terminals are already complete. That to North Charleston is scheduled for completion in 2004. And the authorities have already persuaded the US Congress to appropriate $500,000 to study deepening of the harbour beyond 13.7 m (45 ft) (Port of Charleston 2002b).

The timing of the initial revision might be seen by the outside observer as a reaction to 11 September 2001. Elsewhere in this volume, Slack raises the possibility that this terrorism event, through its effects on consumer demand and investor confidence, might impact severely on container traffic for the foreseeable future. In fact, as indicated above, and as the proposed donation of 22 ha to the city for public use might also indicate, the revised plan was a response to environmental opposition. This force first became evident in Charleston in the 1970s and explains the substantial delay, noted earlier, in completing the Wando Welch Terminal. Although the Wando site was purchased in 1972, construction could not start until 1978 because of environmental arguments, including a court case. In an echo of this hurdle, when the environmental impact assessment of the original Global Gateway proposal was presented to the public in November 1999 it received a very rude hearing.

Environmentalists and local citizens expressed vociferous concern about the sheer magnitude of the 5 km^2 project and its potential impact on traffic congestion, house values, noise, water quality and natural habitat destruction (Bartelme, 2002). All local authorities in the area voted against the plan, and stakeholder suggestions included relocation of the initiative up the Cooper River beyond the existing North Charleston Terminal or on derelict land opposite Daniel Island formerly owned by the US Navy (Wise 2002). South Carolina's General Assembly reacted to public opinion on the Daniel Island revised proposal by enacting a law requiring the SCSPA to obtain its approval before proceeding. Faced with this hostility, the SCSPA's decision to abandon the Daniel Island site and look elsewhere to develop much-needed container handling facilities is understandable. In the event, the Authority has opted to try to develop its *Superterminal* strategy on the former US Navy land opposite Daniel Island. There would appear to be greater support to construct the new terminal there, given the non-residential nature of the area (Bartelme 2003). But even though this is a brownfield site, permission for container terminal development is not assured, and regulatory permits involving a public review of the proposal still need to be acquired.

In conceptual terms, the confrontation over the Daniel Island site can be taken as an indication that, particularly at the *Superterminal* stage, the proposed model of container port development should be developed further to allow for the intervention of environmentalism as a very powerful force. Examples of container developments planned elsewhere in the world, but not yet assessed in the literature, support this view. On Southampton Water in the United Kingdom, for example, Associated British Ports' intention to undertake a very similar scheme to Global Gateway has provoked comparable opposition and is still enmeshed in the public inquiry process (Planning Inspectorate 2003). Pursuing this line of argument means that a link can be developed between the model proposed here and the concept of society and community tolerance limits, first proposed by Pinder (1981, 1984) and subsequently elaborated by Cau (1996).

We must note, however, that the Charleston example also suggests that to view *Superterminal* debates entirely in terms of the community versus development may be a major over-simplification. This is because, in contrast to standard confrontations, there was evidence of vocal community support for the Global Gateway, as well as opposition. Demonstrators at a State Senate hearing in March 2002 included those with banners declaring 'Port = jobs' and 'I'm your neighbor, I work on the waterfront'. The hearing's first speaker proclaimed that 'Much has been said and written that this community does not support port expansion. We are here to say that's absolutely not true.' And when those in favour of the terminal were asked to stand, three-quarters of the 900 people present are estimated to have done so (Bartelme 2002). Whether this support for the port was actually spontaneous rather than contrived is unclear. Bartelme (2002: 2) certainly notes that 'Ports authority officials joined local maritime leaders on a campaign of their own, traveling through the state to enlist the support of manufacturers that use the port and other business groups'. Whatever the reality, the support indicates that a modification of the 'port versus community' perspective should be envisaged. In particular, it is appropriate to recognize that tension and conflict between community factions may become an additional significant element in the decision-making process.

Conclusion

This chapter has presented a model of container terminal development, emphasizing the various processes at work in the application of these technologies, and testing the ideas against the experience of ports along the North American eastern seaboard. All features of the model have been demonstrated at the macro scale. But given the upswing in containerization that has occurred, it is understandable that the evidence currently highlights the importance of processes associated with growth rather than decline or stagnation. At the micro scale, the port of Charleston has been used to illustrate details of the model and demonstrate that not all components may be influential in specific localities. That is to be expected. The usefulness of a model is to simplify a complex reality, in order to deepen understanding of the world by allowing comparisons to be made between that reality and the model. Such a comparison can be highly instructive, and not only about the past. In those places where the final stages have not been reached – as in most eastern seaboard ports – the model may also lead to a better appreciation of the challenges likely to be encountered in the future. These challenges may not be simply technical and financial. One clear message is that they may include the opposition of local interests who question the need for bigger and better facilities made possible by advancing technologies. Even though that opposition may not be unanimous, the model's recognition of environmentalism is salutary, especially in the *Superterminal* context.

The future for all container ports will involve big changes as they jockey to serve the sometimes fickle interests of shippers, shipping lines and special interest groups in port cities. As ships become larger, containerized trade expands and competition between ports heightens, it will be incumbent on each port to redevelop its container handling facilities to cater to the changes. As Charleston makes its concerted effort to exploit technological change and elevate its position in the hierarchy, other ports are pursuing the same objectives and challenges. While Stage 4 consolidation is now quite common on the eastern seaboard, realization of the potential importance of redevelopment leading towards *Superterminal* is also becoming widespread. And while this is apparent on the US east coast, on a broader canvas the challenges are becoming world-wide because of the globalized nature of containerization. Although the model has been developed in the US context, therefore, its utility may be much more widespread.

References

Bartelme, T. (2002) 'Hearing shows controversial issue is far from over', 5 March 2002, available at http://www.charleston.net/pub/news/gateway/spagw0305.htm, (accessed 9 April 2002).

—— (2003) 'SPA has options for new container terminal', 22 February 2003, available at http://charleston.net/stories/022203/scp_businessbartelme3.shtml, (accessed 11 September 2003).

Bird, J.H. (1963) *The Major Seaports of the United Kingdom*, London: Oxford University Press.

Cau, L. (1996) 'Environmental perception and planning: the case of Plymouth's water-front', in B.S. Hoyle (ed.) *Cityports, Coastal Zones and Regional Change: International Perspectives on Planning and Management*, Chichester, UK: Wiley, pp. 61–82.

Hayuth, Y. (1981) 'Containerization and the load center concept', *Economic Geography*, 57: 160–175.

—— (1987) *Intermodality: Concept and Practice*, London: Lloyd's of London Press.

—— (1989) 'Urban waterfronts: a spatial focus for economic, technological and environ-mental change', *Geoforum*, 20: 425–501. [Hayuth was guest editor for this special issue. Seven papers are included.]

Hoyle, B.S., Pinder, D.A. and Husain, S.M. (1988) *Revitalizing the Waterfront: International Dimensions of Dockland Redevelopment*, London: Belhaven Press.

Moise, A. (1991) *History of the South Carolina State Ports Authority*, Columbia, SC: R.L. Bryan.

Pinder, D.A. (1981) 'Community attitude as a limiting factor in port growth: the case of Rotterdam', in B.S. Hoyle and D.A. Pinder (eds) *Cityport Industrialization and Regional Development: Spatial Analysis and Planning Strategies*, Oxford: Pergamon Press, pp. 181–199.

—— (1984) 'Planned port industrialisation and the quest for upward economic transition: an examination of development strategies for the Dutch delta', in B.S. Hoyle and D. Hilling (eds) *Seaport Systems and Spatial Change*, Chichester, UK: Wiley, pp. 277–301.

Pinder, D.A. and Witherick, M.E. (1990) 'Port industrialisation, urbanisation and wetland decline', in M. Williams (ed.) *Wetlands: A Threatened Landscape*, Oxford: Blackwell, pp. 234–266.

Planning Inspectorate (2003) *Dibden Bay Inquiry*, available at www.planning_inspectorate.gov.uk/dibden/ (accessed 21 February 2003).

Port of Charleston (2000) http://www.port-of-charleston.com (accessed 30 January 2000).

—— (2002a) 'Future port development', available at http://www.port-of-charleston.com/constituent/future_plans/futureportdevelopment.asp (accessed 23 March 2002).

—— (2002b) 'Further Charleston deepening studied', available at http://www.port-of-charleston.com/whatsnew/press_room/pressroom.asp?PressRelease=55 (accessed 23 March 2002).

—— (2003) 'State of the Port Address', available at http://www.port-of-charleston.com/whatsnew/press_room/pressroom.asp?PressRelease=69 (accessed 11 September 2003).

Rimmer, P. (1967) 'The search for spatial regularities in the development of Australian seaports, 1861–1961/2', *Geografiska Annaler*, 49B: 42–53.

Slack, B. (1998) 'Intermodal transportation' in B.S. Hoyle and R. Knowles (eds) *Modern Transport Geography*, 2nd edn, Chichester, UK: Wiley.

Taaffe, E., Morrill, R. and Gould, P. (1963) 'Transport expansion in underdeveloped countries: a comparative analysis', *Geographical Review*, 53: 503–529.

Wise, W. (2002) 'Summey vows fight as panel OKs port plan', 4 April 2002, available at http://www.charleston.net/pub/archive/news/04spamain.htm (accessed 9 April 2002).

8 High speed at sea

Evolution and issues

Giovanni Ridolfi

Introduction

Passenger travel and the shipment of goods by sea have traditionally been highly economic but slow, the limit to increased speed being imposed by the high costs of technical innovation and excessive energy consumption. At the same time, the concept of increasing the speed of ships has continued to attract the attention of shipowners because it is a key criterion for the efficiency of marine transportation, and thus for the competitive position of carriers. This has encouraged their constant interest in discovering ways to overcome the limitations, through high-performance propulsion systems and improved hull designs leading to reduced drag. Table 8.1 summarises the major technological advances in propulsion since the early nineteenth century, when the speed of the first steam-powered ships was little better than that of sail.

During much of the twentieth century, the technologies giving the highest speeds were the preserve of naval vessels. In the commercial sphere, meanwhile,

Table 8.1 Propulsion systems and speed at sea

Propulsion	Era	Vessel	Speed (knots)
Sail	Until early 20th century	*Cutty Sark* (1869)	16
Sail and steam engine driving paddle wheel	Early 19th century	*Great Western* (1838)	14
Steam engine driving propeller	Late 19th century	*Napoleon* (1857)	20
Steam turbine with propeller	Early 20th century	*Mauretania* (1907)	25
Diesel engine with propeller	From *c.*1920	*Normandie* (1935)	30
Gas turbine with propeller	1950s onwards	*United States* (1952)	35
Diesel engine with hydrojet	1980s onwards	*Hoverspeed Great Britain* (1990)	37
Gas turbine with hydrojet	1990s onwards	*Destriero* (1992)	53

the spotlight was fixed firmly on the transatlantic crossing, as the leading ocean liner operators vied to establish new records and thus secure the prestigious 'Blue Riband' (the Hales Trophy). Between 1907, when this was captured by the British liner *Mauretania*, and 1952 when it fell to the *United States*, the average speed for the crossing rose from 25 knots to 36.3 – nearly a 50 per cent improvement. Although interest in the transatlantic record then appeared to die with the great ocean liners, as the end of the century approached it was re-kindled by the appearance of very different vessels. In 1990 the catamaran *Hoverspeed Great Britain* raised the average speed to over 37 knots and consequently clipped 2 hours 46 minutes off the *United States'* record of 3 days, 10 hours and 31 minutes. Then, most impressively of all, in 1992 the Italian monohull *Destriero* shattered the record by crossing at 53 knots. The fast ship era had arrived.

Both the *Hoverspeed Great Britain* and the *Destriero* were examples of a new type of ship, the high-speed ferry (Wang and McOwan 2000). In this chapter we explore this important concept, focusing on a series of questions. How has the concept evolved, what have been the dominant innovations driving that evolution, and how are fast ships likely to evolve still further in the foreseeable future? Beyond this, what are their advantages, and how have these assisted operators to exploit not only sources of demand (passengers, cars and freight), but also market opportunities around the world? From these questions it is evident that a main aim of the chapter is to examine and understand success. But, because few innovations are entirely beneficial, the reverse side of the coin is also considered via a further issue. What drawbacks impose limitations that future technological advances must seek to overcome if progress is to be main-tained?

High-speed ferries: the technological milestones

The authoritative specialised review *Fast Ferry International* defines fast ferries as ships capable of transporting at least 50 passengers, or an equivalent combi-nation of passengers and freight, at a minimum cruising speed of 25 knots (46 kph). If we take this definition and ignore transatlantic record breaking, fast ferries can be said to date from the mid-1950s. Since then, four technological milestones mark the growth and diversification of high-speed ferries: the intro-duction of hydrofoils, hovercraft, catamarans and gliding monohulls (Table 8.2).

The first surface-piercing hydrofoil carried 72 passengers at 32 knots (59 kph) and entered service in August 1956 on the route between Reggio Calabria and Messina[1] (Figure 8.1). A year later, in June 1957, the Soviet Union inaugurated the first fluvial hydrofoil service, marking the start of a pro-duction run that would eventually see more than a thousand of these craft built, largely for export.[2] By 1959, Italy's Rodriquez shipyard in Messina, which had built the first PT 20-class hydrofoil for the Reggio Calabria–Messina run, was introducing its more spacious PT 50 variant, with 140 seats. Thereafter, more

Table 8.2 High-speed ferry types: selected examples

Producer	Model	Length (m)	Passengers	Cars	Speed (knots)
Hydrofoils					
Rodriquez	Foilmaster (2000)	31.2	240	0	34
Ordzhonikidze	Kolkhida (1995)	34.5	155	0	34
Boeing	Jetfoil 929-115 (1981)	27.4	316	0	43
Hovercraft					
British Hovercraft	SRN4 Mark 3[a]	56.0	418	60	55
British Hovercraft	AP1 – 88/110 (1990)	24.4	70	0	50
Hovermarine[b]	HM 218 (1985)	18.3	103	0	34
Catamarans					
Finnyards	HSS 1500 (1997)	126.6	1,500	375	40
InCat	Evolution 10b (2002)	97.0	900	267	42
Fjelistrand	Flying Cat 52 (2001)	103.5	427	21	38
Monohulls					
Fincantieri	MDV 3000 (1999)	145.6	1,800	460	40
Austal Ships	Auto Express 86 (2002)	86.6	828	243	37
Alstom Leroux	Corsaire 14000 (2001)	140.0	1,800	442	40

Source: ShipPax (2002).

Notes
a Out of production.
b Sidewall hovercraft.

Figure 8.1 A Freccia del Sole-class hydrofoil, the first in commercial service. (Courtesy of Rodriquez Cantieri.)

or less at the start of every succeeding decade, new construction concepts brought innovations that would increase both the speed and the capacity of the vessels (Blunden 1999).

The 1960s opened with the advent of air cushion vehicles – surface-effect ships or hovercraft[3] – which culminated in the SRN4 Mark 3 hovercraft, built in the United Kingdom by the British Hovercraft Corporation (Figure 8.2). Able to cruise at 55 knots (102 kph) while carrying 418 passengers and 60 cars, this ferry type virtually tripled the passenger capacity, and had nearly twice the speed, of previous models. Operating on the English Channel, SRN4s were able to make the crossing from Dover to Calais in less time than the Eurostar train today.[4] One variant of the hovercraft, the sidewall hovercraft, also appeared at this time, the innovation in this case being that the side 'skirts' were replaced by two solid hulls that were largely raised out of the water as lift pressure rose. Although these sidewall hovercraft never achieved success at the time, they were in many respects the precursors of catamarans, which, as will be shown, now have a substantial share of the fast ferry market. Meanwhile, however, the hydrofoil continued to develop and, indeed, dominate (Figure 8.3). Not least, this reflected a joint venture agreement between Italy's Rodriquez shipyard and two other companies in world regions with major market potential for fast ferries: Hitachi in Japan and Westermoen in Norway. More generally, five countries were building fast ships by the end of the 1960s, and the decade had seen a tenfold increase in production.

Two innovations characterised the early 1970s as understanding of high speed's potential developed. First, catamarans entered the picture in Norway,

Figure 8.2 An SRN4 hovercraft. (Courtesy of the Hovercraft Museum Trust.)

Figure 8.3 The latest generation Foilmaster hydrofoil. (Courtesy of Rodriquez Cantieri.)

with Westermoen's introduction of its Westamaran 86 and 98 models. These asymmetrical catamarans, although slightly slower than hydrofoils, were competitive on Norway's west coast – as well as abroad – because of their higher load capacity. Second, in 1974 Boeing Marine Systems' first Jetfoil appeared on the market. A particular advantage of this new model of hydrofoil was that its completely submerged supporting wings gave excellent seaworthiness, allowing 240 passengers to be carried at 42 knots. Partly through these innovations, but also through continued development of other hydrofoils and hovercraft, during the 1970s the world fleet of fast ferries doubled, while the number of models available increased to seven. Eight countries were now producers, led by Italy as a result of the expertise in hydrofoils established by the Rodriquez company.

Symmetrical catamarans were the chief 1980s innovation, larger than hydrofoils yet just as fast. Originating in Norway, as a development of the asymmetrical catamaran, but within five years their manufacturing focus had shifted to Australia through the initiative of two firms: International Catamarans and Western Australian Lines. Especially important in this technology transfer was the resulting combination of the symmetrical catamaran concept with the companies' existing expertise in lightweight aluminium hull construction. This allowed fast ferries to increase in scale and also to be better adapted to operators' needs, lessons in the use of light alloys that were naturally learned by producers worldwide. Into the early 1990s, catamaran speeds improved, becoming

Figure 8.4 The Incat Evolution 10B wave-piercing catamaran. (Courtesy of InCat Tasmania Pty Ltd.)

comparable with those of hydrofoils, while other technological advances – particularly electronic systems controlling reaction to wave motion – greatly improved their seaworthiness (Figure 8.4).

The 1990s, however, also saw growing competition from a new type of fast ferry: the gliding monohull (Figure 8.5). These retain all the advantages of traditional hulls, but are equipped with advanced stabilisation systems that give them excellent seaworthiness and enable them to operate at high speed even in bad weather (Scarpelli 1996). Demonstrating the capabilities of this vessel type, in 1992 the Italian monohull *Destriero* secured the transatlantic record by making the crossing at an average speed of 53 knots, as mentioned earlier. Two main monohull variants are currently being produced: those specialising in passenger and car transport, and ferries able to accept a wider range of trucks and other freight vehicles. The latter type, a logical development of the traditional freight ro-ro ferry, is arousing growing interest in the freight shipping sector. Currently the largest example is capable of handling up to 1,500 TEU.[5]

Future development trends

The technological trajectory that has been described here – from vessels intended exclusively for passengers into ships with substantial carrying capacity for road vehicles and freight – naturally raises the prospect that high-speed ships will continue to evolve into complete freight carriers, ultimately becoming

Figure 8.5 The Fincantieri Pegasus MDV 3000 monohull. (Courtesy of Fincantieri),
With an overall length of 145.6 m, and powered by two gas turbines or four
diesel engines driving water-jets, the MDV 3000 can carry 1,800 passengers,
460 cars and 30 trucks at a service speed of 40 knots (74 kph). Hull construction is of high-tensile steel. The superstructures of monohulls such as these
commonly employ lighter-weight aluminium alloys, carbon fibre and titanium.

competitive with container ships and multi-purpose vessels on longer routes.
There has been talk for some time of introducing long-distance full-cargo ships.
Proposed areas of operation include the Atlantic, between the United Kingdom
and the United States, and also the Pacific, both within the island archipelagos
(Japan, the Philippines, Indonesia) and between them and mainland countries
such as South Korea and China.

At present, modern container and multi-purpose ships continue to be
competitive on long and medium distances, and it seems unlikely that their load
capacity will be matched by any of the new types of ship in the near future.
Moreover, impediments to progress in this direction are not simply technological. A few marine operators, such as Stena Line,[6] have always been in the
vanguard of replacing conventional ships with fast ones, particularly on reliable
routes where passenger, car and freight flows are distributed more or less uni-
formly throughout the day and year. But such examples are the exceptions, and
there is still widespread scepticism among companies with respect to radical
conversion to high speed. Even so, a new milestone may be on the horizon in
the form of the Philadelphia-based FastShip Atlantic Project. The Kvaerner

Philadelphia Shipyard has signed a memorandum of understanding to build four 1,432-TEU ships capable of 40 knots (74 kph) to operate between Philadelphia and Cherbourg, France. Although financing details for this $1.7 billion project are still under discussion, CP Ships of Canada has already signed an agreement with FastShip to handle sales and customer service, and also take an equity share in the project (FastShip 2003, see also Postscript, page 162).

What is certainly emerging in the freight market is a scenario in which fast vessels complement and support freight flows on the round-the-world routes. How this may work may once again be demonstrated with reference to the Mediterranean. Continued containerisation has made the Mediterranean a sea of global carrier routes, and also the second gateway to a united Europe (Vallega 1998; Ridolfi 1999; Zophil and Prijon 1999). Goods converge on the highly specialised terminal facilities of transhipment ports located either near the sea's entrances (Algeciras, Alexandria, Damietta) or at the centre of the basin (Cagliari, Marsaslokk, Gioia Tauro, Piraeus) from where they require redistribution to their coastal and inland destinations.[7] Transport options for this redistribution clearly include road and the less environmentally damaging use of rail. But, like other semi-enclosed seas, the Mediterranean is also ideally suited to the development of transverse and longitudinal maritime links, not least through the opportunities offered by the Iberian, Italian and Balkan peninsulas projecting southwards into the sea like long wharves (Scorza 1994; Confitarma 1995; CETMO 1995). The combination of this geography and the new-generation fast ferries, now coming into service, opens up the prospect of creating 'superhighways of the sea': routes running parallel to those on land, distributing container traffic swiftly and efficiently, and yet embracing the principles of environmental and social sustainability advocated so strongly by the European Union in response to the Kyoto Protocol (Ridolfi 1999).

Operators, planners and drivers for change

Of the four main types of high-speed ferry discussed, the most numerous – accounting for half the global fleet – are the catamarans, with hydrofoils (25 per cent) ranking second. While hovercraft (less than 8 per cent) have never achieved comparable popularity, the monohull already accounts for 17 per cent of the fleet and is produced in more than a dozen countries[8], despite its recent emergence. As a result of these parallel, and competing, technological developments, there are now more than 1,500 high-speed ferries in operation worldwide. Their total tonnage is almost 900,000 tonnes and their capacity nearly 400,000 passengers and 20,000 vehicles (ShipPax 2002). A further measure of their success is that about 85 per cent of those that have ever been built are still in operation. What has driven this impressive progress?

For operators, a key attraction is that speed can mean major savings on capital investment. In part this is because fewer ships can be required on a given line. Under certain circumstances, in fact, one fast ferry can take the place of two conventional ones. But investment costs – and, indeed, operational costs – are also reduced because there is no sleeping accommodation on board. Speed, of course, reduces the need for this facility, but in any case the Safety for High Speed Ships Code forbids its inclusion. Consequently, load space – for passengers, cars and freight – is maximised, while savings are made because crew costs are reduced. The significance of these factors is readily demonstrated. Even though design and construction costs tend to be high, a fast ferry able to carry 1,000 passengers, and with a cruising speed of 40 knots, has a construction cost of little more than $40 million. This compares with around $100 million for a conventional overnight ferry of the same capacity (G.P. Wild International 1998). Similarly, in day-to-day operations fast ferries make substantial savings in labour inputs, because servicing sleeping accommodation accounts, on average, for a quarter of the total overhead costs of a large conventional ferry. Reduced journey times likewise cut investment and operating costs by eliminating the need for restaurants or entertainment facilities, an economy that also maximises the space available for load.

Fast ferries are also attractive to operators because of their inherent flexibility. This exerts its influence in various ways. First, these ferries' low cost relative to other vessels reduces what would otherwise be a major barrier to market entry. The effect of this emerges clearly from an analysis of ownership structures in the Mediterranean, one of the world's leading arenas for high-speed ferry activity. Although a handful of high-profile companies – Hellas Flying Dolphins, Istanbul Deniz Otobusleri, Aliscafi SNAV and Alilauro Spa – have fleets of up to 40 vessels,[9] they are not typical. Altogether these major companies account for only a third of the fast ferries in service in the Mediterranean and 5 per cent of the operators. In contrast, easy entry has meant that the remaining two-thirds of the fleet is in the hands of no fewer than 86 operators, 60 per cent of which run only one or two vessels (Figure 8.6).

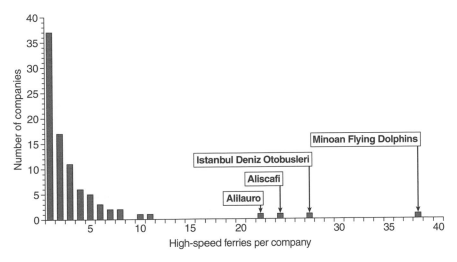

Figure 8.6 Fragmented ownership structures in the Mediterranean's high-speed ferry industry.

Beyond this, the appeal of flexibility is partly that it enables departure schedules to be readily adjusted to demand, with services increased during peak periods and reduced during low seasons. But it is also closely connected with high-speed ferries' suitability for a wide variety of routes. Table 8.3 illustrates this adaptability globally, while Figure 8.7 again focuses on the Mediterranean. Here, significant networks, performing rather different functions, are well developed at a wide variety of scales. Locally, for example, high-speed ferries promote integration and offer alternative transport opportunities for commuters and tourists around the Bay of Naples and along the Amalfi peninsula. Regional isolation is reduced by networks such as that linking the Balearics with the mainland cities of Barcelona and Valencia. In some cases this regional integration has an international dimension, as illustrated by Corsica's links with Italy as well as France. And, at the top of the scale hierarchy, international contact and exchange are promoted by networks such as those radiating from Marseilles to North Africa, and from Venice to Greece and Turkey.

The planning context: transport, integration and the environment

Outside the fast ferry industry, the integrative nature of fast ferries is relevant to quite different interest groups: local, regional and national planners with

Table 8.3 High-speed ferry route characteristics: a global overview

Europe	
Western Europe	Domestic and international services between the British islands, the French coast and the coasts of North and Baltic Sea countries
Southern Europe and the Mediterranean	Coastal services providing connections to and within the Atlantic and Mediterranean archipelagos; interconnection of European, African and Asian shores
Eastern Europe	Fluvial and marine services, domestic and international, between countries along the Danube and the Black Sea
East Asia	
Regional seas of the Pacific and Indian Oceans	Coastal services and connections among the Japanese islands; fluvial and coastal services in China, including connections with Hong Kong, Macao and the Chinese mainland; domestic and international services of South Korea, Singapore, Malaysia, Indonesia, etc.
Australia and New Zealand	Tourist services to the Great Barrier Reef and coastal islands
Rest of the world	
The Americas	Domestic and international services, lacustrine and marine, involving the USA, Canada, Mexico and Central American countries, including the Caribbean islands; coastal and fluvial services in South America
Middle East and Africa	Domestic services for the countries of the Persian Gulf and the Red Sea; fluvial services along the Nile; coastal services in South Africa

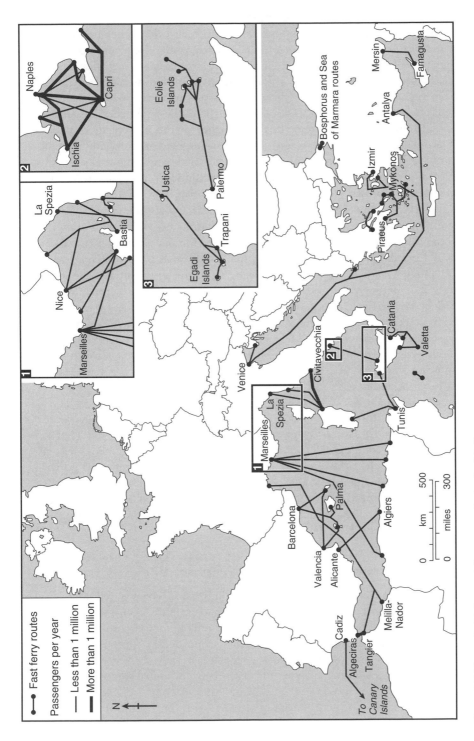

Figure 8.7 The main high-speed ferry networks in the Mediterranean.

responsibilities ranging from local transport to regional development. Increasingly, however, these and similar stakeholders perceive that other benefits can accrue from policies that encourage high-speed ferry development. To a great extent these benefits relate to the environment. Increasing congestion on the roads causes delays and generates pollution in many industrialised countries. This is true in Japan and China, where the railroads are overloaded to the point of collapse, and in the European Union, where the integration process is leading to an enormous increase in the demand for the movement of people and goods. Against this background, there is widespread and growing recognition of the attractions of movement by sea rather than land. Above all, Western and Mediterranean Europe have excellent opportunities to transfer cargo to the sea, since they possess 38,000 km of coastline served by 2,000 ports. Here – and, indeed, in many other maritime regions – the space/time factor is able to create new variable geometries in the transportation networks, with attractive economies of scale and extraordinary advantages for the circulation of passengers and goods (Spiekermann and Wegener 1994; Scorza 1999; Pérez Ramos 2000). In Italy, for example, travel time between the mainland and the major islands, and between the northern and southern regions, has halved since the arrival of fast ferries. Now goods and passengers can travel by sea almost as quickly as they can on the motorways, and certainly in greater comfort and safety (European Union 1997; Ministero dei Trasporti 2000).

Perhaps less obviously, but certainly significantly at the local scale, policies supporting the rapid and tumultuous development of high-speed navigation have brought additional social benefits by revitalising a part of the shipbuilding industry that was suffering a serious lack of orders for conventional ships. Today there are nearly 200 shipyards, in 32 countries, that have the technology for fast ferry construction. Moreover, given a global order book that has recently exceeded 100 additional vessels, prospects are encouraging. For reasons touched upon earlier, the implications of this for the localities affected go well beyond the simple number of jobs created. The increasing technological sophistication of high-speed ferries – affecting aspects of design and construction ranging from their hulls through to electronic control equipment – brings to localities work that is both high value and skilled.

Beyond 2000: towards the globalisation of speed?

Propelled by these advantages, the uptake of high-speed ferries is well on its way to becoming a global phenomenon. Major markets have been established in Japan and other archipelagos of the Asia-Pacific region; in Southern Europe and the Mediterranean; in Northern and Eastern Europe; and in North America and the Caribbean (Figure 8.8). Moreover, recent fast ferry deliveries have reinforced both the established markets and the process of global spread. Half have been brought into service on European routes, evenly divided between Mediterranean and Northern European services, with three-fifths of the remainder being sold to Asian operators and two-fifths to North American companies.

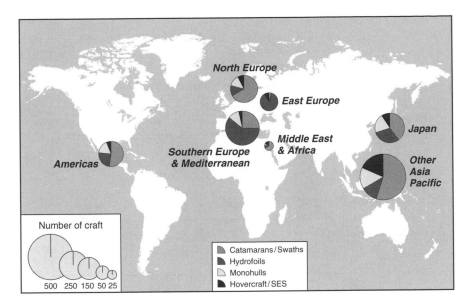

Figure 8.8 Introduction of high-speed ferries worldwide.

Increasingly, therefore, it is arguable that a *globalisation of speed* is taking root. As the following discussion demonstrates, however, for several reasons this concept requires qualification.

First, as Figure 8.8 reveals, the uptake of high-speed ferries is not yet truly global. Large parts of the developing world currently remain untouched by them, often reflecting a combination of factors: initial investment cost, limited demand, obstacles to effective maintenance and, not least, a relative shortage of appropriate waters – particularly semi-enclosed seas.

Second, in those parts of the world where high-speed ferries have been introduced widely, the innovation diffusion process has been more complex than may appear at first sight. Figure 8.8 suggests that global variations in the popularity of the various types of fast ferry amount to little more than a small number of contrasts between major regional markets. In particular, the hydrofoil continues to dominate the cradles of its development – the Mediterranean, the Black Sea and the East European rivers. Outside the Mediterranean and Eastern Europe, the more recent catamaran concept normally accounts for between half and two-thirds of all fast ferries in service. More detailed examination of the data, however, reveal that analysis at this broad scale overlooks substantial intra-regional preferences.

For Asia and the Mediterranean, the two dominant world regions, these contrasts are highlighted by Figures 8.9 and 8.10 respectively. In both cases the methodology has been to calculate, for the region as a whole, the percentage importance of the four different ferry types. This 'profile' has then been deducted from the equivalent profiles of individual countries to identify positive and negative deviations from the regional norm.

For Asia (Figure 8.9), it is immediately apparent that the diffusion of all four ferry types has been very uneven. Hovercraft are strongly concentrated in China and South Korea. Hydrofoils have penetrated poorly in markets such as the Philippines and Singapore, but are a main feature of the Japanese ferry system.

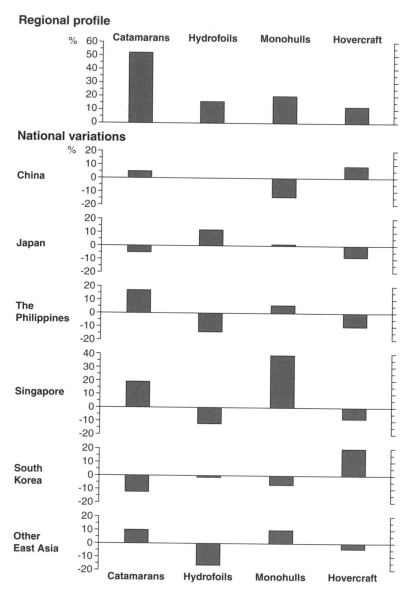

Figure 8.9 Asia: uptake of high-speed ferry types and national deviations from the regional pattern.

Catamarans are especially prominent in the Philippines and the smaller East Asian markets. And monohulls, an usually strong feature of the Singaporean fleet, are virtually absent in China.

Meanwhile in the Mediterranean, uneven uptake between national markets is less characteristic because of the widespread lack of interest in hovercraft, and the relatively uniform advance of monohulls (Figure 8.10). Even so, monohulls'

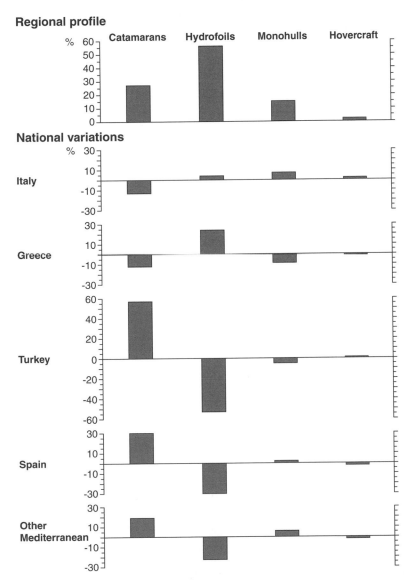

Figure 8.10 The Mediterranean: uptake of high-speed ferry types and national deviations from the regional pattern.

limited progress in Greece is evident. So, too, are strong international contrasts in the adoption of catamarans and hydrofoils. The latter account for 56 per cent of all high-speed ferries operating in the Mediterranean, but almost three-quarters are concentrated in Italy and Greece where – particularly in the latter country – they generate positive deviations from the regional norm. And while the mirror image of this dominance is a relatively limited role for catamarans in the large Greek and Italian markets, this ferry type is the clear leader in Turkey, Spain and a range of other Mediterranean countries.

These results highlight an important research opportunity. Various factors may have contributed to the striking contrasts in market penetration identified above. Possibilities include the stranglehold of hydrofoils in their areas of origin, differential operating costs, the routes and sea conditions to be navigated, the investment costs of latest-generation monohulls, and opportunities for catamaran manufacturers to target markets not already dominated by another type of high-speed ferry. What is extremely unclear, however, is the degree to which these or other factors have acted, individually or in combination, to differentiate the national markets in the ways observed. Investigations into decision making at the operational level are necessary to elucidate this issue.

High-speed ferries: drawbacks and challenges

A further reason to treat the globalisation of speed concept with caution is that – despite the popularity of these new transport media, and despite the advantages discussed earlier – fast ferries have limitations and impose demands. While the former relate to the ferries themselves, the latter set challenges for port systems.

Given the operating standards of the newer vessels, a travel time of one to three hours – or 30–100 nautical miles (55–190 km) – appears to be the economic optimum.[10] Shorter trips reduce the advantage of high speed, making navigation time proportionately too brief relative to total journey time. Journeys in excess of four to five hours, on the other hand, would necessitate equipping the vessel with passenger services – restaurants, entertainment and sleeping facilities – that, as we have seen, would undermine both the constructional and operational economics (Baird 1998). This consideration naturally raises issues in relation to operations away from locations such as semi-enclosed seas, major rivers and inland lakes.

Also relevant is a widespread view that the acceptable premium that fast ferry users are prepared to pay relative to conventional ferries or overland charges is only 10–15 per cent (Lennox 1999). This relates to the point that although fast ferries are cheaper to construct than conventional ones, their speed is rather expensive. As Reynolds notes in Chapter 12, ships' fuel consumption increases rapidly with speed, and consequently fuel costs can be high. There are also cost questions relating to maintenance and life expectancy. For example, because these ferries are generally made with lightweight materials (usually aluminium alloys), they are more susceptible to damage in both low-speed collisions and high-speed debris strike incidents. Aluminium also suffers from corrosion. Operating costs may, therefore, be increased by the need for more frequent repairs, although modern construction techniques – based on high-tensile steel hulls coupled with aluminium, carbon fibre and titanium superstructures – ameliorate this problem.

A further operational limitation is that small- and medium-sized fast ferries, especially, are sensitive to wind and sea conditions. In practice it is often not possible to use these vessels in all weathers and throughout the year, particularly on the more exposed routes such as the North Sea or Norwegian Sea. In parts of the world, therefore, fast ferries are operated only on a seasonal basis to allow for adverse weather conditions. One response to this is that some large ferries even change hemisphere – for example, from the Cook Strait and the Rio de la Plata to the North Sea and the Baltic Sea – in order to maintain the return on investment (G.P. Wild International 1998). This weather dependency has marketing implications, not only for prospective passengers but also for freight. Recently, the movement of commerce towards 'zero stocks' and the 'just-in-time' principle has prioritised to a degree the speed of transport, but has demanded above all its reliability and regularity (Marchese 1993). Where fast ferry services are likely to be weather dependent, therefore, it is highly desirable that there is a safety net, allowing traffic to be diverted on to conventional ferries if the need arises.

Despite the environmental advantages identified earlier, there are also negative impacts. These concern both the marine zone and, especially when the shipping routes are close inshore, the adjacent coasts. High-speed ships raise bow waves, causing strong currents in the water. This wave motion is accentuated in shallow waters, creating discomfort and, at worst, hazards for those pursuing recreational activities such as boating, swimming or scuba diving. Fast ferries are noisy, generating acoustic pollution that disturbs both animal life and humans seeking to enjoy the quiet of the coast. They also emit large volumes of exhaust gases, a problem exacerbated by the increase in fuel consumption associated with high speed.

In the past, little attention was paid to these issues, and the presence of fast ferries was generally accepted. However, following the expansion of services, employing larger vessels in increasing numbers, environmentalists began to react strongly and to promote campaigns hostile to high-speed navigation. The motivation for this can be readily demonstrated by reference to designs produced by the InCat shipyard. In 1990 the standard capacity of its 74-m catamaran was 450 passengers and 84 motor vehicles. The current model, with a length of 96 m, can carry 900 passengers and 260 cars, or 40 cars plus 24 trucks and buses. The next model will measure 120 m and will be able to carry 1,200 passengers plus 460 cars at a cruising speed of 51 knots (94 kph).

The problem of environmental impact is one that is particularly serious in Scandinavian countries, because of the intensity of navigation and the frequency of high-speed ferry services along the coasts, between the islands and along the fjords.[11] It is, therefore, no accident that the Danish Naval Authority has investigated the issues in detail, identifying the extent of the environmental damage produced by high speed at sea, and suggesting rules to limit noise, atmospheric pollution and wake damage (Bennett 2000).[12] Environmental opposition and the threat of regulation have stimulated engineers to seek solutions through design changes to hulls and engines, but without much success. Consequently, the environmental problem is one of the major obstacles to the spread of fast ferries, not only in the Scandinavian countries but also in the United States.

The challenges for ports, meanwhile, are of an exclusively logistical nature stemming from the principle that a ship should navigate as much as possible and spend as little time as possible in port. To enable operators to optimise the productivity of new generations of ferries in this way, ports must increasingly adapt their reception facilities to the scale of the traffic flow and the needs of the passengers. When the first generation of fast ferries was introduced, and passenger throughput was limited to a few dozen or a few hundred people a day, this pressure for change hardly ever arose, or could be resolved easily. But second-generation ferries have much greater capacity for passengers, cars and trucks. For example, the largest in service – the French Corsaire 14000 and the Italian MDV 3000 – can carry 1,800 passengers. Consequently, the situation has changed greatly. These ships require major structural and infrastructural adaptation at their docking points to enable them to handle all the necessary operations efficiently and rapidly. Main ports must therefore develop efficient terminals capable of embarking and debarking intense flows of passengers and vehicles in the most dynamic way possible (Marchese 1993) in order to improve the entire production cycle of transportation and minimise the vessel's time in port. In practice this means that when ports must handle several thousand passengers a day, maritime stations similar to airports are needed to provide seamless interconnectivity between ships and the inland transport network. These infrastructural requirements naturally have far-reaching implications for port authorities as well as operators. Time gained at sea, at high cost, must not be lost in port, but how far this is achieved is critically dependent on the investment response.

Conclusion

This study has demonstrated the impressive technological advances that have underpinned the transformation of the high-speed ferry from an aspirational concept to a widely applied transport medium. In the process it has also shown that progress has not come about simply through the progressive improvement of a single innovation. On the contrary, the problem of achieving high-speed travel at sea has generated a sequence of alternative solutions – the hydrofoil, the hovercraft, the catamaran and the monohull – designed to overcome the limitations of other innovations and enable craft to meet challenging operating conditions as effectively as possible. The importance of this process of progress through alternative solutions is that it has created a competitive environment, which itself stimulates further innovation through positive feedback. Not all the solutions have thrived in the face of this competition – hovercraft, in particular, have not proved popular. But the rivalry of catamarans and hydrofoils has been very productive, and monohulls are now providing an additional stimulus for manufacturers to strive for the cutting edge.

A quite different outcome of the study has been identification of the need for improved insights into innovation dispersal. In this context, the key finding is that understanding of the factors controlling uptake at the global level requires investigation at the local level. When data are aggregated at the broad regional scale they mask substantial intra-regional contrasts in the adoption of different types of high-speed ferry. When these contrasts are exposed through finer analysis, the need for research into corporate decision-making swiftly becomes apparent.

The investigation has also highlighted the way in which technological change can be harnessed to target a broader market than that originally identified, and in the process increase significantly the potential earnings on investment. As Table 8.2 (p. 145) summarises, from an early narrow focus on high-speed passenger travel, the sector has moved on to exploit wider needs, first via the development of car-carrying capacity, and more recently through progression to freight carriage.

Looking to the future, it may be anticipated that continued technological advances will maintain the momentum of high-speed ferry transport. Although the discussion has acknowledged these ferries' limitations, those limitations can be seen as an 'envelope' whose bounds will undoubtedly be moved outwards by research and development – in precisely the same way that the technical frontiers have been pushed back during the past 30 years. Still faster ferries, with greater capacity, may well be realistic, while the widespread appearance of fast ships dedicated to freight is a not-too-distant prospect. In the short term this step would probably complement the great maritime innovation of the late twentieth century – container shipping – by providing fast distributor services. But in the longer term it is quite possible that further technological progress will also bring direct competition between fast ships and 'traditional' container traffic. Within perhaps 20 years, the technological interface between these ferries and containerisation may be benign and supportive on the one hand, yet cut-throat on the other.

While the extension of the limiting envelope in these ways seems likely, it is less clear that equivalent progress will be made with other limitations. Of overriding concern in this connection are the environmental impacts of fast ferries. Technological change has already exacerbated these as designers have striven simultaneously for speed and scale economies. If technological breakthroughs continue to be most successful on the economic front, existing environmental problems are likely to be intensified, and indeed compounded, by new issues such as serious noise pollution of the ocean. From a societal standpoint, squaring the circle to achieve both economic goals and environmental improvements could well be the greatest challenge facing this mode of maritime transport.

Postscript

FastShip now plans a 2008 start; three 1100-TEU vessels; loading and unloading within 6 hours; and 7-day door-to-door delivery time (US–Europe and *v.v.*). Delaware Port Authority will invest $75m in the highly specialised terminal, and the US government $40m (possibly to encourage a strategic rapid military-supply capability).

Notes

1 This first hydrofoil (built by the Rodriquez shipyard in Messina, on licence from the Swiss company Supramar) ran on the Reggio Calabria–Messina route for approximately 30 years. The idea for a ferry of this kind was not really new. At the beginning of the twentieth century the aeronautical engineer Forlanini had constructed and tested, on Lake Garda, a craft equipped with supporting wings. The inventor Alexander Graham Bell had done the same in the United States, and in 1910 had established a world water speed record of 70 knots (130 kph) with his HD-4 prototype (Grosvenor 1957). The interest in winged vessels reawakened in the Second World War in Nazi Germany, and shortly after the war several engineers who had worked on the German project joined Baron von Schertel's Supramar company in Switzerland. Their first model, the PT10, went into service on Lake Maggiore in 1952 as a passenger ferry between Switzerland and Italy. Two years later, the Rodriquez shipyard purchased the construction licence for the new craft. This initiated a long series of variants built in Messina (Baird 1998).
2 Three models were built: the Raketa, the Meteor and the Kometa.
3 The term 'hovercraft' includes a variant, the sidewall hovercraft. Never a major success, this was in many ways a hybrid of the hovercraft and the catamaran.
4 The original SRN4s carried 254 passengers and 30 vehicles. Even these early models consequently had almost double the capacity of previous models. Their speed, 65 knots (120 kph), was actually slightly higher than that of the later, and larger, SRN4 Mark 3. SRN4s remained in cross-Channel service until September 2000.
5 Twenty-foot equivalent units – the standard unit of measurement for container ships.
6 The Stena fleet comprises large catamarans, including the Finnish HSS 1500, which can carry up to 1,500 passengers and 375 vehicles (cars or trailers) at 40 knots (74 kph). The company operates on routes between the United Kingdom, Ireland and the Netherlands (ShipPax 2002).
7 One consequence of this scenario is that it allows for the recovery and further development of ports that previously were unable to capitalise on the container revolution. In Italy the list includes ports in the south of the peninsula, and on the major islands, such as Cagliari, Palermo, Gioia Tauro and Taranto (Ridolfi 1996).
8 Australia, Japan, Norway and Italy are particularly important for monohull construction.
9 The precise fleet sizes in 2002 were: Hellas Flying Dolphins 37, Istanbul Deniz Otobusleri 28, Aliscafi Spa 24 and Alilauro SNAV 36 (ShipPax 2002).
10 While this is the general rule, there are cases – as in the European and Asiatic Mediterranean – of crossings that are necessarily somewhat longer.
11 The problem is not as serious, or not as strongly perceived, in the Mediterranean. Here routes can normally run further from the coasts, so that the noise and wake factors arise only as ferries approach entrance channels and ports. At these points, speeds – and therefore environmental impacts – are necessarily reduced to meet navigational safety standards imposed by port authority controls.
12 The Danish study identified no hazardous effects on marine fauna and flora, and consequently went no further than setting general criteria for safeguarding them.

References

Baird, J. (1998) *The World Fast Ferry Market*, Melbourne: Baird Publication.

Bennett, J. (2000) 'Environmental issues and fast ferries in Denmark', *Cruise and Ferry Info*, 3: 11–13.

Blunden, A. (1999) 'Fast ferries: forty years of developing technology', *Fast Ferry International Executive Briefing*, Boston (typed).

CETMO (1995) *Les Opportunités du cabotage maritime en Méditerranée Occidentale par rapport aux nouvelles pratiques logistiques: document synthèse*, Centre d'Études des Transports pour la Méditerranée Occidentale.

Confitarma (1995) *Libro verde sui servizi di cabotaggio di linea*, Rome: Confitarma.

European Union (1997) *Green Paper on Seaports and Maritime Infrastructure*, Brussels, COM (97) 678, final.

FastShip (2003) [untitled], available at www.fastshipatlantic.com/http (accessed 14 August 2003).

G.P. Wild (International) Ltd (1998) *Tourism and the Future Role of Ferries and Fast Ferries*, Haywards Heath, UK: G.P. Wild (International) Ltd.

Grosvenor, G. (1957) 'Hydrofoil ferry "flies" the Strait of Messina', *National Geographic Magazine*, April, pp. 493–496.

Lennox, R. (1999) 'Market for fast freight by sea', *The Dock and Harbour Authority*, 80 (May/June): 20–22.

Marchese, U. (1993) 'Innovazioni, alte velocità, trasporti marittimi', *II Symposium on High Speed Marine Vehicles*, Naples, 25–26 March, pp. 15–32.

Ministero dei Trasporti e della Navigazione (2000) *Piano Generale dei Trasporti e della Logistica*, Rome: Ministero dei Trasporti e della Navigazione.

Pérez Ramos, D. (2000) 'La alta velocidad marítima en el contexto del transporte interinsular canario', *Actas de las IV Jornadas de Estudios Portuarios y Marítimos*, Universidad de Las Palmas de Gran Canaria (conference paper).

Ridolfi, G. (1996) 'The Italian ports and the wind of change', *Tijdschrift voor Economische en Sociale Geografie*, IGU Special Issue, 87: 348–356.

—— (1999) 'Containerisation in the Mediterranean: between global ocean routways and feeder services', *GeoJournal*, 48, 29–34.

Scarpelli, P. (1996) 'Fast ferries and their application in the Mediterranean', *Seatrade Mediterranean Cruise and Ferry Convention*, Genoa, 17–20 September (conference paper).

ShipPax Information (2002) *HiSpeed 02: Annual Register of Fast Ferries in the World*, Halmstad, Sweden: ShipPax Information.

Scorza, A. (1994) 'Scenari di sviluppo dei porti mediterranei: l'opzione del transhipment', *Studi Marittimi*, 46(17): 57–62.

—— (1999) 'EU – a divided market', *Cruise and Ferry Info*, 11: 12–18.

Spiekermann, K. and Wegener, M. (1994) 'The shrinking continent: new time–space maps of Europe', *Environment and Planning: Planning and Design*, 21: 653–673.

Vallega, A. (1998) 'Pacifico chiama Mediterraneo: un futuro per i nostri porti', *Limes*, 1: 75–88.

Wang, J. and McOwan, S. (2000) 'Fast passenger ferries and their future', *Maritime Policy and Management*, 27: 231–251.

Zophil, J. and Prijon, M. (1999) 'The MED rule: the interdependence of container throughput and transhipment volumes in Mediterranean ports', *Maritime Policy and Management*, 26: 175–193.

9 Energy from the deep
Vessels, technologies and issues

David Pinder

Introduction: towards broader technological perspectives

Studies of the relationship between technological change and advances in shipping have, for several decades, focused chiefly on the impact of containerisation and associated progress with multimodality (OECD 1971; Cooper 1974; Hayuth 1981, 1987; Brookfield 1984; McKenzie *et al.* 1989). Moreover, papers such as those by Cullinane and Khanna (2000), Gilman (1999) and Zophil and Prijon (1999) underline the fact that containerisation's influence on the development of both shipping and ports remains a major research theme. The same is true of the contributions by Slack, McCalla, and Comtois and Rimmer earlier in this volume. The argument underpinning this chapter is that, although the case for the continued investigation of containerisation is strong, there is a danger of undervaluing wider perspectives because technological change has also advanced impressively, and is continuing to advance, in other branches of the shipping sector. Moreover, in some instances the significance of these advances for global societies, and in particular for how they are able to function, is of similar magnitude to that of containerisation.

This contention is explored in the context of energy-sector shipping. Since the oil crises ushered in the post-Fordist era, reducing the pressure for ever-larger supertankers,[1] the importance of researching technological change in this sector has been largely eclipsed.[2] Yet parts of the energy sector are currently witnessing remarkable technological advances, especially in connection with offshore oil and gas (Ghisel 1997; Hayward 1999; Pinder 2001). Moreover, it is becoming obvious that these advances will grow in importance, because pressure is steadily mounting on the industry to operate in increasingly challenging environments in order to secure future supplies. While this is of intrinsic interest for students of technological change, its overriding significance is that the capacity to operate far offshore may become fundamental for both the maintenance of western lifestyles and the energy-demanding development aspirations of many Third World countries.

The nature and importance of today's unsung wave of technological change in energy-sector shipping could be exemplified in relation to a wide range of vessels serving the offshore oil and gas industry. The spectrum extends from high-technology seismic survey ships, through drilling and production facilities, heavy-lift barges and pipelayers to support ships. To demonstrate the principles, two vessel types have been selected for particular attention: drillships and floating production, storage and offloading systems (FPSOs). These have been chosen because, although the FPSO concept might at first sight seem somewhat established and unremarkable, both types of ship in fact illustrate extremely well the importance of technologies in assisting the offshore oil and gas industry to venture successfully into extreme conditions.

While various definitions of extreme conditions could be adopted, the focus selected is the deepwater challenge – operations in water depths of at least 300 m and generally between 500 m and 2,000 m or more[3]. Because the global drillship and FPSO fleets are relatively large and diverse, the chapter does not dwell on their details. Instead, the approach taken has been to highlight the conceptual rationale for these types of vessel, together with key aspects of the fleets' characteristics, ownership and operation. For both drillships and FPSOs, this exploration culminates in the definition of descriptive models summarising the technological essence of advanced deepwater vessels. In the case of drillships this has allowed the analysis to concentrate solely on ships designed for deepwater use. For FPSOs, in contrast, examination of shallow- and deepwater ships has been necessary in order to underline the unique features of the deepwater variants.[4] This modelling approach does not simply assist in sharpening our image of what are shown to be two highly complex sets of ships. It also allows the investigation to test the extent to which there exists a common set of driving forces influencing the development of these two quite different types of vessel. Before we embark on the analysis, however, a brief review of the gathering pace of offshore oil and gas development, and of the key physical challenges to be met, provides essential background.

The push for offshore resources

Despite early offshore excursions in the Venezuelan Gulf of Maracaibo, the mid-Arabian Gulf and the southern Caspian Sea (Odell 1997, 1998), the first major offshore developments focused on the Gulf of Mexico. Here, stimulated by an oil import embargo imposed by the US government from 1959 to 1971, the industry turned to Texas and Louisiana waters. Interest in the North Sea soon followed and was given a powerful impetus by the 1973–4 oil crisis. From these dominant cradles on the US and European continental shelves, the industry has moved on to become global (Figure 9.1). Midway through the first decade of the twenty-first century, North American and European waters are expected to account for less than a third of the world's proven offshore reserves; the Middle East for rather more than North America and Europe combined; Africa (chiefly West Africa) for 13 per cent; Latin America – mainly Venezuela, Brazil and Mexico – for another 13 per cent; and Asia and Australasia for around 17 per cent (Maksoud 2003).

The absolute scale of these known resources should not be exaggerated.

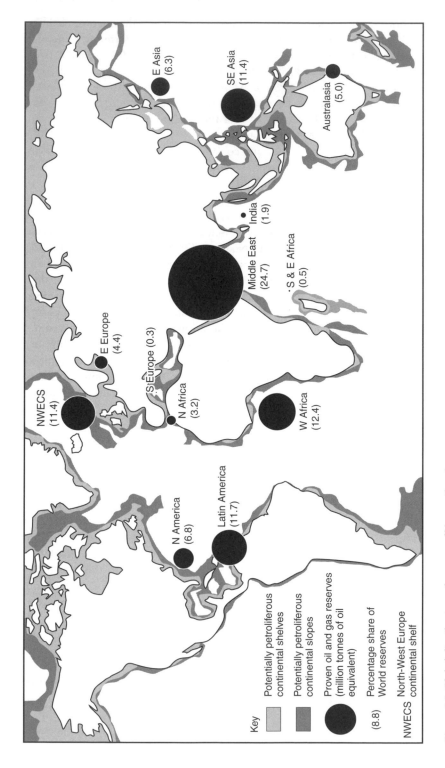

Figure 9.1 Global distribution of proven offshore oil and gas reserves.

Although offshore oil and gas reserves exceeding 14 billion tonnes of oil equivalent (btoe) have now been declared, knowledge of onshore deposits is so well developed that offshore reserves are only about 5 per cent of total known oil and gas resources. However, the utilisation picture is strikingly different. Offshore oil output now satisfies more than a third of total world consumption; for natural gas the figure is around a quarter; and both these proportions will rise as exploration and development continue.

Many of the known offshore fields are in what are now considered relatively shallow regions. Taking 300 m of water as the division between shallow and deep water, the industry journal *Offshore* currently estimates that 80 per cent of oil and gas reserves are shallow-water deposits. Even so, as the most recent *World Deepwater Report* highlights, the attractions of moving into deeper waters are very clear (Douglas-Westwood and Infield Systems 2003). Of central importance is the fact that, while the correlation is far from perfect, the average size of discoveries tends to increase markedly at greater depths (Figure 9.2a). Between 2003 and 2007 the average size of fields found in less than 750 m of water is likely to range between 12 and 20 million tonnes of oil equivalent (mtoe). But beyond the 750 m line the average is expected to be at least 27 mtoe, and between 1,000 and 1,500 m it could be as high as 40 mtoe. Linked with this scale advantage is the attraction of productivity: large fields are more likely to maintain their internal pressure than smaller ones, and consequently will probably achieve higher daily output figures (Figure 9.2b). Thus, average flows from fields in 750–1,000 m of water are likely to be double those for fields in depths of 300 m or less. With more than 1,000 m of water the average is likely to be three times the < 300 m figure (Harbinson and Knight 2003).

In turn, this potential productivity is rapidly feeding through into corporate strategy. Major companies command the large-scale financial resources needed to be able to advance outwards on the depth frontier. Consequently, by 2007 most oil majors are expected to have expanded very substantially their deep-water reserves (Figure 9.2c). Shell, for example, may well nearly triple its known deepwater holdings; for BP the figure is likely to quadruple; and for Exxon-Mobil there may be a five- or sixfold increase. But these gains can be achieved only if appropriate technologies are available, because they require activity to extend out into depths 2,500 m or more. As Pinder (2001) has demonstrated, the technologies in question are numerous, constantly advancing and often interrelated. Within them are nested those maintaining drillships and FPSOs at the leading edge.

Deepwater drillships: concept, practice and models

Drilling on the continental shelves demands the ability both to operate in water and to relocate between sites. Originally these requirements were met by relatively simple 'jack-up' rigs. These comprised a working platform equipped with a drilling rig, which floated during transportation but was then jacked up out of the water in the operational location as legs were lowered and made contact

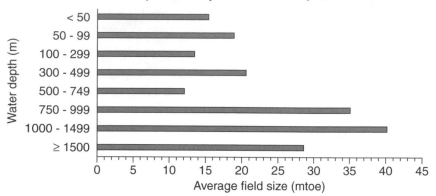

(a) Predicted relationship: water depth and field size, 2003 - 2007

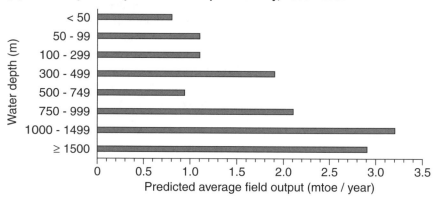

(b) Water depth and predicted field productivity, 2003 - 2007

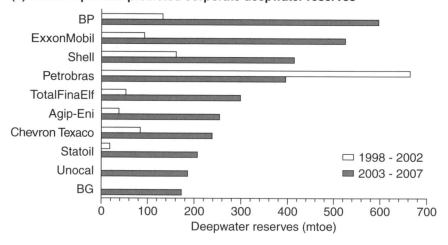

(c) Water depth and predicted corporate deepwater reserves

Figure 9.2 Water depth: relationships with oilfield size, output and ownership.

with the seabed. This solution remains popular in shallow-water conditions, but jack-ups are subject to severe depth limitations,[5] and the push much deeper off-shore has demanded alternative technological approaches.

Numerically the most popular outcome has been the development of semi-submersible rigs: currently these account for around two-thirds of all drilling units with a depth capability exceeding 1,100 m. They have a variety of configurations, but their common principle is that a working platform is mounted on pontoons which can be lowered below, or raised to, the surface by taking in, or pumping out, seawater ballast. Flooding the pontoons leaves only the platform above sea level (hence the term 'semi-submersible'), assisting stability even in severe sea conditions. Semi-submersibles, however, are not true vessels. They do not have traditional hulls and must be towed, at a price, from one location to the next.[6]

These characteristics are central to an understanding of why drillships have emerged to account for the remaining third of the drilling fleet able to operate in more than 1,100 m of water. Drillships are specialised surface vessels whose hulls incorporate open operational wells ('moonpools') through which drilling takes place (Figure 9.3). Although the slowest is capable of only 6 knots (11 kph) under its own power, this is far from typical: the average and modal maximum speeds for the world fleet are 11.6 and 12 knots (21.5 and 22.2 kph) respectively. The capacity for rapid redeployment is consequently a key feature of drillships, which in turn feeds through to high productivity and return on capital invested. This offers an advantage over semi-submersibles – with their substantial towing charges – because typical new-build costs for both types of drilling platform are currently approaching $250 million. Rapid redeployment, it should be noted, is important not simply because it allows work to begin as soon as possible on the next new well to be drilled. Existing wells can also require substantial maintenance, or 'intervention', drilling to maintain flows. Drillships' high mobility, which maximises active drilling time, can clearly be significant for ensuring the efficiency of intervention drilling schedules – with all that this implies for the optimisation of product flows, and thus earnings from reservoirs.

Rapid deployment is also significant in relation to ownership structures. Although oil corporations have been the drivers for expansion and modernisation, they do not own the drillships. Instead, all except one are owned and operated by specialist drilling firms working under contract to the oil companies.[7] For the oil companies, this contracting arrangement has all the advantages of outsourcing. Attention can focus on the core activity of maximising profit from oil extraction, refining and marketing. Financial risk associated with unforeseen drilling delays can be externalised, as can the cost of capital equipment standing idle during the industry's quite frequent downturns in drilling activity. And during these downturns, drilling can usually be contracted at attractively low prices as a result of slack demand. For the drilling companies, these factors emphasise above all the importance of achieving high levels of drillship utilisation, and underline particularly the value of mobility and rapid movement on to station.

Figure 9.3 The drillship *Discover Enterprise*. Constructed in 1999 for Transocean Inc. of Houston, the *Discover Enterprise* is based in the Gulf of Mexico. It is rated to operate in 3,000 m of water, is equipped for 2,400 m and can drill wells up to 10,600 m deep. The overall length is 253 m, with quarters capacity of 130 and a sailing speed of 12 knots. (Photo courtesy of Transocean Inc.)

Drillships' second advantage lies in their maximum depth capability. Since 1995 the design standard for maximum operational water depth has been at least 3,000 m, with a growing number of vessels rated for 3,600 m. This is nearly 20 per cent greater than for the comparable cohort of semi-submersibles. Although in practice most recent drillships are not yet equipped to operate at such depths, but are instead working up to 2,500 m, by a large margin these are the platforms with the greatest potential to carry the industry forward on the extreme deepwater frontier.

An important additional feature of all drillships is their ability, first, to position themselves accurately over the drilling site and, second, to maintain position throughout the drilling operation. Traditionally these problems have been solved through the use of cable moorings, which in their day were technological achievements in their own right. However, the cost and technical challenges of adapting established mooring technologies to increasingly deep conditions have led to the search for alternative solutions. So, too, has the fact that picking up, and casting off, these moorings is a time-consuming process working against rapid redeployment. As drillships have become more advanced, and consequently costly, this time penalty has increased in significance. The alternative solution now universally adopted is to integrate a cluster of technological advances to create dynamic positioning systems (DPS). Various designs are in use,[8] but the principles are constant. The vessel's actual location is sensed continuously, using either precisely positioned seabed transponders or global positioning systems (GPS). On-board computing systems relate its actual position to the planned position, and also control thrusters that automatically bring, and hold, the vessel on station. As might be imagined, this technological breakthrough is also being applied to semi-submersibles. However, whereas all drillships have the advantage of DPS, as yet only about half the semi-submersible fleet is similarly equipped.

While the benefits of DPS are evident in terms of reduced operational costs and increased productivity during normal operations, their linkage with drillships also has other attractions. These relate primarily to weather conditions. Unhampered by moorings, vessels can easily be rotated to minimise the effects of severe sea states. Moreover, with computer control of the thrusters, a vessel's attitude to the sea can be monitored and adjusted continuously. In addition, when very severe weather is forecast, drillships can if necessary move off-station to weather the storm, repositioning themselves rapidly afterwards.[9]

From fleet development to conceptual models

Twenty-seven drillships were operating worldwide in 2002, a number likely to exceed 30 with the completion of orders. The oldest in commission, the *Deepwater Navigator*, was delivered in 1971. Eleven others followed between 1973 and 1982, but the uncertainty caused by the second oil crisis (1979–80) then led to a hiatus (Figure 9.4). This ended as recently as 1995 with the delivery of the *Deepwater Expedition*. Rather more than half the fleet has been launched since then, an impressive burst of construction that has coincided with the offshore industry's rapidly reviving interest in the deepwater frontier. This trend has been so strong that it has also resulted in the large-scale refurbishment of older vessels. Since 1997 all but one of the drillships built before 1983 has been upgraded, so that the fleet as a whole is now either new or modernised, even though the oldest vessel was built over 30 years ago.

Industry reports frequently imply that, rather than viewing deepwater drillships as a homogeneous group, a distinction should be made between new and

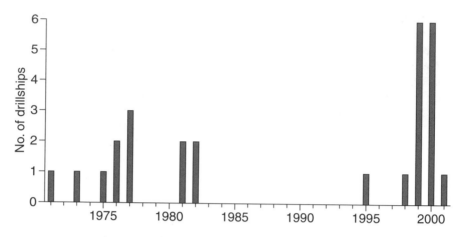

Figure 9.4 Drillship construction eras.

long-established members of the fleet (Gaddy 1998; Hull 2002). The inference is that early drillships – despite their advanced features – can increasingly be considered standard deepsea vessels, whereas the recent construction wave has produced a new and significantly higher league in the shape of their ultra-deepsea descendants. Intuitively, the progress of technological change suggests that this may well be the case. However, the picture is complicated by two factors. The first is the very extensive modernisation wave noted above. The degree to which this has produced significant technological convergence between older and newer vessels is far from evident. Second, the picture is also cloudy because the literature lacks an overall analysis of the characteristics and nature of the complete fleet. Articles relating to specific vessels fail in this respect, and the annual reviews published by *Offshore* present only raw data. The implication that vessel age is the determinant behind the emergence of two distinctive types of drillship – the standard deepwater and ultra-deepwater models – can, however, be tested by comprehensive analysis of these data.

Table 9.1 summarises a range of variables relating to drillships' operational capabilities and their physical characteristics, differentiating between pre-1983 and post-1994 vessels. One key feature of this table is the extent to which the recent averages exceed their earlier counterparts. Three of the six means – for equipped water depth, vessel length and maximum drilling depth – have risen by 40–50 per cent. A fourth, maximum water depth rating, has increased by two-thirds. And the fifth, thruster power, has virtually doubled. Only the quarters capacity average, an index of the scale of the drilling crew, has experienced a modest increase (22 per cent), reflecting the imperative of restraining labour inputs to control operating costs and gain scale economies. These initial indicators of divergence between models are reinforced by the table's second striking feature: the lack of extensive overlap between the parameter ranges of the early

Table 9.1 Early and recent deepwater drillships: comparative parameters

	Water depth rating (m)			Equipped water depth (m)		
	Min.	Av.	Max.	Min.	Av.	Max.
Pre-1983	1,190	1,850	3,030	1,190	1,750	2,420
Post-1994	3,000	3,110	3,640	1,820	2,570	3,030
	Length (m)			Thruster power (HP)		
	Min.	Av.	Max	Min.	Av.	Max
Pre-1983	136	155	188	8,750	17,750	25,080
Post-1994	170	225	254	22,500	34,080	45,250
	Quarters capacity (no. of operatives)			Maximum drilling depth (m)		
	Min.	Av.	Max	Min.	Av.	Max.
Pre-1983	100	122	140	6,060	7,200	9,100
Post-1994	117	149	200	9,100	10,240	11,210

Source: Calculated from *Offshore* annual drillship survey, 2002.

and recent cohorts. Although all variables record maxima for pre-1983 drillships that equal or exceed the post-1994 minima, the overlap is substantial in only one instance: the water depth in which vessels are equipped to operate. Moreover, even for this variable the early drillship maximum (2,420 m) is less than the recent cohort average (2,570 m).

While Table 9.1 demonstrates general divergence between the early and recent cohorts, Table 9.2 brings the existence of extreme contrasts into sharper focus and clearly demonstrates the validity of distinguishing between what may be termed the *standard deepwater* and *ultra-deepwater* models. This table records, for a series of variables, the proportion of each age cohort lying above or below a key threshold. It is evident that to a very high degree the two categories are mutually exclusive. The post-1994 drillship is overwhelmingly synonymous with the *ultra-deepwater model*. Operationally it is rated to work in water depths exceeding 3,000 m. In practice it is highly likely to be equipped to operate in more than 2,200 m of water. Because its equipped depth is less than its rated depth (on average, nearly 20 per cent less), it has reserve capability that can in future be exploited by re-equipment. It is always capable of drilling wells more than 9,100 m deep. It will almost certainly carry more than 125 workers. It is also the faster of the two types, and is thus more swiftly redeployed. These operational characteristics are closely associated with, and dependent on, construction criteria. The ultra-deepwater drillship exceeds 180 m in length, has total power of 40,000 hp or more, and is virtually certain to have thruster power exceeding 25,000 hp. Moreover, its drawworks power – required to withdraw and insert drillpipes and other 'risers' – is consistently more than 4,000 hp.

In comparison, the *standard deepwater model* falls short of all these threshold criteria. What must be emphasised is that this does not mean that the standard deepwater variant is an inferior drillship in terms of the quality of its work. What can be concluded, however, is that this second model's potential is fundamentally constrained – relative to the industry's current cutting-edge needs – by size limitations set when hulls were designed as state-of-the-art investments a quarter of a century or more ago. These hulls have relatively restricted drill-pipe carrying capacity, which is significant because high capacity is essential for the deepest drilling. Their smaller scale is also at variance with the need to support heavier drilling equipment as water depth increases, a problem exacerbated by their limited drawworks power. And by constraining accommodation, small hulls naturally restrict the number of operatives that can be carried. Evidence of the critical importance of hull size is, in fact, provided by a single vessel, the *Glomar Explorer*, which is in many ways the exception proving the rule. Built in 1973, on age grounds this ship should conform closely to the standard deepwater model. However, its hull length – 188 m – is 21 m more than that of its nearest rival in the standard deepwater class, and 36 m more than the class average. As a result, its equipment, capabilities and manning levels meet all the criteria for an ultra-deepwater vessel listed in Table 9.2.

Understanding of the dominant characteristics of the deepwater drillship fleet is, therefore, substantially improved by a modelling approach. Moreover, it also highlights the importance of underlying driving forces echoing those that have been decisive for container ships. As with containerisation, continuing technological advances have been applied to develop a new drillship generation that has eclipsed its predecessor and has allowed the oil industry's deepwater frontier to be radically redefined. But can we assume that this paradigm applies consistently to all types of vessel operating on this frontier, or are alternative paradigms also relevant? The following FPSO analysis is ultimately directed to this question.

Table 9.2 Deepwater drillship model definitions

	Construction pre-1983, N = 12 (%)	Construction post-1994, N = 15 (%)
Length >180 m	8	93
Thruster power >25,000 hp	8	87
Total vessel power >39,000 hp	0	93
Max. speed >11 knots (20 kph)	33	100
Drawworks power >4,000 hp	0	100
Max. water depth rating >300 m	8	100
Equipped for max. water depth >2,200 m	8	87
Max. drilling depth rating >9,100 m	8	100
Quarters capacity >125 operatives	25	93
Equipped to operate up to max. water depth rating	58	33
Operating in Gulf of Mexico or West Africa	8	73

Source: Calculated from *Offshore* annual drillship survey 2002.

FPSOs: neglected technological complexity and the deepwater frontier

At first sight, the FPSO concept is simple and, by today's standards, technologically limited. In many ways, FPSOs appear to be little more than oil tankers moored over oilfields. Risers connect the wellheads to the vessel, carrying crude oil for onboard storage. Shuttle tankers then visit the FPSO periodically – quite often as frequently as every few days – to transship the oil for onward transport to refineries[10] (Murillo 2002).

The simplicity of this concept can be linked through to its popularity. As offshore activity moved from very shallow into deeper waters, the costs of fixed oil production platforms began to rise. Simultaneously, many small and medium-scale oil reservoirs were discovered, too small to justify the investment costs of these increasingly expensive platforms. But, also simultaneously, large-scale tanker surpluses developed in the wake of the oil crises, creating a pool of extremely cheap hulls available for conversion to FPSOs. Between 1977[11] and 2002 the number in service rose to 73, with others undergoing refurbishment. Allowing for new completions, by 2004–5 the world fleet will total almost 100.

As numbers have grown, FPSOs have advanced on the depth frontier. Almost a third are now deployed in more than 300 m of water, and one in five beyond 500 m, with a current record of 2,000 m. An increasingly recognised advantage of deepwater deployment is that they can be installed on fields sooner than would be possible using a fixed platform. This allows reservoirs to be brought into production while development is still in progress, accelerating cash flow to offset high development costs. They may also be installed while the scale and flow-rates of fields are still being assessed, reducing financial risk by allowing production to start before decisions are made as to whether a fixed platform is economically viable. Closely associated with this colonisation of deeper waters, a new geography of deployment has emerged. FPSOs in general are now working worldwide, but those in more than 300 m of water are concentrated primarily on the Brazilian and West African deepwater frontiers (Table 9.3).

This picture of FPSO operations highlights their importance, but conveys no

Table 9.3 Global deployment of floating production, storage and offloading systems (FPSOs) in more than 300 m of water

Brazil	12
West Africa[a]	6
China	2
Norway	2
UK	2
Italy	1
Unspecified	1

Source: Calculated from *Offshore* annual FPSO survey 2002.

Note
a From Equatorial Guinea to Angola.

sense of the cutting edge. In fact, the view that FPSOs are very basic, mundane production platforms is misleading, chiefly because it ignores onboard processing activity. FPSOs are not simply inert and often elderly tankers, but substantial processing facilities that have required significant technological developments. Oil straight from the reservoir normally carries with it 'produced' water. This requires facilities to separate it from the oil before storage and transshipment. In most instances, oilfields require injection wells to maintain their pressure, and consequently FPSOs are commonly equipped to re-inject the produced water after separation. Natural gas is also frequently extracted in association with the oil. This associated gas must also be separated out and, because onboard gas storage is not currently technologically feasible,[12] means must be provided for its safe disposal. Traditionally this has demanded flaring systems, but environmental considerations and the goal of maintaining oil reservoir pressures mean that gas re-injection is also popular, once more requiring specialised injection facilities. All this has demanded the adaptation of technologies originally developed for fixed platforms to transfer them successfully to floating FPSOs, with their quite different space configurations. It has also made necessary the periodic refurbishment of onboard facilities, partly to maintain the efficiency of existing equipment, but also to upgrade it as technology progresses. Virtually all FPSOs with pre-1980 hulls have been upgraded since the mid-1990s, as indeed have most of the more recent vessels. Once again, therefore, modernisation is a key feature of the fleet. Typically, new or refurbished facilities are installed 'topsides', taking advantage of the extensive deck, which often becomes crowded with processing plants (Figure 9.5). Illustrating the reality of this trend, the *Girassol*, due in service off Angola in 2004, will have a topside weight of 30,000 tonnes. Topside investment on any FPSO now entering service is likely to account for 90 per cent of the vessel's total cost (Anon. 2001b).

The technological sophistication of FPSOs has also extended into their design and construction. For example, specialised systems have been required to connect with the risers and also to facilitate mooring. So far as the latter is concerned, the fact that FPSOs are expected to be on station for years at a time might imply that standard anchorage systems would be appropriate. Although a quarter of all FPSOs are certainly 'spread-moored' in this way, there is an in-built disadvantage in that the vessel is unable to adjust its attitude to suit prevailing sea conditions. Consequently, a substantial majority are dependent on much more advanced mooring systems, particularly turrets around which the FPSO is able to rotate. Over 60 per cent of all FPSOs are currently turret moored, using a number of variants. The most popular of these – employed by 40 per cent of vessels – is internal turret mooring. This has required design and construction techniques to be developed to allow the rotatable turret to be incorporated in the hull itself.[13]

Modelling the deepwater FPSO

Since FPSOs are demonstrably far more sophisticated than is usually acknowledged, to what extent is it valid to conceptualise, as has been done for drill-

Figure 9.5 The FPSO *Brasil* undergoing fitting out. Owned by Petrobras, the *Brasil* displaces 255,000 dwt. Stationed in 1,360 m of water off Brazil, mooring is by means of an internal turret. Serving 14 wells, the vessel has an annual production capacity of 4.5 m tonnes.

ships, the emergence of age-related standard and advanced models dominating the deepwater frontier? The initial signs are that FPSO models very similar to those identified for drillships may be appropriate. Although there is no clear break between development phases, two dominant peaks for hull construction stand out: the 1970s and the post-1994 period.[14] More than 75 per cent of the hulls currently in use date from these two eras (Figure 9.6). Similarly, there has been an abrupt transition away from FPSOs based on tanker conversions in favour of new-build projects. Converted hulls date overwhelmingly from the pre-1985 period, with new-build schemes dominating since then. In part, this dramatic shift reflects construction issues. As the FPSO has become increasingly elaborate, it has also become more attractive to build from new to avoid adaptation difficulties – for example, associated with internal turrets. But the change is also a response to a very basic consideration: the growing shortage of tankers suitable for conversion. Here environmental influences have been important, because conversions, based on early tankers, have almost all involved single-skin hulls. Although a few double-hulled tankers, with their greatly reduced risk of accidental spillage, have been converted to FPSOs, in general they are not yet

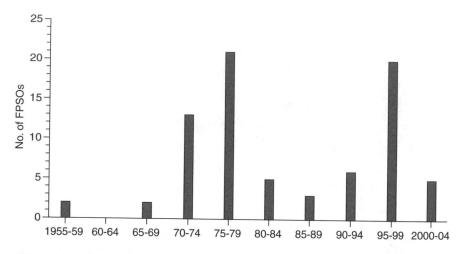

Figure 9.6 FPSO construction eras.

old enough to be relegated for conversion. Consequently, since 1990 the switch to new-build FPSOs has been closely allied to double-hull construction. More than a third of the fleet already has this additional environmental safety measure.

Other age-related distinctions can also be drawn, although they are admittedly less sharp. For example, while the detailed correlation between fabrication year and onboard processing capacity is weak,[15] the typical processing capacity range has shifted upwards (Figure 9.7a). Expressed as averages for the 1970s and post-1994 cohorts, the rise is from 70,000 to 115,000 barrels per day,[16] a 64 per cent increase. Similarly, a slight upward trend in quarters capacity can be observed among the majority of FPSOs – from around 73 to 85 on average (+16 per cent) (Figure 9.7b).

Beyond this, however, the age-based parallel with drillships breaks down rapidly. Although processing capacity and workforces have tended to rise, the overall scale of FPSOs has not increased with time. Thus, the correlation between fabrication year and deadweight tonnage is a mere −0.2. So, too, is the correlation between fabrication year and onboard oil storage capacity. In both cases, therefore, the time variable 'explains' only 4 per cent of the variance. Moreover – and crucially – the correlation between fabrication year and operational water depth is even lower: just 0.042. From these three results it is evident that any FPSO model based on the concept of a recent, large-scale vessel type dominating the deepest waters, with earlier ships relegated to shallower regions, is simply untenable.

What also emerges, however, is evidence that an alternative model – based on a quite different interrelationship between age, scale and operational water depth – can be identified. The keys to this model lie in Figure 9.8. As the previous results have shown, for the vast majority of FPSOs hull size is poorly corre-

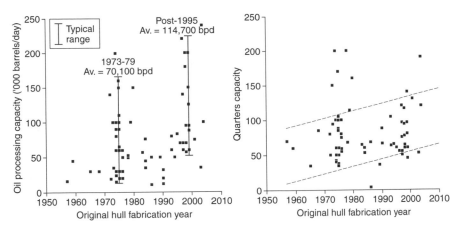

Figure 9.7 Development of (a) FPSO processing capacity and (b) quarters capacity through time.

lated with age: a hull of almost any given age can vary substantially between a few thousand and 200,000 dwt. But this rule is broken by the 1970s hull cohort, because this includes – as a strong outlier in Figure 9.8a – a high proportion of the FPSOs that exceed 200,000 dwt. This 1970s cohort also accounts for many of the vessels with storage capacity greater than 1 million barrels (Figure 9.8b). When these two variables – deadweight tonnage and storage capacity – are related to water depth, the outlying clusters recur, but now point to a clear association between the mammoth 1970s hulls and deployment in deepwater locations (Figure 9.8c and 9.8d). Finally, the sharp peak in Figure 9.8e confirms the strong link between deepwater FPSO operations and 1970s-vintage vessels.

From this and the earlier discussion, it is a short step to propose a reliable model of the deepwater FPSO. Built in the 1970s, it exceeds 200,000 dwt and has more than a million barrels of storage capacity. Operating in at least 300 m of water, it is usually deployed between 700 and 1,500 m. Because of its age it is a converted supertanker, and consequently has a single hull. In other respects, however, it is modernised, with topsides facilities last upgraded after 1995 and often much more recently. Using the industry's broadest definition of deep water – i.e. more than 300 m – this model's explanatory power is admittedly only moderate: 14 FPSOs meet these criteria in full, out of 27 operating beyond the 300 m limit. But beyond 500 m its reliability is impressive: 11 out of 15 vessels (75 per cent) conform totally to its specifications.

The essence of this model is that FPSO operations on the depth frontier currently depend on the marriage of technologies from quite different eras, on modern processing systems coupled with large, elderly – yet still sound – hulls. The drivers behind this counter-intuitive finding are partly practical. Redundant

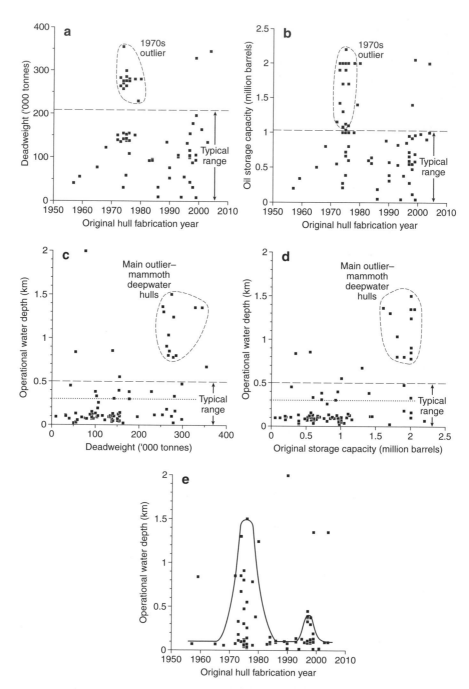

Figure 9.8 Mammoth 1970s hulls: the key to the deepwater FPSO model.

supertankers provide the space to optimise the organisation of large-scale processing facilities. They also have the scale and structural strength to operate indefinitely in open ocean conditions. But the economic factor also looms large. With surplus supertanker hulls available at modest cost in the aftermath of the oil crises, it was unnecessary to resort to the much more expensive option of building very large FPSOs from new. An important consequence of this is that one additional – and disadvantageous – characteristic must be added to our model of the deepwater FPSO. Because it is typically a single-hulled vessel, there is the added risk of serious spillage in the event of a collision.[17]

From technologies to issues

Using the examples of just two types of vessel, this investigation has revealed the important link between shipping technologies and the offshore industry's outward movement on the deepwater frontiers. It has similarly demonstrated that model-based approaches can clarify substantially the complex processes involved. What has also been highlighted, however, is that the models generated may or may not conform closely to intuitive expectations. If containerisation is used as the yardstick, the drillship models identified are not unusual in that they confirm the importance of the paradigm that technological change, advancing with time, leads inexorably to larger, more sophisticated and more efficient vessels inevitably destined to eclipse their predecessors. Yet applied uncritically as an assumption, this finding would at best be a partial predictor of the nature of the typical deepwater FPSO. This clearly indicates the need to avoid such assumptions and instead apply the modelling approach to other specialist ships serving the offshore industry and, indeed, to other types of specialist vessel in the shipping sector as a whole.

Beyond this, a range of issues must finally be added to the discussion. While several of these relate primarily to the likely trajectory of innovation within the offshore industry itself, they also extend the argument into new territory by identifying societal questions concerning the distribution of costs and benefits linked with offshore technological change.

An appropriate starting point is that, because the industry is so dynamic, models will inevitably evolve. Drillships have already provided one outstanding example: the standard deepwater model identified would undoubtedly have been considered cutting edge in the late 1980s, yet little more than ten years later it is now mainstream compared with its ultra-deepwater successor. Currently there are signs that, by the end of the decade, the deepwater FPSO model specified above will also require major revision. Large FPSOs converted from supertankers will still exist, but for the first time there will also be a generation of new-build vessels in deep waters. It is the need to ensure that hulls have the integrity to withstand 'greenwater' conditions,[18] are able to accommodate increasingly complex processing facilities, and have the environmental safeguards offered by double-sided or doubled-hulled construction that points to this conclusion. Indications that this change is already in progress are provided by Figures 9.8a, 9.8b and 9.8e, with their sprinklings of recently constructed yet exceptionally large vessels. In the vanguard are examples such as the *Girassol*, which entered service in 1999, and the *Dalia*, due to be commissioned in 2004. Designed to operate on the West African deepwater frontier off Angola, both are well in excess of 300,000 dwt and will work in 1,350 m of water.

Change, however, is unlikely to be limited to the refinement and improvement of existing concepts, as two further examples demonstrate. First, ideas are emerging which may lead to the hybridisation of drillships and FPSOs (Furlow 1999). This innovation would add drilling capability to an FPSO, creating a floating drilling, production, storage and offloading system (FDPSO). Particular attractions are concurrent drilling and production in the early phases of field development, followed later by the ability to undertake maintenance drilling while simultaneously sustaining flows of oil, water and gas through the unaffected production and injection wells. Capital sunk into such vessels would be invested more efficiently and profitably – a major consideration when even a day's lost production might cost $2 million or more (Constantinis and Mortlock 2001). While it is not envisaged that this trend would render drillships obsolete, an important consequence of any movement towards FDPSOs would be at least the partial convergence of existing models, as opposed to their continued separate evolution.

Second, there is now a real prospect that the FPSO concept will be developed into a quite different vessel, producing liquified natural gas. The step change to floating liquefied natural gas (FLNG) operations is challenging.[19] None the less, the attractions of FLNG – especially bringing into production gas reservoirs whose reserves currently cannot be landed economically – is generating widespread interest. Shell, Chevron/Texaco, Mobil, Statoil and a range of smaller companies have all been examining the problems since the mid-1990s, and specific solutions are now starting to emerge (Bliault 2001; Crook 2001b; Finn 2002; Furlow 2002). Given the progress made, and the strength of global natural gas demand, Shell's assessment is that the concept has moved from 'if' to 'when', and a time-span of five to six years is currently being quoted for the development of the company's first FLNG vessel (Bliault 2001). What is certain is that this will not be designed for the rigorous sea conditions found in deep water. However, there is no doubt that the long-term intention is to develop the concept to survive those conditions in order to tap significant gas deposits beyond the reach of economic pipelines. Conceptually, therefore, the future may well entail not simply the convergence of models – as between FPSOs and drillships through the FDPSO concept – but also divergence, as the FLNG transforms the basic FPSO idea into a quite different vessel exploiting an entirely different fuel.[20]

If internally the industry is likely to witness these and similar trends facilitated by technological change, what implications are there for the world at large? As was indicated at the outset, the consequences are in one sense positive, in that improved access to offshore oil and gas assists the continuation of western lifestyles, and also makes available energy resources expected to be required for Third World development. Yet viewed from a quite different perspective, the distribution of socio-economic costs and benefits associated with the deepwater frontier is a significant issue.

Globalisation and offshore vessel production: winners and losers

The issue of the distribution of costs and benefits relates partly to global organisational structures. The shift in basic shipbuilding capacity away from western economies to newly industrialised countries has affected FPSOs and drillships just as much as other commercial vessels. Today it is countries such as South Korea and China that are the most popular producers of these ships. In this sense, oil-sector development is clearly contributing to the globalisation process, encouraging falling capacity and job losses in traditional production areas, and opening up new opportunities elsewhere. Yet this interpretation is misleading, because construction is not normally completed in a single location. As we have seen, finished FPSOs and drillships are highly sophisticated, and this is reflected in the geography of their fabrication. Basic hull construction may take place in countries such as South Korea, but fitting out is often completed in the West. The significance of this is that, especially for FPSOs, the fitting-out process involves the installation of highly complex processing modules, all of which are high value, and many of which are produced in the advanced industrial countries. Thus, the FPSO hull for Nigeria's Bonga field, although fabricated in South Korea, was fitted out on Tyneside in the United Kingdom, with topside modules being produced in the local region and in the Netherlands. Similarly, the South Korean FPSO hull for Angola's Kizomba field has topsides units manufactured in the United Kingdom, the Netherlands and the United States. By these means the large majority of the value added, and the lion's share of skill development, benefit the advanced economies. Superficially, the industry underpins a more even distribution of industrial capacity at the global scale; in reality it reinforces the polarisation of profits and high-order skills within the traditional global core.

Related to this, there is the final issue of the ways in which developing countries become involved in opening up resources on new frontiers. New producing regions in developing areas are virtually all brought into production by the western oil companies that monopolise the industry's expertise. The resource-owning countries may opt to secure income through the sale of licences and the imposition of royalties and other taxes. But it is also common for them to enter into participation agreements with the western companies, in order to share in profits. Angola, for example, takes a 20–25 per cent equity stake in offshore activity. It is in this context that problems can arise, because participation entails proportional up-front investment before any profits accrue. This investment is normally on a very large scale, and is amplified by the need to contribute – for example – to essential projects such as the construction of highly sophisticated FPSOs, each costing perhaps $400 million or more (Maksoud 2001; Thackeray 2000).

The result can be major strains for a developing country,[21] as the majority of its investment flows into the advanced industrial economies that are predominantly responsible for adding value to vessels. The developing countries affected naturally make attempts to counter this problem by pressing for agreements guaranteeing the inclusion of significant local content in such projects, but in this they are rarely successful on any significant scale. For example, because of the high proportion of foreign work involved in the original plan, in November 2000 Angola pressed for an agreement whereby the state oil company, Sonogal, would supply the Kizomba FPSO (Quinlan 2001). In the end, the country was awarded the fabrication of run-of-the-mill items such as the helideck, the boat landing, suction anchors and an off-loading buoy (Beckman 2002a). In Nigeria likewise: local content for the Bonga FPSO was limited primarily to fabrication of the flareboom, the gas metering system and one basic module.

Finally, therefore, relating offshore technological change to the interests of emergent oil-producing countries in the developing world sounds a clear, and very necessary, note of caution. The technological achievements essential to enable the industry to find and extract increasingly inaccessible resources are, by any standards, impressive. What is essential is that we are not dazzled by these achievements. Offshore activity is not surgically separated from onshore economies, and where these are fragile the industry's progress – largely driven by the West's self-interest – may at best be a mixed blessing.

Acknowledgement

I am grateful to Mr Barry Harding of Harding Resources, Inc., for his advice and to Claire Pinder for constructing the databases used for the drillship and FPSO analyses.

Notes

1 From the early 1950s to the 1970s, the development of supertankers reduced oil transport costs through economies of scale. Whereas in 1950 the typical crude oil tanker was less than 30,000 dwt, by the mid-1960s the norm had risen to 120,000 dwt. By the 1970s very large crude carriers (VLCCs) and ultra-large crude carriers (ULCCs) of 200,000 to 400,000 dwt had arrived (Hayuth and Hilling 1992). This made a significant contribution – especially in western Europe – to a steady decline in the real cost of oil, and thus to a fundamental transition from coal to oil as society's energy linchpin. Crude oil carriers consequently took centre stage in analyses of the impact of technological change on shipping and ports (van den Bremen 1981; Molle and Wever 1984a, b; Odell 1986; Pinder 1992).

2 Interest has tended to revive only when tanker disasters have hit the headlines or new national or international regulation has been introduced (Quon and Bushell 1994; Hysing and Torset 1994; Rosenblatt 1995; Talley 1995).

3 Until recently there was general agreement that depths exceeding 300 m should be considered deep water. Continued technological advances have encouraged the view that the definition should be 500 m or more. Although this chapter retains the more liberal definition, in practice it is chiefly concerned with depths well beyond 500 m.

4 The data sources employed for both modelling exercises are the detailed comprehensive surveys of drillships and FPSOs published annually by the leading industry journal *Offshore*.

5 These limitations become severe in more than 100 m of water (Kota *et al.* 2000).

6 Generally it is best to engage two smaller tugs, rather than one large one, because of the safety margin provided in the event of tug failure. However, the decision can also involve a wide range of other factors, including the towing distance, tug availability, the degree of urgency to reach the new location, weather conditions and the towing characteristics of particular semi-submersibles (personal communication, Mr Barry Harding, Harding Resources, Inc., 2003).

7 The one exception is owned by the Brazilian state oil corporation, Petrobras. While ownership of other drillships is spread between ten contracting firms, a single corporation is dominant: Transocean Inc. of Houston. This controls half the total fleet, with investments divided between both the early and recent construction waves.

8 Currently there are eight dynamic positioning system variants in use.

9 Despite this flexibility, time is required to retrieve drill pipes, etc, deployed below the vessel.

10 While various configurations are used for the shuttle tanker link, the standard is for the shuttle to ride in tandem astern of the FPSO.

11 This was the year in which the first FPSO entered service. Deployed in the Mediterranean, it was a converted oil products carrier and had throughput capacity of less than 1 million tonnes per year (Pinder 2001).

12 The discussion returns to the possibility of floating gas production systems in the section 'From technologies to issues' (p. 181).

13 A development of this system, the disconnectable turret, can be employed. The concept is particularly useful in hazardous environments. Prime examples are provided by the typhoon-prone South China Sea and the Terra Nova oilfield in 'Iceberg Valley' off Canada's east coast. The *Terra Nova* FPSO serves the latter and has as its ultimate line of defence a quick-release turret. This enables controlled decoupling within four hours, and emergency decoupling in just 15 minutes. This is achievable even though all risers for production and injection wells for this complex field pass through the turret (Crook 2001a). For a report on a conference focused on FPSO design for harsh conditions, see Beckman (2002b).

14 When FPSOs are converted tankers, hull construction dates are the original building dates, not those when conversion took place.

15 For the Pearson and Spearman coefficients the correlations are +0.36 and +0.32, respectively.

16 These figures are equivalent to 3.5 million and 5.7 million tonnes per year.

17 Much greater protection in this respect is to be found in less than 300 m of water. Here the number of fields requiring an FPSO has outstripped the supply of surplus hulls suitable for conversion, creating the main new-build market. In these shallower waters, therefore, new-build hulls, all with the additional environmental safety margin of double-sided or full double-hull construction, currently account for half the vessels deployed.

18 Greenwater conditions are defined as 'unbroken waves overtopping the bow, side or stern of the vessel'. One recent study of 15 large FPSOs in the North Sea reported an increasing greenwater threat. Although no overtopping incidents were recorded before 1995, 17 have subsequently occurred, indicating a growing probability of damage (Anon. 2001a).

19 FLNG requires the development of onboard liquefaction units, for two reasons a challenge in its own right. First, there are major safety issues associated with the production process and the product itself. Second, onboard processing would require production plants to be scaled down substantially compared with land-based liquefaction 'trains'.

20 The fact that many oilfields produce associated gas is also encouraging research into the FONG – floating oil and natural gas – system. This would add gas liquefaction plants to FPSOs, enabling them to market both oil and gas. This would, of course, represent a development of the FPSO concept, though admittedly a quite radical one (Furlow 2002).

21 These strains can be intensified still further when multinational companies wish to accelerate development even though the country would prefer to decelerate in order to lessen investment demands and extend the period in which benefit will be gained from the industry.

References

Anon. (2001a) 'Greenwater grabs attention', *Offshore Engineer,* January, p. 27.
—— (2001b) 'Floating production: getting to grips with project performance', *Offshore,* May, p. 26.
Beckman, J. (2002a) 'Bonga, Kizomba set benchmark for large FPSO vessels', *Offshore,* March, pp. 68–70, 108.
—— (2002b) 'FPSO designs adapt to harsh northerly/sub-tropical conditions', *Offshore,* May, p. 97.
Bliault, A. (2001) 'Shell floating LNG plant, technology ready for project development', *Offshore,* May, pp. 102–104.
Brookfield, H.C. (1984) 'Boxes, ports and places without ports', in B.S. Hoyle and D. Hilling (eds) *Seaport Systems and Spatial Change,* Chichester, UK: John Wiley.
Constantinis, D. and Mortlock, D. (2001) 'Inspection, evaluation methods help FPSOs, FSOs avoid drydockings', *Offshore,* May, pp. 84–88.
Cooper, M.J.M. (1974) 'Container shipping and regional economic growth', *New Zealand Geographer,* 30: 54–65.
Crook, J (2001a) 'FPSO first in "Iceberg Valley"', *Petroleum Review,* 55(9): 46–47.
—— (2001b) 'Doubt surrounds Timor gas project', *Petroleum Review,* 55(11): 26–27.
Cullinane, K. and Khanna, M. (2000) 'Economies of scale in container shipping: optimal size and geographical implications', *Journal of Transport Geography,* 8: 181–196.
Douglas-Westwood and Infield Systems (2003) *The World Deepwater Report 2003–2007,* Canterbury, UK: Douglas-Westwood and Infield Systems.
Finn, A.J. (2002) 'New FPSO design produces LNG from offshore source', *Oil and Gas Journal,* 100: 56–62.
Furlow, W. (1999) 'Independent tension deck for FDPSO supports dry trees', *Offshore,* December, pp. 55–57, 108.
—— (2002) 'Shell launches new floating concept processing oil and gas in remote areas', *Offshore,* May, pp. 50, 142.
Gaddy, D.E. (1998) 'Next-generation drilling equipment pushes back water depth barrier', *Oil and Gas Journal,* 96: 74–78.
Ghisel, R.G. (ed.) (1997) *Fifty Years of Offshore Oil, Gas Development,* Houston: Hart Publications.
Gilman, S. (1999) 'The size economies and network efficiencies of large container ships', *International Journal of Maritime Economics,* 1: 39–59.
Harbinson, D. and Knight, R. (2003) 'Future deepwater prospects', *Petroleum Review,* 57(2): 12–15.
Hayuth, Y. (1981) 'Containerization and the load center concept', *Economic Geography,* 57: 160–188.
—— (1987) *Intermodality: concept and practice,* Colchester, UK: Lloyd's.
Hayuth, Y. and Hilling, D. (1992) 'Technological change and seaport development', in B.S. Hoyle and D.A. Pinder (eds) *European Port Cities in Transition,* London: Belhaven, pp. 40–58.

Hayward, A.B. (1999) 'Exploration frontiers for new century determined by technology, politics', *Oil and Gas Journal*, 97: 42–44.

Hull, J.P. (2002) '*Discoverer Enterprise* ahead of the pack at Thunder Horse', *Offshore*, July, pp. 36, 109.

Hysing, T. and Torset, O.P. (1994) 'Reduction of oil outflows at collisions and groundings through improved vessel design arrangement', *Marine Pollution Bulletin*, 29: 368–374.

Kota, R., Maloney, J. and D'Souza, R. (2000) 'MOPUs evolving to meet greater depth, flexibility challenges', *Offshore*, February, pp. 94–96, 129.

McKenzie, D.R., North, M.N. and Smith, D.S. (1989) *Intermodal Transportation: The Whole Story*, Omaha: Simmons.

Maksoud, J. (2001) 'West Africa: continuing discoveries + stability + infrastructure = rising investment', *Offshore*, October, p. 30.

—— (2003) 'International report: West Africa major focus of future E&P spending', *Offshore*, May, pp. 26–48, 144.

Molle, W. and Wever, E. (1984a) *Oil Refineries and Petrochemical Industries in Western Europe: Buoyant Past, Uncertain Future*, Aldershot, UK: Gower.

—— (1984b) 'Oil refineries and petrochemical industries in Europe', *GeoJournal*, 9: 421–430.

Murillo, V. (2002) 'Options vary for GoM shuttle service', *Offshore*, June, pp. 68–69.

Odell, P.R. (1986) *Oil and World Power*, 8th edn, Harmondsworth, UK: Penguin.

—— (1997) 'The exploitation of offshore mineral resources', *GeoJournal*, 42: 17–26.

—— (1998) 'Hydrocarbons: the pace quickens', in G.H. Blake, M.A. Pratt and C.H. Schofield (eds) *Boundaries and Energy: Problems and Prospects*, Dordrecht, the Netherlands: Kluwer Law International, pp. 28–42.

Organisation for Economic Cooperation and Development (OECD) (1971) *Developments and Problems of Seaborne Container Transport, 1970*, Paris: OECD.

Pinder, D.A. (1992) 'Seaports and the European energy system', in B.S. Hoyle and D.A. Pinder (eds) *European Port Cities in Transition*, London: Belhaven, pp. 20–39.

—— (2001) 'Offshore oil and gas: global resource knowledge and technological change', *Ocean and Coastal Management*, 44: 579–600.

Quinlan, M. (2001) 'Angola: a grown-up oil country develops', *Petroleum Economist*, 55, February, pp. 6–9.

Quon, T.K.S. and Bushell, G.E. (1994) 'Modelling navigational risk and oil-spill probabilities', *Journal of Navigation*, 47: 309–402.

Rosenblatt, M. and Son Inc. (1995) 'Tanker structure behaviour during collision and grounding', *Marine Technology and SNAME News*, 32(1): 20–32.

Talley, W. (1995) 'Vessel damage severity of tanker accidents', *Logistics and Transportation Review*, 31: 191–207.

Thackeray, F. (2000) 'Lots of potential – but lots of problems', *Petroleum Review*, 54(7): 32–33.

van den Bremen, W.J. (1981) 'Aspects of maritime transport and port development under the influence of changes in the energy supply in the next decades: Western Europe as a case study', in C. Muscara, M. Soricillo and A. Vallega (eds) *Changing Maritime Transport*, vol. 1, Naples: Istituto Universitario Navale and Istituto di Geografia Economica for the International Geographical Union, pp. 40–73.

Zophil, J. and Prion, M. (1999) 'The MED rule: the interdependence of container throughput and transhipment volumes in Mediterranean ports', *Maritime Policy and Management*, 26: 175–193.

Part III

The environment – towards a new harmony?

10 Integrated environmental management of ports and harbours

The European experience – from policy to practice

Chris Wooldridge and Tim Stojanovic

Introduction

Environmental management of ports and port areas concerns the functional organisation of activities and operations specifically to attain high standards of environmental protection and the goal of sustainable development. Effective environmental management requires science-based evidence on which to make decisions, the identification of key performance indicators by which to demonstrate achievement, and appropriate monitoring in order to assess both the efficacy of management and the quality of the environment itself. This chapter examines how seaports within Europe have been developing towards this level of environmental practice. Two important trends in port environmental management from the past ten years are identified. The first is policy based. This involves ports collaborating on the topic of the environment as a pre-competitive issue in order to share knowledge and solutions. The second is technology based. On the one hand, this concerns the use of technology and improved information processing for the integration of port information systems; on the other, it relates to the integration of environmental performance and monitoring data within environmental management information systems (EMIS).

Each seaport may be considered unique in terms of its geographical, hydrographical and commercial profile. In addition, the diversity of form and function can be further compounded by considerations of ownership, politics, culture and legislation. This means that the environmental management and auditing tools need to be capable of being tailored to the special circumstances of each port. Without these flexible tools, ports may lack the evidence or structures to implement environmental management within the working practices of the port organisation, as envisioned in the goal of sustainable development. The fact that European ports themselves are seeking to develop collaborative, in-house solutions for environmental management, as an alternative to legislation-driven approaches, indicates the importance of the environmental issue to the port sector as a factor within business risk. Towards the end of the chapter, therefore, we move on to discuss models for the networking of environmental tools and methodologies evolved through port-inspired European research and development projects. The scope of the findings concentrates on environmental practices in pioneer European ports, but lessons may be usefully applied to any ports operating within an institutional system of structured environmental management.

Concepts, practice and the integrated environmental management of ports

Since 1990 the experience of European seaports is that the topic of environmental management has developed from small project- or issue-based investigations to become an important consideration within the corporate business plan. However, the challenge for many seaports remains that of translating conceptual strategies into practical, applied environmental management. There is growing awareness among port managers of the significance of the environmental aspects of their ports' activities and operations, and of the liabilities and responsibilities associated with them. Progressive port authorities are playing an increasingly active role as partners in coastal zone management initiatives. However, there are some misgivings as to the most appropriate form of management option to pursue in balancing the sometimes conflicting demands of, on the one hand, port development and the commercial imperative with, on the other, the requirement for environmental protection. Pragmatic port managers have a strong preference for practical, non-bureaucratic and cost-effective environmental programmes.

Integrated environmental management has been defined as an approach to reconcile conflicting interests and concerns, and to coordinate institutional actions and fragmented efforts. It seeks to integrate with the processes of planning and decision-making those aspects of management that impact on assessment and evaluation (Born and Sonzogni, 1995). It embodies a number of concepts and guiding principles that can make possible the successful implementation of environmental management within ports. It encourages the selection of relevant approaches, comprehensive or incremental, to enable ports to focus on significant environmental aspects of their activities (International Organization for Standardization (ISO) 1996). An integrated approach offers several advantages in efficiency compared to *ad-hoc* or problem-solving approaches since monitoring, research and enforcement efforts can be harmonised (Barrow 1999). From a business perspective, an integrated approach is required to undertake a strategic assessment of environmental risks. These days, the business sector also acknowledges that there are value-added benefits for customer and public relations in taking an integrated approach (International Chamber of Commerce 1993).

Figure 10.1 depicts the environmental regime within a medium-sized commercial port, and indicates the nature of environmental challenges in the port context. Various common operational activities such as cargo handling, dredging and waterfront discharges have potential impacts on land, water, suspended sediment and air. Environmental aspects may impact on any or all media, and their effects can be trans-boundary. Furthermore, port authorities are often

Figure 10.1 Land, sea, air, industry and environmental impacts in a port. (Courtesy of Instituto Portuario e dos transportes Maritimos-Delegação dos Portos do Norte.)

landlords to large industrial and manufacturing estates located within the port-city complex, with the attendant environmental impacts and issues typical of major industrial developments.

To a certain extent, ports may be considered unique businesses, and the coastal zone as a location with specific issues. Ports represent a concentration of human activity as nodes in the logistic chain and points of transfer within transport networks. Furthermore, the legal basis for environmental management is complicated by the fact that the law regards the coastline as a legal boundary. This means that both maritime law and the ordinary law of the land are of relevance to ports. Responsibilities and liabilities may range from dredging to issues related to the safety of navigation and, under some types of ownership, environmental protection. Port jurisdiction can provide a further raft of environmental responsibilities requiring positive management, with the attendant demands to provide adequate resources for enforcement and reporting. Such an amalgam of intensity of use, profusion of agencies and stakeholders, multiplicity of uses, and potential conflicts for space can present complex environmental problems. An integrated approach is required to address and assess the interrelated causes, effects and management options.

The emergence of port environmental management: an overview

What progress is being made towards this integrative goal? While it is misleading to describe environmental practice as if it is common to all ports, there have been dominant trends. These have been driven by legislation, greater awareness of the impacts of port activities, and changes in business practices, all of which reflect shifting attitudes to the environment within broader society.

The overriding concern of health and safety legislation in ports during the 1970s encouraged at least some monitoring of environmental conditions that could be harmful to port employees. But ports were primarily concerned with the effects of environmental dynamics and conditions on their activities, rather than with the impact of port operations on the environment. When they looked outwards, the emphasis was on environmental factors affecting human health, such as noise and dust. Such environmental duties as were recognised tended to be carried out as adjuncts to the work of engineering or survey sections, or added to the list of activities to be carried out by the 'Harbour Master'. Environmental management, when it was practised at all, was based on technical rather than environmental standards. It was a quite different activity – spatial planning – which encouraged strategies to maintain the environment within the port and to deal with the environmental aspects of development, landscaping, excavation and landfill.

In many ports, specific environmental issues have been important drivers in the subsequent inception of an environmental programme. At the port of Dover – a UK ferry port handling 16 million passengers a year (Dover Harbour Board 2001) – dredging activity in the early 1990s produced the first initiative towards the development of environmental monitoring by the port. In other cases, a negative incident such as an oil spill, or a positive experience of cooperation with an environmental research institute (e.g. as part of an engineering contract for port development), has acted as a trigger for a port to develop and implement its environmental management activities.

More systematically, as Reynolds reviews in Chapter 12, regulation has been significant. For example, the MARPOL (73/78) convention has included provisions for adequate waste reception from ships, and this has been implemented by ports during the 1980s and 1990s through waste management plans. These have incorporated practices such as the designation of waste storage facilities for different types of material, and the establishment of contractors for recycling or disposal. Another important legislative influence in Europe has been the EU's Environmental Impact Assessment Directive (EC85/337), requiring environmental assessments for the development of ports capable of receiving vessels over 1,350 tonnes. Although these assessments are commonly prepared by consultancies, this has led to the growth of expertise on environmental mitigation in the port sector. The EU Habitats Directive (EC92/43) has further raised the requirements of port managers to understand the environmental aspects of port activities, including their impact on sensitive species or habitats in the coastal environment.

	1970s	1980s	1990s	2000s
FOCUS OF ENVIRONMENTAL APPROACHES IN PIONEERING PORTS	Health and safety (i.e. human environment) Spatial planning in the port area	Waste management Environmental impact assessment	Environmental auditing Participation in coastal zone management	Integrated port environmental management Environmental management systems
EXAMPLE UK/EU GLOBAL DOCUMENTS and INITIATIVES	Health and Safety at Work Act (UK) 1974 MARPOL International Convention 73/1978	EC 85/337 EIA Directive UNCTAD UNCTAD/ SHIP/494(2) Spatial Planning in Port Area	EC 92/43 Habitats Directive ESPO (1994) Environmental Code of Practice ABP (1999) Humber Port Estuary Management	ECOPORTS (EU DG TREN) Initiative 2002-2005

Figure 10.2 Timeline of important ideas in port environmental management.

Meanwhile, the role of ports in the environmental management of the coastal zone has been enhanced by the participation of many European ports in estuary and coastal management initiatives. In response to the pressures for the use of space in coastal zones, ports are now commonly represented on committees of management or research groups as they plan the development and environmental management of coastal areas.[1] The Humber estuary (UK), the Ebbro delta (Portugal) and the Wadden Sea (Netherlands/Germany/Denmark) are three examples of locations where ports have made a significant contribution to the funding or research activities of coastal initiatives. Since ports are major stakeholders in the coastal zone, they are able to influence human activities, and this has led to the practical application of a number of techniques by ports, such as the zoning of space uses, or the regulation of activities with environmental impacts by using legal powers (ABP 1999).

Until the 1990s, much port environmental policy was the by-product of sectoral legislation, and reflected the need for ports to detail their own procedural protocols for the environmental aspects of their activities, such as the preparation of oil spill response plans. The point is that ports were essentially preparing action plans in response to individual pieces of legislation, rather than considering the environment in an integrated way as a component of their operations (Couper 1992). A classic example of the argument for a more integrated approach is the need for a port to consider anthropogenic factors beyond the port boundaries, such as those arising further inland. In the case of a port that has a river draining into its area, an integrated approach enables the port to understand, for example, whether pollutants arise from its own activities or from those further upstream[2] (Vandermeulen 1996). Progress towards an integrated approach has been assisted in several instances by the appointment of port environmental managers or the designation of environmental responsibilities to port managers, although this is by no means universal.

Whitehead (2001: q133) describes some of the attitudinal changes to environmental issues during the 1990s. He relates the growing awareness of UK port managers in accepting the need to find out more about what is happening in the environment for which they have responsibility, together with their realisation that this entails a good level of knowledge about the environmental aspects of port activities. Furthermore, at a European policy level he notes that the environmental code of the European Sea Ports Organisation (ESPO) (1994) has influenced changes in practice, such as increased preparation of environmental plans and policies within ports.[3] Thus, many managers have come to accept the ethical, economic and profitable option[4] arguments for making investments in environmental management.

Ports are also increasingly attending to environmental and sustainability issues as they formulate business policies and propose new developments. Global environmental issues have appeared on the agenda of port managers making proposals for developments in the 2000s. Proposals commonly consider the global evolution of transport networks, and the role of ports in environmentally friendly logistics chains. A key point here is that ports are able to support environmentally favourable forms of transport. For example, because of reduced fossil fuel consumption, ships make lower inputs to the environment than alternative modes of transport, thereby lowering emissions and reducing the contribution to global warming. Such considerations have encouraged ports to lobby for structural adjustment and investment in infrastructure to promote sea transport.

A major recent step has been to rationalise different port environmental initiatives and their common information requirements into integrated environmental management programmes (Eco-Information 1999). Tools such as audits, reports and environmental management systems (EMS) may all form elements of these programmes and have particular requirements for implementation in the port sector (Valencia Port Authority 2002). Each port faces different environmental circumstances and has a different starting point for developing environmental management, but Table 10.1 illustrates – for the Port of Dover – the post-1990 evolution of tools utilised by the Harbour Board to support environmental management activities. These tools illustrate the extent to which ports can become involved in environmental management on a procedural level. They are complemented by structural changes that have taken place in the port to appoint an environmental manager (as part of the safety and environmental management group) and designate a surveyor with specific environmental monitoring responsibilities. The list contains a number of tools

Table 10.1 Tools and information resources used by the Dover Harbour Board for environmental purposes

Output	Date of inception	Environmental function
Environmental database	1992–	Store and analyse environmental data and records
Environmental Review of the Marine Environment	1993–	Provide an initial or preliminary review of the impact of activities and operations, and establish an environmental baseline
Environmental research programme	1994–	Collaborative R&D programmes with universities and research establishments in data collection and environmental science
Environmental Database Reference Manual	1995–	Standardise monitoring and reporting and implement quality assurance for data
Surveys of water quality	1996–	Track trends in water quality and assess against guidelines/standards
Environmental policy	1997–	Influence corporate environmental practice and programmes
Waste Management Plan	1997–	Plan collection, storage and disposal of waste in an environmentally efficient manner
Environmental review	1997–	Statement of policy and environmental actions
Directory of Coastal Environmental Management	1998–	Outline other relevant initiatives and organisations, their work and contact details
Environmental Reference Manual	1998–	Detail protocols for environmental activities such as monitoring procedures
Self-Diagnosis Methodology	1998–	Review the environmental management performance using EU/Eco-information tools
Environmental Incidents Database	1999–	Record environmental incidents
Habitat Monitoring Atlas	1999–	Establish the status of flora and fauna in the port in order to identify indicator species, establish baseline, map habitats and track trends
Environmental Report	1999–	Produce a summary of environmental plans, actions and performance
Geological handbook	1999–	Build a knowledge base to complement development, operation and dredging of the port. Understand factors behind environmental quality (e.g. drainage).
Port Environmental Review System	2003–	Prepare and structure an annual environmental report, externally reviewed and certified for validity. Start of EMS.

Note
The table shows a progression of tools and reports compiled during the evolution of an environmental programme. Port environmental managers are seeking to provide a framework that integrates these individual components in order to avoid duplication and to improve access to, and interpretation of, data.

that may be common to other ports. Indeed, some are based on European port-sector standards such as the Port Environmental Review System (PERS) (Eco-Ports 2003). However, the exact design of the various components of an environmental programme or EMS will naturally vary according to the circumstances of the individual port.

Monitoring environmental performance: technologies and data collection methodologies

In the context of assessing and regulating environmental and human health impacts of anthropogenic activities, specifically the introduction of wastes, ICES (1989) defines monitoring as 'the repeated measurement of an activity or of a contaminant or of its effects, whether direct or indirect, in the environment'. Monitoring is increasingly being used as an investigative, diagnostic and environmental management tool. Indeed, it has been described as 'the sensory component of environmental management' (NRC 1990). Indicators themselves are quantified information that demonstrates environmental quality and management performance over time. The argument now pursued is that production of these performance indicators first entails collecting data on human activities, or monitoring of the environment, and the most efficient way of making these measurements is within an integrated monitoring network. The large volume of data produced will then require dedicated information management so that it can be properly collated, stored and interrogated. This can be achieved via EMIS – a toolbox of applications that are related to the functional requirements of port managers (e.g. waste management, contingency planning, spatial planning).

The European Sea Ports Organisation's environmental review (2001) recommended that ports should consider what environmental monitoring is required in order to assess their environmental progress. It also stressed the need to establish a number of relevant indicators, with targets, to measure such progress. Today, an increasing number of port authorities are including such recommendations in their environmental (and/or annual) reports and reviews. Table 10.2 lists a typical set of indicators now used by European ports.

As previously noted, port operators have in the past been more concerned with the effect of the environment on their activities than with the effects and impacts of their operations on the environment. Atmospheric, oceanographic and hydrodynamic components have traditionally been monitored for their effect on the safety of navigation, berth performance, manoeuvring and navigable depth. Today, however, an increasing number of ports are monitoring environmental quality and their own environmental performance for a variety of reasons, including a direct response to legislation and the expectations of a range of stakeholders. Monitoring in order to demonstrate compliance with legislation has been a major driver as port authorities seek ways to confirm conformity and reduce the possibility of prosecution, with all the implications that would have in terms of penalties and poor public relations. Evidence of the achievement of policy objectives can be validated only by reference to carefully

Table 10.2 Selected examples of parameters for monitoring key port issues

Issue	Parameter	Technique	Significance	Rank[a]
Health and safety	Total days per annum lost to injury or accident	Reporting form and database	Calculation of the economic costs of health and safety failures	1
Waste management	Mass of materials (kcal/kg) in waste stream	Dedicated waste reception facilities and management system	Assessment of requirements for storage and landfill	2
Dredging	Spatial tracking of vessel	Real-time monitoring of dredging activity: GPS, logger and database	Assessment of disturbance of seabed	3
Water quality	Faecal streptococci organisms/ 100ml	Standard water quality analysis for bacteria	Comparison against EU Directive levels	4
Noise	Complaints about noise per 1,000 population	Structured complaints procedure and database of complaints	Assess in combination with compliance monitoring	5
Soil contamination	Heavy metals, e.g. cadmium (ppm wet weight)	Grab sampling and laboratory analysis	Trends in relative toxicity of sediments in parts of port	6
Dust	Particulates (e.g. grain dust) $\mu g \ m^3$	Impingers, air bubblers or gravimetric pump	Identification of potential health concerns, assessment against standards	7
Air quality	Concentration of SO_2: 98 percentile daily averages ($\mu g/m^3$)	Spectroscope or integrators	Tracking the source of air pollution and monitoring impacts of new technology	8
Habitat loss	Areal coverage of habitats (ha)	Remote sensing, trawls, traps, underwater photography, dive surveys	Assessment of changes in areal coverage of habitats	9
Energy use	Electricity consumption (kWh per degree day)	Metering and audit system	Eco-efficiency of buildings and work practices	10
Traffic volume	Emission factors for road traffic (CO_2/NO_x (g/km)	Monitoring, surveillance and recording of road movements	Health and safety implications of regularly high concentrations of emissions	11

Note:
a Rank refers to the priority given to the issue within the Port Self-Diagnosis Methodology (SDM) (1998). In total, 30 issues were reported.

monitored targets. The reduction of environmental risk can best be addressed by monitoring to establish patterns and trends of specific pollutant pathways, and thus early warning of significant changes or impacts. The build-up of information on specific issues derived from monitoring can be used to support decision-making processes, and repeated measurements of significant criteria can be used to construct baselines of data for comparison over time, the establishment of benchmarks, and the verification of standards.

Port authorities face a range of challenges and dilemmas in selecting effective monitoring strategies and identifying appropriate indicators. Major environmental issues may not necessarily be the direct responsibility of the authority. However, as in the case of identifying significant environmental aspects for purposes of EMS documentation under ISO 14001, many ports are taking some action to monitor on the basis that they may be considered to 'have influence' over the related activities, or that the issue itself is of pronounced local significance. Ports are increasingly accepting the notion that it is in the best interests of the sector, and the individual port itself, to monitor selected impacts of their own activities (and some of those of their clients or tenants) in order to demonstrate due diligence; avoid fines and costly clean-up or remedial operations; provide baseline, mitigating and reference data; and facilitate the implementation of environmental standards and award schemes. Legally adequate and scientifically sound criteria for use as indicators can serve the goals of environmental protection by providing not just the standards by which achievements can be tested, but also the units of assessment for comparison in the often contentious debate between conservation and profit, legislation and self-regulation, sustainability and development. However, informed decision making and appropriate management response options can be achieved only on the basis of a reasonable scientific understanding of the various interactions involved and the identification of relevant determinants by which environmental quality and performance can be assessed. The performance of carefully selected indicators derived from an appropriate monitoring programme can add objectivity to the debate on environmental quality – an area of concern often dominated by emotion, dogma and subjectivity.

With the realisation of the importance of relevance, ports are increasingly seeking a rationale to counter the 'if it moves, measure it' philosophy, a description with which some research monitoring was often branded. This is because exhaustive monitoring is unrealistic in the pragmatic and cost-conscious world of commercial ports and shipping. Also, it is unnecessary to monitor everything that may be considered to be a pollutant, let alone every parameter that may possibly affect the pollution process (McMullon 1997). Instead, systematic scoping of the monitoring criteria, methods and equipment should be carried out in order to ensure focus on the significant issues. Table 10.2 provides selected examples of parameters monitored for priority port environmental issues, and the associated monitoring techniques. Tabor (1990) points out that monitoring programmes require analytical and bioassay data that are scientifically sound in terms of accuracy and precision, and that the methodology must be free of artefacts and interferences. The port sector can demonstrate strategies and techniques based on point source, diffuse, effect and baseline monitoring. The latter, 'the description of conditions existing at a point in time against which subsequent changes can be detected through monitoring' (Beanlands 1988), has been a particularly useful approach for ports developing the first phases of environmental management as it has assisted in determining pollutant and activity cause–effect relationships.

In terms of actually executing monitoring programmes, ports have in the past cited lack of resources and in-house expertise, as well as legal requirements, as reasons for not spending time and budget on such activities. However, several factors have encouraged ports to adopt a more proactive approach to monitoring in recent years. The development and reporting of monitoring programmes by an increasing number of port authorities have reflected the availability of a wide range of relatively user-friendly and cost-effective sensors; the real-time capability of many systems; the 'value-added' aspect in that many of the indicators and parameters measured are also useful for the management of health and safety issues (and vice versa); and the perceived value of being able to demonstrate voluntary self-regulation of environmental responsibility. Many initiatives for port environmental management acknowledge that ports require a dedicated database of information for surveillance of activities, monitoring and auditing (International Navigation Association 1999). The development of such databases has been enhanced in many cases by the recognition that not all information needs to be directly monitored by the port itself. Ports are increasingly aware of the wealth of data held by regulatory authorities and other interested parties such as NGOs and special interest groups. To gain these economies, many ports are actively forging monitoring links at local, regional, national and international levels, both within the sector and with other industries and agencies.

Monitoring tools can be most effectively organised within a well-designed monitoring network. Ports can also use data from other programmes, such as local government agencies responsible for monitoring water quality, or research programmes to model pollutant pathways. They can contribute to, and collaborate with, wider monitoring strategies for coastal zones (Tyler-Walters 1997). However, their own monitoring strategies must consider both local and regional trends in order to provide useful information. For example, water quality sampling within a port might concentrate on local suspected sources of contaminants, and areas of ecological importance; the least contaminated areas might also be chosen to provide some kind of reference value. In addition, however, regional sampling is required to assess the inputs to the marine system from upstream, the natural variability of the seas, and the extent to which impacts are cascading throughout the system. Beyond this there is the time dimension. In order to understand the significance of environmental impacts arising from port activities, monitoring and assessment of the system's long-term response – and of other factors affecting biological, physical and chemical interactions within the ecosystem – are required (Townend 2002).

Environmental management information systems in ports: rationale and experiences

Even when the focus is strictly on relevant criteria, today's advanced data collection and monitoring technologies used in response to environmental imperatives may produce an information glut. This is one major reason why IT-based EMIS are an essential tool for modern management. But there are also other drivers. Such systems do not simply cope with the scale of information available; they also allow for a consistent approach to environmental control from one port to another. Ports are keen to share technical, managerial and legal solutions to environmental problems in order to minimise duplication of effort and reduce environmental management costs. There is also a political desire – especially in Europe – for standardisation and cooperation in knowledge management between ports to reduce disparities in environmental efforts.

An EMIS has been described as 'a case-book or collection of tools organised into a system to support the administration of environmental management and planning tasks by . . . making information available to executives and the public through co-ordinating existing systems and investments by a common architecture' (Gunther 1998: 160). There is an emphasis on using information about human activity and the human interactions with the environment, and it is this that distinguishes EMIS from environmental information systems (EIS).[5] Ports already have extensive and positive experiences of managing complex information, for example in relation to vessel traffic management systems (Hanekamp 2000) as well as in the use of intelligent systems to integrate quay management, vessel loading and electronic data interchange (UNCTAD 1993). With this experience, theoretically it should be simple to link systems that manage the relevant environmental data. In practice, however, the task is extremely complex and frequently fails in large organisations[6] because of the magnitude of the challenge of linking common tools within a toolbox. Consequently, the following discussion focuses on a number of important factors relating to this task of integrating, within the port setting, major tools such as audits, reports, databases and decision support systems. Figure 10.3 presents a model for networking existing port tools, collaborative data – in this case European – and standard methods within a port EMIS.

A recent EU DG TREN research programme has focused on developing a flexible and incremental approach to EMIS on a European scale (EcoPorts 2003). A number of major findings are now emerging from this and other recent research projects designed to assess and improve the environmental performance of seaports and terminals (EcoPorts 2003). One important result is that large-scale technological solutions for port environmental information systems will become widely used only if they are flexible enough to incorporate existing tools used by ports. The previous sections have alluded to the considerable investments that many ports have already made in environmental management, and it is the capability of EMIS to act as an intelligent architecture to link these existing tools that forms the most efficient solution.

A second significant conclusion is that the development of the technical

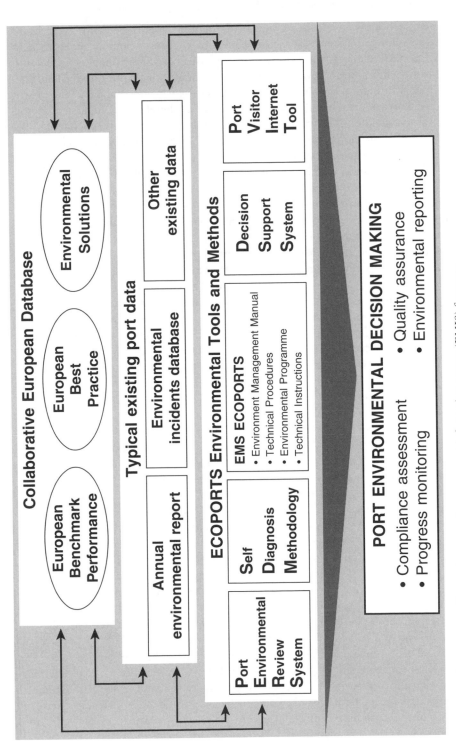

Figure 10.3 Components of an environmental management information system (EMIS) for ports.

aspects of systems, without accompanying human support elements, often leads to the failure of systems or their rejection by the port community. Since it is transportation that is the primary function of ports, many employees do not have a background in environmental management; nor do they understand the unique information processing requirements for environmental data. The provision of environmental and technical education is, therefore, an important factor in the successful implementation of EMIS. Success may also be encouraged by in-house applications that enable information systems to reflect working practices in ports more accurately.

The information science literature also attests to the fact that many IT projects take a technocentric approach to developing information systems, and neglect the informal, human elements (Mayda 1997). There is a need for research that assesses not only the capability of IT tools, but also their ability to aid broader 'human' information systems. The technical specifications for integrated environmental management systems, although necessarily specialised for the port and marine environment, are within modern technological capabilities. However, the organisational changes required to enable staff to implement port environmental management are a more comprehensive undertaking.

In sum, information systems have the potential to provide an economically efficient and effective toolbox for ports undertaking environmental management. Specific technical solutions are required to network environmental tools, and these can work if they allow ports to incorporate the output of existing environmental management programmes. Optimisation, however, requires a focus on the human element, providing adequate training support, and modelled accurately on port working practices.

What has not yet been considered, but must not be overlooked, is that information systems also have a role to play in the final phase of the information cycle: dissemination. Ports are under growing pressure to demonstrate their environmental credentials through transparency of action and the publication of environmental strategies and performance data. Increasingly, environmental legislation encourages ports to organise their environmental information in a form that is relevant to shareholders, regulators, clients, insurers and the public. Evidence of ports' environmental achievements (or otherwise) needs to be provided through the promulgation of appropriate performance indicators.

Traditionally, of course, this has been achieved via printed documents. Best practice in this regard is perhaps provided by the Scandinavian countries, which have imposed some of the most exacting reporting standards. In Sweden, for example, the Environmental Code (chapter 9, §6, section 1) requires all harbours and docks accessible to ships of more than 1,350 GRT to provide an annual environmental report. These reports are guided by advice from the Swedish Environment Protection Agency (General Advice 96: 1). Typically they provide a formal review of licences and permits issued, and report data on emissions and waste. Crucially, they aim to balance the danger of reader overload with the provision of sufficient information to allow the port to verify the report's claims and demonstrate precautionary measures taken (Fortes and

Akerfeldt 1999; Port of Göteborg 2002). Inevitably, however, even best-practice hard-copy reports tend to have a restricted circulation, which increasingly means that transparency and accountability tend to fall further behind the rising expectations set by current societies. Against this background it is appropriate to return to the theme of IT applications pursued earlier in this chapter. One particularly effective way of communicating environmental commitment and achievement to stakeholders, regulators and the public should be the Internet. What evidence is there that this potential is being exploited?

Table 10.3 lists the results of an online global survey of a random sample of

Table 10.3 Environmental reporting on port Web sites, 2003

A	*Do ports provide evidence of environmental management or planning online?*			
	Americas	*Europe*	*Oceania*	*Total*
Positive result:	15/22	14/19	9/9	38/50
	68%	74%	100%	76%

B	*Do ports publish an environmental policy online?*			
	Americas	*Europe*	*Oceania*	*Total*
Positive result:	11/22	7/19	7/9	25/50
	50%	37%	78%	50%

C	*Do ports publish an environmental report online?*			
	Americas	*Europe*	*Oceania*	*Total*
Positive result:	2/22	3/19	3/9	8/50
	9%	16%	33%	18%

D	*Do ports put environmental monitoring data online?*			
	Americas	*Europe*	*Oceania*	*Total*
Positive result:	4/22	5/19	7/9	16/50
	18%	26%	78%	32%

E	*Do ports advertise achievement of ISO/EMAS/other certification of environmental management system?*			
	Americas	*Europe*	*Oceania*	*Total*
Positive result:	0/22	2/19	5/9	7/50
	0%	11%	56%	14%

Note
Figures indicate the number of affirmative statements from the total number of Web sites analysed.

50 port Web sites. In some respects the data are encouraging. A large majority of the ports sampled provided information relating to environmental management and planning, while half set out their environmental policies. However, only a third put environmental monitoring data online, and less than a fifth gave access to a complete environmental report or publicised an environmental management system certified by ISO, the Eco-Management and Audit Scheme (EMAS) or any similar agency.[7] Overall, the high proportion providing at least some environmental information indicates that more ports are reporting publicly in a very accessible manner, as recommended by various codes of practice such as EMAS. The credibility of these reports depends on the quality of the environmental performance data and the inclusion of science-based evidence from environmental monitoring. It is evident that in these respects there is still much that remains to be done. In this sense, major shortfalls remain with respect to ports' environmental accountability to the public.

The fact that much remains to be done should not be taken to indicate that the process ports use to address environmental demands has stalled. Progress continues to be made with new technology-based management tools, and reporting is on an upward curve. Moreover, in Europe at least, considerable momentum has been developed in recent years as ports have collaborated on a broad front to implement a plan of action. The vehicle for this collaboration has been the ESPO, formed in 1993 as the EU member states' independent port sector representative organisation. Funded and run by its roughly 700 members, ESPO can be considered a role model for collaboration.

ESPO collaboration and improved environmental management

One of ESPO's first activities was to produce an environmental code of practice (ESPO 1994) that combined recommendations on a management approach with objectives and targets for priority issues such as dredging, port planning and development, and emergency response plans. The code attempted to take into account the remarkable diversity of the sector as expressed in terms of the location, size, type, ownership, and local and national policies of its membership of around 700 ports. Benchmark environmental initiatives driven by ESPO include the setting up of Environmental Challenges for European Port Authorities (ECEPA) (de Bruijn 1998), to provide a vehicle for initiating joint environmental research projects between ports from different member states. Another contributory activity has been the commissioning of ESPO's Environmental Survey in 1996, aimed, first, at assessing the sector's response to major environmental management issues and, second, at establishing benchmark performance for future monitoring of progress. There has also been active participation in the EU Eco-Information project (1996–9) which was co-funded by several major European port authorities. This research and development initiative established a network of cooperation on environmental issues between port partners and resulted in practical tools for reviewing environmental management performance such as the 'Self-Diagnosis Methodology' (SDM'98).

ESPO published an environmental review in 2001 as a follow-up to its original code. Today the collaborative momentum is being maintained by the involvement of ESPO ports in the co-funded EU EcoPorts Project (2002–5), the main goals being to harmonise the approach of port administrations in Europe to environmental management and to exchange best practices in respect of port-related environmental issues. The significance of these initiatives is that they have produced tangible tools and methodologies to assist implementation of publicly declared sector policies. They include a database of practical solutions, a new (2003) SDM for reviewing environmental management performance, and a PERS designed to assist development of an EMS.[8] A methodological guide to practical solutions applied to the port-city area, a forum for the exchange of experience, and a Web site[9] for networked access to news, developments and results are also available to participating partners. In the near future, EMIS and training support are envisaged products of the continuing project.

ESPO's overall declared policy towards environmental management is to encourage compliance with legislation and the attainment of high standards through voluntary schemes of self-regulation. Ports in the organisation wish to create a 'level playing field' by limiting consideration of the environment as a competitive factor. The strategy for implementation is based on 'ports helping ports' through networked exchange of shared experience, together with the provision of tools and methodologies to assist with putting in place the recommendations of the ESPO code. One way to judge the extent to which these port-inspired initiatives have been successful is to evaluate, through independent analysis, port managers' perceptions of progress in environmental management (Wooldridge 2000). Port authorities are now commenting favourably on the benefits of implementing a positive environmental programme. They include in these benefits cost savings; reduced environmental impact; improved public image and fewer complaints; an enhanced safety regime; wider port development opportunities; improved stakeholder relationships; and better

Table 10.4 Progress in port environmental management, 1996-2003

Management Component	1996 (%)	2003 (%)	Increase (%)
Does the port authority have an environmental plan?	45	62	+17
Does the plan aim for 'compliance-plus'?	32	45	+13
Does the plan aim to raise environmental awareness?	44	56	+12
Is environmental monitoring carried out in the port?	53	69	+16
Does the plan involve community and stakeholders?	53	56	+3

Source: Derived from surveys in 1996 and 2003 by the European Sea Ports Organisation. Results for 2003 are as yet interim. As the numbers and identity of respondent ports are not the same in the two surveys, the trends of progress are more significant than the percentage values imply.

compliance with legislation. Moreover, as Table 10.4 demonstrates, the period since ESPO's formation has been marked by increasingly positive attitudes to the environment among port operators, attitudes that have led to a clear improvement in standards. By 2003, around two-thirds of respondents reported that their ports engaged in environmental management and had an environmental plan. A majority indicated that their plans were intended to improve environmental awareness and involve the community and other stakeholders. And almost half were aiming for 'compliance plus'.

Conclusion

Progress in European port environmental management has been driven by increasing legislation and regulation, and through recognition of the common challenges posed by environmental issues. Additional drivers have been the impact of societal expectations and, most recently, the emergence of the deliberate policy that the environment should be a pre-competitive factor among European ports. While port sector activity in this field initially produced a wide range of responses, mostly issue led, an impressive recent trend has been a shift towards mutual assistance through collaboration. The fruits of this – which are admittedly still developing – have been structures and methodologies with the potential to standardise approaches to environmental management and remove the environment as a competitive factor.

An upturn in levels of environmental reporting arguably demonstrates another positive change in attitude towards environmental management by port professionals. Progress towards an integrated approach, with all its attendant benefits, is being made through a series of iterative steps. This reflects the diversity of approach, resources, awareness and attitudes within the port sector. Policy at a European level is well established and widely accepted. However, the major gap between policy objective and environmental quality is the critical phase of implementation at the local level. It is at this local level that technical developments will play an important role. Tools and methodologies derived from collaborative research and development (such as environmental management systems, decision support systems, Self-Diagnosis Methodology, the Port Environmental Review System and databases, auditing and performance analyses) increasingly provide the mechanism for implementation. Particularly significant is the fact that these developments frequently place environmental issues in the business plan itself and, in the process, acknowledge the benefits of an integrated approach to information management – benefits that can accrue to both the individual port and the sector.

Yet despite this progress, for commercial port managers and designated environmental managers the challenges remain substantial and varied – depending, of course, on the existing approaches in each port. The establishment of environmental performance and monitoring programmes, and key indicators, is crucial to producing the evidence and understanding that will support practical environmental management. There is increasing pressure from regulators and the local community for port authorities to demonstrate unambiguous evidence of their claims regarding sustainable development and compliance with legislation. The result is that the sector has begun to identify port-specific performance indicators of both environmental quality and environmental management activity. Various physical, chemical, biological and managerial indicators are emerging and are being applied over a growing number of port areas. These in turn require the development of environmental management information systems in order to structure information into a retrievable format and maximise the components that allow an integrated response.

EMIS can be developed in a number of ways, but experience suggests that a networked and incremental approach will allow maximum flexibility to accommodate the existing individual tools that ports have developed. Experience in developing and validating an EMIS approach also demonstrates the importance of taking into consideration the human dimension. In themselves, technological 'solutions' are not sufficient. Continued progress to ensure the user-friendliness of EMIS is a key goal if these tools are to be accepted and used by the port community. Also key in the human context is capacity building among European port professionals. Despite the advances of recent years, there are still opportunities among port staff for increased understanding of environmental solutions and environmentally friendly practices. As ports seek to make progress on these fronts, it may well be that useful lessons – positive or negative – can be learned from elsewhere in the world. What is certainly evident is that, while the European experience has great relevance for port management in other continents, there is still considerable scope to refine the quality of the knowledge we are currently able to export.

Notes

1 Some European ports have even gone as far as to engage in conservation in order to enhance the working environment for their employees or gain positive public relations. The port of Bristol, for example, includes wildlife corridors within the port area, as well as an owl conservation initiative.

2 This kind of environmental information has the potential to become more easily available to ports as environmental agencies take an increasingly networked approach to managing their own data.

3 The Eco-Information (1999) survey estimates that the number of European ports having an environmental plan increased by 17 per cent (from a baseline of 44 per cent) between 1996 and 1999.

4 Profitable options refer to the capital benefits of a healthy environment, which can be degraded. For example, the possibility of using the port area for recreational purposes is lost if there is a severe reduction of water quality.

5 Environmental information systems are likely to contain more extensive pure science information, such as that needed to resolve questions of environmental impact, than is the case with EMIS.

6 A failure rate of 60 per cent has been quoted by Coopers and Lybrand (1996) in a recent international study of organisational systems development.

7 When the data are broken down by broad global region, they suggest that Oceania tends to lead the Americas and Europe. With only nine ports sampled in Oceania, however, this difference could be more apparent than real.

8 PERS has the option of applying voluntarily for a Certificate of Validation based on independent review and attainment of the specified standard of management.
9 www.ecoports.com.

References

Associated British Ports (ABP) (1999) *Humber Ports and Estuary Strategy*, Southampton: ABP.

Barrow, C.J. (1999) *Environmental Management: Principles and Practice*, London: Routledge.

Beanlands, G. (1988) *Scoping Methods and Baseline Studies in EIA*, in P. Warthern (ed.) *Environmental Impact Assessment: Theory and Practice*, London: Unwin Hyman, pp. 33–46.

Born, S.M. and Sonzogni, W.C. (1995) 'Integrated environmental management: strengthening the conceptualisation', *Environmental Management*, 19: 161–181.

Coopers and Lybrand (1996) *Managing Information Systems and Systems Risk: Results of an International Survey of Large Organisations*, London: Coopers and Lybrand.

Couper, A.D. (1992) 'Environmental port management', *Maritime Policy and Management*, 19: 165–170.

de Bruijn, H. *Forward Programme for Environmental Research*, Proceedings of ESPO Environmental Conference, Lisbon, 29 May 1998, Gare Maritima de Alcantara: European Sea Ports Organisation.

Dover Harbour Board (2001) *Annual Report and Accounts*, Dover: DHB.

Eco-Information (1999) *Eco-Information in European Ports: Sharing Knowledge Towards Environmental Regulation in the Port-City Area. Final Report*, EC Transport RTD Programme, The Hague: Eco-Information Secretariat.

EcoPorts (2003) 'Environmental management information system', available at http://www.ecoports.com/ports/tools/index.asp (accessed 1 May 2003).

European Sea Ports Organisation (ESPO) (1994) *Environmental Code of Practice*, Brussels: ESPO.

—— (2001) *Environmental Review*, Brussels: ESPO.

Fortes, H.J. and Akerfeldt, K. (1999) *Environmental Reporting in Sweden*, London: Middlesex University Business School.

Gunther, O. (1998) *Environmental Information Systems*, Berlin: Springer-Verlag.

Hanekamp, H.B. (2000) 'The port of Rotterdam: how ECDIS, GIS, EPFS and AIS technologies can help in developing a vessel traffic management and information service', *Port Technology International*, 9: 17–22.

International Chamber of Commerce (ICC) (1993) 'Business Charter for Sustainable Development: principles for environmental management', *Environmental Conservation*, 20: 82–83.

International Council for the Exploration of the Seas (ICES) (1989) *Report of the ICES Advisory Committee on Marine Pollution, 1988*, Co-operative Research Report no. 160, Copenhagen: ICES.

International Navigation Association (PIANC) (1999) *Environmental Management Framework for Ports and Related Industries*, Report of PIANC PEC Working Group 4, Brussels: International Navigation Association.

International Organization for Standardization (ISO) (1996) *ISO 14001. Environmental Management Systems: Specification with Guidance for Use*, Brussels: European Committee for Standardization (CEN).

McMullon, C. (1997) 'The Validity of Scientific Criteria for the Environmental Auditing of Port and Harbour Operations', unpublished PhD thesis, University of Wales, Cardiff.

Mayda, J. (1997) 'Policy and decision-making as a focus for integrated data management', in N.B. Harmancioglu and M.N. Alpaslan (eds) *Integrated Approach to Environmental Data Management Systems*, Dordrecht, the Netherlands: Kluwer Academic, pp. 67–78.

National Research Council (NRC) (1990) *Managing Troubled Waters: The Role of Marine Environmental Monitoring*, Marine Board, NRC, Washington, DC: National Academy Press.

Port of Göteborg (2002) *Environmental Report, 2002*, Göteborg: Port of Göteborg.

Tabor, M.W. (1990) 'Chemical analysis for assessment and evaluation of environmental pollutants: fact or artifact?', in S.S. Sandhu, W.R. Lower, F.J. De Seres, W.A. Suk and R.R. Tice (eds) *In situ Evaluations of Biological Hazards of Environmental Pollutants*, Environmental Scientific Research vol. 38, New York: Plenum Press.

Townend, I. (2002) 'Marine science for strategic planning and management: the requirement for estuaries', *Marine Policy*, 26: 209–219.

Tyler-Walters, H. (1997) 'Monitoring programme design and implementation in coastal management initiatives in England and Wales', unpublished MSc dissertation, University College of Wales, Aberystwyth.

United Nations Conference on Trade and Development (UNCTAD) (1983) *Planning Land Use in Port Areas: Getting the Most Out of Port Infrastructure*, UNCTAD Monographs on Port Management, UNCTAD/SHIP/494(2), Geneva: UNCTAD.

—— (1993) *Computerized Container Terminal Management*, UNCTAD Monographs on Port Management, UNCTAD/SHIP/494(10), Geneva: UNCTAD.

Valencia Port Authority (2002) *Guide for the Implementation of Environmental Management Systems in Port Facilities*, Valencia: Port Institute for Studies and Cooperation (IPEC).

Vandermeulen, J. H. (1996) 'Environmental trends of ports and harbours: implications for planning and management', *Maritime Policy and Management*, 23: 55–66.

Whitehead (2001) quoted in *Select Committee on Environment, Transport and Regional Affairs, Minutes of Evidence. Evidence given on Wednesday 14 February 2001*, London: The Stationary Office.

Wooldridge, C.F. (2000) 'Quality assurance in European port operations', *BIMCO Bulletin*, Baltic and International Maritime Council, 95(1) (February): 55–58.

11 Port development and implementation challenges in environmental management

The case of Venice

Stefano Soriani

Introduction

Over the past few decades, environmental issues in coastal areas have acquired an ever-greater importance. Coastal environments provide the setting in which new conflictual relationships between different economic uses (transport, manufacturing, fishing, aquaculture, tourism, outdoor recreation, etc.) take place. At the same time there is broad recognition of the important role that coastal ecosystems, in particular wetlands and other shallow estuarine and coastal habitats, play in providing and maintaining biodiversity and productivity (Pinder and Witherick 1990).

From these two perspectives it is clear that the position of ports is crucial (Allen 1996; Vallega 1996; Vandermeulen 1996; World Bank 1990). Their role in sustaining the globalisation of economies and in shaping global traffic flows is of basic importance, while their territorial and environmental impacts are strong. Dredging and mud disposal, traffic congestion, air pollution and land consumption represent important threats to coastal environments despite some reductions in the pressures on water, air and land from some traditional port-related industrial activities. Moreover, while the local or regional economic importance of ports has generally decreased as a result of a dispersal along the whole logistics chain (owing to their changed role in transport networks and to technological and organisational improvements), their environmental and territorial impacts still remain strongly localised (Pinder 2002; Slack 2002; Soriani 2002).

The challenges brought about by the interplay of economic and environmental forces, together with the pressures from environmentalists in the most developed countries, have given rise to ever more severe environmental regulations at a multitude of scales. At the same time, there is a lower social tolerance of environmental problems (Pinder 2002). As a consequence, environmental policies and management arrangements at a variety of scales (local, regional, national and international) have become mandatory strategic considerations for port policy and planning. Today, environmental issues and regulations are as much factors shaping the success of ports as are the more traditional economic forces of competition (Couper 1992; Finney and David 1995; Slack 2002).

The present chapter explores how the relationships between port development and environmental protection have changed recently in a very particular territorial case: the lagoon of Venice. Here, because of the very specific nature of the city and its lagoon, development and conservation goals have been in sharp conflict for many decades. It is only recently that a prescription for a more sustainable form of port development has begun to emerge (Soriani and Zanetto 2002). The chapter pays particular attention to the ways in which economic and market tendencies, political arrangements and cultural/social values can interact in order to reconcile port development and environmental protection in the lagoon.

The discussion is organised as follows. Attention is given first to the most important features of the port and industrial development in the lagoon during the twentieth century, and how this development contributed to the modification of the lagoon ecosystem. This review provides a picture of how port activity has consistently played a role in ordering and regulating natural processes in the lagoon (mainly the deposition of sediments coming from the mainland), and producing direct and severe environmental impacts as the result of the modernisation of port activities. The following section identifies the most important contemporary environmental problems, based upon three decades of studies and research which started after the flooding in November 1966[1] (Soriani 1996; Zanetto and Soriani 1998). The analysis then turns to the environmental policy proposals that have been presented recently. These provide a general context in which the port has to operate and have clear implications for its future development. Discussion focuses next on the recent evolution of local port activity, aiming to understand how the local port function is changing, and how this may contribute to environmental sustainability in the lagoon. These changing functions may allow the port to grasp new market opportunities while helping reconcile development and protection goals. The environmental management measures that the Venice Port Authority is promoting to address its important challenges are then reviewed. These challenges include the search for new areas for expansion, the problem of dredging and canal maintenance, and the problem of how to manage polluted mud. In evaluating the relevance of the port's measures to protect the environment, the penultimate section considers the role that the Venice Port Authority is playing at the present time as an 'environmental manager' (Bryant and Wilson 1996). In particular, it examines the Authority's contribution to the spread of a new environmental discourse[2] regarding relationships between (i) economy/market and governance and (ii) environmental gains in the lagoon. The chapter concludes by showing how the Venice experience may shed light on the broader debate concerning port development and environmental protection and management.

Port-industry development in the lagoon of Venice: main features

There has always been a strong symbiotic relationship between Venice and its lagoon. On one hand, without the lagoon that separates the fragile urban fabric from the sea, Venice could not have survived and developed. On the other hand, it is through the efforts of the city that the natural tendency towards siltation has been counteracted and through which the lagoon has been maintained to facilitate navigation and trade. The lagoon, therefore, can be regarded as the product of centuries-long human intervention that has been aimed at balancing terrestrial and maritime forces.

It is possible to argue that the lagoon worked as a locally sustainable system up to the twentieth century: organic wastes could be easily disposed of and recycled; the state of technology in maritime transportation did not require a large amount of space for infrastructures or deep canals; and the port function was based on commercial activities which could easily find a home in the city (Zanetto and Soriani 1998). This picture radically changed with the port-industrial development which occurred in the interior edge of the lagoon in the twentieth century. The reclamation of about 500 ha of marshes led to the establishment of the 'first industrial area', which came into operation at the end of the First World War. After the Second World War the 'second industrial zone' was built (1,500 ha). Then, in the 1960s, a new expansion area, the 'third industrial zone', was planned. At the end of the 1960s the 'oil canal' was dredged to allow larger and larger tankers and commercial vessels to enter the port without passing through the San Marco basin (Figure 11.1).

All these operations precipitated severe environmental impacts. As well as contributing significant air pollution (Cossu and de Fraja Frangipane 1985), port-industrial development greatly modified the lagoon's morphology. The construction of new coastal defences led to a clean-cut separation between land and water. The building of new roads and the impressive urbanisation which followed the development of the port-industrial complex along the margins of the lagoon, during the 1950s and 1960s, sharpened the boundaries still further. The increasing size of vessels called for the construction of deep linear channels in the lagoon, and the progressive strengthening of the inlet jetties (Zanetto and Soriani 1998). Finally, groundwater take for industrial purposes, combined with natural subsidence and eustasy, resulted in the reduction of Venice's lagoon beds. One result has been that the high tide (acqua alta) phenomenon has steadily increased in frequency and magnitude (Carbognin *et al.* 1993; Zanda 1991).

It is interesting to place the early-twentieth-century development of Porto Marghera within the context of the cultural and political debate concerning the preservation of the city of the lagoon from the envisaged effects of the modernisation of port activities. Even in the early part of the century it was clear that the city of the lagoon could not be home to a 'modern' port. For that reason, Porto Marghera was promoted by its developers as the only way to protect the historic city. It was argued that building 'modern Venice' on the mainland was essential for ensuring the physical and economic survival of 'ancient Venice' (Volpi 1939). Even as late as 1967, referring to the operations that reclaimed part of the lagoon for new sites for industrial development, some of Porto Marghera's industrialists wrote, 'Where it was a barren and inhospitable nature,

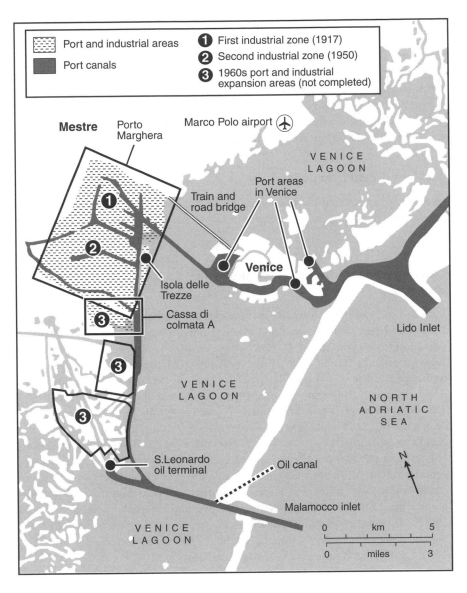

Figure 11.1 The Venice lagoon: main port channels and port and industrial areas. The 'first industrial zone' is the commercial sector of the port of Venice on the mainland. The 2000 Port Planning Scheme envisages the expansion of the commercial port on redundant industrial sites in this zone. Chemicals and petrochemicals are the main activities in the 'Second industrial zone'. The 1984 Special Law for Venice considers the Cassa di Colmata to be appropriate for commercial port activities.

now it is economic improvement, social progress and a well-preserved Venice' (Associazione Industriali della Provincia di Venezia 1967). Yet only a few years later, surveys conducted on the evolution of the lagoon ecosystem made it clear that what had been intended to protect the city from the effects of industrial development had turned out to be the most serious threat for both the city and the lagoon. The degradation of ecosystems, and the worsening of the high tide phenomenon, can now be seen as the unintended effects of policies designed to accommodate the needs of port and industrial development while trying to pre-serve the historical urban settlements in the lagoon.

The lagoon environment

In order to understand the context in which the port operates, it is necessary to review the most important environmental challenges as they are recognised today.

Lowering of the lagoon beds and the 'acqua alta' *(high tide) phenomenon*

Venice is increasingly threatened by flooding. At the beginning of the twentieth century St Mark's Square was flooded seven times a year. Today, unusually high tide conditions occur about 40 times per year, with seven events exceeding 1 m above mean sea level. While at the beginning of the twentieth century the return period for very high tides (such as that of 1966) was about 800 years, now it is about 200 years (Zanda 1991; Consorzio Ricerche Laguna 1999). This worsening high-tide phenomenon was caused by the reduction in the height of the land with reference to sea level (about 23 cm), that occurred during the twentieth century. This fall was due to the joint effect of eustasy (11 cm) and subsidence (12 cm). Subsidence was partly natural (4 cm), owing to structural geomorphologic changes (consolidation of alluvial deposits), but was chiefly induced by water drained from aquifers by Porto Marghera's industries during the period 1930–70 (8 cm, with the highest peaks occurring in the 1960s). In connection with the later discussion, it is important to note that this human-induced subsidence stopped in the 1970s as the systems for providing water for urban and industrial uses were improved.

Sea level rise

Still controversial are the predictions of future sea level rise. Three different sce-narios have been recently produced, based on studies produced locally and by the Intergovernmental Panel on Climate Change (Consorzio Ricerche Laguna 1999). The first scenario is based on the fact that in the past two decades no eustatic change occurred; therefore, it foresees a sea level rise of about 5 cm, due only to natural subsidence, during the twenty-first century. The second scenario extrapolates the tendencies of the last century (eustasy and natural subsidence), producing an expected sea level rise of between 16 and 20 cm. This would bring about 37 high tide events per year that exceed 1 m. The third scenario considers the potential impacts for the north Adriatic Sea of global climate change due to greenhouse gas emissions. In this case, and according to different hypotheses, sea level rise increase would range between 22 and 31 cm. It is worth noting that a change of about 30 cm would lead to St Mark's Square being flooded about 360 times a year, with more than 120 tide events exceeding 1 m.

Morphological simplification

Over recent decades the lagoon has become increasingly flat and deep. The depth of the water has increased by an average of 30 cm. Having been protected for centuries by *siltation* and what may be referred to as *continentalisation*, the lagoon nowadays suffers more and more from *maritimisation*. While a key factor is the lowering of the seabed, this has been accentuated by the decreased contribution of sediments from the mainland and the creation of deeper and more linear port channels. It is recognised that the excavation of the latter (such as the 'oil canal') reinforced erosion and marsh degradation in the lagoon (Rinaldo 1997). As a result, about 50 per cent of the marshes that existed at the beginning of the twentieth century have been degraded and eventually lost (Consorzio Venezia Nuova 1997a).

Pollution, water quality and sediments

The quality of water in the lagoon depends on land uses in the drainage basin (1,872 km^2) and on local sources of pollution. As for the latter, the introduction of increasingly strict environmental regulations and technological improvements (together with the closing down of many basic industries) have reduced the pollution contributed by Porto Marghera industries in the past few decades. The process of degradation of water quality peaked in the 1970s and appears to have undergone a turnaround. However, the situation is still very serious in many parts of the central lagoon, as well as in most of the port channels (Zanetto and Soriani 1998). While the environmental problems of reclaiming redundant industrial sites are significant, one of the most important challenges is the management of polluted sediments in port channels. Here, the main threat is the beds' erosion dynamics, since erosion causes the dispersal of pollutants (Consorzio Venezia Nuova 1997a). In addition, there are increasing problems related to air pollution brought about by vehicular traffic and congestion, and also by greater port activity (see p. 222).

Environmental protection policies and implications for port activity

This section reviews recently proposed environmental protection policies and their potential implications for navigation.

Flooding and sea level rise countermeasures

Two types of measures have been prescribed to protect the city from flooding. The first involves maintaining and reinforcing the land interface and, where possible, raising the land surfaces. This action, which mainly affects the lower areas of Venice and of the other inhabited islands (Murano, Burano and Chioggia), has no potential implications for navigation and port activity. Second, the closure of the port entrances with mobile flood barriers (the MOSE project) aims to protect the city when tides exceed 1 m above sea level (today, this occurs about seven times a year). This is the most important measure. Its original version was based on a modular series of mobile gates hinged to a bottom base, with no intermediate piers, overhead structures or locks. The project as proposed now focuses on mobile gates for three main reasons: to safeguard landscape values; to minimise the potential impacts on navigation; and to reduce the impacts of the gates on the water exchange between the lagoon and the sea during normal tide conditions, thus avoiding the concentration of pollutants coming from the mainland (Consorzio Venezia Nuova 1997a).

This project is highly controversial, and many criticisms have been voiced (Penning-Rowsell *et al.* 1998). The most important objections include the arguments that:

- The project is too costly for a system that is designed to operate occasionally when the tides exceed 1 m.
- Even if the project has been designed with the goal of minimising the potential impacts on navigation, the construction phase, estimated to take seven years, will severely constrain shipping, according to the Venice Port Authority.
- Sea level rise predictions are still uncertain; this makes it difficult to assess the period of time beyond which such a project might prove inadequate.
- The focus of the project has been mainly on technical aspects (engineering and construction methods), while little attention has been paid to non-technical – yet still extremely important – questions such as public participation, stakeholders' involvement in the definition of coastal issues, environmental perception and communication.
- The evaluation procedure and the following debate have suffered from a lack of information.

Until now, the discussion has been marked by many conflicts, in particular between the Ministry of Public Works and the Ministry of the Environment, and between the Municipality of Venice and the Veneto Region. The National Commission for Environmental Impact Analysis opposed the project in 1998 (Ministero dell'Ambiente 1998). More recently, the project has regained attention at the national scale, and it is likely that some technical upgrading of options (mainly aimed at gaining support from the port industry) will be proposed and assessed.

Morphological restoration and improvements of the lagoon habitat

The morphological restoration of the lagoon is being pursued mainly through the creation of new salt marshes, using the sediments from the digging of the lagoon's navigation channels (this issue will be addressed on p. 225) and from new channels in areas that were previously silted up. The goal is to encourage the circulation of water in the inner parts of the lagoon. More than 300 ha of salt marshes and mud flats have been reconstructed in recent years using compatible sediments. Such measures are designed to mitigate the force of the sea, restore the lagoon habitat and encourage reduction of the nutrients discharged into the drainage basin by farming activities via phytodepuration (Consorzio Venezia Nuova 1997a).

The re-naturalisation concept and the increasing popularity of 'soft' approaches to environmental management

The concept of 're-naturalisation' (i.e. to recreate marshes, or re-meander canals, or 'let nature do the work' in coastal defence programmes) is gaining acceptance everywhere as a new paradigm of sustainable environmental management. This is in contrast to traditional approaches based on 'hard' engineering (French 1997). In Venice the debate about re-naturalisation has focused on measures such as the reopening of fish farms to tidal flows in order to extend the areas filled by high tides; the reconstruction of salt marshes in order to restore the typical lagoon habitats and improve ecological values; the re-meandering of the channels in order to reduce marine dynamics and to restore the lagoon as it was in the nineteenth century; and the reduction in depth of port canals and lagoon inlets.

These approaches assume that only a more 'natural' lagoon can protect the city from the Adriatic waters. These views have become very popular recently and are propagated by the green movement. However, it must be pointed out that there are serious questions about the efficacy of these proposals. The restoration of lagoon morphology by filling in the most important port channels would require the capability to place and stabilise an enormous quantity of mud, and the technical and economic feasibility of such operations have never been assessed. Furthermore, as has been noted, the main cause of flooding is not the deepening of port channels, but the lowering of the lagoon beds as result of the combined effects of subsidence and eustasy (Rinaldo 1997). Finally, re-naturalisation measures could hardly protect the city against sea level rise should this occur. This suggests, therefore, that new artificial forms of separation between the lagoon and the sea should be designed and implemented independently from other 'soft' measures of environmental management.

Environmental management measures: implications for the port

The proposed interventions will have important effects on local port activity. The restoration of the lagoon morphology to the state it was in the nineteenth century would make it impossible for the lagoon to accommodate a modern port. The proposed infilling of the oil channel and the reduction of the lagoon inlets' depth would pose substantial constraints for the functioning of the port as it operates today. Also, the MOSE project has been criticised by the port industry for its potential impacts on navigation. The debate on the project is presently at a standstill and it is not possible to predict the future outcome.

It is important to remember that the proposals were developed during the 1980s. At that time, the Venetian industrial complex was experiencing a deep crisis which led to significant job losses and a pending threat of the transfer of the oil traffic. At the same time, the commercial activities of the port were sluggish, while the tourist industry in Venice was growing, thereby helping the Venice region pass through a period of severe economic dislocation. Furthermore, other north Adriatic ports, such as Ravenna and Trieste, were experiencing expansion. In the 1980s Ravenna was one of the most dynamic ports in Italy, thanks to its private management and its available sites for expansion. The port of Trieste has always benefited from state financial support, owing to its geopolitical importance. In addition, the realisation of new infrastructure[3] enabled Trieste to become the only Italian port in the north Adriatic Sea where fourth-generation container vessels could operate. It was also during the 1980s that important intermodal initiatives were undertaken in the Veneto region, including the inland combined transport node of Verona and the Padua *interporto* for containers, which have become major logistics centres (Robiglio Rizzo 1996, 2002; van Klink and van den Berg 1998; Zanetto *et al.* 1999). Thus, it may be seen that the MOSE project was developed at a time when the prospects for the port of Venice were somewhat low, and when new transport nodes in the region were developing and attracting political and financial support. For these reasons, the interests of the port were not treated with much consideration when the environmental strategies for the Venice lagoon were being conceived.

A further controversy that has arisen recently concerns the costs that the port should bear with the introduction of limitations to navigation (such as the closure of the port entrances with mobile gates and without locks to guarantee movement between the lagoon and the Adriatic). The original proposal put forward by the Consorzio Venezia Nuova concluded that the mobile barriers would not hinder port activities, owing to the fact that the system would operate only in the case of severe high tides, and moreover, during such events the gates would completely block navigation only for a few hours (Consorzio Venezia Nuova 1997b). The issue has subsequently been subject to several evaluations. The most reliable research was carried out in 1982 and revised in 1992. It concluded that the most important consequence for the port would be the so-called shadow effect: the perception by commercial shipping lines of constraints on arrival and departure that would be particularly evident for the container and ro-ro shipping lines, owing to their need to maintain a regular schedule (Canestrelli *et al.* 1992). Almost 20 years later, the growing competition between ports and the increasingly important role of liners in directing traffic flows (Slack 1993, 2002) would appear to confirm the relevance of the above considerations.

It was in the context of this controversy that Venice Port Authority commissioned a study in 1997 to estimate the port's economic impact on the Venice area (COSES 1998). The results confirmed that port and port-related functions are still one of the main activities of the municipality. Undoubtedly, these findings contributed to further questioning of the project as proposed by the Consorzio Venezia Nuova. Should the MOSE solution remain the focal point of the protection strategy, it is likely that, in order to get the port industry's support, it would have to ensure that at least one of the lagoon inlets would include a lock system for allowing ships passage during high tide conditions.

Port activity trends and implications for the harmonisation of port development and environmental protection

Recent functional changes in local port activity are now outlined and considered in the context of how the port can contribute to environmental sustainability.

For decades, the most important function performed by the port of Venice was to sustain local industrial activity. The environmental debate that emerged after the 1966 flooding, the difficult employment conditions, and the significant restructuring processes which occurred in Porto Marghera industries all had important consequences for the port. Oil and industrial goods shipments have steadily declined since the late 1970s. The port's non-bulk traffic sector also stagnated during the 1970s and 1980s, because of port organisation problems experienced during the new era of containerisation. This latter problem was common to most Italian ports in this period (Ridolfi 1995, 1996).

The picture changed during the 1990s. As shown in Table 11.1, the port's commercial sector recorded a sharp increase in the second half of the last

Table 11.1 Venice: port throughput, 1984–2001

	Commercial		Industrial		Oil		Total	
	('000 t)	*(%)*	*('000 t)*	*(%)*	*('000 t)*	*(%)*	*('000 t)*	*(%)*
1984	3,584	14.4	9,542	38.4	11,704	47.2	24,830	100
1986	3,883	15.0	8,970	34.3	13,199	50.7	26,052	100
1988	4,282	17.0	9,686	38.2	11,390	44.9	25,358	100
1990	4,865	20.2	9,190	38.0	10,116	41.8	24,171	100
1992	4,751	19.4	8,504	34.7	11,252	45.9	24,507	100
1994	6,142	26.9	6,780	29.6	9,947	43.5	22,869	100
1996	7,363	30.3	6,445	26.6	10,458	43.1	24,266	100
1998	9,436	35.3	5,392	20.2	11,913	44.5	26,741	100
2000	10,305	36.6	7,290	25.9	10,581	37.5	28,176	100
2001	11,470	39.8	6,681	23.2	10,658	37.0	28,809	100

Source: Autorità Portuale di Venezia.

Table 11.2 Passenger traffic in Venice, 1992–2001

Year	Traditional ferry passengers	Cruise passengers	High-speed ferry passengers[a]	Total passengers
1992	49,687	165,767	28,157	234,611
1993	62,459	205,868	50,028	318,355
1994	57,519	214,426	52,832	324,777
1995	182,396	242,884	36,070	461,350
1996	222,934	262,762	44,024	529,720
1997	331,950	299,450	76,647	708,047
1998	365,207	335,483	58,514	759,204
1999	361,296	97,398	43,514	502,208
2000	468,026	337,475	67,738	873,239
2001	415,541	526,436	80,819	1,022,796

Source: Autorità Portuale di Venezia.

Note

a Dominantly tourists carried by catamarans and hydrofoils between Venice and Dalmatia and Istria.

decade, and by 1996 it surpassed industrial traffic for the first time. During the same period the port has become one of the most important home ports for the Mediterranean cruise industry (Table 11.2) and has also closed the gap with other north Adriatic ports in the container trade (Table 11.3).

The transformation has come about for a number of reasons (Zanetto *et al.* 1999). First, the Venice Port Authority has successfully completed the difficult process of privatisation according to the 84/1994 law (Ridolfi 1996). Port terminals are now completely privately owned, allowing the Authority to be more focused on strategic planning (e.g. regulation and planning tasks, marketing policies). These changes have improved labour relations and have given the port greater market orientation. Second, the port has benefited greatly from the development of new container feeder services in the Mediterranean, especially those established after the creation of the Gioia Tauro hub. Third, the conflict

Table 11.3 Container traffic in Venice, Ravenna and Trieste, 1992–2001

Year	Venice ('000 TEU)	Ravenna ('000 TEU)	Trieste ('000 TEU)
1992	106.5	157.1	138.1
1993	117.6	170.6	155.9
1994	114.7	181.0	146.1
1995	127.9	193.4	151.7
1996	168.8	190.8	176.9
1997	212.0	188.2	204.3
1998	206.4	172.5	174.1
1999	199.8	173.4	189.3
2000	218.0	181.4	206.1
2001	246.2	158.4	200.6

Sources: Autorità Portuale di Venezia, Autorità Portuale di Trieste, Autorità Portuale di Ravenna.

in the former Yugoslavia, and geo-economic changes in the Mediterranean area (in particular the rise of trade with Turkey and Greece), have resulted in a strong increase in ro-ro traffic (Zanetto *et al.* 1999; Dall'Agata and Soriani 2000). Finally, as far as passenger traffic is concerned, the port has greatly benefited from the recent development of the Mediterranean cruise market (the second largest in the world after the Caribbean). This is due to the tourist attraction of Venice itself, as well as to the spread of so-called 'fly and cruise' products (which, incidentally, have raised Venice airport to rank third in Italy).

The recent dynamism of the port's commercial activity is due to two interrelated factors. First, growth has been shaped by the expansion of the world economy and technological developments. Second, organisational improvements have permitted the exploitation of local advantages, in particular the economic dynamism of the industrial districts in north-east Italy. However, it must be stressed that in the case of Venice these growth tendencies have taken place in a context of the need to harmonise economic development and environmental protection goals. The underlying belief is that there are new development opportunities in the market for local port activity which, if grasped, would allow the port to enhance its position in the transport and distribution sector, while enforcing environmental protection goals. A basic objective of the Port Authority is to demonstrate that there are ways to pursue development goals while contributing to the improvement of the environmental situation. The debate over the environmental management of the lagoon often brings into question the ability of the port to continue to operate in so fragile and threatened an environment. Because of this dynamic, in the past few years the Port Authority has strongly promoted the commercial and passenger segments, which are regarded as less dangerous and more benign for the lagoon environment than are the industrial and oil sectors. This is not to say, of course, that commercial activity does not produce environmental problems. For example, a recent survey has found that little awareness still exists in the field of environmental auditing and reporting, in particular for the most problematic aspects related to dry bulk cargoes (Dall'Agata and Soriani 2000). However, the Port Authority, and most of the other actors who have responsibility in port affairs, argue that port growth can be realised in those sectors that can contribute to environmental sustainability.

Port development and environmental management

To assess how the port is trying to improve its environmental performance, two broad issues deserve attention: how to find new areas for port expansion, and how to manage dredging and the disposal of polluted mud.

Expansion sites

As with many other ports, Venice has to find new areas for expansion because of the recent growth of its commercial traffic. The special legislation for Venice (in particular the 1984 law) would allow the port to build new commercial facilities in the Cassa di Colmata A (see Figure 11.1) – one of the areas that were reclaimed for industrial expansion in the 1950s and 1960s, but which were eventually abandoned. It is clear, however, that the use of new port sites in the lagoon, even for commercial purposes only, appears to be both politically and socially unacceptable. The problem has been clearly acknowledged by the Port Authority. In drafting the new port plan it envisages the expansion of the port within the boundaries of the first industrial zone (Figure 11.1), through the modernisation of existing infrastructure and docks, and especially the redevelopment of some redundant industrial areas which border the commercial sector of the port (Autorità Portuale di Venezia 2000). This solution has been made possible thanks to an agreement with the Municipality of Venice. The most recent town plan of the Venice Municipal Council has provided for the utilisation of abandoned industrial areas by the port, in exchange for simultaneous urban redevelopment of some parts of the Stazione Marittima that it presently uses[4] (Comune di Venezia 1996). In the first industrial zone's expansion areas – which total approximately 80 ha – approved projects favour the sectors that have recently been the most dynamic (containers and ro-ro). This project (presently under construction) is an important example of functional and spatial restructuring, an option that recognises environmental concerns and attitudes, and the need to harmonise port and coastal planning (Charlier 1992; Charlier and Maliziéux 1994; Soriani and Zanetto 2002).

Dredging, canal maintenance and the problem of polluted mud

It is important to stress that the redevelopment of redundant industrial areas in the 'first industrial zone', while being an important step in the reconciliation between port development and environmental protection, makes the dredging of the Porto Marghera channels even more urgent. This gives rise to the problems of mud disposal and other environmental issues.

Dredging operations and the depth of port channels play a fundamental role in the biophysical health of the lagoon. The 1965 port plan established that the depth of the straight channel leading from the San Leonardo oil terminal to the first and the second industrial zones, and then to the different internal harbour channels, should not exceed 12 m. These channel depths are confirmed in the latest plan for both Porto Marghera and the Stazione Marittima (Autorità Portuale di Venezia 2000). In fact, marine accessibility has been problematic for more than a decade, with jurisdictional conflicts resulting in channels becoming silted up, making port operations more difficult and costly (Ente della Zona Industriale di Porto Marghera 1997). The situation changed with the establishment of the Venice Port Authority, and dredging operations started again in 1995–6. But, as the maintenance of port channels proceeded, it became clear that sediments were highly polluted and consequently represented a hazard for the ecosystem (Della Sala *et al.* 2000; Mannino *et al.* 2002).

In 1999 the issue was dealt with by a National Government Decree (Decreto

Presidente Consiglio dei Ministri, 12 February 1999) that endorses the Local Framework Agreement on the Reconversion of Chemical Industries in Porto Marghera. According to this, the Venice Water Authority and the Port Authority are held responsible for studying the state of deterioration of the canal beds and for the clean-up and stockpiling of the mud. It has since emerged that an estimated total of 6.9 million m³ of mud need to be dredged (Magistrato alle Acque, Autorità Portuale di Venezia 1999). According to national guidelines, the total has been divided into four levels of toxicity on the basis of the concentration of pollutants including heavy metals,[5] total hydrocarbons, polyaromatic hydrocarbons (PAHs), polychlorinated biphenyls (PCBs) and pesticides.

About 0.5 million m³ (only 7 per cent) has been classified as being in the least dangerous category (A). In this case, the mud can be used in operations to restore the lagoon's morphological balance and offset erosion. Second, 1.8 million m³ (a quarter) is considered to be class B and can also be used for restoring the lagoon's morphology; in this case, however, the mud must be stored in such a way as to avoid its submersion during normal high tides. Third, 3.1 million m³ (45 per cent) is designated as class C. This category poses more serious problems requiring the dredged material either to be subjected to preliminary treatment and then stocked in landfills, or to be used in the lagoon to raise the level of permanently emerged islands. Under no circumstances must class C material come into contact with the water. Lastly, 1.5 million m³ (no less than 22 per cent) is in the most hazardous class (over C). In this case, the mud has to be stocked in landfills situated outside the lagoon boundaries, in line with the strictest existing laws on wastes.

Up to now, the mud belonging to the less dangerous classes has been first dredged and then reused for morphological restoration, or stocked in a permanent emerged island (Isola delle Trezze) close to Porto Marghera's industries. Costs are borne by the Venice Port Authority, which benefits from national funds (the Ministry of Transport and Navigation and the Ministry of Public Works). It is important to note that the dredging of the most dangerous mud is still at the early stages, yet the capacity of the Isola delle Trezze as a home for dredged materials is already nearing its limit. This means that the port will have to rely more and more on the availability of other landfills in the region. This operation will be extremely costly, and it is likely that the problem of finding suitable landfill sites will be great. In order to cope with these complex issues, the Port Authority is promoting cooperation agreements with the ports of Hamburg and New York, and with the American Environmental Protection Agency, for experiments involving new technological treatment methods. These should allow the more hazardous mud to be used (following pre-treatment operations) to produce building materials (tiles and bricks) or to create ground for sale. The search for beneficial uses of contaminated material appears to represent a priority of the Port Authority.

Changing attitudes to economic development: the port authority as a 'partner' in the environmental management process

Since the late 1960s the idea that port and industrial development are incompatible with the lagoon has increasingly inspired public opinion and perceptions. Porto Marghera is now often seen as a legacy of the past. Moreover, the impressive growth of tourism in the area has reinforced the perception that, although Porto Marghera may be a very important port and industrial area, it is in the wrong place![6] In this difficult social and political situation, the Venice Port Authority has begun to play a role as an environmental manager within the context of the debate about how economic development and environmental protection goals can be successfully harmonised in the lagoon.

First of all, the Port Authority is trying to foster and spread a new image for the port as a 'partner' in the process of improving environmental conditions. Its role in promoting beneficial uses, such as the development of 'clean' technologies to transform mud into business opportunities, and its efforts to improve environmental conditions through the reconstruction of lagoon morphology, are examples. At the same time, the Port Authority sees itself as fostering port competitiveness by the reconversion of abandoned industrial areas, which also offers a 'green' solution.

The dynamic role the port is playing as a partner in the search for improving environmental conditions goes in parallel with the promotion of new governance instruments, including public–private partnerships, the search for consensus, and multi-level governmental cooperation. These are becoming important tools for approaching and solving problems. Greater attention is paid to environmental communication. Increased funds are being spent by the port to promote round tables, conferences and events intended to help reconcile the port with the territorial context in which it operates[7] (Autorità Portuale di Venezia 2000).

Great emphasis is placed on the positive impacts for the environment, as well as for the economy of the area, which result from the exploitation of new market opportunities. For example, the development of new container feeder services is regarded as a fundamental feature of the port's future, since such services allow the port to improve its market position and attract new port-related functions, while resisting the need for deeper channels. The same approach is evident in the Port Authority's emphasis on the evolution of the geo-economic situation in the Mediterranean, which is expected to support the development of new high-speed ferry services, and on the development of the Mediterranean cruise market. These elements are regarded and promoted as important sources of new revenue, helping the transition to a 'safer' and 'cleaner' port. They fit in with the public's perceptions that tend to regard the commercial and passenger segments of port traffic as intrinsically more environmentally friendly than other traffic components.[8]

Thus, the Venice Port Authority has become a very dynamic leader in the promotion of a new environmental discourse, one that involves the port improving environmental conditions while pursuing new economic development goals. This vision requires cooperation between the different agents involved and a willingness to solve problems, leaving behind the ideological conflicts which characterised past debates that separated the protection of the lagoon from market considerations. This evolution of the relationship between port development and the lagoon environment shares many elements with the 'ecological modernisation' political programme (Gouldson and Murphy 1996). This concept suggests that economic and environmental goals can be combined with synergistic effects, with an appropriate mix of tools such as entrepreneurship for environmental gains; organisational/technological improvements; market-oriented approaches; new environmental policy tools based on a search for consensus and pragmatism; and voluntary agreements and new governance schemes.

These efforts are just beginning in Venice, and it is not easy to say how this vision can inspire environmental practices and which environmental goals can be achieved. At the moment, the vision appears to be a rhetorical discourse whose importance derives mainly from the positive contribution it brings to the difficult conditions of the social and political climate in which the port operates. It must be stressed again that in Venice the ability of the port to continue operating in such a fragile and complex environment is often questioned. The Port Authority's role as an environmental manager also has fundamental social and cultural implications, since it aims to develop and spread community trust and consensus concerning its ability to solve problems, as well as to avoid the traditional prioritisation between economic and environmental goals. It is clear, however, that too many elements are out of the port's control. For instance, the re-utilisation of dredged materials for beneficial uses is controversial in the sense that the market and technological viability are yet to be fully confirmed. Moreover, the idea that it is possible to develop a more efficient and 'cleaner' port by exploiting market opportunities ignores increasing market competition, and conflicts with the fact that ports are not major partners in the decision chain (Slack 1993, 2002). There is also the problem of the economic sustainability of such a transformation. For instance, the economic implications for the port's balance sheet of a reorganisation of oil traffic in the north Adriatic has never been evaluated properly. Moreover, this future vision of the port is clearly optimistic, since it tends to underestimate the redistributive effects on the port of the envisioned functional transformation.

Conclusion

As in other coastal areas, the port and the port-related industrial development of Venice have been responsible for the depletion of extremely valuable natural resources and for the declining quality of the environment. From the late 1960s onwards this created an extremely contradictory framework, with the port and industrial activities being increasingly regarded by most of the public as responsible for the environmental degradation of the lagoon. Meanwhile, Venice has become increasingly important as a tourist market on a global scale. As the debate developed over how to safeguard Venice, the historical city became an icon of urban environmental challenge. This led to a period of deep ideological conflict over the means to 'save' the city and the lagoon, and on the role of the port in the future development of the region.

It is clear that, in response, environmental problems and environmental management options have become one of the main concerns for local port policy. Regarding the search for new expansion sites, the very particular situation of Venice in terms of social attitudes and values towards the environment has forced the port authority to focus on modernising *in situ* as well as redeveloping redundant industrial sites. The experience of Venice well illustrates the role that environmental perception and concerns can play in determining the use of infrastructures and areas. Reconciling port planning with coastal management has brought to light critical issues over the problem of dredging and canal maintenance in the area of Porto Marghera, plus environmental management problems relating to mud removal and disposal.

The Port Authority is playing a very dynamic role as an environmental manager in these issues. It has developed an 'environmental vision' that recognises that environmental protection can be compatible with new development goals. Technological and organisational improvements, new marketing approaches and regulatory schemes are regarded as appropriate tools for developing further local port activity, as well as improving environmental conditions. It believes that local functional change and environmental protection can go hand in hand.

Ports everywhere face environmental challenges. The case of Venice, however, is marked by the fact that the very future of port activities will depend on political decisions made to cope with flooding. The intrinsic value of the historical city amplifies the problems considerably and makes it extremely difficult to secure consensus on the measures to adopt. Environmental problems of the lagoon may impose substantial constraints on the future of the port, regardless of the steps it takes to improve its environmental or economic performance. Furthermore, the environmental management options for Venice are not based merely on scientific and technical considerations. Public opinion and perceptions of the local inhabitants and those beyond who wish to 'save Venice and its lagoon' are of the utmost importance. They strongly influence the debate about what Venice has to be and why, and who has to decide . . . and for whom.

Finally, the problem of geographic scale is a crucial element. Up to now, most attention has been placed on the search for solutions primarily at the local scale. Little attention has been devoted to the links between the lagoon and the north Adriatic coastal zone. This is true, in particular, for environmental problems. The issue of port activity and environmental impacts would take on new dimensions if the scale of the North Adriatic coastal area was considered, in terms both of the definition of the problems and of the costs and benefits of the different options for the different agents involved. This suggests that new coastal management approaches should be adopted, aimed at the identification of coastal issues, stakeholders, participatory procedures, and ecosystemic and economic gains and losses according to different scenarios and on different spatial scales (Sorensen 1997). In the case of Venice, adopting multiple scales when considering problems would appear to be necessary not only for the identification of the best or most viable solutions, but, even more basically, for correctly defining the terms with which to deal with the problems.

Acknowledgements

I would like to thank Stefano Della Sala, Andrea Rumor and Sergio Nardini (Venice Port Authority), Stefania Bertazzon (Calgary University, Canada) and Ilda Mannino (University of Venice) for their helpful suggestions and indications on the topic. They bear no responsibility for opinions and conclusions stated herein. MURST funds 2000 – MM11361573 are acknowledged.

Notes

1 On 4 November 1966, as a consequence of particular atmospheric and marine conditions, the water reached 1.94 m above mean sea level. With that dramatic event began the contemporary scientific, political and cultural debate on how to 'safeguard Venice' and its lagoon. More and more attention was placed on the need to harmonise economic development (strongly dependent up to the late 1970s on port and port-related industrial activities) and protection goals. In this sense, the case of Venice can be regarded as a forerunner in the debate about sustainable development, at least at the local scale.

2 An 'environmental discourse' has been defined as a 'framework that includes whole sets of ideas, words, concepts and practices' with respect to the way society–nature relationships are interpreted (Benton and Short 1999).

3 Infrastructure investments have been particularly important in the container segment. Operations for the realisation of a new facility (the Molo, or Pier, VII Container Terminal) started in the early 1970s. Today the terminal covers an area of 400,000 m^2 and has approximately 2,000 m of quay. The maximum depth is 18 m. The terminal is equipped with post-Panamax portainer cranes, and its annual handling capacity is in the region of 400,000 TEU. It must be said, however, that the port has never gained complete benefit from this infrastructure, owing to the increasing peripherality of the Adriatic Sea relative to the emerging networks of maritime routes.

4 This redevelopment is to be undertaken in such a way that the Stazione Marittima, in the western part of historic Venice, will continue to perform some of its present port functions, particularly the handling of passengers and mixed (passenger/car/lorry) ferries. Most of the area, however, will be converted to alternative uses (mainly university departments and offices).

5 The heavy metals include arsenic, cadmium, chromium, copper, mercury, nickel, lead and zinc.

6 The question of whether the lagoon can continue to be home for 'traditional' industries is very often an issue in political debates. For example, an Italian minister who visited Venice in November 2000 argued, 'The city must change, according to the era we have entered. Venice has to leave its industrial past behind. I can't believe that the lagoon is the home of a "highway" for tankers. The "oil canal" has had its time.' (*Il Gazzettino*, 26 November 2000, p. I).

7 As examples, the Port Authority launched in the second half of the 1990s the

campaign '*Porte aperte*' (Open Doors), in which people (in particular students) were invited to see how the port is contributing to the revitalisation of Porto Marghera as well as to the restoration of the lagoon; how the Authority is partner in, and sponsor of, many research programmes and centres in the field of sustainable development in the Mediterranean; and how Venice is today the headquarters of SedNet, a European network of port authorities and research institutions for studying the environmental, technological and economic problems related to mud disposal and re-utilisation.

8 Recently this traffic segment has also been questioned on environmental grounds. The problem is the potential contribution that the wash of large ships can give to the *moto ondoso* (groundswell). In order to answer criticisms and to show that even the largest ships do not pose problems when passing through the San Marco Basin and the Giudecca Canal, the Port Authority commissioned a survey in 2001. The report stated that the wash caused by small craft, such as boats used for public transport, motorboats, transport boats, etc., is sometimes higher than that of big ships, because of their higher speed. The following statement by the President of Venice Port Authority clearly shows the complexity of the social context which the port has to confront: 'The commitment of the port authority [in commissioning the survey] was to dissipate the myths and the misunderstandings which often confuse those who deal with the port of Venice, obscuring its image and creating traffic diversions with dangerous and noxious announcements' (Autorità Portuale di Venezia 2002: 11).

References

Allen, R. (1996) 'The environmental consequences of port development', in J. Taussik and J. Mitchell (eds) *Partnership in Coastal Zone Management*, Cardigan, UK: Samara Publishing, pp. 21–27.

Associazione Industriali della Provincia di Venezia (1967) *Interventi tenuti in occasione delle cerimonie per il cinquantenario di Porto Marghera*, Venice: Associazione Industriali della Provincia di Venezia.

Autorità Portuale di Venezia (2000) *Piano Operativo Triennale, 2000–2002*, Venice: Autorità Portuale di Venezia.

——— (2002) *News and Sailing List*, Venice: Autorità Portuale di Venezia.

Benton, L.M. and Short, J.R. (1999) *Environmental Discourse and Practice*, Oxford: Blackwell.

Bryant, R.L. and Wilson, G.A. (1996) 'Rethinking environmental management', *Progress in Human Geography*, 22: 321–343.

Canestrelli, E., Costa, P., Marguccio, A. and Muscarà, C. (1992) 'Regolazione delle maree in laguna: effetti sull'attività portuale veneziana', in P. Costa (ed.) *Venezia: Economia e Analisi Urbana*, Milan: Etaslibri, pp. 173–200.

Carbognin, L., Frankenfield Zanin, J. and Ramasco, C. (1993) *A Guidebook on the Lagoon of Venice: Environment and Problems*, Venice: ISDGM-CNR.

Charlier, J. (1992) 'The regeneration of old port areas for new port uses', in B.S. Hoyle and D.A. Pinder (eds) *European Port Cities in Transition*, London: Belhaven Press, pp. 137–154.

Charlier, J. and Maliziéux, J. (1994) *Les Stratégies de Redéveloppement Portuaire en Europe Occidentale*, Le Havre: Association International Villes et Ports.

Comune di Venezia (1996) *La pianificazione urbanistica come strumento di politica industriale: la variante al prg per Porto Marghera*, Rome: Urbanistica Quaderni.

Consorzio Ricerche Laguna (1999) *Scenari di crescita del livello del mare per la Laguna di Venezia*, Venice: Consorzio Ricerche Laguna.

Consorzio Venezia Nuova (1997a) *Measures for the Protection of Venice and its Lagoon, Report,* Venice: Consorzio Venezia Nuova.

—— (1997b) *Studio di impatto ambientale (SIA) del Progetto di Massima della Chiusura Mobile delle Bocche di Porto,* Venice: Consorzio Venezia Nuova.

COSES (1998) *Analisi della funzione portuale veneziana,* Report no. 20, Venice: Maggio.

Cossu, R. and de Fraja Frangipane, E. (1985) *Stato delle conoscenze sull'inquinamento della Laguna di Venezia,* Venice: Sistema Informativo Consorzio Venezia Nuova.

Couper, D.A. (1992) 'Environmental port management', *Maritime Policy and Management,* 19: 165–170.

Dall'Agata, G. and Soriani, S. (2000) 'Infrastrutture e servizi per il traffico marittimo: i risultati di un'indagine sul porto di Venezia', *Economia e Società Regionale,* 1: 42–81.

Della Sala, S., Pietrogrande, A., Wenning, R. and Zanotto, E. (2000) 'Sediment characterisation and ecological risk assessment of Venice Port canals for the environmental clean up plan of the Porto Marghera area', *Consoil,* 1: 635.

Ente della Zona Industriale di Porto Marghera (1997) *Relazione anno 1996,* Venice: Ente della Zona Industriale di Porto Marghera.

Finney, N. and David, Y. (1995) 'Environmental zoning restriction on port activities and development', *Maritime Policy and Management,* 22: 319–329.

French, P.W. (1997) *Coastal and Estuarine Management,* London: Routledge.

Gouldson, A. and Murphy, J. (1996) 'Ecological modernisation and the European Union', *Geoforum,* 27: 11–21.

Magistrato alle Acque, Autorità Portuale di Venezia (1999) *Rapporto sullo stato di compromissione dei fondali,* Venice: Autorità Portuale di Venezia.

Mannino, I., Soriani, S. and Zanetto, G. (2002) 'Management of port dredged material: an environmental political issue', *Littoral 2002, The Changing Coast, Porto, EURO-COAST & EUCC,* 3: 75–79.

Ministero dell'Ambiente (1998) *Parere di Compatibilità della Commissione per le Valutazioni di Impatto Ambientale,* Rome: Ministero dell'Ambiente, 9 December.

Penning-Rowsell, E., Winchester, P. and Gardiner, J. (1998) 'New approaches to sustainable hazard management for Venice', *Geographical Journal,* 164: 2–18.

Pinder, D.A. (2002) 'Le principali implicazioni del cambiamento delle funzioni portuali per gli ambienti costieri', in S. Soriani (ed.) *Porti, città e territorio costiero: le dinamiche della sostenibilità,* Bologna: il Mulino, pp. 185–198.

Pinder, D.A. and Witherick, M. (1990) 'Port industrialization, urbanization and wetland loss', in M. Williams (ed.) *Wetlands: A Threatened Landscape,* Oxford: Blackwell, pp. 234–246.

Ridolfi, G. (1995) 'Public policy and port development: the Italian case', *Maritime Policy and Management,* 27: 73–95.

—— (1996) 'Italian ports and the wind of change', *Tijdschrift voor Economische en Sociale Geografie,* 87: 348–356.

Rinaldo, A. (1997) *Equilibrio fisico e idrogeologico della Laguna,* Rapporto di Ricerca 09.97, Progetto Venezia 21, Venice: Fondazione Eni Enrico Mattei.

Robiglio Rizzo, C. (1996) 'Combined transport in Italy: the case of the Quadrante Europa, Verona', in B.S. Hoyle (ed.) *Cityports, Coastal Zones and Regional Change: International Perspectives on Planning and Management,* Chichester, UK: John Wiley, pp. 248–270.

—— (2002) 'Nodi interni e attività logistiche: alcune nuove tendenze nella Padania orientale', in S. Soriani (ed.) *Porti, città e territorio costiero: le dinamiche della sostenibilità,* Bologna: il Mulino, pp. 161–183.

Slack, B. (1993) 'Pawns in the game: ports in a global transportation system', *Growth and Change*, 24: 579–588.

—— (2002) 'Globalizzazione e trasporto marittimo: competizione, incertezza e implicazioni per le strategie di sviluppo portuale', in S. Soriani (ed.) *Porti, città e territorio costiero: le dinamiche della sostenibilità*, Bologna: il Mulino, pp. 67–83.

Sorensen, J. (1997) 'National and international efforts at integrated coastal management: definitions, achievements and lessons', *Coastal Management*, 25: 3–41.

Soriani, S. (1996) 'The Venice port and industrial area in a context of regional change', in B.S. Hoyle (ed.) *Cityports, Coastal Zones and Regional Change: International Perspectives on Planning and Management*, Chichester, UK: John Wiley, pp. 235–248.

—— (2002) 'La transizione postindustriale della portualità tra dinamiche di mercato e vincoli-opportunità territoriali', in S. Soriani (ed.) *Porti, città e territorio costiero: le dinamiche della sostenibilità*, Bologna: il Mulino, pp. 19–65.

Soriani, S. and Zanetto, G. (2002) 'Portualità e dinamiche sostenibili. Il caso veneziano', in S. Soriani (ed.) *Porti, città e territorio costiero: le dinamiche della sostenibilità*, Bologna: Il Mulino, pp. 255–285.

Vallega, A. (1996) 'Cityports, coastal zones and sustainable development', in B.S. Hoyle (ed.) *Cityports, Coastal Zones and Regional Change: International Perspectives on Planning and Management*, Chichester, UK: John Wiley, pp. 295–306.

Vandermeulen, J.H. (1996) 'Environmental trends of ports and harbours: implications for planning and management', *Maritime Policy and Management*, 23: 55–66.

van Klink, H.A. and van den Berg, G.C. (1998) 'Gateways and intermodalism', *Journal of Transport Geography*, 6: 1–9.

Volpi, G. (1939) *Venezia antica e moderna*, Rome: Tipografia Parlamento.

World Bank (1990) *Environmental Considerations for Port and Harbor Development*, Technical Paper 126, Transport and the Environment series, Washington, DC: World Bank.

Zanda, L. (1991) 'The case of Venice', in R. Bruttomesso (ed.) *Impact of Sea Level Rise on Cities and Regions*, Venice: Marsilio, 51–59.

Zanetto, G. and Soriani, S. (1998) 'Economic development and environmental management in the government of Venice', in F. Salvatori (ed.) *Italy's Seas: Problems and Perspectives*, Rome: Società Geografica Italiana, pp. 221–234.

Zanetto, G., Soriani, S., Roson, R. and Dall'Agata, G. (1999) 'Medium size ports and inland transport nodes', development in a context of regional change: the case of Veneto Region', *Rivista Geografica Italiana*, 106: 311–334.

12 Operational pollution from shipping

Sources, environmental impact and global contribution

Gillian Reynolds

Introduction

Pollution from shipping has traditionally been thought of in terms of oil pollution resulting from catastrophic tanker accidents, or smaller slicks associated with day-to-day ship operations. Generally less newsworthy, but recognised internationally as a source of pollution since the 1970s, has been the loss of other environmentally damaging cargoes carried in chemical tankers or in containers, and the discharge of ship-generated wastes, primarily sewage and garbage.

The ship itself as a source of pollution received scant consideration until the early 1990s, when first air pollution, and subsequently antifouling paints and ballast water, were flagged as major operational pollutants. It is now acknowledged that shipping is associated with a broad range of environmental issues (Figure 12.1). Most 'land-based' environmental concerns – including sewage, garbage, exhaust emissions, volatile organic compounds, chlorofluorocarbons (CFCs) and halon firefighting media – are associated with shipping. But beyond this, ships give rise to additional concerns relating to:

- damage to the hull and loss of fuel oils or cargo;
- the transfer of live organisms and chemical pollutants in ballast water; and
- coating of the hull with biocides to keep it free of fouling.

Ship-generated pollutants are associated with a range of environmental impacts and may be of concern at a local, regional and/or global level. All stages of the ship's life cycle, from construction through to scrapping, impact on the environment. However, this chapter will focus on day-to-day operations because – although they were relatively neglected until recently – they are widely considered to be of greatest significance in terms of emissions and discharges to the environment. Against this background, the chapter is primarily concerned to demonstrate the breadth of the problem of shipping-related pollution and the challenges still to be met. To do so, discussion is structured around the following pollution categories: emissions to air, discharges to water and waste streams. Accidental pollution is largely excluded.

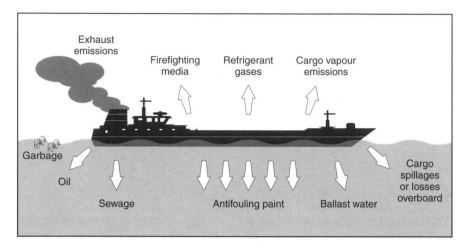

Figure 12.1 Operational pollution from shipping.

Emissions to air

Exhaust emissions

Composition and environmental impact

Of primary interest are exhaust emissions from diesel engines, currently the major provider of propulsive power in the marine industry. Emissions largely comprise nitrogen, oxygen, carbon dioxide (CO_2) and water vapour, together with smaller quantities of carbon monoxide, oxides of nitrogen (NO_x), oxides of sulphur (SO_x), partially reacted and non-combusted hydrocarbons, and particulate material (Figure 12.2). Trace quantities of organic micropollutants such as polyaromatic hydrocarbons (PAHs), dioxins and heavy metals are also present.

Of especial concern are NO_x, SO_x and CO_2, plus particulate material and various micropollutants. The formation of oxides of nitrogen occurs as a result of the oxidation either of molecular nitrogen in combustion air, or of organic nitrogen in fuel. Nitric oxide (NO), the principal reaction product, nitrogen dioxide (NO_2) and nitrous oxide (N_2O) are primarily formed. Adverse effects due to NO_x are diverse: NO_2 affects respiration and vegetation, as well as contributing significantly to acid deposition. NO_x and volatile organic compounds (VOCs) can produce tropospheric ozone, which adversely affects human health, crop yield and natural vegetation. At a global level, N_2O plays a small role in both stratospheric ozone depletion and global climate change.

Carbon dioxide and oxides of sulphur derive, respectively, from the oxidation of hydrocarbons and sulphur in the fuel. Oxides of sulphur principally

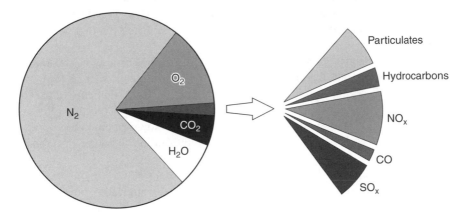

Figure 12.2 Marine diesel exhaust emission composition.

consist of sulphur dioxide (SO_2), with much lower quantities of sulphur trioxide (SO_3). Concern over SO_2 emissions arises from their detrimental impact on human respiration, vegetation and building materials. Although traditionally not regarded as a pollutant, CO_2 has become of increasing concern because of its importance as a 'greenhouse gas' and the possibly far-reaching consequences of rising CO_2 concentrations for global climate change.

The particulate fraction of exhaust gases represents a complex mixture of inorganic and organic substances largely comprising elemental carbon, ash minerals and heavy metals, plus a variety of non- or partially combusted hydrocarbons from ships' fuel and lubricating oils. An intermittent discharge of accumulated deposits from the exhaust system may also be encountered. With the exception of the latter, the majority of diesel particulates are likely to be less than 1 μm in diameter, readily transportable by air currents and of low settling velocity. Potentially detrimental effects may thus be encountered away from the immediate vicinity of the exhaust gas plume. Although study of the marine diesel particulate composition is limited, the extrapolation of results from other diesel applications would suggest that not only general respiratory problems, but also more serious toxic, mutagenic and carcinogenic effects, may be associated with these emissions.

The term 'micropollutants' generally refers to those pollutants present in trace quantities, typically at the parts per billion level, which demonstrate severe adverse effects even at low concentrations. In the context of diesel exhaust emissions, micropollutants encompass both organic micropollutants and heavy metals. The former typically include such trace organic contaminants as polyaromatic PAHs, dioxins and furans. With respect to combustion processes, the presence, and in many cases carcinogenicity, of PAHs in the exhaust gas stream are well documented. Highly mutagenic nitrated PAHs have also been identified and are believed to originate from chemical reaction between PAH and

NO_x in the exhaust gas system. In addition, highly toxic emissions of polychlorinated biphenyls (PCBs), polychlorinated dibenzodioxins (PCDDs) and polychlorinated dibenzofurans (PCDFs) have been reported (Lloyd's Register 1993).[1]

Heavy metals include many transition elements such as cadmium, chromium, copper, mercury, nickel and zinc; some non-transition metals such as lead; and the metalloids arsenic and selenium. The presence of these elements in marine exhaust emissions generally reflects concentrations in the oil fuels combusted. This in turn reflects the component oil blends plus any elements incorporated during storage and transfer, but minus those removed in the course of onboard treatment.

The significance of heavy metals is that they are well-known inhibitors of biological processes, with toxic effects mediated through the poisoning of enzymes involved in biochemical reactions. Consequently, their widespread impacts range from reduced diversity of aquatic ecosystems, through fish kills to renal dysfunction and cancer in humans.

Marine emissions estimates

The focus on marine diesel exhaust emissions throughout the 1990s was accompanied by significant progress in constructing inventories of key components. Internationally accepted emission factors were established (Lloyd's Register 1995). Detailed methodologies for constructing inventories of ship emissions were developed by the UNECE Task Force on Emission Inventories and published in the Atmospheric Emission Inventory Guidebook (EEA 2002). A number of inventories were undertaken on both regional and global bases (Table 12.I). Despite variations in the results,[2] comparison of global emissions from shipping with those from all other sources indicates that marine emissions of CO_2, NO_x and SO_x amount to around 2 per cent, 10–15 per cent and 4–6 per cent respectively of global anthropogenic emissions (Endresen *et al.* 2003a). Beyond this, there is a geography to the pollution: most ship-generated emissions take place in the northern hemisphere. Corbett *et al.* (1999) report that 85 per cent of shipping emissions occur there, with 52 per cent impacting on the North Atlantic and Northern Europe, and 27 per cent on the North Pacific.

Some information also exists on regional and global estimates of other emission components of significant environmental interest, for example PAH, heavy metals and nitrous oxide (N_2O). However, the emission factors on which these estimates are based tend to be derived from very limited data sets, and/or to be adopted from other industries or transport modes. Consequently, they must be treated with caution.

Control mechanisms

Mechanisms for controlling diesel engine exhaust emissions tend to focus either on specifically reducing SO_x or NO_x emissions, or on the introduction of fuel

Table 12.1 Summary of shipping exhaust emission estimates (M tonnes/annum)

	Reference	Base year	NO_x	CO	Hydrocarbons	SO_2	CO_2
Worldwide	Endresen et al. (2003a)	1996/2000	10.8/11.9	1.0/1.1	0.33/0.36 (NMVOC)	6.1/6.8	461/501
	Ship & Ocean Foundation (2001)	1997					387
	Skjølsvik et al. (2000)	1996	10.3	1.0	0.33 (NMHC) 0.04 (CH_4)	5.8	438
	Corbett et al, 1999	1993	10.1			8.5	
	Olivier et al. (1996)	1990	8.6[a]	0.1	0.02 (CH_4)	4.9	350
	Lloyd's Register, pers. comm. (2002)	1990	11.3			6.4	
	Bremnes (1990) and Melus	1986	5.085			4.58	
European area							
North Sea/Baltic	Whall et al. (2002)	2000	1.074		0.039	0.763	41
North Sea	Jerre et al. (1994)	1990				0.269	
Southern North Sea	CONCAWE (1994)	1992				0.206	
NE Atlantic, Black and Mediterranean Seas	Whall et al. (2002)	2000	2.543		0.095	1.815	116
NE Atlantic	Lloyd's Register (1995)	1990	1.94	0.17	0.04	1.37	
Baltic Sea	Lloyd's Register (1998)	1990	0.35	0.03	0.008	0.23	
Baltic Sea	Alexandersson et al. (1993)	1987	0.163			0.084	
Mediterranean and Black Seas	Lloyd's Register (1999)	1990	1.73	0.15	0.04	1.25	

Sources: Individual references cited

Note:
a Amended figure, T.G.J. Olivier, personal communication (2002).

economy measures that provide 'across-the-board' emission reduction. There are two approaches to reducing SO_x: reducing fuel sulphur content and treating the exhaust gas stream. Reducing fuel sulphur levels can provide benefits in terms of reduced maintenance costs and increased reliability and availability of the engine. There are also savings associated with the reduced requirements for fuel treatment equipment and the absence of quantities of sludge. These benefits are, however, associated with the combustion of cleaner fuel such as marine diesel oil rather than the use of desulphurised residual fuel. Moreover, problems may be encountered with the availability and high cost of low-sulphur distillate fuel.

Exhaust gas cleaning systems have received little attention, owing to concerns such as corrosion problems caused by the generation of dilute sulphuric acid, and the washing of other emission components – particularly highly toxic organic micropollutants and heavy metals – into the marine environment. Shipboard trials are being initiated, however, and these may demonstrate that exhaust gas cleaning is a viable approach to SO_x emission control.

As with SO_x, there are currently two different approaches to reducing NO_x emissions. Primary methods involve either modifications to the engine or the introduction of pollution-reducing substances into it. Secondary methods treat the exhaust emissions generated.

Primary methods include optimising fuel injection and ignition timing, exhaust gas recirculation, the use of fuel–water emulsion, direct water injection and the 'humid air motor' concept. Although there is an extensive literature relating to these measures (BMT 2000; Croner 2000; Marintek 2000; MER 1999; Fleischer 1996), the information presented is often conflicting in terms of the effectiveness of NO_x reduction. Moreover, most measures appear to be associated with increased fuel consumption, which is neither environmentally nor economically recommended. The use of NO_x-optimised slide valves does, however, appear to be an exception: both NO_x reduction and fuel savings have been reported. Even so, all data are very preliminary and are rarely based on in-service experience.

Possible secondary methods of NO_x control include selective catalytic reduction (SCR) of the exhaust stream and non-thermal plasma systems. The SCR system is currently the only available technology proven at full scale to meet 90 per cent NO_x reduction levels, but obstacles are that its capital investment and operating costs are high. Moreover, analysis of through-life environmental cost has still to demonstrate an overall environmental advantage to its use.

The less well known non-thermal plasma technique is potentially capable of at least matching an SCR system in marine applications. Moreover, there is the prospect that it will be a simpler, more robust and more compact system, without the requirement for separate (catalytic) consumables. The plasma is a partially ionised gas comprising a neutral mixture of atoms, molecules, free radicals, ions and electrons. This constitutes an extremely reactive medium that breaks down the exhaust components into simpler molecules. Trials of both SCR and plasma systems have indicated that non-thermal plasmas compare favourably with SCR in terms of emission reduction efficiency, costs, installation and operational efficiency. The system does, however, consume approximately 5 per cent of the power produced by the engine, effectively increasing fuel consumption.

The available literature provides some estimates of the costs of implementing the various options for controlling NO_x emissions but, given that NO_x reduction methods are not widely used, reliable market-based cost information is limited, except for SCR systems. While costs are likely to fall as the uptake of NO_x emission technologies increases, many owners are unlikely to invest until reliable data on the various control measures are available. The task of making reliable estimates of the cost of emission abatement is further complicated as it is generally a function of operating hours and/or distance travelled. The financial cost is thus dependent upon the individual ship, its efficiency and its trading pattern. For example, capital costs for SCR systems have been calculated to vary from $27,500 to nearly $1.8 million, with annual operating costs ranging between $8,000 and $533,000 dependent upon ship type and installed power (BMT 2000).

In addition to those measures specifically targeted at reducing NO_x or SO_x, fuel economy measures will achieve an 'across the board' reduction in emissions. Energy savings can be obtained on new ships by good hull design and the use of a variety of unconventional propeller arrangements. Up to 20 per cent reductions in fuel consumption can reportedly be achieved by these means, although such economies have been difficult to demonstrate in practice. For ships in service, fuel savings of up to 5 per cent can be made through best-practice maintenance to retain 'as-built' hull smoothness, and also by maintaining propeller finish.

Operational measures such as slow steaming, weather routing, fleet planning and cargo handling can also result in significant fuel savings. Above all, speed reduction is the most effective in reducing emissions since fuel consumption increases with the square of the speed. Despite the economic pressures for maximisation of asset use and fast delivery, the latter discussed by Slack in Chapter 2, there may be scope for fuel savings by weather routing and speed reduction within the scope of client commitments. Although these measures are no doubt taken for economic reasons, environmental gains are an important additional benefit. Conversely, of course, the quest for high speed in some parts of the shipping sector – detailed by Ridolfi in Chapter 8 – currently entails significant emission increases and thus environmental costs.

In the longer term, design options such as measures to reduce ship resistance by, for example, modification of the hull's surface geometry and 'whale tail propulsion' are at a preliminary stage of development. Harnessing renewable energy is also being considered by some. The greatest potential, however, appears to be in the use of fuel cells for propulsion and auxiliary power. These could potentially provide a means of dramatically cutting emissions associated with ship propulsion and on-board electrical generation. However, progress in this context will be dependent on the source of hydrogen. Although fuel cell power generation in shipping is at present theoretically possible,[3] capital costs are as yet extremely high and there are other practical problems to resolve, such as the safety of hydrogen storage. Even so, in sensitive markets (e.g., ecologically vulnerable areas targeted by the cruise industry; see Hall, Chapter 6) auxiliary power provided by fuel cells could be viable for passenger ships in ten years.

Refrigerants and firefighting agents

Environmental impact

Chlorofluorcarbons (CFCs) and hydrochlorofluorocarbons (HCFCs) have, until recently, been in widespread use in the shipping industry as refrigerants and in insulating foams. Halons (brominated fluorocarbons) have also been used extensively as firefighting agents in both fixed extinguishing systems and portable extinguishers. Both groups of compounds are now considered environmentally unacceptable because of their significant ozone depletion potential (ODP) and greenhouse warming potential (GWP) (Table 12.2). Consequently, following the Montreal Protocol on Substances that Deplete the Ozone Layer and subsequent amendments, the use of CFCs and halons – the agents of key concern – is now prohibited in new ships. But HCFCs such as R-22 are still permitted in existing plant, and R-22 continues to be used widely. With this solution still available, utilisation of the more environmentally acceptable hydrofluorocarbons (HFCs) has been slow to be adopted. Some success has been achieved in specific applications – particularly refrigerated containers (R134a) and reefer ships (R407c) – and, more generally, R404a. More recently, R410a has been adopted for use in air-conditioning systems. However, the unfamiliarity of the industry with these refrigerants, and concerns over their availability

Table 12.2 Environmental factors for selected refrigerant gases

Refrigerant no.	Name	ODP[a]	GWP[b]
R-11	Trichlorofluoromethane ($CFCl_3$)	1.000	4,000
R-12	Dichlorodifluoromethane (CF_2Cl_2)	1.000	8,500
R-22	Chlorodifluoromethane ($CHClF_2$)	0.055	1,700
R-134a	1,1,1,2-Tetrafluoroethane (CF_3CH_2F)	0.000	1,300
R-407c	Blend of R-32/125/134a ($CH_2F_2/CF_3CH_2/$ CF_3CHF_2F)	0.000	1,610
R-717	Ammonia (NH_3)	0.000	0
R-170	Ethane (CH_3CH_3)	0.000	3
R-290	Propane (C_3H_8)	0.000	3
R-600	Butane (C_4H_{10})	0.000	3

Source: British Standards Institution (2000)

Notes
a Ozone depletion potential.
b Global warming potential.

Table 12.3 Environmental factors for selected gaseous fire-extinguishing agents as alternatives to halon 1301

Trade name	Chemical formula	ODP[a]	GWP[b] (100 year)	Atmospheric lifetime (years)
Halon 1301	$CBrF_3$	12–16	4,900	65
CEA410	C_4F_{10}	0	7,000	2,600
FE13	CHF_3	0	11,700	264
FM200	C_3HF_7	0	2,900	36.5

Source: Department of Trade and Industry (2001)

Notes
a Ozone depletion potential.
b Global warming potential.

worldwide, has militated against their extensive use. Furthermore, although they are non-ozone-depleting, HFCs do have a significant GWP and will themselves ultimately be phased out. This may lead to a resurgence in the use of natural refrigerants, such as carbon dioxide, ammonia and hydrocarbons.

Similarly, the manufacture of halon firefighting agents has been phased out. Although their use in existing vessels is still permitted, this is gradually diminishing, owing to the impracticality of obtaining additional halon for 'topping up' existing cylinders or replacing those that have been discharged. Alternative halocarbon compounds (e.g. FM-200) have been developed as more environmentally benign, but they still exhibit significant GWP (Table 12.3), and there are concerns on health and safety grounds due to the toxicity of their degradation products. They are also expensive, and consequently their use tends to be confined to smaller ships. Water (deluge or mist), CO_2 or foam are the most frequently used alternatives at present, dependent upon the application. Replacement of halon systems in existing ships generally necessitates replacement of the entire firefighting system.

Marine emissions estimates

The available data for regional or global emissions of refrigerant gases and firefighting agents are limited. However, emissions of CFCs from the world shipping fleet were estimated at 3,000–6,000 tonnes in 1990 – equivalent to between 1 and 3 per cent of total global emissions. Halon emissions from shipping for the same year were estimated to be 300–400 tonnes, or around 10 per cent of the world total (International Maritime Organization, personal communication). Although more recent figures are not readily available, it is likely that new surveys would show a significant reduction in CFC and halon emissions because of the phase-out of these compounds.

Control mechanisms

Control strategies centre around the selection of more environmentally benign refrigerant gases or firefighting media (see 'Environmental impact', pp. 240–241) combined with effective loss-minimisation strategies. The latter are particularly important for refrigerant gases, for which high leakage rates have previously been reported. However, leak detection and preventive maintenance are now widely practised on a voluntary basis to reduce discharge to the environment from operational systems. Venting of refrigerants and CFC or HCFC foam-blowing agents to the atmosphere is also illegal under the Montreal Protocol. Where insulating foam has been blown using CFC or HCFC, the foam should be removed, degassed and the gas recovered, prior to disposal. Similarly, refrigerant gas must be recovered during maintenance, or prior to scrapping, using appropriate recovery equipment. While recovery does generally occur during maintenance, refrigerant gas and blowing agent recovery is unlikely to be well established in most ship scrapping facilities at present.

Cargo vapour emissions

Environmental impact

Emissions of volatile organic compounds (VOCs) from oil and chemical tankers are of increasing concern, due to the part they play in the formation of photo-chemical oxidants such as ground-level or tropospheric ozone. Ozone has no significant anthropogenic sources in the atmosphere. It, and other photochemical oxidants, are generated by chemical reaction involving nitrogen oxides and VOCs in the presence of sunlight.

Ozone is a strong oxidising agent and one of the most aggressive of the common air pollutants. Exposure can harm human health, reduce forestry and crop yields, and damage materials, including natural and synthetic rubber, paints, varnishes and textiles. Ozone also acts as a greenhouse gas, although its warming potential is uncertain.

Marine emissions estimates

Most estimates of global emissions of VOCs from the handling and transport of crude oil and oil products are in the range of 1.7–1.8 million tonnes per year. This is equivalent to 0.1–0.15 per cent of all cargo transported (Martens 1993; Endresen *et al.* 2003a). Emissions are generally geographically limited, partly because oil transport takes place within a well-defined system of international sea routes, but also because most of the evaporation takes place during loading.

Control mechanisms

The primary mechanism for control of cargo vapour emissions is the use of vapour emission control systems (VECS), which act to condense vapour and return it to the onshore tank or service vessel. This requires compatible ship- and shore-based installations, for which both the US Coast Guard and the International Maritime Organization have published essentially equivalent standards. VECS are now commonplace in the United States and their use is increasing in Europe. As an alternative to the combined ship- and shore-based systems two other innovations – a self-contained shipboard VOC recovery plant and a system that substantially reduces VOC formation during loading – have been developed. What may be noted is that, as with slow steaming and fuel economy, the drivers for the oil industry in this context may not be purely environmental: the cost of losses in transit is considered sufficiently serious to warrant detailed monitoring and annual reviews in, for example, the *Petroleum Review*. None the less, even if the motivation is economic, the consequential environmental benefits are genuine.

Discharges to water

Ballast water

Environmental impact

Ships require ballast for stability. This is taken on and discharged as required. In the past a number of materials have been used as ballast, but now water, primarily from ports and coastal areas, is used almost exclusively. Millions of tonnes are transported around the world annually.

Two major environmental problems are associated with ballast water:

- the uptake of ballast from chemically polluted waters (containing, for example, heavy metals, persistent organics and nutrients) and its subsequent discharge into a 'clean' environment; and
- the transfer of live organisms from one region to another. This is of major concern since, if conditions are right in the port of discharge, non-native or pathogenic organisms may survive and establish themselves. Potentially this can lead to severe disruption of the local marine ecology or the introduction of disease, particularly in situations where the natural predators normally present in the home port are absent and consequently cannot keep the organisms in check.

This second problem is widely recognised as being one of the most serious impacts affecting the marine environment. Many organisms can potentially be transported in ballast water. All that is needed is for them to be present in the water or sediment alongside the vessel when it is ballasting and be able to pass through the intake grill. Many organisms have been introduced to the United Kingdom, including microscopic plankton, barnacles and Chinese mitten crabs. So far these have caused only localised problems, such as fouling of jetties, outcompeting local species and damaging embankments. However, elsewhere in the world, organisms introduced via ballast water have had major economic, ecological and health impacts.

The havoc caused by the introduction of the European zebra mussel into the American Great Lakes is well known. Some estimates put the costs of cleaning fouled pipes and generally controlling the zebra mussel invasions at $400–$500 million a year in the Great Lakes alone. However, the problem is not exclusive to North America. In the Black Sea a carnivorous comb jellyfish introduced from North America is now present in huge numbers and, by feeding on anchovy larvae, has caused the collapse of this fishery. Human health can also suffer: cholera is known to have been transported from Asia to Latin America in this way, and microscopic dinoflagellates, which cause paralytic shellfish poisoning, have been introduced into Australia.

Ballast water is unique among the environmental issues associated with shipping in that it is associated with detrimental effects caused by living organisms. The densities and composition of organisms carried by individual vessels are extremely variable, and there is no simple relationship between the quantity of ballast discharged and environmental impact. The origin of the water, the environmental compatibility of uptake and discharge ports, and the interaction discharged organisms have with native species are also of key importance in assessing the risk of non-native organisms becoming established. Given the potential threat, it is understandable that tools for estimating the potential risk of introducing non-native species have been recently developed (IMO 2002d).

Discharge estimates

For commercial reasons, vessels will strive to operate with maximum cargo and minimum ballast at all times. Ballast water capacity varies as a function of cargo carrying capacity and ship type, with typical values ranging from 25 to 40 per cent of the dead weight tonnage (Carlton *et al.* 1990, 1995; Hay *et al.* 1997; Endresen *et al.* 2003b). Assuming ballast water on average amounts to 30 per cent of the cargo transported annually, global transfer quantities are estimated to be approximately 2.7–2.8 billion tonnes (Endresen *et al.* 2003b; Lloyd's Register, personal communication, 2002). The greater part of the discharge is geographically limited, owing to the well-defined system of international sea routes. Information on estimated quantities discharged nationally and worldwide is presented in Table 12.4. Information is also available on typical discharge quantities by different ship types (e.g. Hay *et al.* 1997; Carlton *et al.* 1990). As with other sources of pollution, variation between these estimates may be attributable to factors such as the use of different base years, calculation methodologies and fleet segments.

Control mechanisms

Because the potential seriousness of the ballast water problem is acknowledged, international regulations to lessen the risk of introducing non-native organisms

Table 12.4 Ballast water discharge estimates[a]

	Volume discharged (M tonnes/annum)	Reference
USA	79	Carlton *et al.* (1995)
	101	Endresen *et al.* (2003b)
Australia	121	Australian Bureau of Statistics (1997)
	58	Jones (1991)
	98	Endresen *et al.* (2003b)
New Zealand	3.7–5.0	Hay *et al.* (1997)
Netherlands	7.5[b]	Gotje *et al.* (1998)
	26	Endresen *et al.* (2003b)
Worldwide	3,000–5,000	IMO, pers. comm. (2002)
	2,700	Endresen *et al.* (2003b)
	2,800	Lloyd's Register, pers. comm. (2002)

Sources: Individual references cited

Notes
a Variations between estimates may be attributable to factors such as the use of different base years, calculation methodologies and fleet segments.
b Stated to represent 42 per cent of ballast water discharged in Europe.

have been under discussion for over a decade (IMO 1997). At present the primary method for controlling such transfers is by mid-ocean ballast water exchange. This relies on the fact that deep ocean water contains few organisms and those that do exist are unlikely to survive removal to a coastal or freshwater environment. However, the exchange procedure can be a hazardous operation. Few ships have been designed with ballast exchange at sea in mind, and the process of pumping out and refilling tanks in sequence can compromise longitudinal strength if the ship is not designed with this in mind. Also, if sea conditions pick up when the tanks are partially emptied, sloshing damage can occur. In some cases, bulkheads can be completely destroyed.

The alternative to sequential exchange is continuous flushing in which at least three times the tank volume is pumped through the tank. But this procedure is not ideal, since it can leave behind much of the sediment that tends to host the most undesirable organisms. It can also be impractical, because ballast tank air pipes are not designed for continuously overflowing ballast water. It may therefore be necessary to route the overflow through opened manholes, but this is not always feasible, particularly where these are located in holds or storerooms. Other options for controlling the transfer of organisms are consequently being investigated. They include the retention of ballast water on board; designs which eliminate the need for ballast water; discharge to reception facilities; and treatment by filtration, ultraviolet irradiation, chemical disinfection or heat. While there are isolated cases of water treatment plant being installed on ships, effective commercially applicable techniques are some way off. In the interim, ballast water exchange at sea is likely to remain the most widely used option.

Antifouling paints

Environmental impact

Antifouling systems are applied to the wetted surface of ships' hulls to prevent settlement of marine organisms, thus aiding fuel efficiency. These systems are traditionally paints containing one or more biocides which act to kill organisms attempting to settle on the hull. They may also be non-biocidal 'non-stick' coatings or systems working on a different principle altogether, but the marine environmental impact of coatings generally relates to their biocidal content.[4] The active components in these are primarily tributyl tin (TBT), copper and organic booster biocides such as triazines. Conventional coatings emit biocides constantly, and 80–90 per cent will leach into the sea within three to five years.

Since its introduction in the late 1960s, TBT has been the most effective and most widely used antifoulant. While it is intended to act at the surface of the ship's hull, TBT will leach into the sea and accumulate in the biota and sediment. Adverse impacts were initially reported in the 1970s, particularly in commercial oyster beds, where severe shell malformations were apparent, making the oysters unfit for human consumption. Population levels also declined, leading to multi-billion-dollar losses in the mariculture industry. TBT was subsequently found to be responsible for the decline of the dogwhelk, *Nucella lapillus*, in the vicinity of marinas – exposure resulting in the inability to reproduce following the development of male sexual characteristics by females ('imposex').

Discharge estimates

It has been estimated that TBT-based antifouling paint is used on 70 per cent of the world's fleet (Mayell and Swanson 1998). While Isensee *et al.* (1994) estimated annual TBT input to the marine environment to be between 1,400 and 2,400 tonnes, Endresen and Sørgård (1999) calculated that in 1996 the global input – mainly from oil tankers, bulk carriers and general cargo vessels – was in the range 750–1,500 tonnes. This calculation was based on a leaching rate of $2–4\,\mu g/cm^2/day$ and an estimated total wetted area of about 148 million m^2.

Because attention has focused on TBT, few data are available on the input of other antifouling biocides into the marine environment. However, by definition, any biocide used for antifouling purposes is likely to have an adverse environmental effect. Consequently, with the planned phasing out of TBT-based paints (see the following) it is becoming increasingly important to monitor rising inputs of other biocides from alternative antifouling coatings. How this can be done effectively is uncertain; however, it may be possible to derive an approximation from the biocide content of paint sold for marine application.

Control mechanisms

Concern over the input of TBT into the environment has led to the International Maritime Organisation's International Convention for the Control of Harmful Anti-fouling Systems on Ships (IMO 2001). This should ensure decreasing inputs of TBT into the marine environment. Yet at present none of the alternatives provides a clearly preferable alternative solution. There are also implications for atmospheric pollution. It has been estimated that a switch from TBT to modern tin-free coatings would attract an environmental penalty of around 5 million tonnes of CO_2 resulting from the increased fuel requirements associated with the current performance of alternative antifouling coatings relative to TBT-based paints.

Currently the main alternatives are copper-based paints, but these still carry environmental risks, and their concentrations in the marine environment are likely to rise as the use of TBT declines. 'Non-stick' coatings, which prevent adhesion of fouling organisms, have been under development for some time. Although these are beginning to be used commercially, experience of application and performance in service is limited. They are also relatively expensive. Natural biocides provide another possibility, but they are far from the commercial marketplace. A different approach – the physical removal of fouling by periodic scrubbing – is considered by some to be a potential short-term solution. Popular though this is with some environmentalists, however, the feasibility and costs of establishing sufficient scrubbing capacity, as well as the overall environmental effects, are uncertain.

Oil

Sources and scale of pollution

The public commonly associates marine oil pollution with losses of crude oil or refined petroleum products as a result of tanker groundings and collisions. Best known are incidents such as those involving the *Torrey Canyon* and *Exxon Valdez*, which respectively spilled 107,000 tonnes of oil off the coast of Cornwall, England, in 1967 and 30,000 tonnes into Prince William Sound, Alaska, in March 1989. Partly because of the public perception factor, more information on accidential spillages is available than for any other cause. For example, the International Tanker Owners' Pollution Federation makes available a regularly updated database of oil spilled in the marine environment (ITOPF 2002). Similarly, Oil Spill Intelligence Report (Aspen, weekly) provides information on accidental pollution from marine transport.

In reality, tanker accidents are responsible for only a minor proportion of oil entering the marine environment. Precise data for other sources are rare

Table 12.5 Inputs of oil to the marine environment, 1990

Source	Tonnes	Per cent
Municipal/industrial	1,175,000	50
Transportation	564,000	24
Atmosphere	305,000	13
Natural sources	258,500	11
Offshore production and exploration	47,000	2
Total	2,350,000	

Source: Etkin *et al.* (1998).

compared with those for accidents, but a 1990 survey showed that as much as 50 per cent of the oil entering the seas and oceans was land based (Table 12.5). Moreover, little more than 20 per cent of ship-generated oil pollution was the consequence of accidents, the remainder being caused by discharges during normal ship operations (Table 12.6).

One of the major sources of oil entering the marine environment as a consequence of normal shipping operations is the discharge of crude oil and products during tank cleaning, a problem caused primarily by older, single-hulled, tankers that use tanks for both cargo and ballast water. Quantitatively greater than this, however, are the losses arising from ships' fuel tanks and bilges. As

Table 12.6 Estimates of oil entering the marine environment from shipping, 1989/90

Source	Discharge (tonnes/year)	Discharge (%)
Operational discharge of oil cargo from tankers	158,600	27.9
• *Crude oil: long haul*	*45,600*	*8.0*
• *Crude oil: short haul*	*20,300*	*3.6*
• *Product oil: long haul*	*20,800*	*3.7*
• *Product oil: short haul*	*71,900*	*12.6*
Dry docking	4,000	0.7
Marine terminals (eg bunker operations)	30,000	5.3
Bilge and fuel oil	252,600	44.4
• *Machinery space bilges*	*64,400*	*11.3*
• *Fuel oil sludge*	*186,800*	*32.9*
• *Oily ballast from fuel oil tanks*	*1,400*	*0.2*
Accidental spillage	121,000	21.2
• *Tanker accidents*	*114,000*	*20.0*
• *Non-tanker accidents*	*7,000*	*1.2*
Scrapping of ships	2,600	0.5
Total	568,800	100

Source: IMO (1990).

Table 12.6 demonstrates, these two forms of discharge have together typically accounted for 40–50 per cent of ship-generated oil pollution, made manifest as slicks at sea, oiling of seabirds and sea mammals, and chronic pollution of beaches with tar-like deposits. Inevitably there is a geography to these impacts, since – while discharges are subject to restrictions in terms of distance from land[5] – operational oil pollution tends to be concentrated around the main shipping and oil transportation routes.

Controls and pollution trends

The relative importance of accidental and other discharges will naturally vary from year to year, depending on the severity of tanker accidents. As a long-term trend, however, significant reductions in both accidental and operational pollution should occur as a reflection of improved technologies and regulation. Of particular importance is Annex I to the International Convention for the Prevention of Pollution from Ships, MARPOL 73/78. This covers the handling of oil leakages and oily wastes in the engine room, and the minimisation of discharges from oil tanker cargo tanks.

All ships encounter leakages from machinery, whether routinely or during maintenance. This oil will tend to collect in the ship's bilges, where it may lie or be transferred to a bilge water holding tank. In line with MARPOL Annex I, this oily bilge water may then be discharged ashore, for which a charge is generally made, or discharged to sea through an oily water separator or filter which theoretically reduces the oil-in-water content to a maximum value of 15 ppm. Larger ships, or those trading in designated special areas such as the Baltic, are also required to monitor the concentration of oil in water and to cease discharging if the 15 ppm oil-in-water threshold is reached. Additional treatment, such as the use of filtration to further reduce the oil content of the water discharged, is sometimes used, but this is rare at present. All discharges are subject to restrictions in terms of distance from land and location outside special, environmentally vulnerable, areas.

Other oily wastes such as the sludge resulting from fuel purification, which cannot be passed through the oily water separator, will be stored on board in a dedicated tank until they can be discharged ashore. In order to reduce operational oil pollution associated with the cleaning of cargo/ballast tanks, procedures have been developed by the oil industry and subsequently incorporated into international legislation. These include a particular sequence of tank washing, termed the 'load on top' procedure, which acts to minimise the discharge of oil to the sea in tank washings. A system of crude oil washing has also been developed whereby cargo tanks are washed with cargo using highly controllable tank washing machines. In this process the lighter fraction of the crude oil acts as a solvent, washing the heavier fractions from the tank walls. By this means, cargo out-turn can be greatly increased.

Despite these measures, assessing the scale of progress remains difficult. Reliable surveys are few and far between, and evidence can be contradictory. Thus,

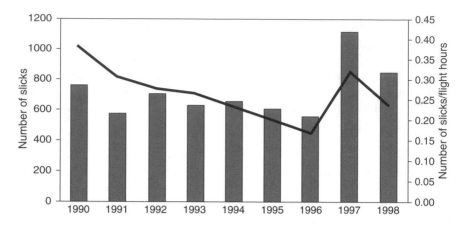

Figure 12.3 Annual number of oil slicks from illegal discharges observed by aerial surveillance in the North and Baltic Seas. (Source: EEA 2001.)

it has been estimated that following the adoption of Annex I to MARPOL, operational oil pollution fell by almost two-thirds between 1981 and 1990 – from approximately 1.4 million to 0.56 million tonnes a year (Patin 2002). However, the annual number of slicks recorded between 1990 and 1998 in the North and Baltic Seas – areas in which official vigilance is high – did not show a consistent decline (Figure 12.3). For this reason, the recent work of Koops and Huisman (2001), which has produced advances in estimating the volume of individual operational oil discharges, is to be welcomed because of the potential for improvements in both data availability and reliability.

Waste streams

Composition and environmental impact

Shipboard waste streams comprise sewage or 'black water', domestic waste water or 'grey water', oily wastes and garbage. The latter is particularly diverse and can include plastics, packing, glass, crockery, metal, rags, food wastes, cargo residues, medical waste, ropes, paint, equipment, and so on. As oily wastes from bilges and oil cargo residues have been covered in the previous section, they are not considered here.

For the purposes of this chapter, wastes disposed of ashore will be assumed not to cause environmental pollution. The environmental impact of wastes discharged to sea will be diverse, consistent with their diverse composition and the disposal route. Although some wastes will be discharged directly to the marine environment, particularly outside coastal or various 'special areas', other wastes will be actively managed. Sewage and garbage may, for example, be discharged to reception facilities ashore, treated prior to discharge or incinerated. Grey water is exceptional in that its discharge is not restricted by international law and it is most commonly discharged directly to the environment.

Some streams – and especially garbage – tend to be unsightly, but often there are other impacts. Discarded ropes or nets are hazardous to wildlife onshore and at sea. Other items of garbage – paints, equipment and medical wastes – may contain marine pollutants. Sewage and grey water have a high biological oxygen demand (BOD) that depletes receiving waters of oxygen. Sewage and grey water also introduce nitrate and phosphate into receiving waters, potentially causing rapid algal growth where waters are static and enclosed. Sewage is naturally likely to carry pathogenic microbes, including *E. coli*. The danger of some coliform bacteria is demonstrated in the recent deaths associated with *E. coli* food poisoning.

Quantification and control of ship-generated wastes

Quantification of ship-generated wastes – sewage, grey water and garbage – is reasonably well covered. Figures are available from several sources on wastes generated per person per day for the various ship types (Norwegian Environmental Department 1994; Schnitler 1995; EMARC 1998). Waste factors – in combination with time spent at sea, ship size and type, and crew and passenger numbers – have been used to derive annual figures for waste production by shipping on a regional basis (Table 12.7). Some information is also available on the amounts of washing agents, on biological oxygen demand (BOD) and nitrogen and phosphorus nutrients discharged in sewage and/or grey water in the Baltic Sea (Swedish Shipowners' Association 1995).

Control of pollution from shipboard wastes has primarily been achieved through international regulation, specifically the MARPOL 73/78 Convention, which addresses prevention of pollution by sewage and garbage in two of its (currently) six annexes. Management of garbage is generally achieved by compaction and storage on board prior to disposal ashore, or by the controlled disposal to sea of certain categories of waste in line with restrictions specified in the

Table 12.7 Estimates of sewage and garbage waste generated annually by shipping in Europe

	Sewage ('000 cu m)	Garbage ('000 tonnes)
Eastern Mediterranean	916	12
Iberian Peninsula	3,437	44
Northern Europe	4,141	51
Southern Europe	9,300	112
Scandinavia	4,887	61
UK/Eire	3,667	45
Total	26,348	325

Source: EMARC (1998).

Convention. Alternatively, waste may be incinerated on board. Control of pollution by sewage is achieved either by retention on board and discharge ashore, or by passage through an approved sewage treatment plant, certified to meet international requirements with regard to performance and effluent quality. However, while the release of sewage is not allowed within 4 nautical miles (7.4 km) of the coast, even if it has been comminuted and disinfected, outside the 12-mile (19-km) limit untreated sewage may be freely discharged to sea.

Although, as noted earlier, there is no international requirement to control grey water discharge, some more environmentally proactive authorities, such as Alaska, are introducing local or national legislation. This has resulted in some ships, particularly cruise ships and military vessels, taking steps to treat grey water on board prior to discharge using systems similar to, or the same as, those used for sewage treatment. A development of this approach is that, in addition to waste management systems processing specific wastes, integrated waste management systems are beginning to emerge. Using a combination of technologies, these systems can process most wastes produced on board including sewage and grey water; bilge water; metal, glass, paper, plastics and food waste; and clinical and sanitary wastes (Smith *et al.* 2002).

Conclusion

This chapter has underlined the extent of the range of environmental problems associated with day-to-day shipping operations that affect both the atmosphere and the marine environment. It has also indicated relationships between these problems and the other dominant themes in this volume: globalisation and technological change. Ships working at the local and regional scales naturally contribute to environmental pollution at local, regional and, indeed, global levels. But in addition there are the problems related to the increasing globalisation of trade, such as the potential for non-native organisms to be transported many thousands of miles in ships' ballast water. These global impacts are in turn linked with the necessity for environmental pollution produced by ships to be regulated internationally.

Regulation can, however, rarely achieve an instantaneous solution. Instead, progress is usually a much more incremental process, brought about by pressure on different sectors at different points in time and by different institutions, often as new priorities come to be appreciated. This is well illustrated by Alaska's recent unilateral decision to impose local controls on grey water discharge into the state's highly sensitive waters – while geographically more widespread legislation is not yet being considered by the international community.

Significant lead times are also intimately linked with technological factors. Although in some instances legislation can limit pollution effectively in the short term, technological advances are frequently required before control becomes a realistic proposition – for example, to reduce emissions to the atmosphere or process wastes. Inevitably, these advances take time. Moreover, even when appropriate technologies become available, progress may still be retarded by the technical difficulties, and/or cost, of applying them to existing vessels. This dictates the necessity for measures such as phase-out periods and 'grandfather clauses', whereby legislation is not applied to existing ships. Despite such obstacles, however, there is no doubt that technological change has a key role to play in the reduction of vessel pollution, a role complementing other technological advances – such as those reviewed in Part II of this book – aimed primarily at economic efficiency.

Acknowledgement

Many of the data on emission and discharge estimates quoted in this chapter were compiled in the context of the Technologies for Reduced Environmental Impact from Ships (TRESHIP) thematic network, under contract to DG-XII of the European Commission. The contribution of the network participants and colleagues at Lloyd's Register to the information reported here is gratefully acknowledged.

Notes

1 Significant concentrations of polychlorinated compounds are only likely to be associated with isolated incidents of chemical contamination of fuels.
2 This variation can be attributed to such factors as the use of different base years, calculation methodologies, emission factors, fleet segments and geographical limits for the different inventories.
3 The application of fuel cell technology is much further advanced for road vehicles.
4 VOC emissions during coating application can also be of significance, though this relates to air, rather than water, pollution.
5 No discharge is allowed within 50 nautical miles (92.6 km) of land or within a special area. Beyond 50 nautical miles, discharge is permitted when a tanker is *en route*, subject to rate and volume restrictions. Special areas currently include the Mediterranean, the Black, Baltic and Red Seas, the 'Gulf area', the Gulf of Aden, and Antarctic and North-West European waters. The latter comprise the North, Irish and Celtic Seas, the English Channel and western approaches, and the north-east Atlantic immediately west of Ireland.

References

Alexandersson, A., Flodström, E., Öberg, R. and Stålberg, P.(1993) *Exhaust Gas Emission from Sea Transportation*, TFB report 1993/1, Goteborg: MariTerm AB.
Aspen Publishers Inc. (weekly) *International Oil Spill Statistics*, Oil Spill Intelligence Report, New York: Aspen Publishers Inc., available at www.aspenpublishers.com (accessed 8 January 2004).
Australian Bureau of Statistics (1997) *4605.0 Australian Transport and the Environment*, available at www.abs.gov.au (accessed 8 January 2004).
BMT (2000) *Study on the Economic, Legal, Environmental and Practical Implications of a European Union System to Reduce Ship Emissions of SO₂ and NO$_x$*, European Commission Contract B4–3040/98/000839 /MAR/B1, available at: www.europa.eu.int/comm/environment/enveco/studies2.htm#27 (accessed 8 January 2004).

Bremnes, P.K. and Melhus, Ø. (1990) *Exhaust Gas Emission from International Marine Transport*, Trondheim, Norway: Marintek.

British Standards Institution (2000) *BS EN 378–1:2000, Refrigerating Systems and Heat Pumps – Safety and Environmental Requirements – Part 1: Basic Requirements, Definitions, Classification and Selection Criteria*, Annex E, Table E1, London: British Standards Institution.

Carlton, J.T., Reid, D.M. and van Leeuwen, H. (1990) *The Role of Shipping in the Introduction of Non-indigenous Aquatic Organisms to the Coastal Waters of the United States (other than the Great Lakes) and an Analysis of Control Options*, Report no. CG-D-XX-92, Mystic, CT: Williams College.

—— (1995) *The Role of Shipping in the Introduction of Non-indigenous Aquatic Organisms to the Coastal Waters of the United States (other than the Great Lakes) and an Analysis of Control Options*, Shipping Study I, USCG Report No. CG-D-11–95, Springfield, VA: National Technical Information Service.

CONCAWE (1994) *The Contribution of Sulphur Dioxide Emission from Ships to Coastal Deposition and Air Quality in the Channel and Southern North Sea Area*, Report no. 2/94, Brussels: CONCAWE.

Corbett, J.J., Fischbeck, P.S. and Pandis, S.N. (1999) 'Global nitrogen and sulfur inventories for oceangoing ships', *Journal of Geophysical Research*, 104: 3457–3470.

Croner, P.A. (2000) 'A company perspective: designing and managing ships in an environmentally friendly way', *Conference Proceedings: Managing Environmental Risk in the Maritime Industry*, London: LLP Ltd.

Department of Trade and Industry (UK) (2001) *Phase-out of Halons: Advice on Alternatives and Guidelines for Users of Fire-fighting and Explosion Protection Systems*, available at www.dti.gov.uk/publications (accessed 8 January 2004).

EMARC (1999) *MARPOL Rules and Ship Generated Waste*, Report of the 'EMARC' project, contract no. WA-95-SC.097, funded by the European Commission under the Transport RTD Programme of the Fourth Framework Programme, available at http://www.cordis.lu/transport/src/emarc.htm (accessed 8 January 2004).

Endresen, Ø. and Sørgård, E. (1999) *Reference Values for Ship Pollution*, Technical Report 99–2034, Oslo: Det Norske Veritas.

Endresen, Ø., Sørgård, E., Sundet, J.K., Dalsøren, S.B., Isaksen, I.S.A., Berglen, T.F. and Gravir, G. (2003a) 'Emission from international sea transportation and environmental impact', *Journal of Geographical Research*, 108(D17): 4560.

Endresen, Ø., Sørgård, E., Behrens, H.L. and Andersen, A.B (2003b) 'How much ballast?', *Ballast Water News*, issue 14 (July–September 2003): 6–7, London: Global Ballast Water Management Programme, International Maritime Organization.

Etkin, D.S., Wells, P., Nauke, M., Campbell, J., Grey, C., Koefoed, J., Meyer, T. and Johnston, P. (1998) 'Estimates of oil entering the marine environment in the past decade: GESAMP Working Group 32 project', *Proceedings of the 21st Arctic and Marine Oilspill Program Technical Seminar*, pp. 903–910, available at http://www.environmentalresearch.com/publications/statistics.htm (accessed 8 January 2004).

European Environment Agency (EEA) (2001) 'Environmental consequences of transport: accidental and illegal discharges of oil by ships at sea, 2001', available at http://themes.eea.eu.int/Sectors_and_activities/transport/indicators/consequences/discharges/index.htmp (accessed 8 January 2004).

—— (2002) *Joint EMEP/CORINAIR Atmospheric Emission Inventory Guidebook*, 3rd edition October 2002, Copenhagen: European Environment Agency, available at: http://reports.eea.eu.int/EMEPCORINAIR3/en (accessed 8 January 2004).

Fleischer, F. (1996) 'NO$_x$ reduction: a technical challenge for marine diesel engine man-ufacturers', *Proceedings of the Tenth International Maritime and Shipping Conference*, London: Institute of Marine Engineers, pp. 37–43.

Gotje, W., Heinis, F., Janmaat, L.M. and Derksen, J.G.M. (1998) *Ballast Water: Overview of Available Data and Estimation of Possible Risks*, Report no. 98.1162, Ams-terdam: Ministry of Transport, Public Works and Water Management, North Sea Directorate, AquaSense.

Hay, C., Handley, S., Dodgshun, T., Taylor, M. and Gibbs, W. (1997) *Cawthron's Ballast Water Research Programme Final Report 1996–97*, Nelson, New Zealand: Cawthron Institute.

International Maritime Organization (IMO) (1990) *Petroleum in the Marine Environ-ment*, MEPC 30/INF.13, submitted by the United States, London:International Mar-itime Organization.

—— (1997) *Ballast Water Guidelines A. 868 (20)*, available at: http://globallast.imo.org/ (accessed 8 January 2004).

—— (2001) *Anti-fouling Systems*, available at http://www.imo.org/home.asp, London: International Maritime Organization (accessed 26 February 2004).

—— (2002) 'Risk assessments underway', *Ballast Water News*, 8 (January–March): 6–7, available at http://globallast.imo.org/BallastWaterNews8.pdf (accessed 26 February 2004).

International Tanker Owners' Pollution Federation Limited (ITOPF) (2002), statistics, available at www.itopf.com/stats.

Isensee, J., Watermann, B. and Berger, H. (1994) 'Emission of antifouling biocides into the North Sea: an estimate', *German Journal of Hydrography*, 46(4): 355–365.

Jerrc, J., Barret, K. and Styve, H. (1994) *The Contribution from Ship Emission to Acidifi-cation on The North Sea Countries: The North Sea as a Special Area – Phase II*, Report no. 94-3437, Oslo: Det Norske Veritas.

Jones, M.M. (1991) 'Marine organisms transported in ballast water: a review of the Aus-tralian scientific position', *Bureau of Rural Resources Bulletin*, 11: 1–45, Canberra: Australia Government Publishing Service.

Koops, W. and Huisman, J. (2001) 'Problems in estimating the quantity of operational oil discharges from ships', Congress Proceedings, *The Marine Environment: How to Preserve*, London: Institute of Marine Engineers, pp. 234–242.

Lloyd's Register (1993) *Marine Exhaust Emissions Research Programme, Phase II, Tran-sient Emission Trials*, London: Lloyd's Register of Shipping.

—— (1995) *Marine Exhaust Emissions Research Programme*, London: Lloyd's Register of Shipping.

—— (1998) *Marine Exhaust Emissions Quantification Study – Baltic Sea*, Report no. 98/EE/7036, London: Lloyd's Register of Shipping.

—— (1999) *Marine Exhaust Emissions Quantification Study –Mediterranean Sea*, Report no. 99/EE/7044, London: Lloyd's Register of Shipping.

Marintek (2000) *Study of Greenhouse Gas Emissions from Ships*, Final Report to the Inter-national Maritime Organisation, Trondheim, Norway: Marintek.

Martens, O. (1993) 'Solutions to hydrocarbon gas emission from tankers: marine system design and operations', Paper 22, ICMES 93, Conference on Marine System Design and Operation, Technical University of Hamburg and Harburg, pp. 231–242.

Mayell, H. and Swanson, C. (1998) 'Ban considered on anti-fouling ship paint', *Environ-mental News Network*, 24 December, available at http://www.enn.com/news/enn-stories/1998/12/122498/tbt765.asp (accessed 8 January 2004).

MER (1999) 'Coming clean on exhaust gas emissions', *Marine Engineers Review*, May, pp. 19–24.

Norwegian Environmental Department (1994) *Reception of Waste from Ships*, Report no. T-1026: (in Norwegian), Oslo: Norwegian Maritime Directorate.

Olivier, J.G.J., Bouwman, A.F., van der Maas, C.W.M., Berdowski, J.J.M., Veldt, C., Bloos, J.P.J., Visschedijk, A.J.H., Zandveld, P.Y.J. and Haverlag, J.L. (1996) *Description of EDGAR Version 2.0*, Report no. 771060 002, The Hague: National Institute of Public Health and the Environment (RIVM). Also available as TNO-MEP Report no. R96/119.

Patin, S. (2002) 'Oil pollution of the sea', Offshore-environment Web site available at http://www.offshore-environment.com/oilpollution.html (accessed 8 January 2004).

Schnitler, P. (1995) *Modelling of Sources and Quantities of Waste Oil from Ship Operations*, Research Report no. 95–3738, Oslo: Det Norske Veritas.

Ship and Ocean Foundation (2001) *Study on Estimation and Reduction of GHG Emissions from Ocean-going Vessels*, IMO MEPC Report no. 47/4/5, Tokyo: Ship and Ocean Foundation, available at http://www.sof.or.jp/english/project/report/mepc47e.html (accessed 8 January 2004).

Skjølsvik, K.O., Andersen, A.B., Corbett, J.J. and Skjelvik J.M. (2000) *Study on Greenhouse Gas Emissions from Ships*, Report to the International Maritime Organisation, Report no. Mtoo A23–038, Trondheim, Norway: Marintek, Det Norske Veritas, Centre for Economic Analysis (ECON) and Carnegie Mellon University.

Smith, G., Kenny, S., Roynon, K. and Thomas, N. (2002) 'Waste management at sea: the drive towards an environmentally independent ship', *Proceedings of the International Conference, ENSUS 2002*, Newcastle upon Tyne: School of Marine Science and Technology, University of Newcastle upon Tyne.

Swedish Shipowners' Association (1995) *Environmental Effects from the Discharge of Grey Water from Ferries in the Baltic Sea Area*, Göteborg: Swedish Shipowners' Association.

Whall, C., Cooper, D., Archer, K., Twigger, L., Thurston, N., Ockwell, D., McIntyre, A. and Ritchie, A. (2002) *Quantification of Emissions from Ships Associated with Ship Movements between Ports in the European Community*, Report to the European Commission, Northwich, UK: Entec.

13 Trade and environmental management in the Straits of Malacca

The Singapore experience

Mark Cleary and Goh Kim Chuan

The Straits of Malacca, as one of the world's busiest waterways, plays a crucial role in international trade and shipping, as well as in the development of the three littoral states of Malaysia, Indonesia and Singapore. Economic growth and development in these three countries, and most notably in the case of Singapore, is heavily dependent on the flows of goods shipped through the Straits. Over the past two decades, strong export-led growth in the Malaysian and Singaporean economies has significantly increased both traffic in the Straits and the volume of goods moving through the major ports of the region. However, the increasing volume of vessel traffic, and the rapid development of the littoral zone in the past three decades, have made the Straits highly vulnerable to sea-based pollution.[1] This situation is exacerbated by the fact that the waterway is a semi-enclosed sea. It is within the very constricted and busiest southern part of the Straits, with its maze of islands centred on Singapore, that the issues of tracking shipping and marine pollution take on national importance, particularly for the island republic of Singapore.

Recognition by Singapore, Malaysia and Indonesia of the need to grapple with these problems is long established. Well before the adoption of the UN Convention on the Law of the Sea (UNCLOS) in 1982, a Joint Statement on the safety of navigation in the Straits of Malacca and Singapore was issued by the three states in November 1971 (Sunardi 1998). This was followed by the formal establishment of the Tripartite Technical Expert Group (TTEG) on safety of navigation in the Straits in 1977, and a host of other arrangements were made in subsequent years. Consequently, this is not simply a region in which the tensions between development and the interests of the environment are very apparent, but also one in which there is momentum to establish effective environmental protection. Against this background, this chapter has two main concerns. The first is to review the pressures on the maritime environment of the Straits, emphasising a range of issues that extends from the loss of wetland, through marine contamination by heavy metals, to the hazards of intensive navigation. The second is to examine environmental management responses to these issues, focusing in particular on the role of Singapore, essentially the lead nation in this context. In the conclusion we extend the discussion to argue the need for still more international collaboration in the future management of these economically vital yet environmentally vulnerable waters. At the outset, however, a brief analysis of the Straits region is appropriate.

The Straits region

In terms of maritime law, the Straits of Malacca can be said to extend from Port Klang at the mouth of the Klang River in Malaysia through to Tanjong Piai and the island of Little Karimun where the Singapore Straits begins (Leifer 1978). However, for the purposes of this chapter the Singapore Straits are also included. Under this definition, the Straits have a funnel-shaped opening to the Andaman Sea and the Indian Ocean to the north, and taper to the south-east and the waters around Singapore island. They extend for some 300 km from north to south; at their widest, around Penang, they are about 230 km across, narrowing to around 17 km at Little Karimun (Figure 13.1).

Although politically divided between three littoral states – Singapore, Malaysia and Indonesia – the Straits of Malacca share a range of cultural, historical, economic and environmental characteristics. Historically, they have long been an important artery for the migration of peoples, cultures, traded goods, navies, money and diseases. Changing patterns of trade, technology and polit-

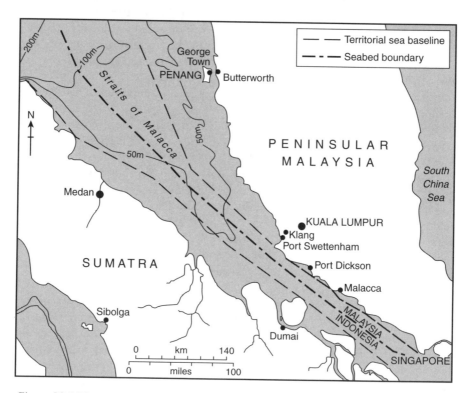

Figure 13.1 The regional setting of the Straits of Malacca.

ical influence can be read in the landscapes, cities, ports and hinterlands of the region (Cleary and Goh 2000). Despite the political division of the Straits between the three states – largely a legacy of the 1826 Treaty of London between the British and Dutch – that which unites the region is greater than that which divides it. Environment and ecology – the low-lying mangrove fringes, peat swamp areas, shallow warm coastal waters, and monsoon wind conditions – have given the region a strong shared identity in both the past and the present (Cleary and Goh 2000; Hamzah 1997).

Historically, the Straits were the focus both for the movement of goods between Europe, the Near East, India and China and for the establishment of important port cities with their attendant trading and tributary territories. For the kingdom of Srivijaya, centred around the city of Palembang in southern Sumatra, control of the Straits' shipping lanes helped the kingdom to tap into a rich intercontinental trade (Wolters 1967; Reid 1988). The emergence of Malacca as a key power, which was to give its name to the Straits from the early years of the fifteenth century, also reflected the pivotal role of both short- and long-distance trade through these waters (Sandhu and Wheatley 1983). European colonial powers – first the Portuguese, then the Dutch, later the British – saw control of the Straits and their hinterlands as the key to commercial prosperity in the region. The rise of Johor-Riau in the southern waters, the emergence of Singapore as a pre-eminent city-state, and the development of the economies of colonial Malaya and the Dutch East Indies all served to accentuate the historical importance of the Straits region (Cleary and Goh 2000).

Our notion of the Straits as a single human and physical unit is further reinforced by the impact of colonial powers on the trade and territories of these waters. Dutch colonialism in Sumatra and Java had important effects in changing trade patterns through, for example, the development of plantations and the expansion of existing ports such as Malacca and Batavia (Jakarta). The British had a particular impact on the rise of Singapore, which was established as a free port by Raffles on the site of an existing Malay *kampong* in 1819, and on the economic development of the Malay states. The development of rubber, tobacco and tea plantations, the expansion of tin mining, and the creation of new ports and transport infrastructures modified the physical environment of the regions abutting the Straits in significant ways (Trocki 1979; Turnbull 1990).

These similarities in historical experience are, in part at least, shaped by the physiographic character of the Straits region. The almost parallel north-east–south-west alignment of both mountain ranges which run the length of the Straits creates a natural basin in the region. Submarine contours show a steady deepening of the Straits towards the northern end. Coasts on both sides of the Straits face isolated erosion problems coupled with accretion, creating extensive mangrove swamps, especially on the Sumatran side. The Straits' topography, particularly the constrained southern end, means that in terms of waste materials and pollutants it constitutes an enclosed sink (Hanus *et al.* 1996). Flushing and dispersal of pollutants is both slow and difficult, making issues of marine management especially challenging.

Economic growth and shipping in the Straits

In both west-coast Malaysia and coastal Sumatra, post-1945 economic development initially focused on small-scale artisanal and industrial activity, coupled with the intensification of agricultural production. The expansion of plantation production (rubber, tobacco, oil palm) on both sides of the Straits was vital to ensure export revenues for Indonesia and Malaysia. That expansion was largely concentrated on regions abutting the Straits, and was naturally heavily dependent on ports and shipping. In addition, the continued development of mineral production (notably the historically important tin industry in the Malaysian state of Perak) increased the need for international trade.

Major changes in the economies of the region came with the shift in economic strategies in Malaysia and Singapore in the mid-1960s from import substitution to more aggressive export-oriented production. By the mid-1980s, Singapore had emerged as the economic powerhouse of the region, developing high-value-added industry in the electronics, biotechnology and computer sectors (Rigg 1997). While economic expansion in Malaysia came rather later, by the early 1990s Singapore and west-coast Malaysia were the key foci of economic growth, rural–urban migration and urban industrial expansion.

Economic changes initiated in this period have had a number of important implications for the management of the marine environment of the Straits (Hamzah 1997: 46–47). An important consequence of the growth of the region's 'tiger' economies, the expansion of its hydrocarbon production and the more general advance of globalisation has been a major increase in shipping volumes using the Straits. Trade comprises a wide range of goods that are potentially environmentally damaging, including hydrocarbons to East Asia, notably Japan, and bunkering traffic through the port of Singapore. Hydrocarbon tanker traffic is of major significance: some 70 per cent of eastbound laden tankers in the late-1990s used the Straits rather than the longer Lombok–Macassar route. Hydrocarbon products constituted some 90 per cent of all bulk cargo entering Singapore in 2001, and such products made up around 36 per cent of the port's total cargo traffic (MPA statistics).

Table 13.1 shows estimated shipping flows through the Straits and charts the very substantial increases over the past decade and a half. Cargo throughput at

Table 13.1 Shipping flows through the Straits of Malacca

Year	Arrivals at Singapore	Estimated through traffic
1982	36,361	43,633
1985	36,531	43,837
1990	60,347	72,416
1992	81,340	96,000
1997	130,333	No data
2000	145,383	196,000

Source: Cleary and Goh (2000); Maritime and Port Authority of Singapore.

Singapore, the pre-eminent port in the region, has grown by over 300 per cent in the past decade. Despite the importance of hydrocarbons, the continuing high productivity of the Singapore container port has been important in securing a major share of both global and Asian trade (Song and Cullinane 2000). In addition, many regional ports have a traffic volume that makes a sizeable contribution to regional shipping, especially in Malaysia (Figure 13.2). Thus, the port of Johor, and its new container terminal at the Port of Tanjung Pelapas, has

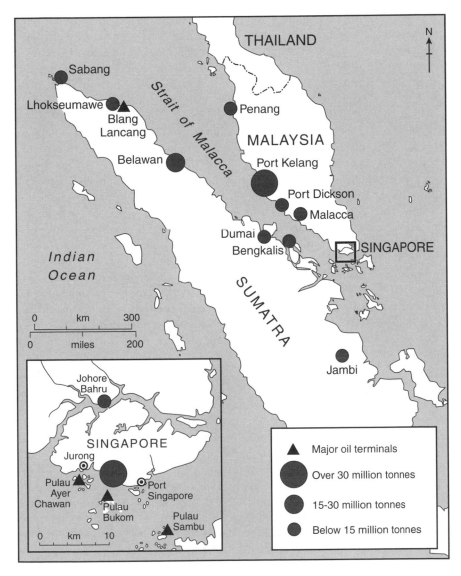

Figure 13.2 Port activity in the Straits.

attracted increased traffic into the southern part of the Straits, in direct competition with Singapore.

Shipping, ports and environmental issues in the Straits

As Singapore is the most developed urban region abutting the Straits, and has a role as a global transshipment centre, it is understandable that it has a particularly high stake in the environment of this part of the waterway and how that environment is managed. While the general state of the environment in the entire waterway is of concern to Singapore within the context of the tripartite littoral states arrangements, it is within the congested southern portion – where the Republic's jurisdiction is most apparent and its national interest paramount – that the marine environment is most threatened. Thus the discussion will focus, first, on the nature of the threats from a Singaporean perspective and, later, on Singapore's role in the environmental management of this part of the sea lane.

Although Reynolds (Chapter 12) identifies air pollution as an issue associated with inland seas, in this region emissions from ships are not a dominant problem. One recent study concluded that sulphur oxides from this source accounted for only 3.7 per cent of total emissions (Zafrul 1999). This figure, however, is slightly deceptive, because although the remaining 96.7 per cent came from land-based sources, many of these – particularly power stations, oil refineries and other industries such as petrochemicals – are located in the general port industrial area and consequently are related to maritime activity.

Historically, this port industrialisation, and associated city development, have been major drivers behind a quite different environmental problem: the consumption of wetland as a result of reclamation. Over the past three decades Singapore's land area has been expanded by some 10 per cent, or approximately 83 km², and eventually this will increase to some 25 per cent of the original land size of some 640 km². A further 15 per cent will have been added by 2010. Very few stretches of coastline still retain their natural indented nature (Pinder and Witherick 1990). Clusters of islands have also been amalgamated to create larger islands for industrial purposes, a good recent example being that of four separate southern islands south-west of Singapore that have now become one single large piece of land for a major petrochemical and industrial complex. In Indonesia, with the implementation of the Singapore–Johor–Riau growth triangle, the Riau Province islands (Batam, Bintan and Karimun) have similarly seen the rapid opening up of land for industrial sites and coastal resorts, as well as intensive quarrying activity to support infrastructural and building work. Reclamation such as this extends to developing areas a major problem created by port development in the advanced economies: the large-scale loss of fragile wetland environments rich in both flora and fauna. Moreover, in Singapore's case there have been further impacts beyond the reclaimed areas: increased turbidity and siltation have harmed coral reef growth and the coastal habitats of the smaller islands (Low and Chou 1994). The tensions between development and the environment are made all too apparent by these physical expansion projects.

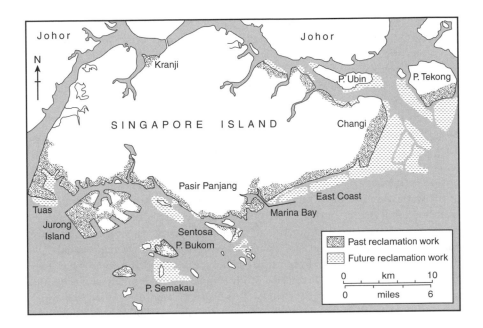

Figure 13.3 Coastal reclamation projects in Singapore.

Industrialisation is also a major source of marine pollution, especially by heavy metals. The Port of Singapore is the area worst affected by metallic pollutants in the entire region, followed by the Johor Straits (Orlic *et al.* 1994). High copper and zinc levels have been reported in Singapore's Keppel Harbour in particular, while high concentrations of lead, nickel and cobalt have been recorded in waters near petroleum refineries off the island's south coast[2] (Grace *et al.* 1987). Around the southern coast of Johor, abutting the Straits, high levels of arsenic and mercury have also been noted (Dow 1997), although research does suggest that these levels have now stabilised (Tang *et al.* 1996). As in many ports, the issues surrounding heavy metals are not simply associated with their release into the marine environment by (largely) port-based industries. Port dredging activity regularly exacerbates the problem by disturbing polluted mud, thus increasing its contact with marine life, in order to maintain or deepen access channels – not least to remain attractive to ever-larger container ships. Beyond this, because the Port of Singapore is so attractive to shippers, and because its port-based oil refining industry has been the basis for the world's largest supply of ships' bunker fuel[3] (Pinder 1997) accidental discharges provide a further water pollution problem. These may involve hazardous cargoes or fuel transferred during bunkering operations. Even in small quantities they can accumulate insidiously, to pose particular threats to shallow waters close to land. The precise effects of these various water pollutants – metals, oil products, etc. – on marine life in Singapore's coastal waters are difficult to estimate. However, indications can be gained from the Red List of species declared extinct, or on the verge of extinction. Numbers on this list are high, given the small area of marine environment. Included are 52 species of fish, 13 species of coral and sea anemones and 12 species of crustaceans. Moreover, more than 50 other species of marine life are considered threatened (MPPMEAS 1996).

Added to these problems is the ever-present risk of maritime accidents. One mid-1990s study showed that in 1993 alone there were 32 such accidents in the Straits as a whole (Hamzah 1997). A combination of factors – including the high volume of east–west shipping traffic, heavy criss-cross traffic by a diversity of vessels that vary in size, capacity and condition, the highly constricted nature of the waterway, and the position of Singapore within a narrow configuration of islands – renders the southernmost portion of the Straits of Malacca the most congested of the entire international waterway. Hence, this area is the most vulnerable to ship collision and resulting pollution. Any accident entails the danger of marine pollution from cargo or fuel tanks, but this danger is naturally greatest with oil tankers. Hamzah's study suggests that a laden tanker would pass some sort of vessel in the Straits once every 14 minutes. Moreover, a risk assessment of accidents resulting in a major oil spill (>1,500 tonnes) showed a risk frequency value of 0.0029 per cent of the total number of tankers passing through the waterway. The total number of vessels transiting the Straits in 1993 was estimated at about 99,000, and approximately 33 per cent of these were tankers. Based on these data, the risk of a major oil spill was estimated at one per year[4] – and 1993 did indeed witness one major spill, from the *Maersk Navigator*. Such estimates must, of course, be treated with caution because of random variation through time. For example, the number of serious spills could have been higher in 1993 because the total number of accidents involving tankers in that year was 9. Similarly, in 1997 a major spill resulting from a collision between the oil tanker *Evoikos* and the *Orapin Global*, an empty very large crude carrier (VLCC), was one of three separate maritime accidents that occurred in the Straits within only two months. This incident, which occurred in Singaporean waters and involved the release of 28,500 tonnes of crude oil, was the worst yet faced by the Republic.

From this review, the range and scale of the environmental challenges to be addressed in the Straits is clear. In responding to the needs of shipping and the economy, ports have damaged the environment by, for example, creating extensive and irreparable wetland loss. Industrial development closely related to trade has generated marine pollution. And the intensity of navigation in the Straits means that there is an ever-present risk of major pollution incidents caused by accidents. How, then, has the difficult task of implementing environmental legislation been approached?

Environmental management

The strategic economic importance of the Straits, coupled with dramatic increases in traffic over the past three decades, has meant that both the Singapore government and its neighbours have had to research, develop and fund a range of shipping and environmental management measures. It is clear that the routeway through the Straits of Malacca and Singapore will remain the dominant route for some time to come. Hence, policies, strategies, legislation, institutions and a host of other support infrastructures have to be in place to ensure that the waters are well managed to allow both the safe navigation essential to economic growth, and a clean, sustainable marine environment. Despite the popularity of the 'polluter pays' principle elsewhere, the costs of these measures are borne largely – but not exclusively – by the littoral states. The imposition of charges for users to support such measures is generally seen as a difficult proposition to implement legally and would, of course, be unpopular with users. The states have consequently chosen to avoid the risk that increased navigation costs would have repercussions on shipping in and through the Straits and, therefore, on economic activity.

Marine protection agencies and regulation

The responsibility for protecting the marine environment of Singapore rests primarily with the Maritime and Port Authority of Singapore (MPA). The role of the MPA is crucial in that it administers a comprehensive set of marine pollution legislation in line with UNCLOS 82 and International Maritime Organisation (IMO) conventions. This legislation covers areas such as prevention, preparedness and response to marine pollution emergencies, and compensation for oil pollution damage due to spills of persistent oil. Through the Prevention of Pollution of the Sea Act (PPSA), Singapore has given effect to the International Convention for the Prevention of Pollution from Ships 1973, modified later by the Protocol of 1978 (MARPOL 73/78). The PPSA has been translated into explicit definitions of vessel-based pollution through the various parts of the Act. For example, Part 2 prohibits the discharge of oil from land or apparatus on vessels, as well as defining the penalties for doing so. Part 3 extends the prohibition to the discharge of noxious liquid substances (chemicals), as well as refuse, garbage, plastics, wastes, marine pollutants in packaged form or trade effluent. This applies to Singapore ships in any part of the sea and to ships of other nationalities in Singapore waters. Part 4 introduces a different dimension by stipulating the waste reception facilities for oil and noxious liquid substances that must be provided by the relevant agencies, including the MPA and terminal operators. We return to these facilities, and their role in pollution prevention, later.

While the role of the MPA is paramount, other agencies also have environmental management responsibilities. Thus, the Ministry of the Environment operates waste disposal facilities for ships' oil and chemical residues, controls the design, construction and equipment of these reception facilities, and handles the final disposal of the wastes that are collected. The Urban Redevelopment Authority acts as the national planning authority and national conservation authority; the Primary Production Department is responsible for marine fisheries and aquaculture; and the National Parks Board develops and maintains coastal parks and coastal nature reserves respectively. Each of these bodies thus plays a part in designing and implementing environmental strategies in the Straits.

Managing shipping flows

The earliest regulatory measures were primarily concerned with controlling shipping flows and thereby minimising the risk of collisions and resultant marine and coastal pollution. As early as 1981 a routing system was adopted by the IMO for the Straits of Malacca, and three Traffic Separation Schemes (TSSs) were demarcated. Two of these are within the Straits of Singapore: the Singapore Strait itself (a stretch of some 72 nautical miles (133 km)) and at the Horsburg Lighthouse area (some 15 nautical miles (28 km)) (Figure 13.4).

These TSSs were agreed jointly by the three littoral states of Indonesia, Malaysia and Singapore. To enhance safety, further measures were recommended by the three parties, including the extension of the TSS from One Fathom Bank to Pulau Pisang, and a joint resurvey of critical areas, wrecks and shoals in the Malacca and Singapore Straits. The TSS extension, as well as changes to the existing routing system, came into force in December 1998

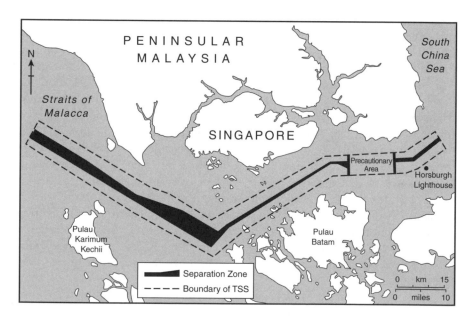

Figure 13.4 Vessel routing schemes.

(Wee 1999). As far as the Straits of Singapore is concerned, the modified system included:

- classing a new deepwater route (DWR) off Tanjung Medang as a precautionary area where 'ships must navigate with particular caution and within which the direction of traffic flow may be recommended'.
- a reduced speed limit of 12 knots for VLCCs in specified areas.
- the implementation of a compulsory reporting system, known as STRAITREP, to facilitate traffic control. This is now obligatory for all ships exceeding either 300 GT or 50 m in length entering the operational area (Chee and Johansen 2000).
- restrictions on overtaking in the DWR in the Singapore Strait and Philip Channel.
- a rule whereby vessels with defects affecting operational safety must ensure that they are rectified before entering the Straits of Malacca and Singapore.

Pollution response

While these measures emphasise pollution prevention, particularly from oil and oil products, Singapore has also acted to achieve effective response and remediation when incidents do occur. An important aspect of this approach is to ensure that stakeholders are prepared for pollution incidents and are able to cooperate and respond rapidly. One important requirement for terminal operators handling oil in bulk is to maintain a stock of not less than 10,000 litres of readily usable dispersants prescribed by existing regulations. A minimum set of equipment for oil recovery (e.g. craft for anti-pollution operations, equipped with dispensing spray units, knapsack sprayers, dispensing pumps and oil content barrier equipment) must also be provided at such terminals. The role of the MPA is crucial in providing a comprehensive emergency response plan within Singapore waters, through its Marine Emergency Action Procedures (MEAP) and contingency plans. Should a major spill occur, the MPA can also call on the assistance of the Ministry of Defence, the Ministry of the Environment, the Police Coast Guard, the East Asia Response Pte Ltd, salvage companies and other organisations. Outside Singapore waters, the MPA will also help to coordinate emergencies when called upon to assist.

These measures are supported by adherence to the 1992 Protocol to the International Convention on Civil Liability for Oil Pollution Damage, 1969. Singapore's Instrument of Accession to the Protocol was placed with the IMO on 18 September 1997, enabling the Protocol to enter into force one year later. Its key regulation is that shipowners are required to take out liability insurance for pollution damage caused by oil spills. The requirement is for cover higher than the legal minimum, and applies both to Singapore-registered oil tankers and to foreign tankers calling at Singapore while they are in the Republic's waters. This is one instance in which regulation does rely on the 'polluter pays' principle. Evidence as to the value of Singapore's emphasis on quick response and well-funded remediation measures is demonstrated by, for example, the aftermath of the collision between the oil tanker *Evoikos* and the VLCC *Orapin Global* discussed on p. 264. Studies carried out to assess the consequences of this 28,500–tonne oil spill, and the use of dispersants in clean-up operations, showed that the effects on seawall molluscan communities and corals were negligible (Tan *et al.* 1999).

Improved navigation and pollution control technology

In a narrow, shallow and congested waterway such as the Straits, the use of improved navigation technology has become important in reducing collision risk. A comprehensive radar and computer-based Vessel Traffic Information System (VTIS) covering the Singapore Strait Traffic Separation Scheme has been in operation since October 1990. Although only 20–30 per cent of through traffic participates in the scheme, it is a useful mechanism for improving the safety of navigation, and the system has recently been substantially upgraded to cope with increased traffic. Also, the use of a differential global positioning system (DGPS) to provide more accurate positioning data for ships plying the region was introduced in Singapore in October 1998. This free service is offered to shipping on a round-the-clock basis.

To complement the above measures, the Maritime Port Authority of Singapore is partially reliant on patrols to police its waters and combat pollution. However, the use of satellite remote sensing is also becoming an increasingly effective tool in oil-spill monitoring, and for random checks to detect deliberate discharges of pollutants into the sea. This technique can be used effectively to track pollution in either the Straits of Singapore or the main part of the Straits of Malacca. The basis for this technological advance is collaboration between the MPA and the Centre for Remote Imaging, Sensing and Processing (CRISP).

The effectiveness of this technique was demonstrated, in conjunction with the application of oil spill modelling, in the case of the oil tanker *Song San* in mid-August 1996, when dark patches of oil were detected in port waters off Singapore. More patches were evident in the next few days, but the pollution source could not be located. Based on the lead samples provided for the oil spill model, a satellite image clearly showed a shaped plume, and revealed the position of the ship. On the basis of GPS data, as well as the MPA's multi-radar VTIS, the culprit vessel was identified as the *Song San*. The case was brought to court, and the ship's owner, agent, master and chief officer were sentenced for pollution offences (Toh and Sheri 1999).

Improved waste disposal measures

For reasons that are self-evident, much of the regulation and technology-based pollution prevention strategy is a response to the threats posed by oil, oil products and chemicals. As Reynolds has stressed in Chapter 12, however, ships can be the source of other significant pollution 'streams'. Given that Singapore is the world's busiest port, this too is a significant issue. As the earlier discussion has noted, the PPSA is a central measure in this context, through its requirement for land-based waste reception facilities.

A range of facilities is provided for the comprehensive task of collecting, receiving, treating and disposing of waste. Reception facilities in the Republic were first set up on the island of Sebarok in 1972 by the Port of Singapore Authority (now known as PSA Corporation). In July 1993 a private company, Singapore Clean Seas Pte Ltd, was formed to take over the facilities on Sebarok. This company's facilities are very extensive and include sludge treatment plants; a slop treatment system; an oily water treatment plant; a specialised oil distillation unit; mechanical equipment including disk stacks and hydroclones; thermal process equipment; a mobile sludge treatment unit; steam, electricity, desalination and other utility support; two dedicated jetties; and two specialised oil tankers. For Chua *et al.* (1997), the biggest contribution of Singapore towards enforcing the prevention of vessel-sourced pollution is this reception facility on Pulau Sebarok for different types of waste.

Oily waste reception facilities are also available elsewhere, at five refinery-based terminals operated by multinational oil companies. These terminals receive oily ballast water, tank washings, oily bilge water and oil purifier sludge from tankers unloading at refineries. Chemical wastes are received at two terminals, but can also be unloaded at facilities where agreement has been made with the unloading terminal to receive them. Stringent conditions are applied, one being that when a shipyard signs a contract with a shipowner for repair in Singapore, the contract contains a clause binding the shipowner to declare that the incoming ship is in 'clean condition'. A potential problem with this approach is that tanker cleaning contractors may seek to reduce their costs by discharging wastes outside port limits, a practice that is particularly difficult to monitor and control. Consequently, Singapore has sought to eliminate such activities by imposing, since April 1993, stringent regulations on tanker cleaning contractors. These include the registration of contractors with the Ministry of the Environment, a requirement to indicate that wastes have been properly disposed of, and set rules relating to cleaning and disposal techniques.

Garbage disposal, meanwhile, is organised through an MPA contractor, PSA Marine Pte Ltd. Daily collections are carried out. These 'comb' the port's extensive anchorage systematically, resulting in the collection of about 240 tonnes of waste from some 7,200 vessels per month. To encourage use of the system, garbage collection is free of charge, although the costs are actually included in the port dues collected by the MPA.[5]

Conclusion: progress, issues and the international context

It is evident that substantial efforts have been, and are being, made to improve marine environmental protection. These efforts depend on regulation – improved control of the shipping lanes, the requirement for pollution clean-up insurance, legal penalties for pollution, etc – supported by strategies such as investment in facilities to receive wastes that might otherwise find their way into the marine environment. While the costs of this are borne partly by users – either directly through charges at, for example, oily waste disposal facilities, or indirectly as in the case of garbage – there is also substantial state investment, particularly in the traffic management systems. Despite this progress, however, in various respects there remains much that has not yet been addressed.

First, even the elaborate traffic management systems are not comprehensive. In particular, there is the problem of the diversity of vessels that criss-cross the Straits and, of course, its major shipping lanes. In such a narrow waterway, the hazard posed by these vessels, which hitherto have not been regulated in their movement by any international rules, will indeed be a major challenge for the littoral states in the future.

Second, there remains scope to support the traffic management schemes through both capacity building and the additional use of technology. Issues such as training and the standardisation of qualifications for shipmasters, crew and port officials; ship condition and maintenance, and adherence to mandatory ship reporting; and the use of automatic transponder systems on vessels all provide opportunities in these respects.

Third, the greatest efforts have been invested in achieving environmental protection through the regulation of shipping, with the result that there is arguably a lag in mitigating the impact of port development. Admittedly, there are now interesting signs that opposition to port expansion schemes may be starting to emerge. A proposed reclamation project on the island of Ubin, north of Singapore's main island, is currently under review because of concerns over the ecological value and international status of the rich mud and sand flats on that island. At the international scale, another current reclamation scheme on Tekong Island has generated controversy between Malaysia and Singapore. This project is controversial because, while it is located in Singapore's territorial waters, it may result in silting in the deep shipping channel into the Malaysian port of Pasir Gudang, and may also impact negatively on both fishing conditions and erosion risk on the Johor coast. Such controversies signal the need for reclamation schemes to receive attention similar to that focused on shipping and pollution.

Finally, there is the need for even greater levels of international collaboration than have been achieved in the past. This is not to underrate progress. The chapter has reviewed a number of international arrangements, and a host of others over the years have underlined growing awareness among the three littoral states of the importance of the Straits to their economies and security. This awareness has underpinned cooperative efforts extending from bilateral agreements, through ASEAN conventions, to IMO charters and conventions. Various platforms are now in place for cooperation, ranging from research into marine ecosystems and the impact assessment of oil spills, to regional oil spill preparedness and response systems and the work of the Malacca Straits Council involving Japan (Cleary and Goh 2000: 145–151). Yet as the earlier discussion has demonstrated, the pace in this sphere has been set by Singapore, and there is undoubtedly scope for a more uniform approach across the region. To cite just one example, it would be highly advantageous for all three states to ratify UNCLOS and IMO conventions and their protocols, so that a more harmonious and coordinated implementation of the regulations and standards could be carried out. In important respects, therefore, the challenge in this area of cooperation still lies ahead. As in many other heavily used stretches of water in the world, the future of the maritime environment is likely to rest on the ability of the key littoral states to collaborate and cooperate in the task of managing both the port-based and maritime developments which have the potential to damage such a sensitive environment.

Notes

1 While this chapter is concerned with pollution related to shipping and ports, it should be noted that land-based impacts on the marine environment are also substantial. High rates of economic growth, urbanisation and population growth have created a range of pollution issues for the Straits. Urban waste discharges from the growing cities of the region (especially Singapore and the Klang valley growth region in Malaysia); the growth of agricultural pollutants (especially from the rubber and oil-palm sector); and river channelisation and dam construction have all led to measurable changes in water quality in the rivers flowing into the Straits (Chua *et al.* 1997; Cleary and Goh 2000). Hydrocarbon production (most notably around Dumai in Sumatra) has also greatly increased the potential for pollution in the Straits from land-based sources (Valencia 1985; Yu *et al.* 1997). As far as Singapore is concerned, government efforts to clean up the Singapore and Kallang rivers, and the high standards of environmental quality set through a series of legislative and long-term 'Green Plan' initiatives, have meant that pollution from land-based sources on the island has been severely curtailed. Agricultural effluents have been a particular target: pig farming is now banned in the Republic because of its impact on waste management, and greater restrictions on poultry farming have been implemented (Ministry of the Environment 1989).
2 The west and east coasts of Singapore, furthest from the industrial port area, were the least polluted.
3 Bunker deliveries vary annually, but have exceeded 11 million tonnes a year.
4 The calculation for this probability is: 99,000 multiplied by 0.0029 and divided by 3 to reflect the fact that only a third of the ships were tankers.
5 The garbage is eventually disposed of at the Sebarok facility.

References

Chee, B.T. and Johansen, O. (2001) 'Development of a new VTS for the Port of Singapore', *Maritime Technology*, 8: 1–8.

Chua, T.-E. S., Ross, A. and Huming, Y. (1997) *Malacca Straits Environmental Profile*, Quezon City Philippines: GEF/UNDP/IMO Regional Programme for the Prevention and Management of Marine Pollution in the East Asian Seas.

Cleary, M. and Goh, K.C. (2000) *Environment and Development in the Straits of Malacca*, London: Routledge.

Dow, K. (1997) 'An overview of pollution issues in the Straits of Malacca', in A. Hamza (ed.) *The Straits of Malacca: International Cooperation in Trade, Funding and International Safety*, Kuala Lumpur: Pelanduk Publications, pp. 61–102.

Grace, L.M., Woo, K.H. and Chou, L.M. (1987) 'Singapore Country/Status Report', in Anon (ed.) *Development and Management of Living Marine Resources Workshop on Pollution and Other Ecological Factors in Relation to Living Marine Resources*, Singapore: ASEAN–Canada Cooperative Programme on Marine Sciences, pp. 188–274.

Hamzah, A. (ed.) (1997) *The Straits of Malacca: International Cooperation in Trade, Funding and International Safety*, Kuala Lumpur: Pelanduk Publications.

Hanus, V., Spichak, A. and Vanek, J. (1996) 'Sumatran segment of the Indonesian subduction zone: morphology of the Wadati-Benioff zone and seismotectonic pattern of the continental wedge', *Journal of Southeast Asian Earth Science*, 13: 39–60.

Leifer, M. (1978) *International Straits of the World: Malacca, Singapore and Indonesia*, Amsterdam: Sithoff and Noordhoff.

Low, J.K.Y. and Chou, L.M. (1994) 'Fish diversity of Singapore mangroves and the effect of habitat management', in S. Sudara, C.R. Wilkinson and L.M. Chou (eds) *Proceedings of the Third ASEAAT–Australian Symposium on Living Coastal Resources*, vol. 2: *Research Papers*, Bangkok: Department of Marine Sciences, Chulalonghorn University, pp. 465–469.

Maritime Port Authority of Singapore (MPA) *Annual Reports*.

Ministry of the Environment Singapore (1989) 'Country report on the assessment of pollution from land-based sources and their impact on the marine environment', presented at the UNEP–COBSEA *Seminar on the Assessment of Pollution from Land-based Sources and Their Impact on the Environment*, 25–27 January 1989, Singapore.

MPPMEAS (1996) *Regional Programme for the Prevention and Management of Marine Pollution in the East Asian Seas: From Planning to Action, 1996*, MPPMEAS Technical Report no. 8, Manila: Global Environment Facility/UNDP/IMO Regional Programme for the Prevention and Management of Marine Pollution in the East Asian Seas.

Orlic, I., Makjanic, J. and Tang, S.M. (1995) 'Multimetal analysis of marine sediments from coastal region by PIXIE and XRF', in D.K. Watson, S. Ong and G. Vigers (eds), Advances in Marine Environmental Management and Human Health Protection, Singapore: ASEAN-Canada Cooperative Programme on Marine Science. Proceedings, 24–28 October 1994, pp. 314–326.

Pinder, D.A. (1997) 'Deregulation policy and revitalisation of Singapore's bunker supply industry: an appraisal', *Maritime Policy and Management*, 24: 219–231.

Pinder, D.A. and Witherick, M.E. (1990) 'Port industrialization, urbanization and wetland decline', in M. Williams (ed.) *Wetlands: A Threatened Landscape*, Oxford: Basil Blackwell, pp. 234–266.

Reid, A. (1988) *Southeast Asia in the Age of Commerce, 1450–1680*, vol. 1: *The Lands Below the Winds*, New Haven, CT: Yale University Press

Rigg, J. (1997) *Southeast Asia: The Human Landscape of Modernisation and Development*, London: Routledge.

Sandhu, K. and Wheatley, P. (eds) (1983) *Melaka: The Transformation of a Malay Capital c.1400–1800*, Kuala Lumpur: Oxford University Press.

Song, D-W. and Cullinane, K. (2000) 'Asian container ports and productivity: implications for the new millennium', *Singapore Maritime and Port Journal*, 126: 149–161.

Sunardi, K. (1998) 'Prospects for sub-regional, regional, and international cooperation in implementing Article 43 of UNCLOS', *Singapore Journal of International and Comparative Law*, 2(2) (special feature): 442–451.

Tan, K.S. *et al.* (1999) 'An assessment of the impact of the Evoikos oil spill on the marine environment in Singapore', *Singapore Maritime and Port Journal*: 69–73.

Tang, S.M., Orlic, I., Makjanic, J., Wu, X.K., Ng, T.H., Wong, M.K., Lee, K.K. and Chen, N. (1996) 'A survey of levels of metallic and organic pollutants in Singapore coastal waters and marine sediments', in Anon. (ed.) *ASEAN Marine Environmental Management: Quality Criteria and Monitoring for Aquatic Life and Human Health Protection*, ASEAN–Canada, CPMS11 End of Project Conference, 24–28 June 1996, Penang: Pelandruk.

Toh, A.C. and Sheri, K.L. (1999) 'Combating oil pollution using technology', *Singapore Maritime and Port Journal*, 125(3): 46–49.

Trocki, C. (1979) *Prince of Pirates: The Temmenggongs and the Development of Johor and Singapore, 1784–1885*, Singapore: Singapore University Press.

Turnbull, C.M. (1990) *A History of Singapore, 1879–1988*, Singapore: Oxford University Press.

Valencia, M.J. (1985) *Southeast Asian Seas — Oil under Troubled Waters: Hydrocarbon Potentials, Jurisdictional Issues and International Relations*, Singapore: Oxford University Press.

Wee, H.L. (1999) 'Revised routing system and traffic separation scheme in the Malacca and Singapore Straits', *Singapore Maritime and Port Journal*, 125(1): 7–15.

Wolters, J. (1967) *Early Indonesian Commerce*, Ithaca, NY: Cornell University Press.

Yu, H., Sung L.N., Minh, S. and Lee, D. (eds) (1997) *Oil Spill Modelling in the East Asian Region with Special Reference to the Straits of Malacca*, Quezon City: United Nations Development Programme.

Zafrul, A. (1999) 'Regional and global sulphur cap and control of fuel quality and their impact on the bunkering industry', *Singapore Maritime and Port Authority Journal*, 125(3): 54–61.

Index